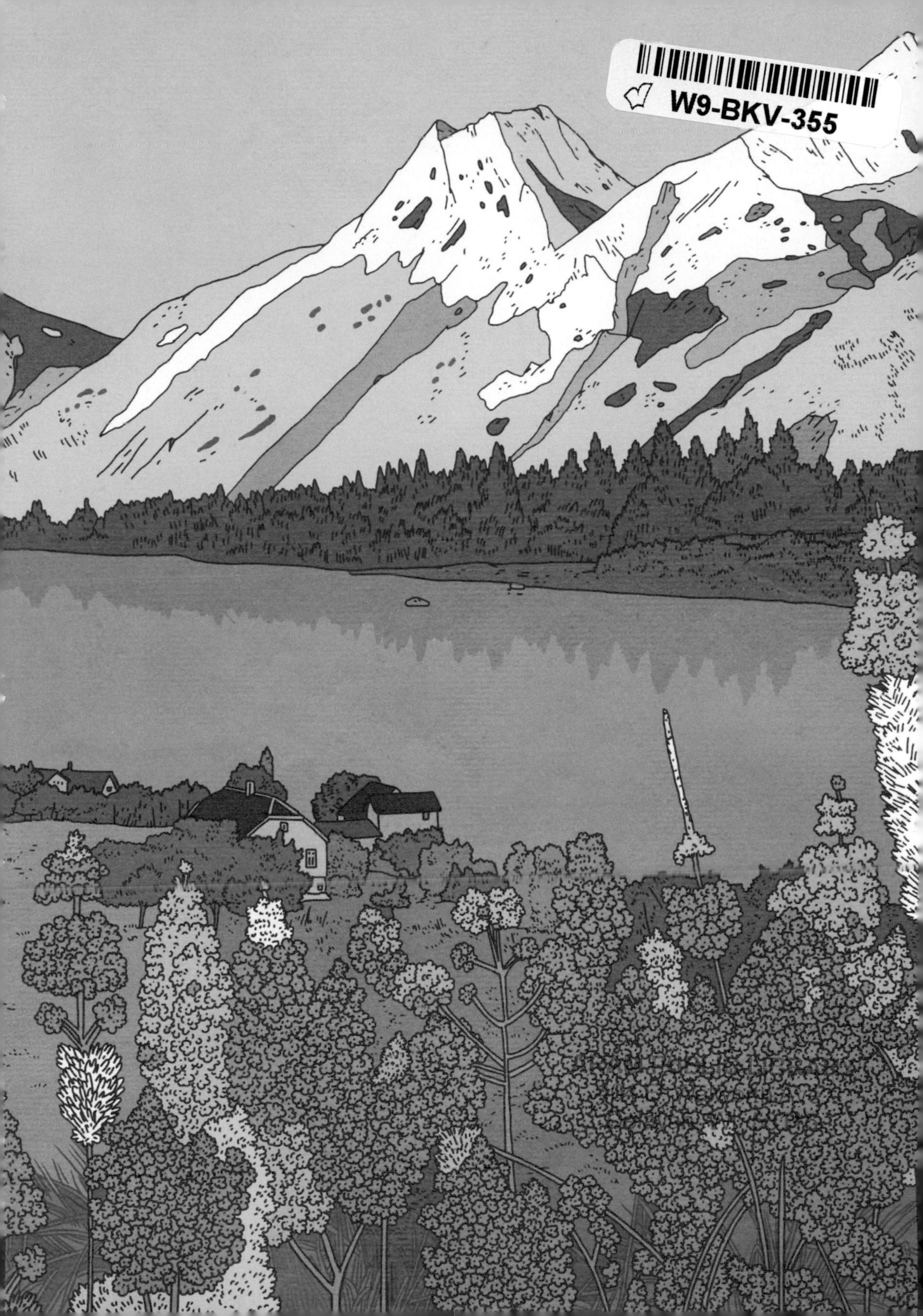

THE PROPERTY
RUTU MODAN

Translation by Jessica Cohen

DRAWN & QUARTERLY

To Michali

"With family, you don't have to tell
the whole truth and it's not considered lying."
—MICHAELA MODAN

DAY ONE

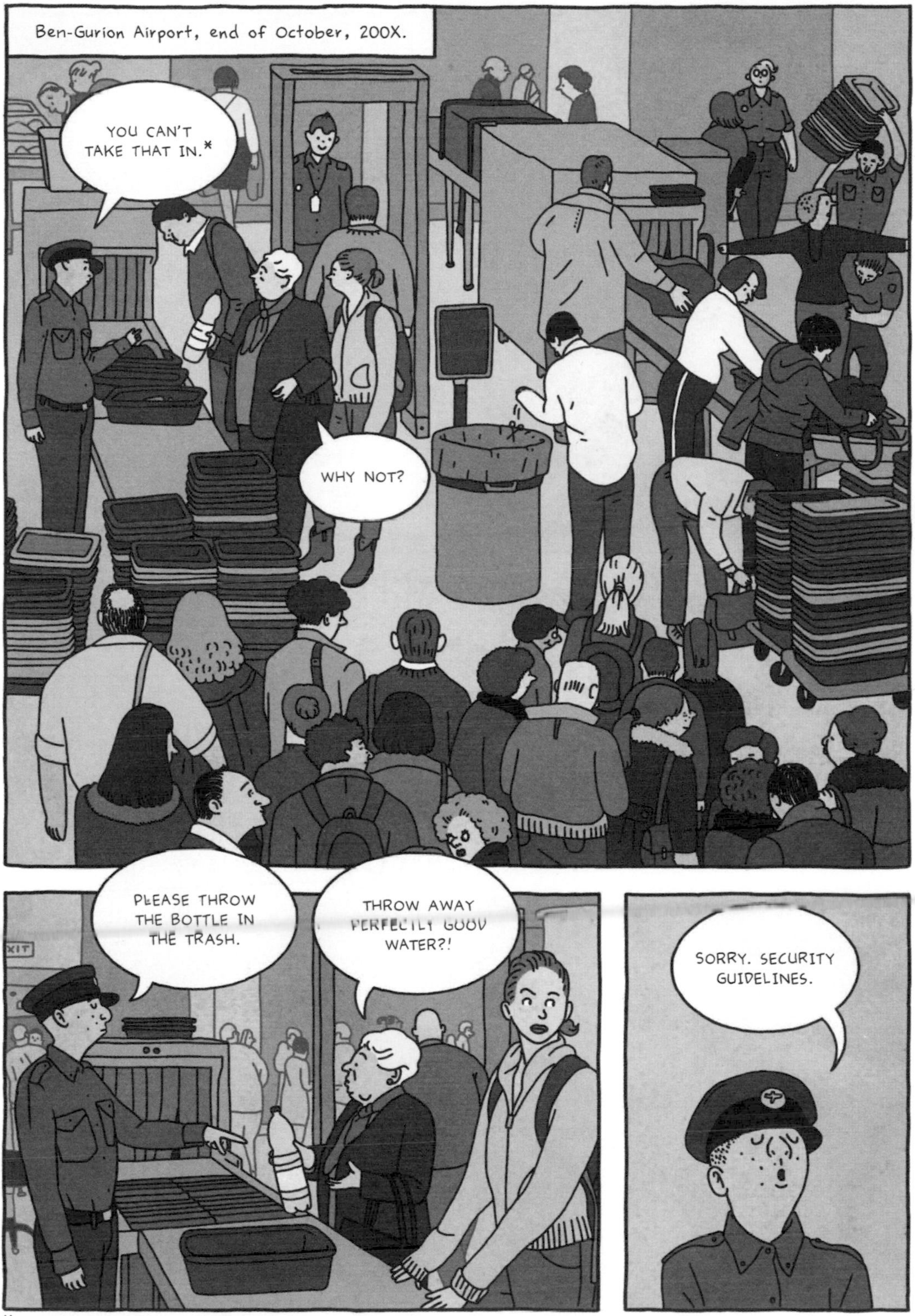
Ben-Gurion Airport, end of October, 200X.
YOU CAN'T TAKE THAT IN.*
WHY NOT?
PLEASE THROW THE BOTTLE IN THE TRASH.
THROW AWAY PERFECTLY GOOD WATER?!
SORRY. SECURITY GUIDELINES.

*Capitalized text represents Hebrew.

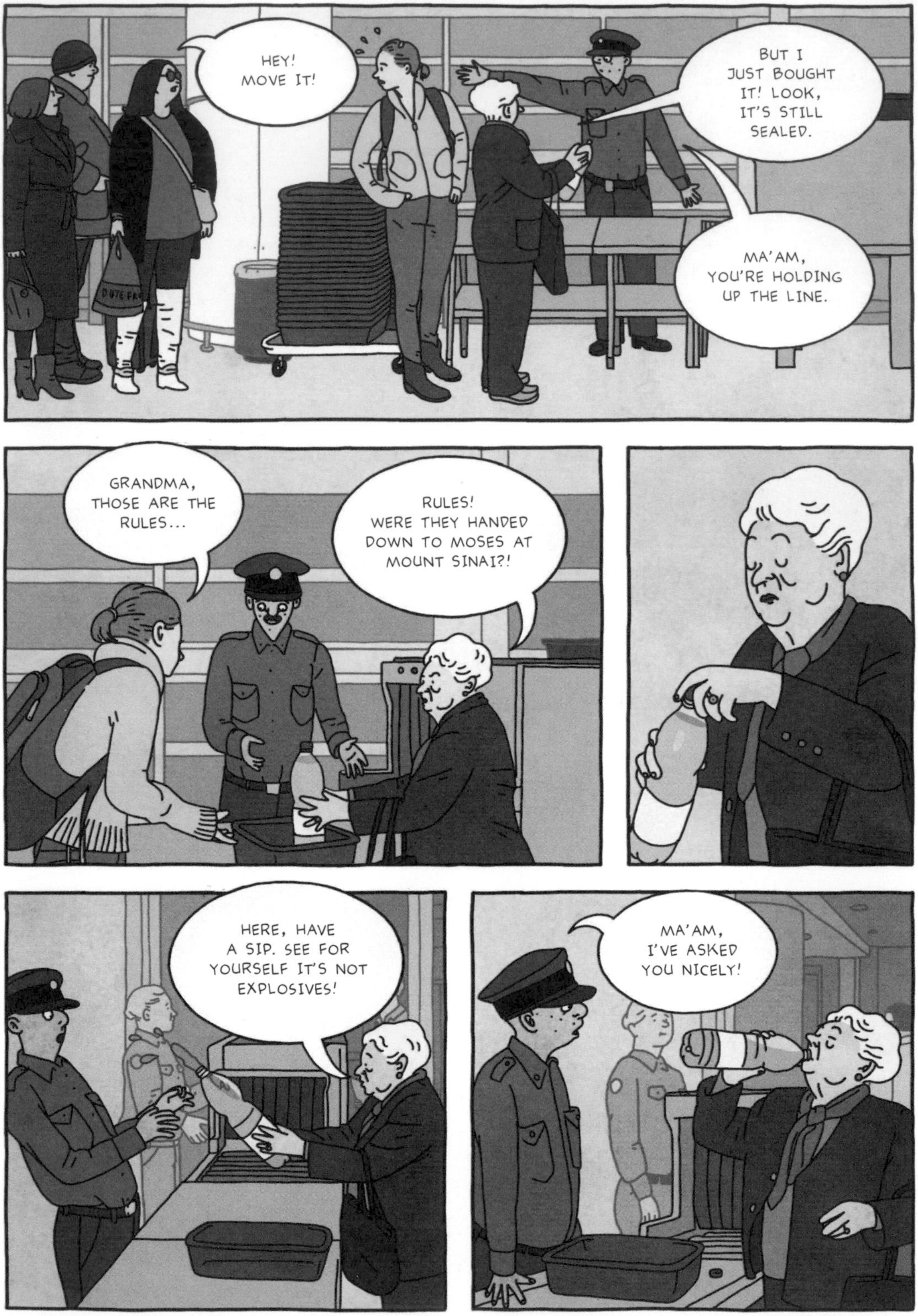
HEY! MOVE IT!
BUT I JUST BOUGHT IT! LOOK, IT'S STILL SEALED.
MA'AM, YOU'RE HOLDING UP THE LINE.
GRANDMA, THOSE ARE THE RULES...
RULES! WERE THEY HANDED DOWN TO MOSES AT MOUNT SINAI?!
HERE, HAVE A SIP. SEE FOR YOURSELF IT'S NOT EXPLOSIVES!
MA'AM, I'VE ASKED YOU NICELY!

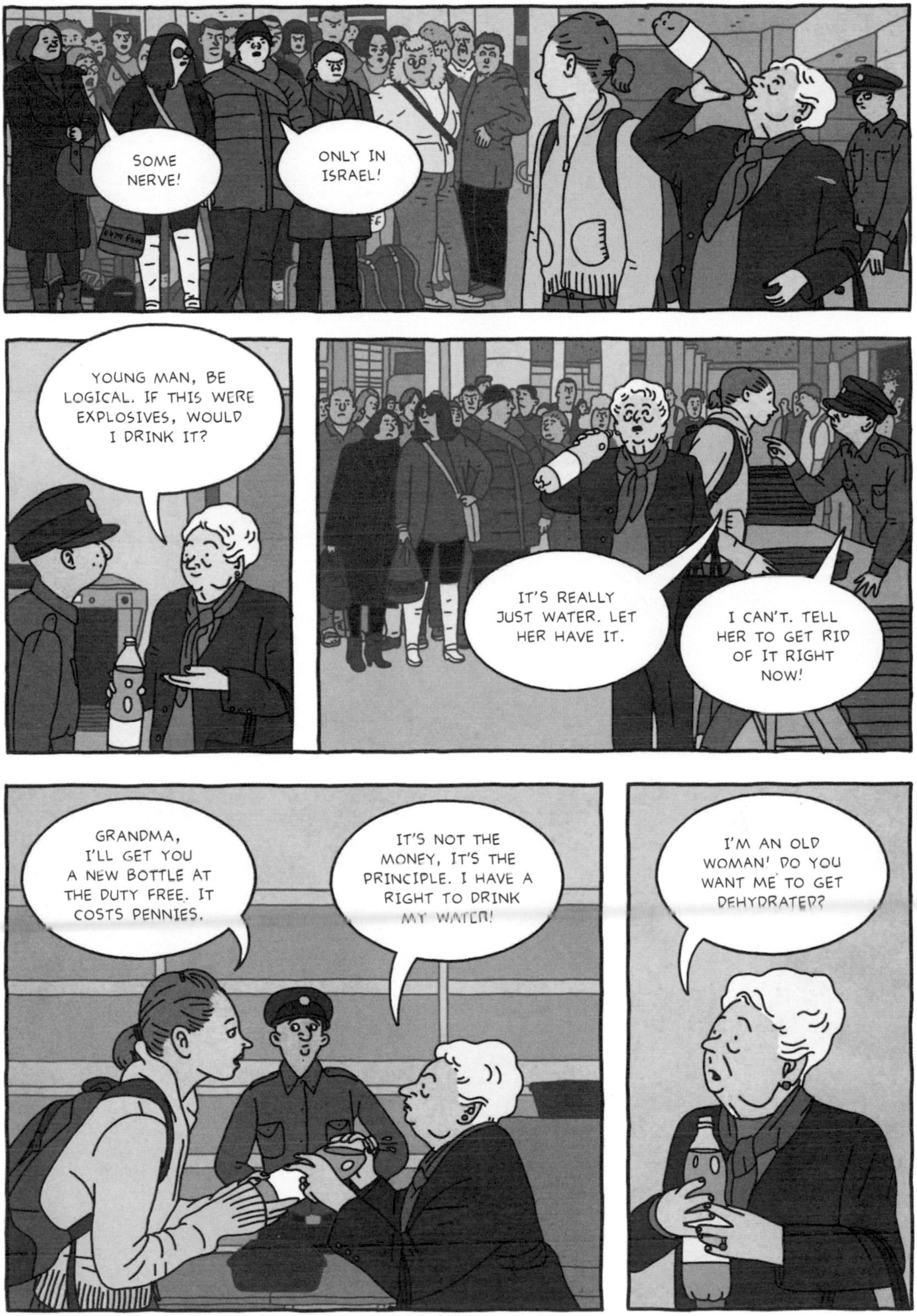
SOME NERVE!
ONLY IN ISRAEL!
YOUNG MAN, BE LOGICAL. IF THIS WERE EXPLOSIVES, WOULD I DRINK IT?
IT'S REALLY JUST WATER. LET HER HAVE IT.
I CAN'T. TELL HER TO GET RID OF IT RIGHT NOW!
GRANDMA, I'LL GET YOU A NEW BOTTLE AT THE DUTY FREE. IT COSTS PENNIES.
IT'S NOT THE MONEY, IT'S THE PRINCIPLE. I HAVE A RIGHT TO DRINK MY WATER!
I'M AN OLD WOMAN! DO YOU WANT ME TO GET DEHYDRATED?

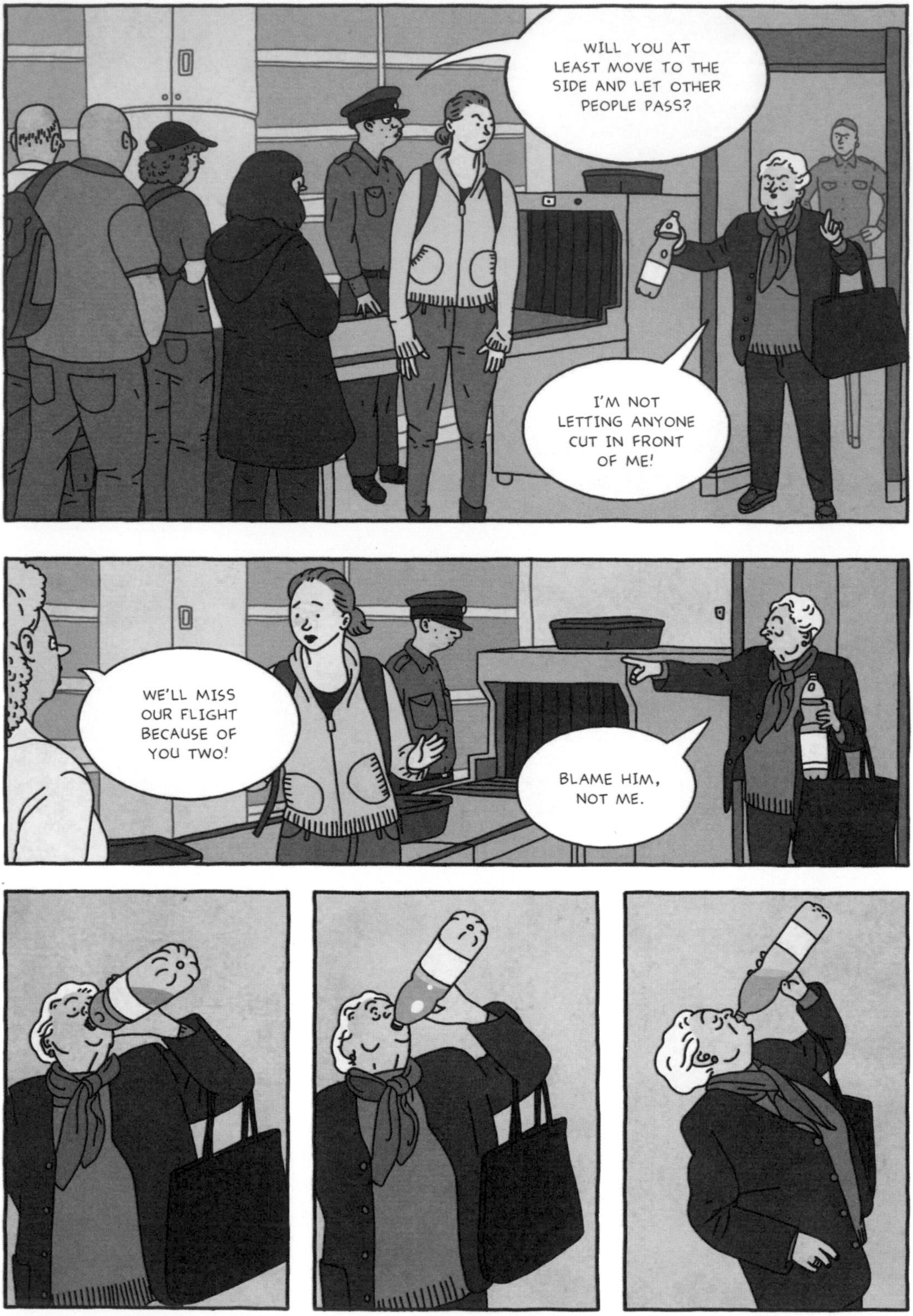
WILL YOU AT LEAST MOVE TO THE SIDE AND LET OTHER PEOPLE PASS?
I'M NOT LETTING ANYONE CUT IN FRONT OF ME!
WE'LL MISS OUR FLIGHT BECAUSE OF YOU TWO!
BLAME HIM, NOT ME.

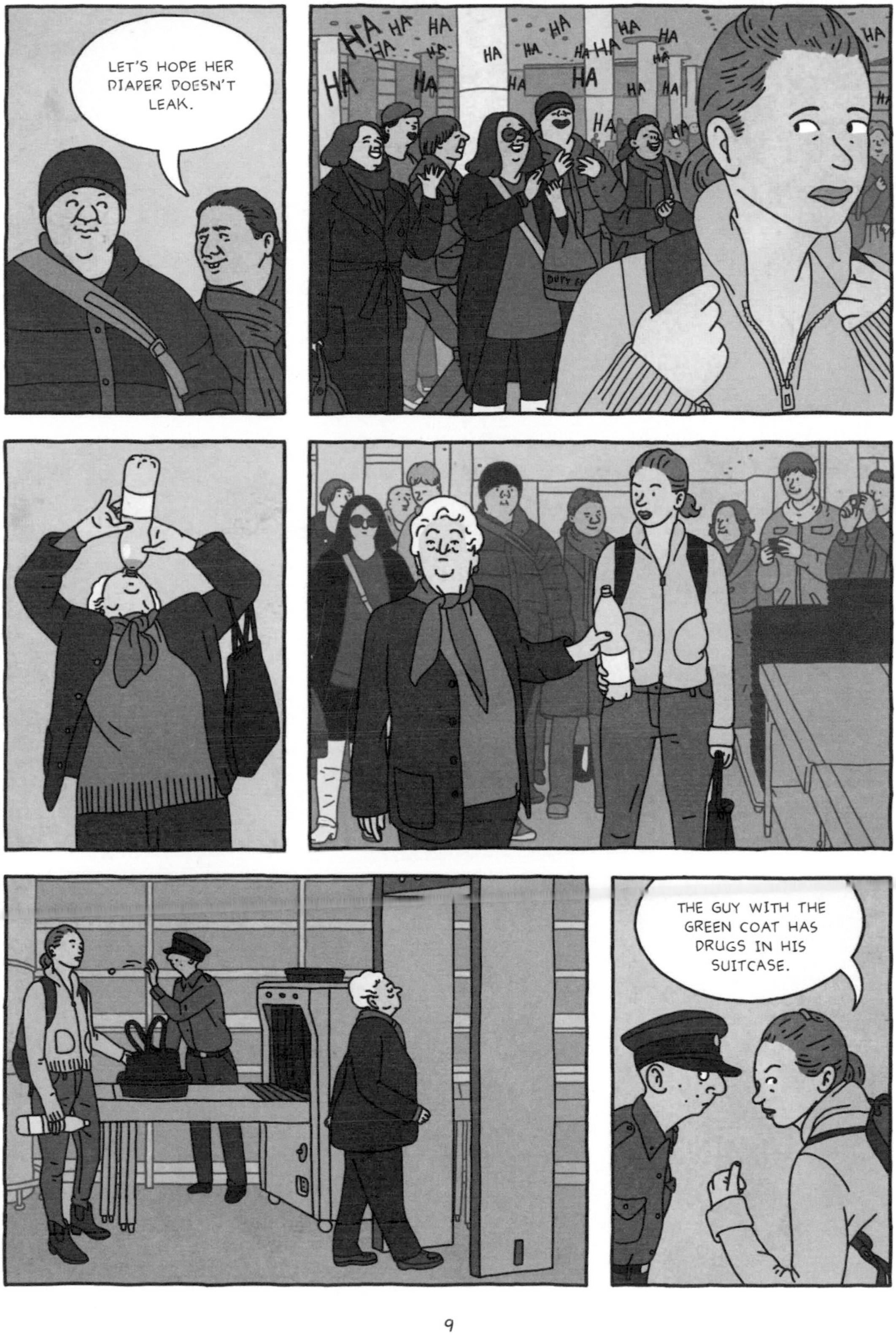
LET'S HOPE HER DIAPER DOESN'T LEAK.
HA HA HA HA HA HA HA HA HA HA HA HA HA HA HA HA HA HA HA HA HA
THE GUY WITH THE GREEN COAT HAS DRUGS IN HIS SUITCASE.

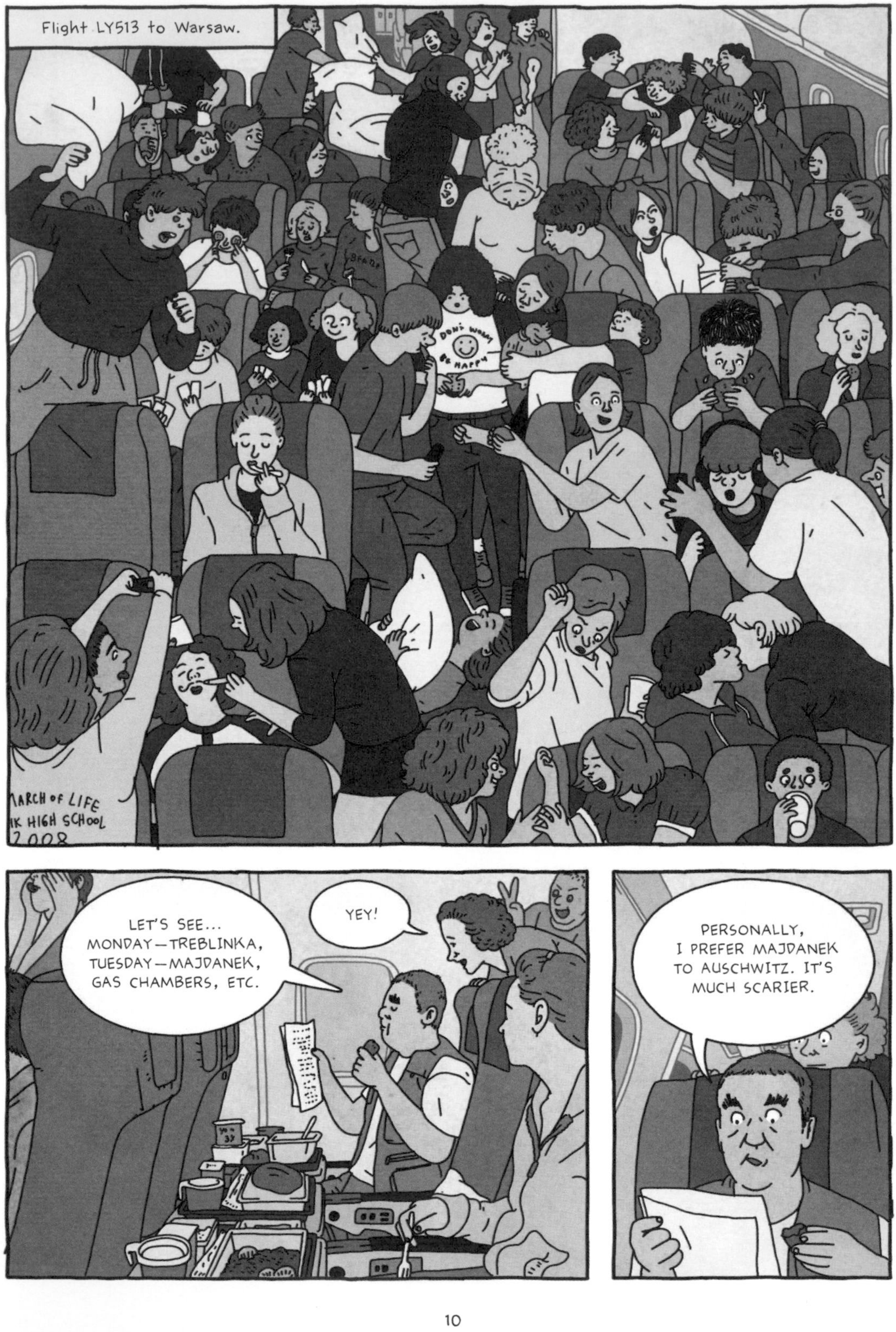
Flight LY513 to Warsaw.
MARCH OF LIFE
LET'S SEE... MONDAY—TREBLINKA, TUESDAY—MAJDANEK, GAS CHAMBERS, ETC.
YEY!
PERSONALLY, I PREFER MAJDANEK TO AUSCHWITZ. IT'S MUCH SCARIER.

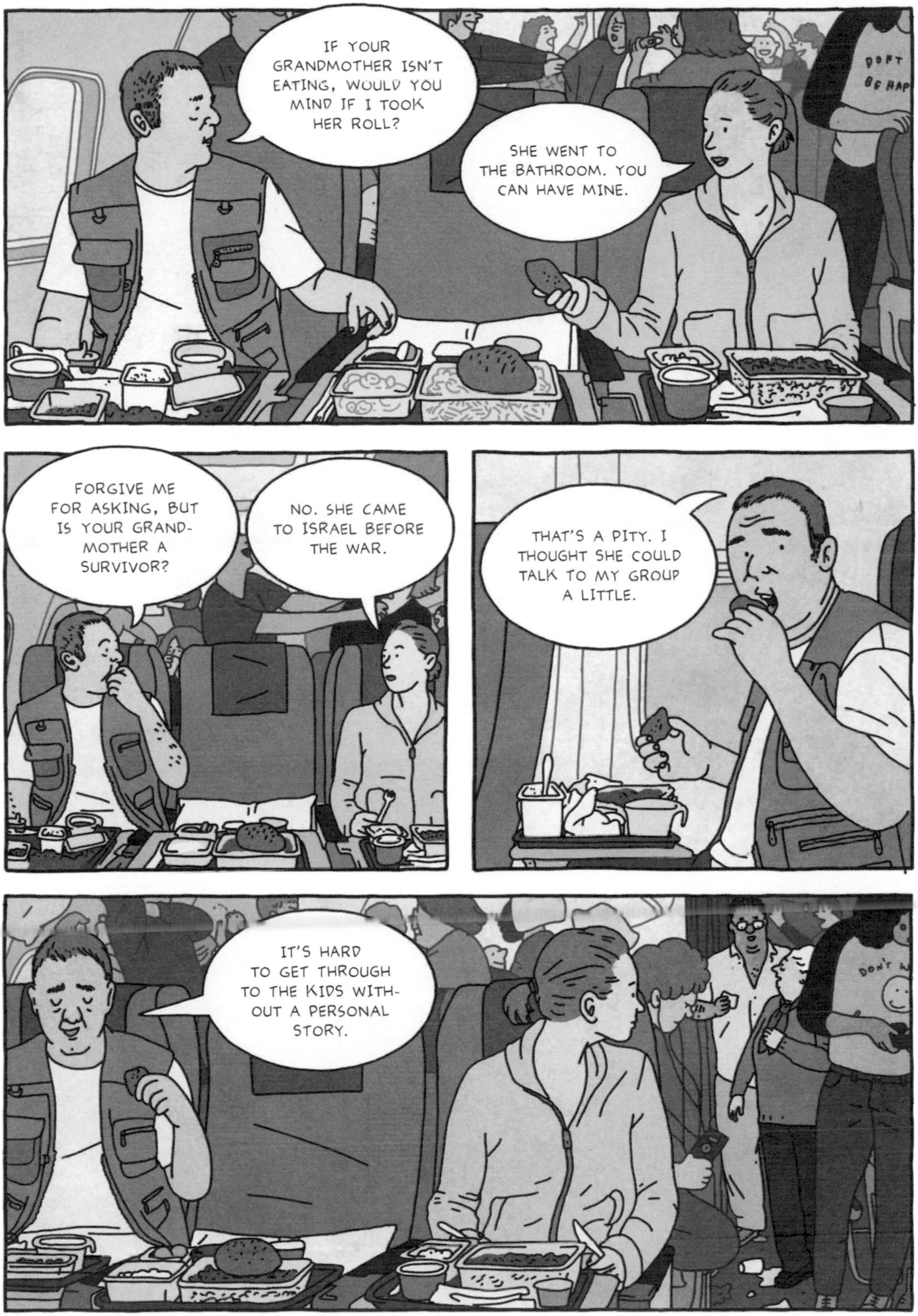
IF YOUR GRANDMOTHER ISN'T EATING, WOULD YOU MIND IF I TOOK HER ROLL?
SHE WENT TO THE BATHROOM. YOU CAN HAVE MINE.
FORGIVE ME FOR ASKING, BUT IS YOUR GRAND-MOTHER A SURVIVOR?
NO. SHE CAME TO ISRAEL BEFORE THE WAR.
THAT'S A PITY. I THOUGHT SHE COULD TALK TO MY GROUP A LITTLE.
IT'S HARD TO GET THROUGH TO THE KIDS WITH-OUT A PERSONAL STORY.

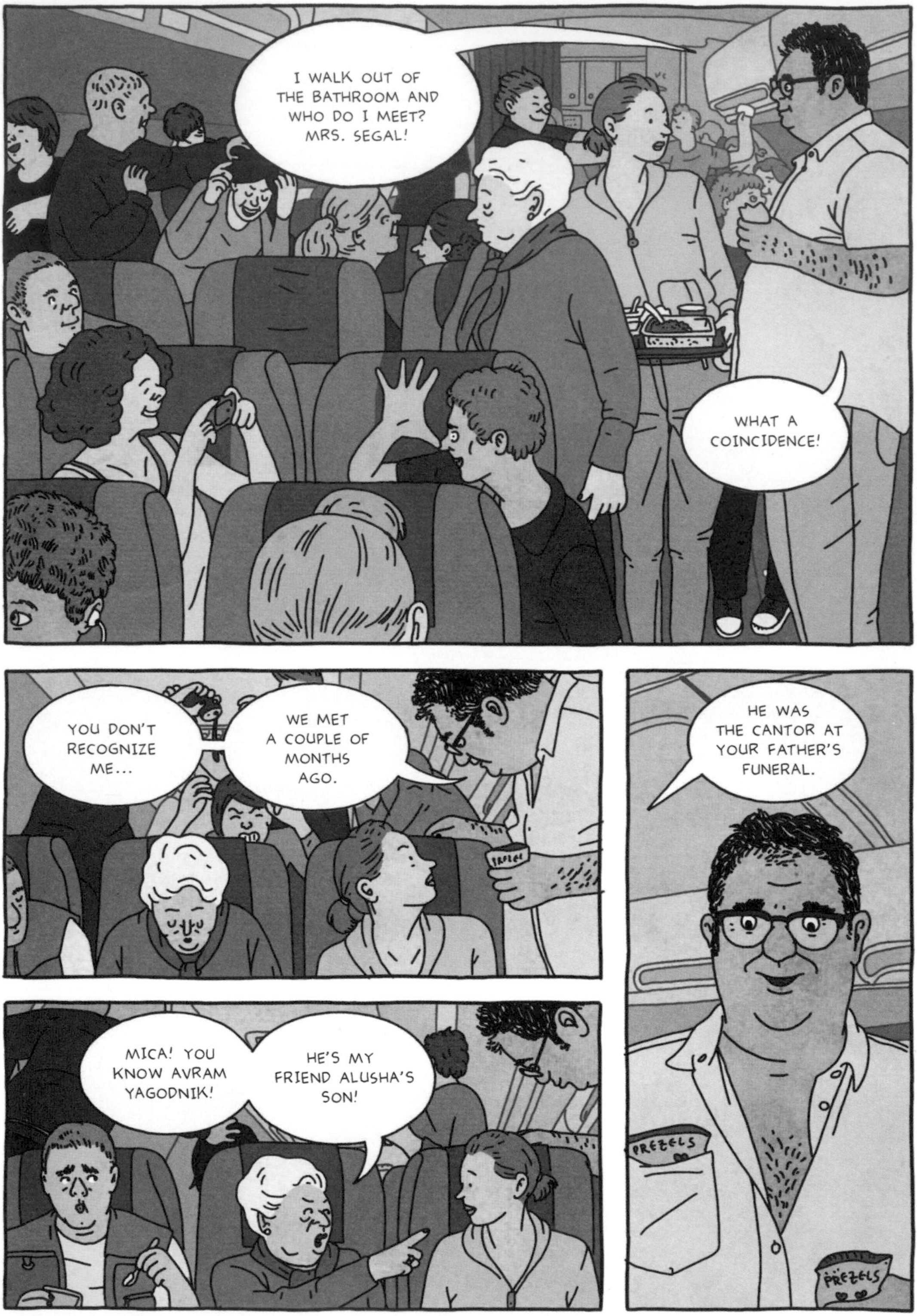
I WALK OUT OF THE BATHROOM AND WHO DO I MEET? MRS. SEGAL!
WHAT A COINCIDENCE!
YOU DON'T RECOGNIZE ME...
WE MET A COUPLE OF MONTHS AGO.
HE WAS THE CANTOR AT YOUR FATHER'S FUNERAL.
MICA! YOU KNOW AVRAM YAGODNIK!
HE'S MY FRIEND ALUSHA'S SON!
PREZELS
PREZELS

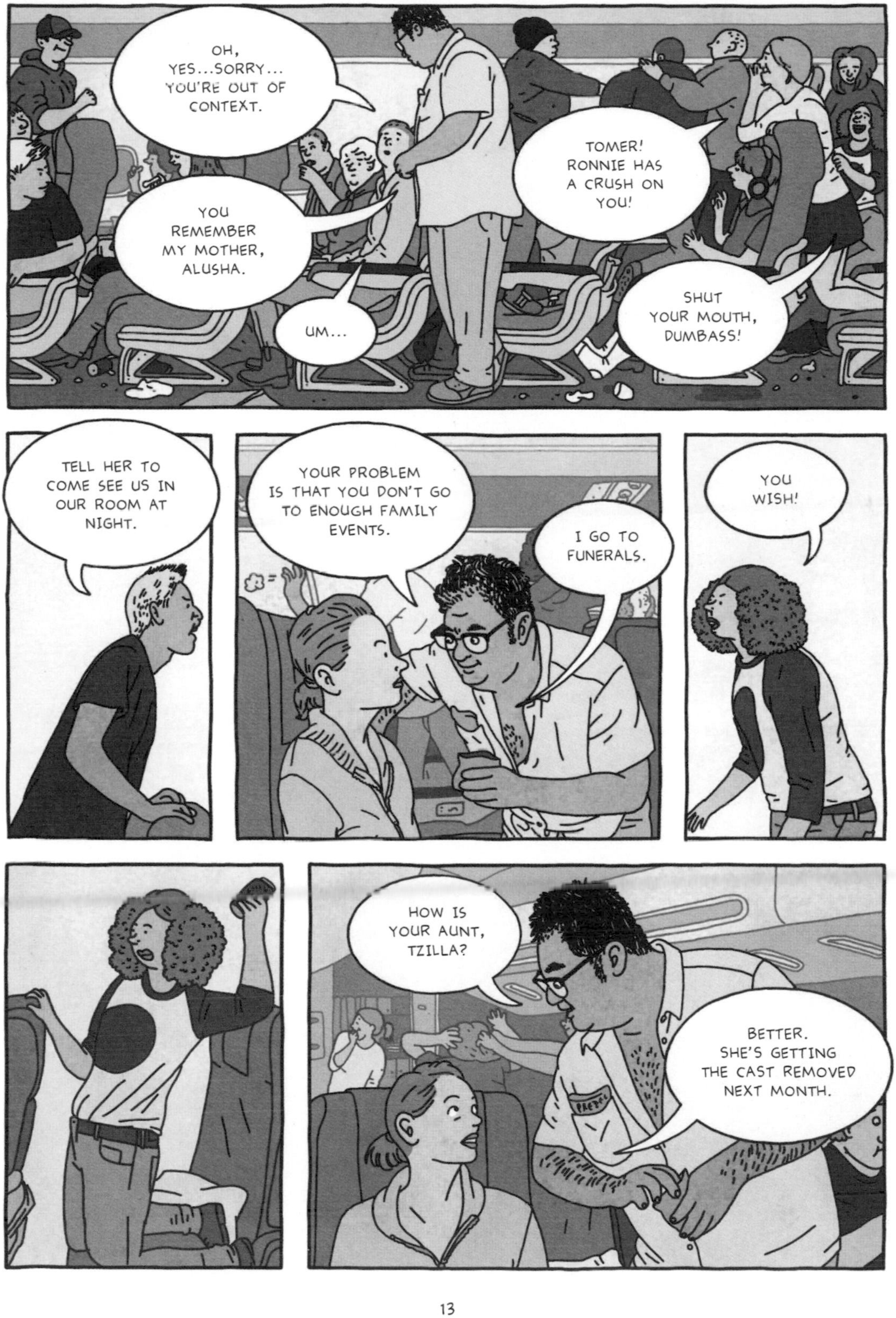
OH, YES...SORRY... YOU'RE OUT OF CONTEXT.
YOU REMEMBER MY MOTHER, ALUSHA.
UM...
TOMER! RONNIE HAS A CRUSH ON YOU!
SHUT YOUR MOUTH, DUMBASS!
TELL HER TO COME SEE US IN OUR ROOM AT NIGHT.
YOUR PROBLEM IS THAT YOU DON'T GO TO ENOUGH FAMILY EVENTS.
I GO TO FUNERALS.
YOU WISH!
HOW IS YOUR AUNT, TZILLA?
BETTER. SHE'S GETTING THE CAST REMOVED NEXT MONTH.

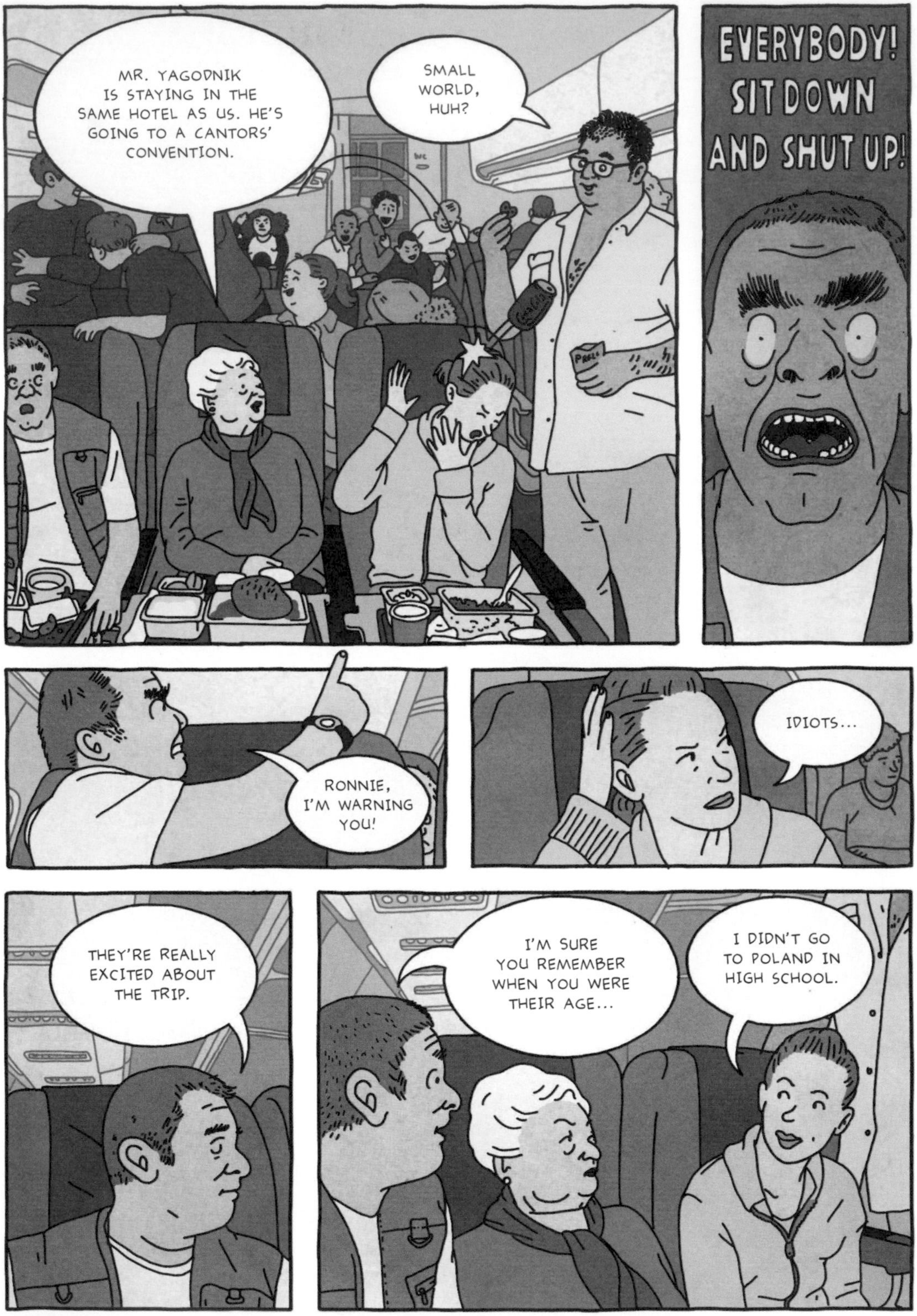
MR. YAGODNIK IS STAYING IN THE SAME HOTEL AS US. HE'S GOING TO A CANTORS' CONVENTION.
SMALL WORLD, HUH?
EVERYBODY! SIT DOWN AND SHUT UP!
RONNIE, I'M WARNING YOU!
IDIOTS...
THEY'RE REALLY EXCITED ABOUT THE TRIP.
I'M SURE YOU REMEMBER WHEN YOU WERE THEIR AGE...
I DIDN'T GO TO POLAND IN HIGH SCHOOL.

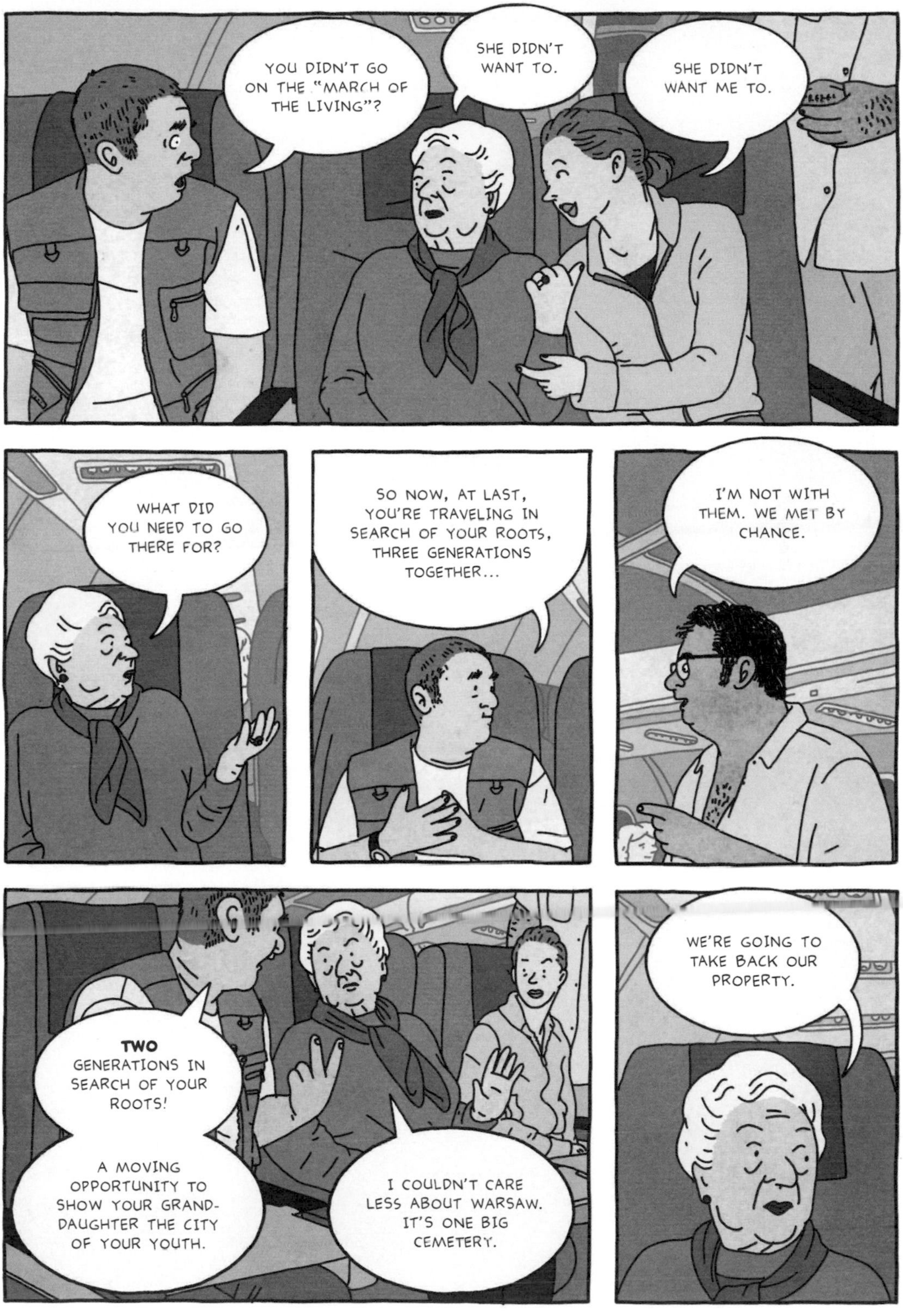
YOU DIDN'T GO ON THE "MARCH OF THE LIVING"?
SHE DIDN'T WANT TO.
SHE DIDN'T WANT ME TO.
WHAT DID YOU NEED TO GO THERE FOR?
SO NOW, AT LAST, YOU'RE TRAVELING IN SEARCH OF YOUR ROOTS, THREE GENERATIONS TOGETHER...
I'M NOT WITH THEM. WE MET BY CHANCE.
TWO GENERATIONS IN SEARCH OF YOUR ROOTS!
A MOVING OPPORTUNITY TO SHOW YOUR GRAND-DAUGHTER THE CITY OF YOUR YOUTH.
I COULDN'T CARE LESS ABOUT WARSAW. IT'S ONE BIG CEMETERY.
WE'RE GOING TO TAKE BACK OUR PROPERTY.

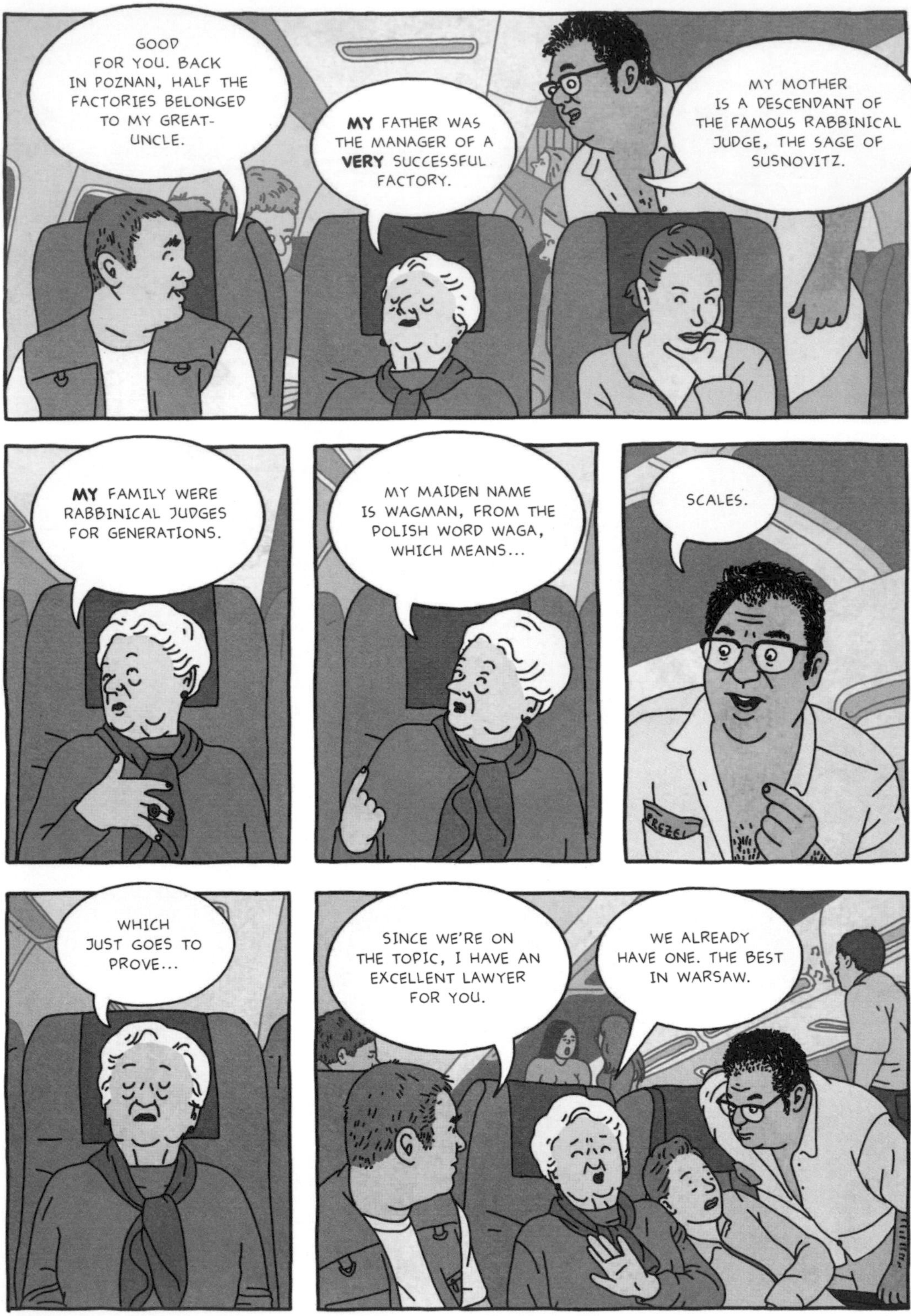
GOOD FOR YOU. BACK IN POZNAN, HALF THE FACTORIES BELONGED TO MY GREAT-UNCLE.
MY FATHER WAS THE MANAGER OF A VERY SUCCESSFUL FACTORY.
MY MOTHER IS A DESCENDANT OF THE FAMOUS RABBINICAL JUDGE, THE SAGE OF SUSNOVITZ.
MY FAMILY WERE RABBINICAL JUDGES FOR GENERATIONS.
MY MAIDEN NAME IS WAGMAN, FROM THE POLISH WORD WAGA, WHICH MEANS...
SCALES.
WHICH JUST GOES TO PROVE...
SINCE WE'RE ON THE TOPIC, I HAVE AN EXCELLENT LAWYER FOR YOU.
WE ALREADY HAVE ONE. THE BEST IN WARSAW.

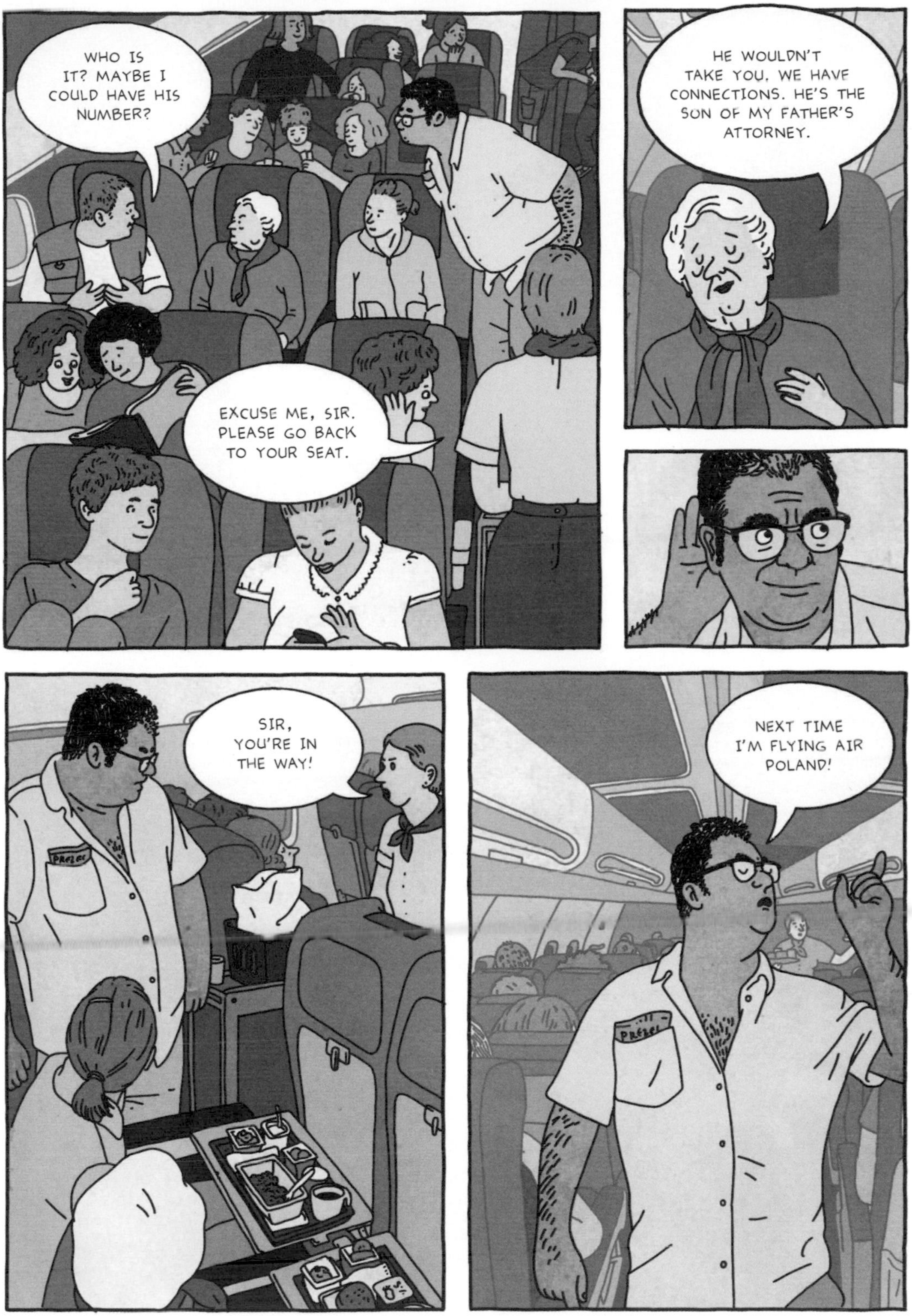
WHO IS IT? MAYBE I COULD HAVE HIS NUMBER?
EXCUSE ME, SIR. PLEASE GO BACK TO YOUR SEAT.
HE WOULDN'T TAKE YOU. WE HAVE CONNECTIONS. HE'S THE SON OF MY FATHER'S ATTORNEY.
SIR, YOU'RE IN THE WAY!
NEXT TIME I'M FLYING AIR POLAND!

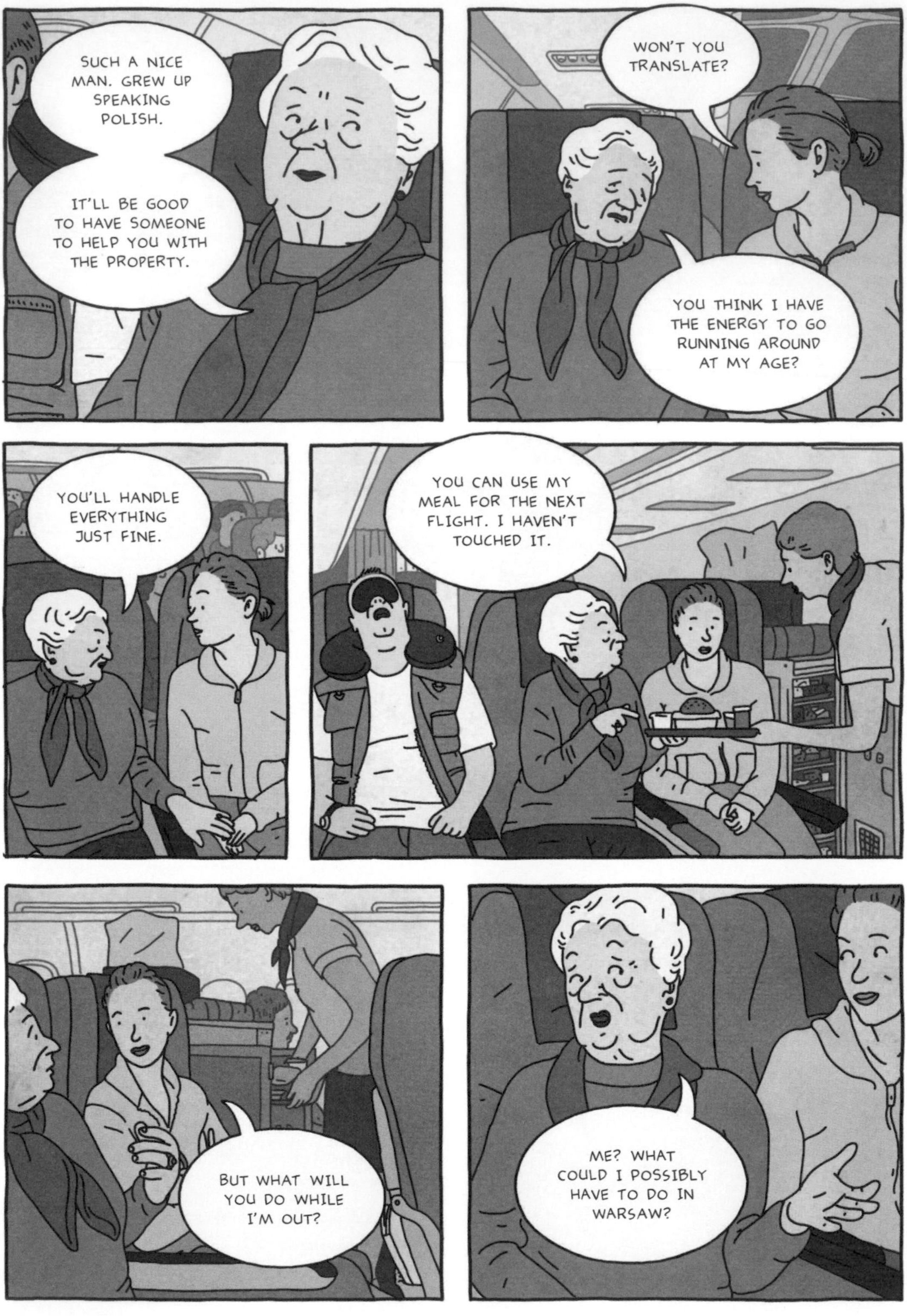
SUCH A NICE MAN. GREW UP SPEAKING POLISH.
IT'LL BE GOOD TO HAVE SOMEONE TO HELP YOU WITH THE PROPERTY.
WON'T YOU TRANSLATE?
YOU THINK I HAVE THE ENERGY TO GO RUNNING AROUND AT MY AGE?
YOU'LL HANDLE EVERYTHING JUST FINE.
YOU CAN USE MY MEAL FOR THE NEXT FLIGHT. I HAVEN'T TOUCHED IT.
BUT WHAT WILL YOU DO WHILE I'M OUT?
ME? WHAT COULD I POSSIBLY HAVE TO DO IN WARSAW?

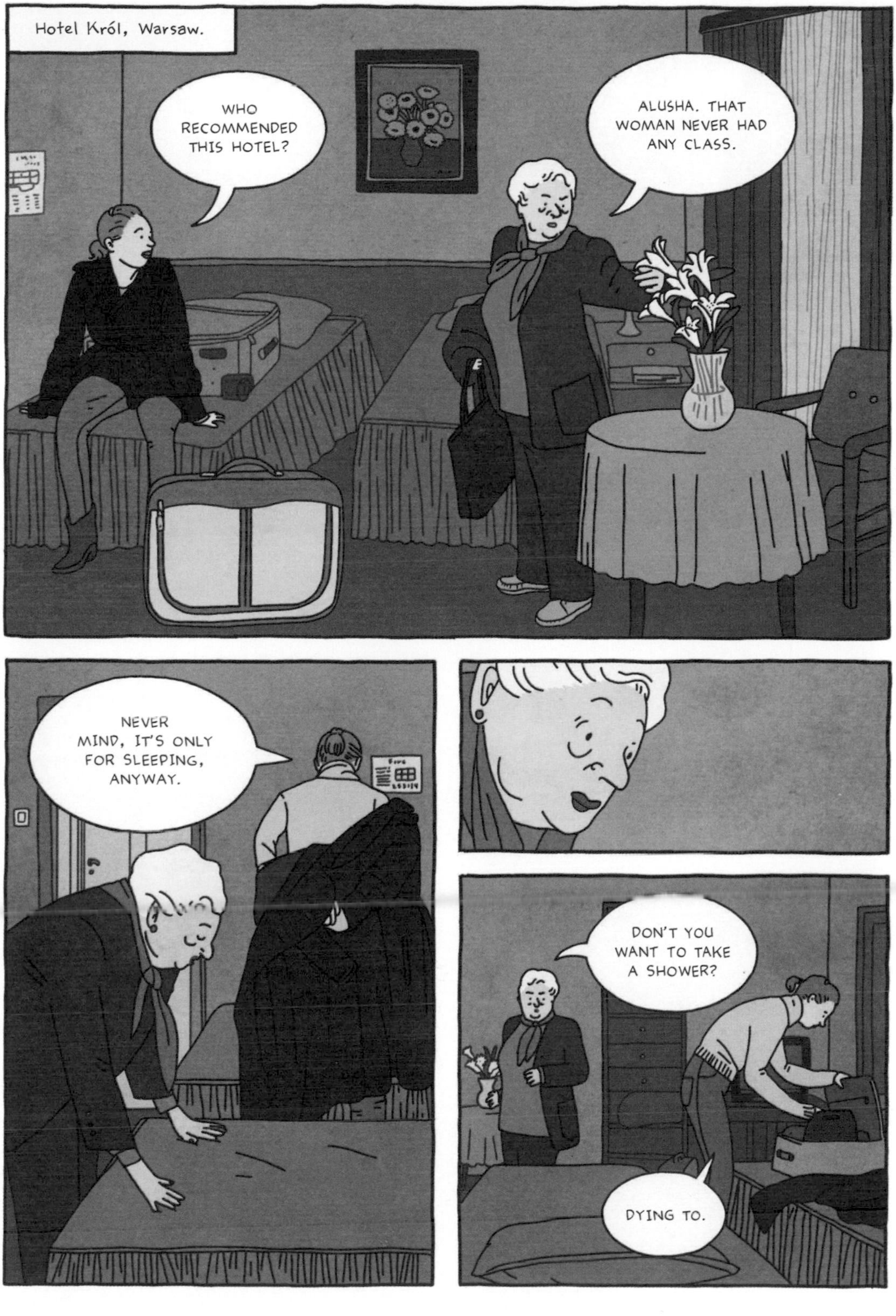
Hotel Król, Warsaw.
WHO RECOMMENDED THIS HOTEL?
ALUSHA. THAT WOMAN NEVER HAD ANY CLASS.
NEVER MIND, IT'S ONLY FOR SLEEPING, ANYWAY.
DON'T YOU WANT TO TAKE A SHOWER?
DYING TO.

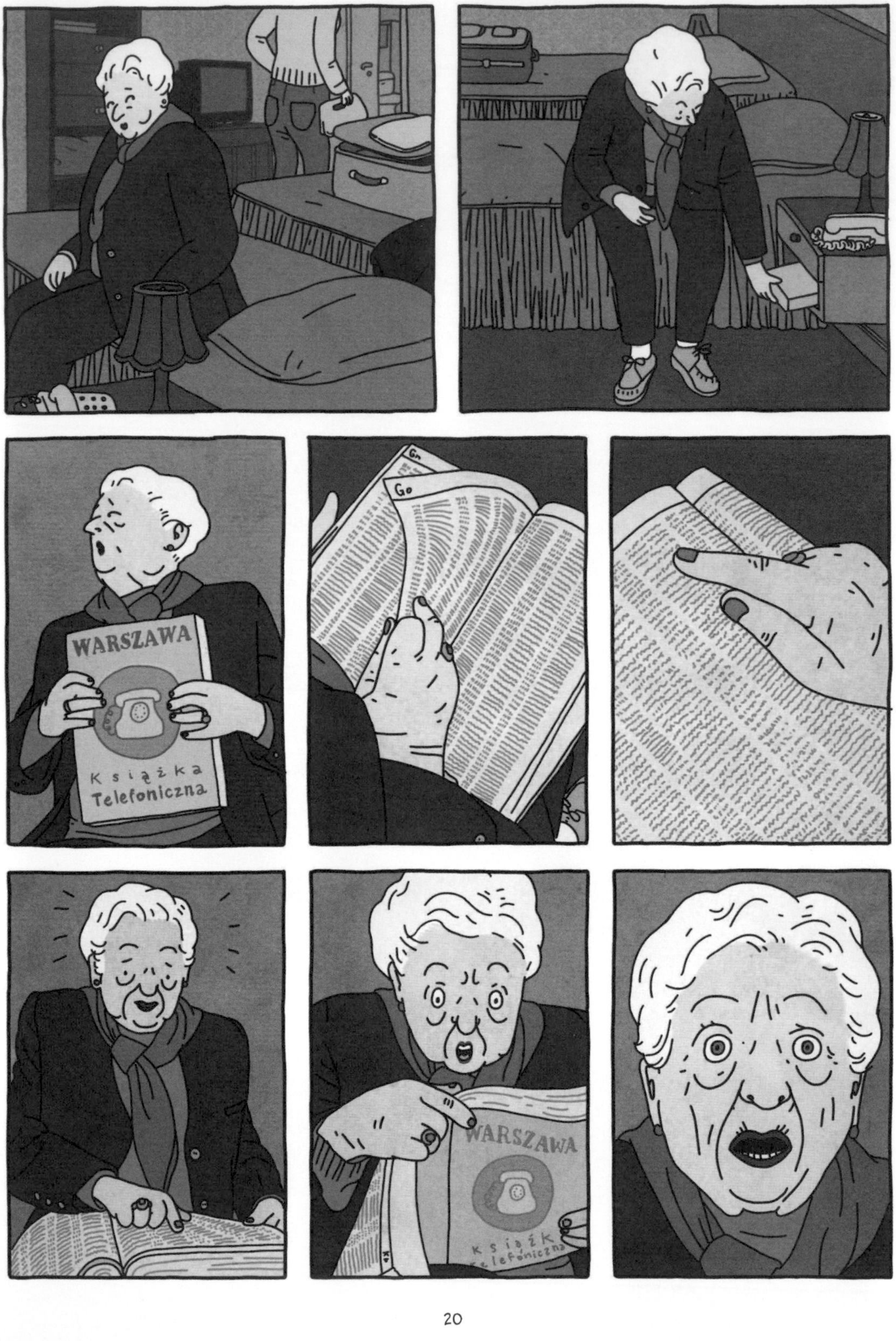
WARSZAWA
Książka
Telefoniczna
Gr
Go
WARSZAWA

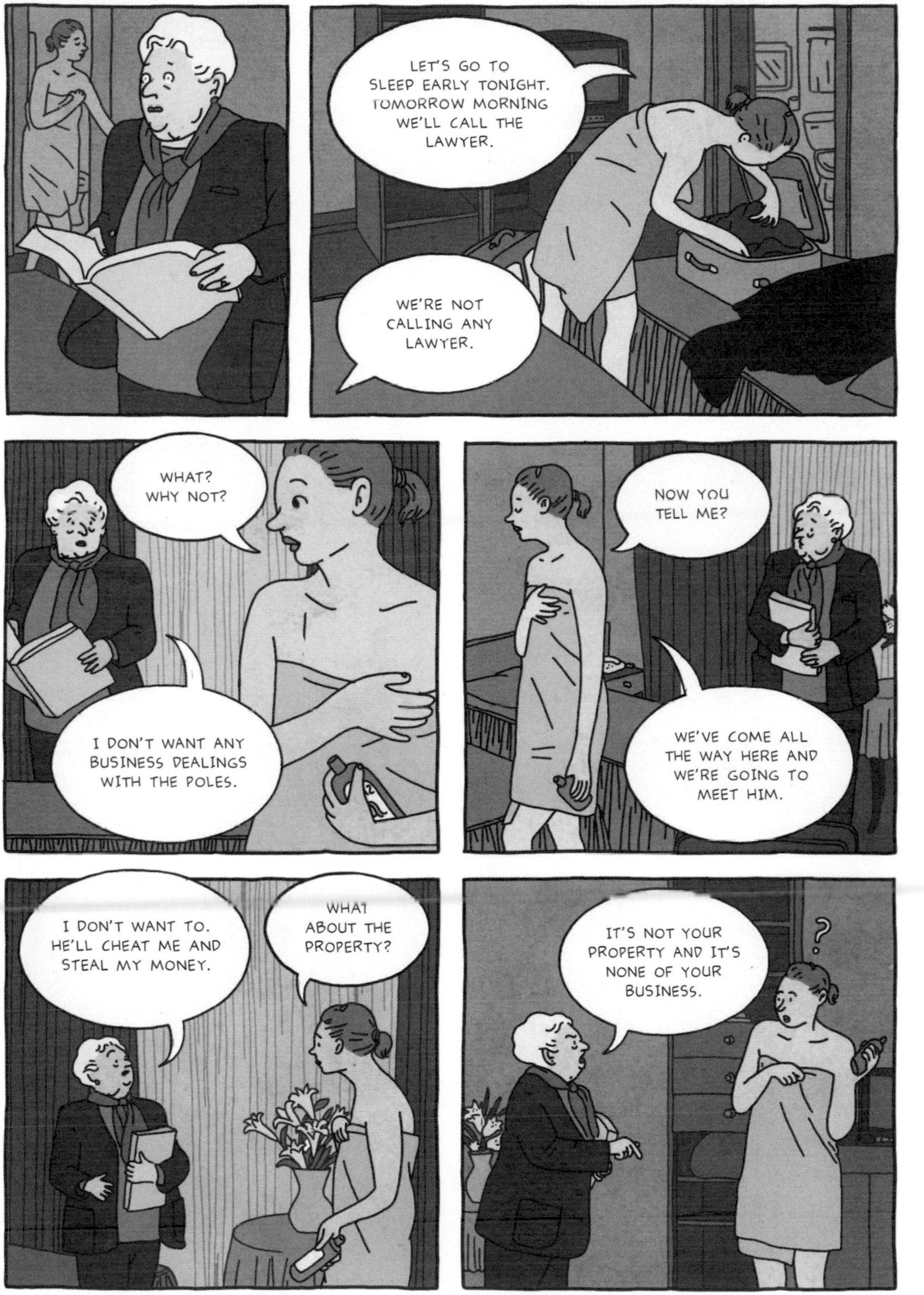
LET'S GO TO SLEEP EARLY TONIGHT. TOMORROW MORNING WE'LL CALL THE LAWYER.
WE'RE NOT CALLING ANY LAWYER.
WHAT? WHY NOT?
I DON'T WANT ANY BUSINESS DEALINGS WITH THE POLES.
NOW YOU TELL ME?
WE'VE COME ALL THE WAY HERE AND WE'RE GOING TO MEET HIM.
I DON'T WANT TO. HE'LL CHEAT ME AND STEAL MY MONEY.
WHAT ABOUT THE PROPERTY?
IT'S NOT YOUR PROPERTY AND IT'S NONE OF YOUR BUSINESS.
?

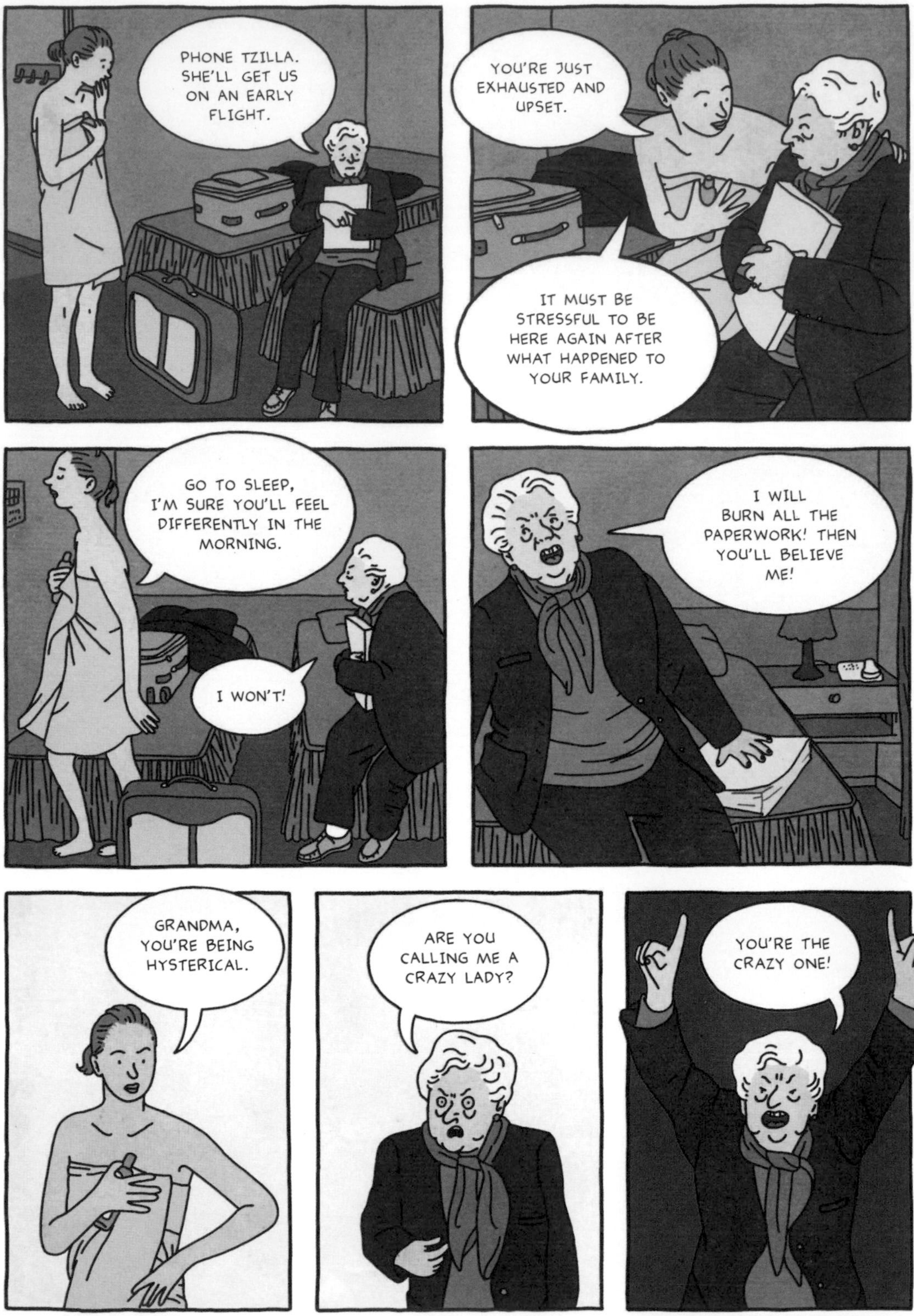
PHONE TZILLA. SHE'LL GET US ON AN EARLY FLIGHT.
YOU'RE JUST EXHAUSTED AND UPSET.
IT MUST BE STRESSFUL TO BE HERE AGAIN AFTER WHAT HAPPENED TO YOUR FAMILY.
GO TO SLEEP, I'M SURE YOU'LL FEEL DIFFERENTLY IN THE MORNING.
I WON'T!
I WILL BURN ALL THE PAPERWORK! THEN YOU'LL BELIEVE ME!
GRANDMA, YOU'RE BEING HYSTERICAL.
ARE YOU CALLING ME A CRAZY LADY?
YOU'RE THE CRAZY ONE!

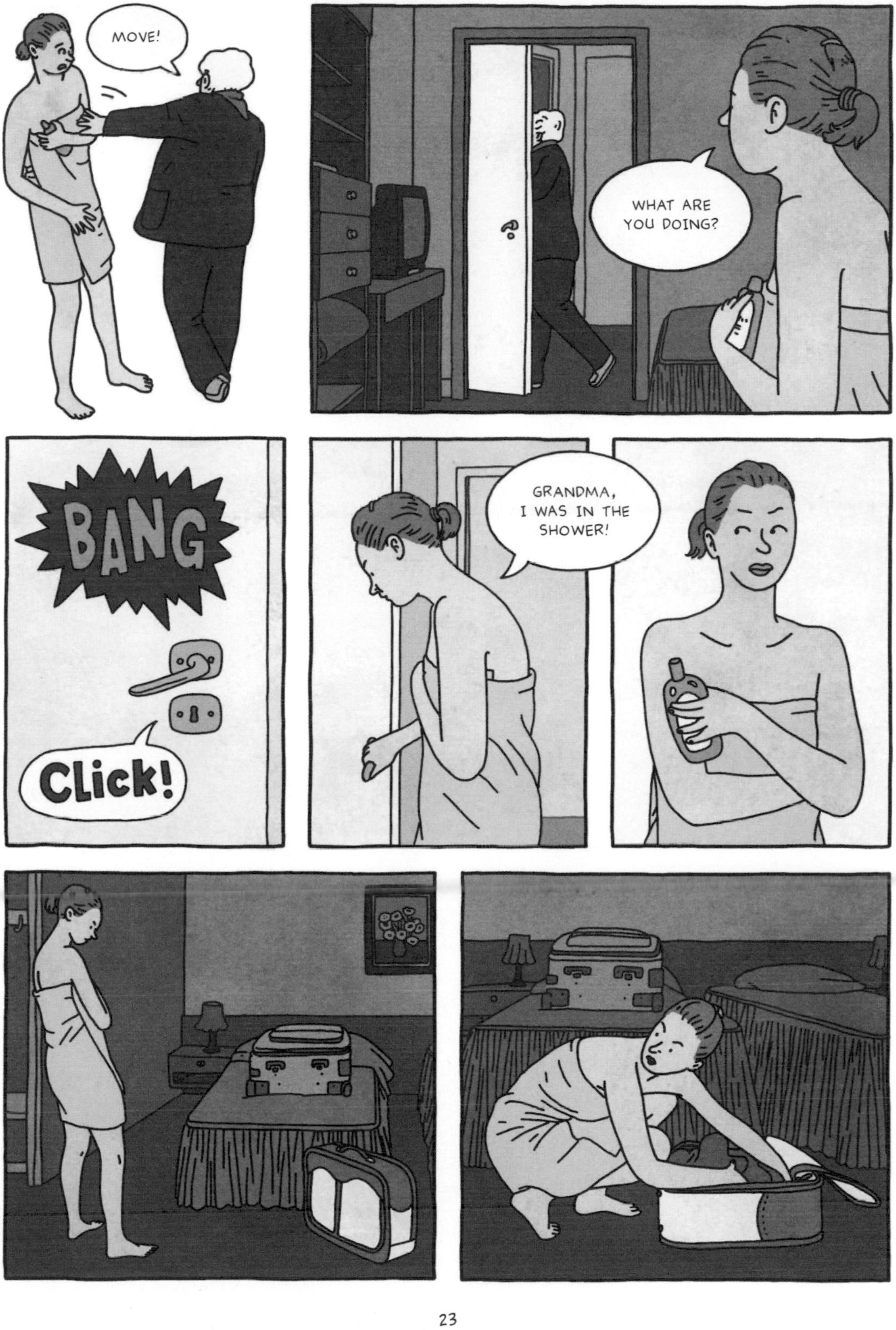
MOVE!
WHAT ARE YOU DOING?
BANG
Click!
GRANDMA, I WAS IN THE SHOWER!

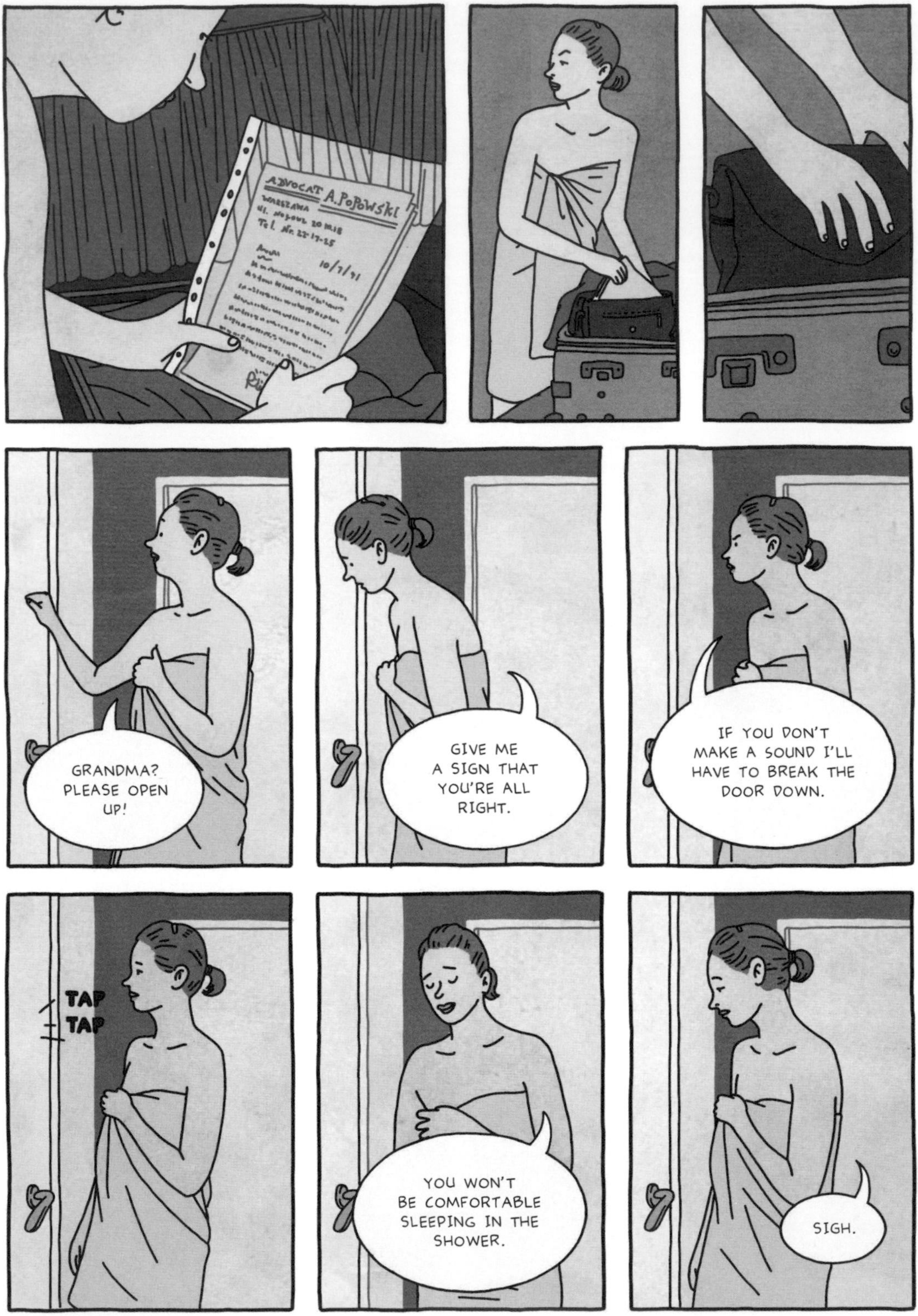
ADVOCAT A.POPOWSKI
GRANDMA? PLEASE OPEN UP!
GIVE ME A SIGN THAT YOU'RE ALL RIGHT.
IF YOU DON'T MAKE A SOUND I'LL HAVE TO BREAK THE DOOR DOWN.
TAP TAP
YOU WON'T BE COMFORTABLE SLEEPING IN THE SHOWER.
SIGH.

Later...

Górska Barbara Żelazna
Górski Ewa Ciepła 3......
Górski Roman Nasza 31...
Górski Ta   Śliska 20...
óruk Ire   warda 21...
aba Ja   Długa 30...
bajto
barcz
ias t

DAY TWO

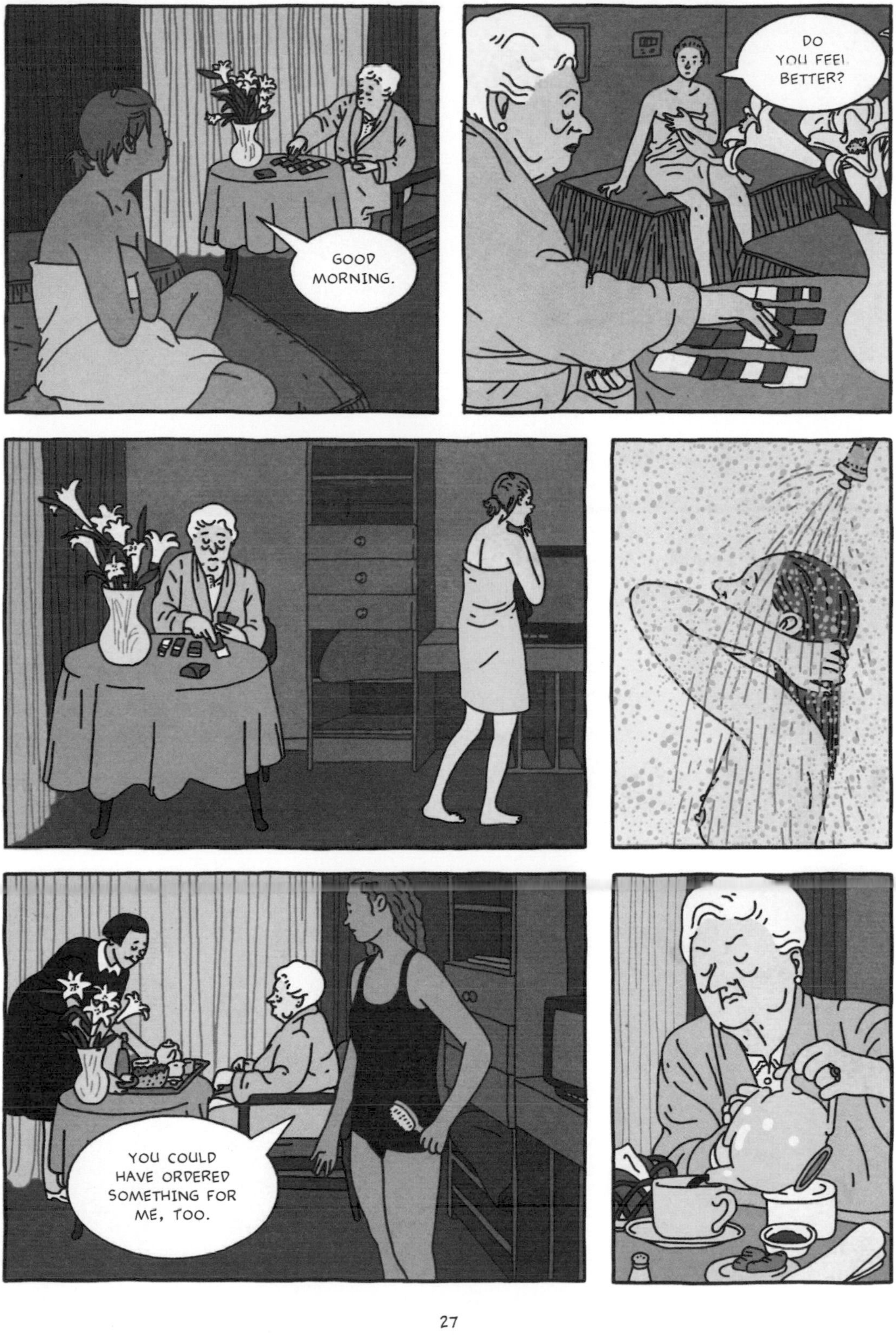
GOOD MORNING.
DO YOU FEEL BETTER?
YOU COULD HAVE ORDERED SOMETHING FOR ME, TOO.

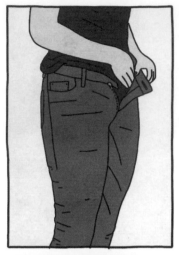

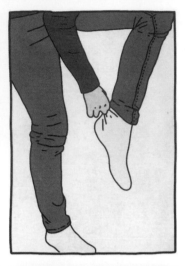

CAN WE TALK REASONABLY FOR A MINUTE?

FINE.

I'M GOING DOWN TO EAT.

31 Nasza Street.

Ring ring...

Hello?*

May I speak with Mr. Gorski?

One moment...

Father!

Ma'am?

Mr. Gorski is busy.

Give me your name and he'll get back to you.

Beeep...

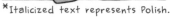
*Italicized text represents Polish.

29

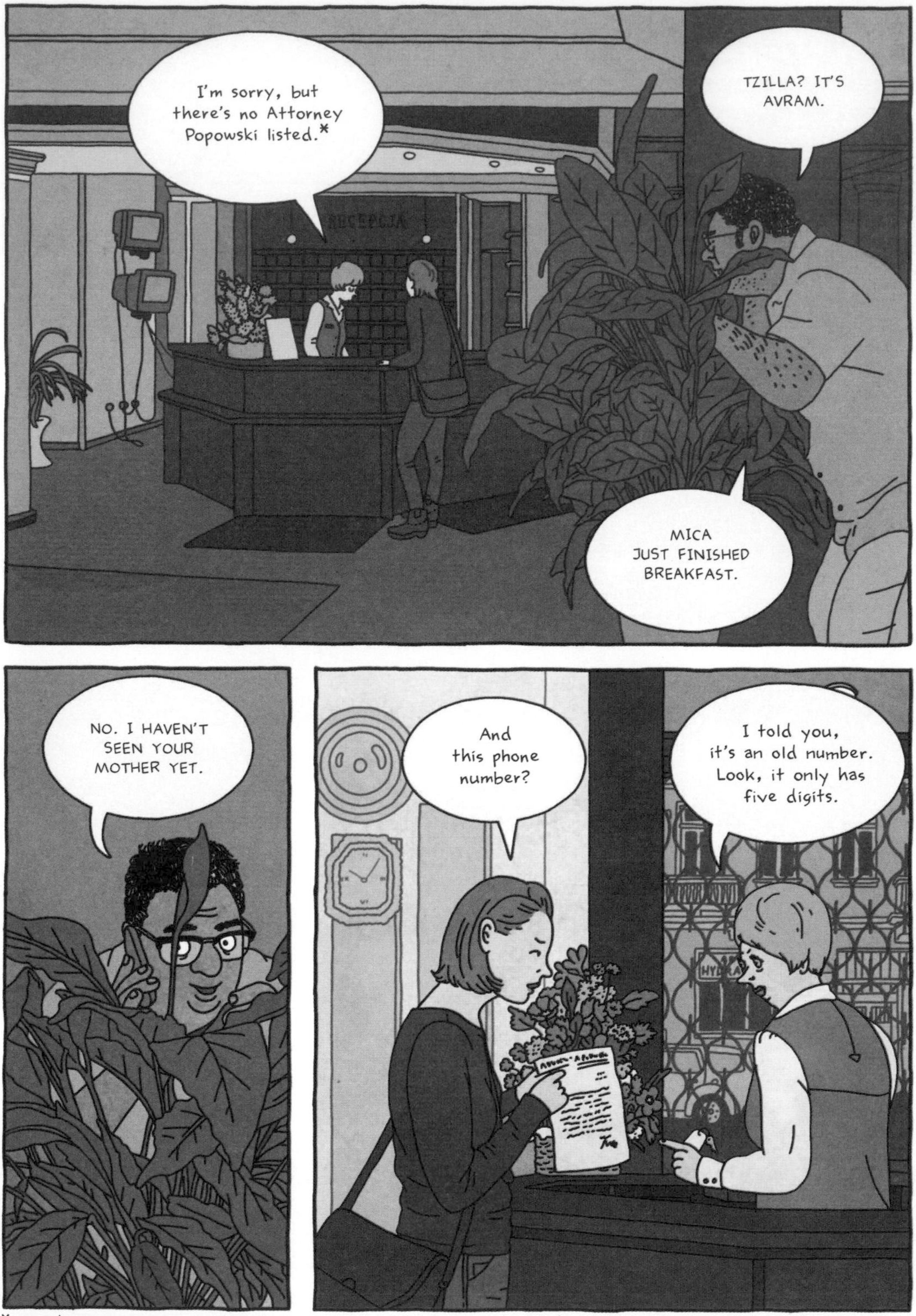
I'm sorry, but there's no Attorney Popowski listed.*
TZILLA? IT'S AVRAM.
MICA JUST FINISHED BREAKFAST.
NO. I HAVEN'T SEEN YOUR MOTHER YET.
And this phone number?
I told you, it's an old number. Look, it only has five digits.

*Mixed case represents English.

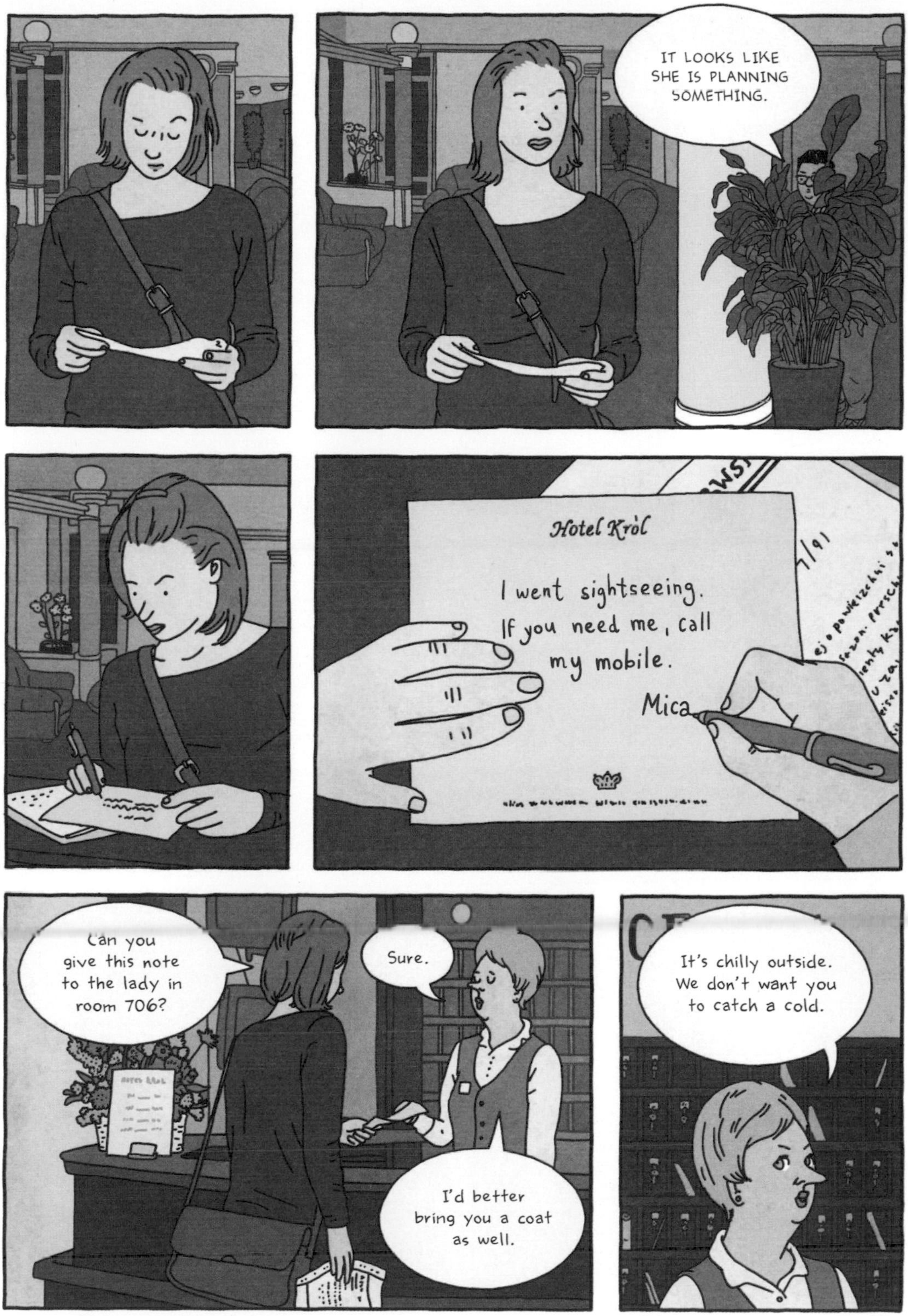
IT LOOKS LIKE SHE IS PLANNING SOMETHING.
Hotel Król
I went sightseeing. If you need me, call my mobile.
Mica
Can you give this note to the lady in room 706?
Sure.
I'd better bring you a coat as well.
It's chilly outside. We don't want you to catch a cold.

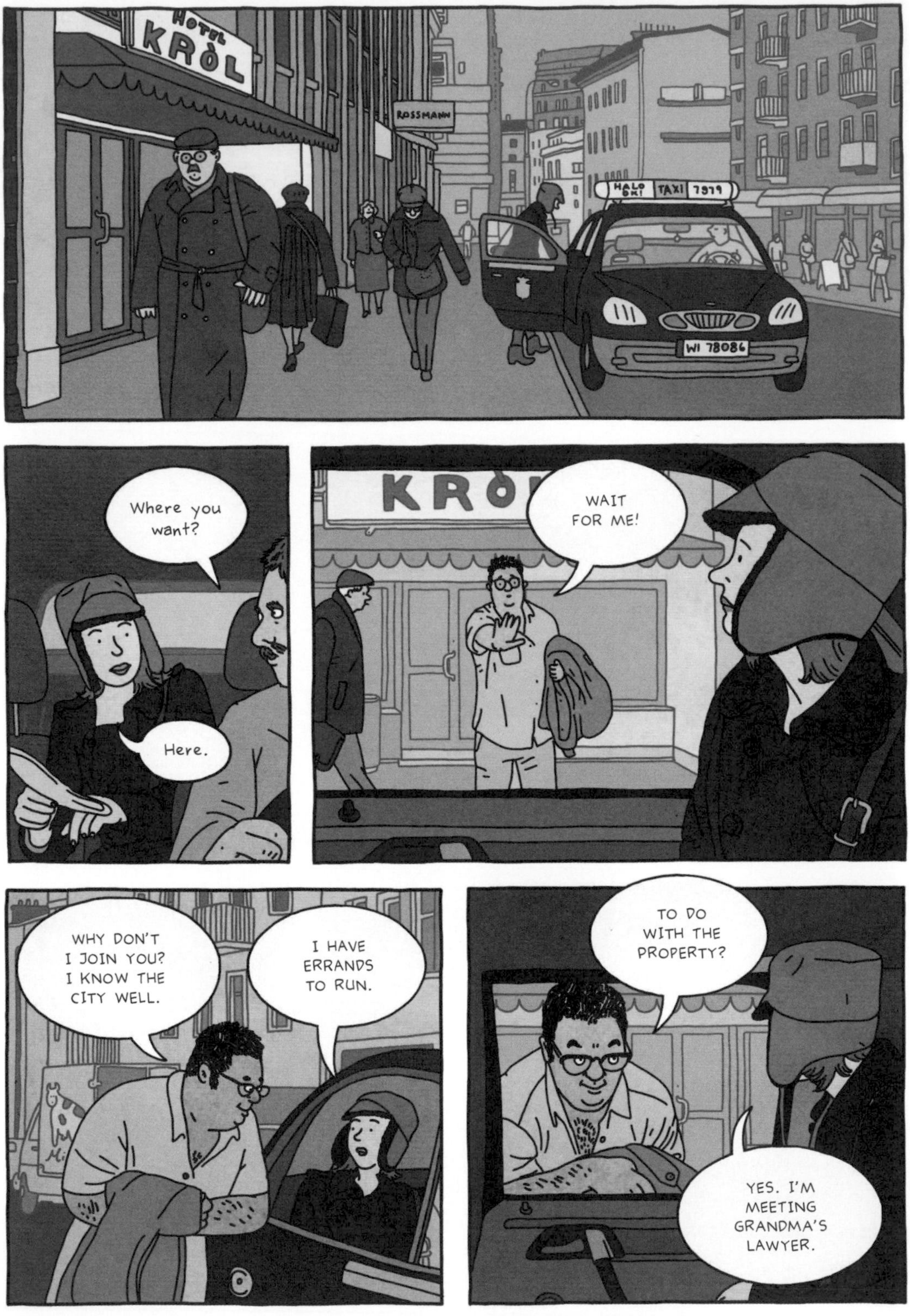
HOTEL KRÒL
ROSSMANN
TAXI 7979
WI 78086
Where you want?
Here.
KRÒL
WAIT FOR ME!
WHY DON'T I JOIN YOU? I KNOW THE CITY WELL.
I HAVE ERRANDS TO RUN.
TO DO WITH THE PROPERTY?
YES. I'M MEETING GRANDMA'S LAWYER.

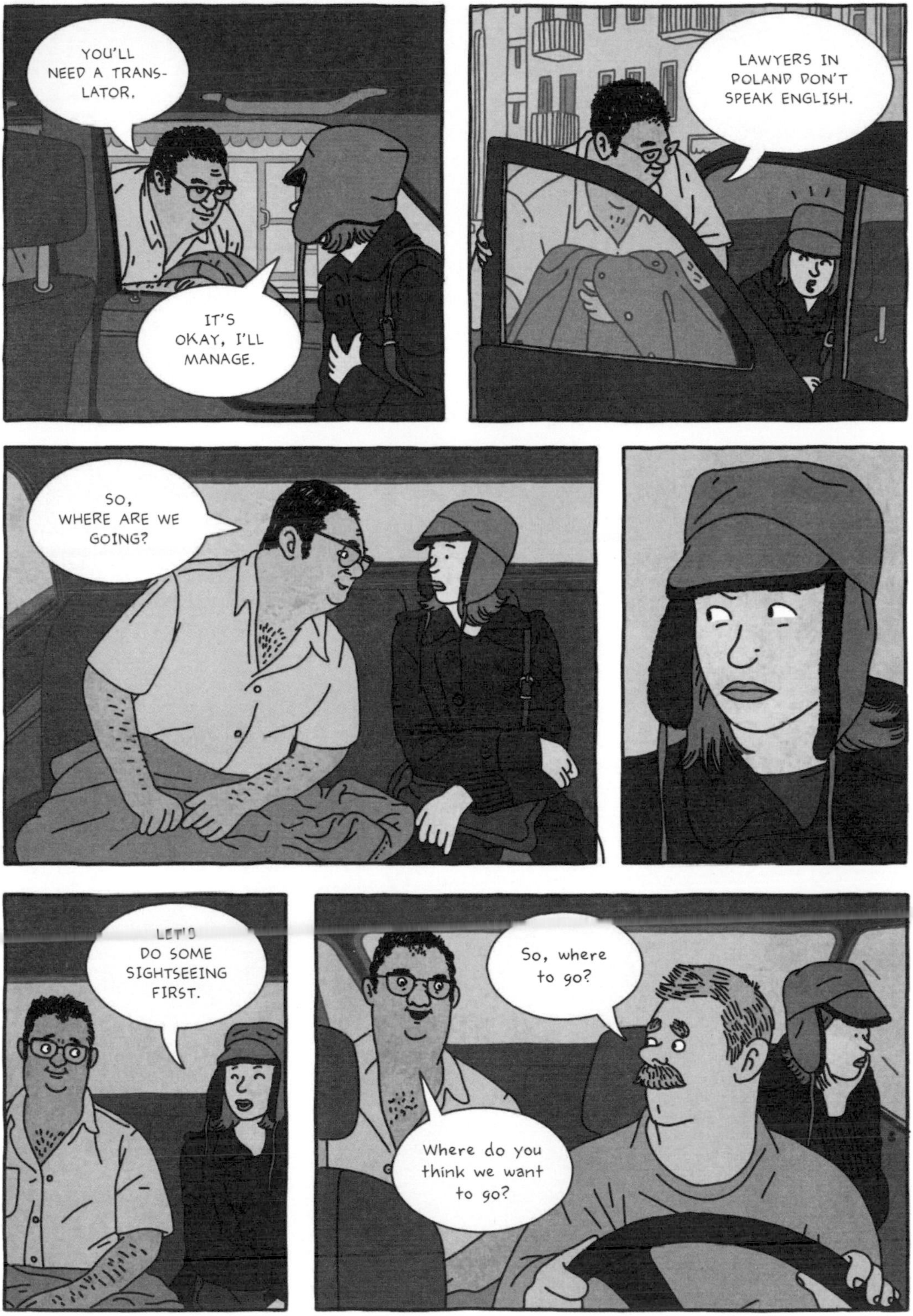
YOU'LL NEED A TRANSLATOR.
IT'S OKAY, I'LL MANAGE.
LAWYERS IN POLAND DON'T SPEAK ENGLISH.
SO, WHERE ARE WE GOING?
LET'S DO SOME SIGHTSEEING FIRST.
So, where to go?
Where do you think we want to go?

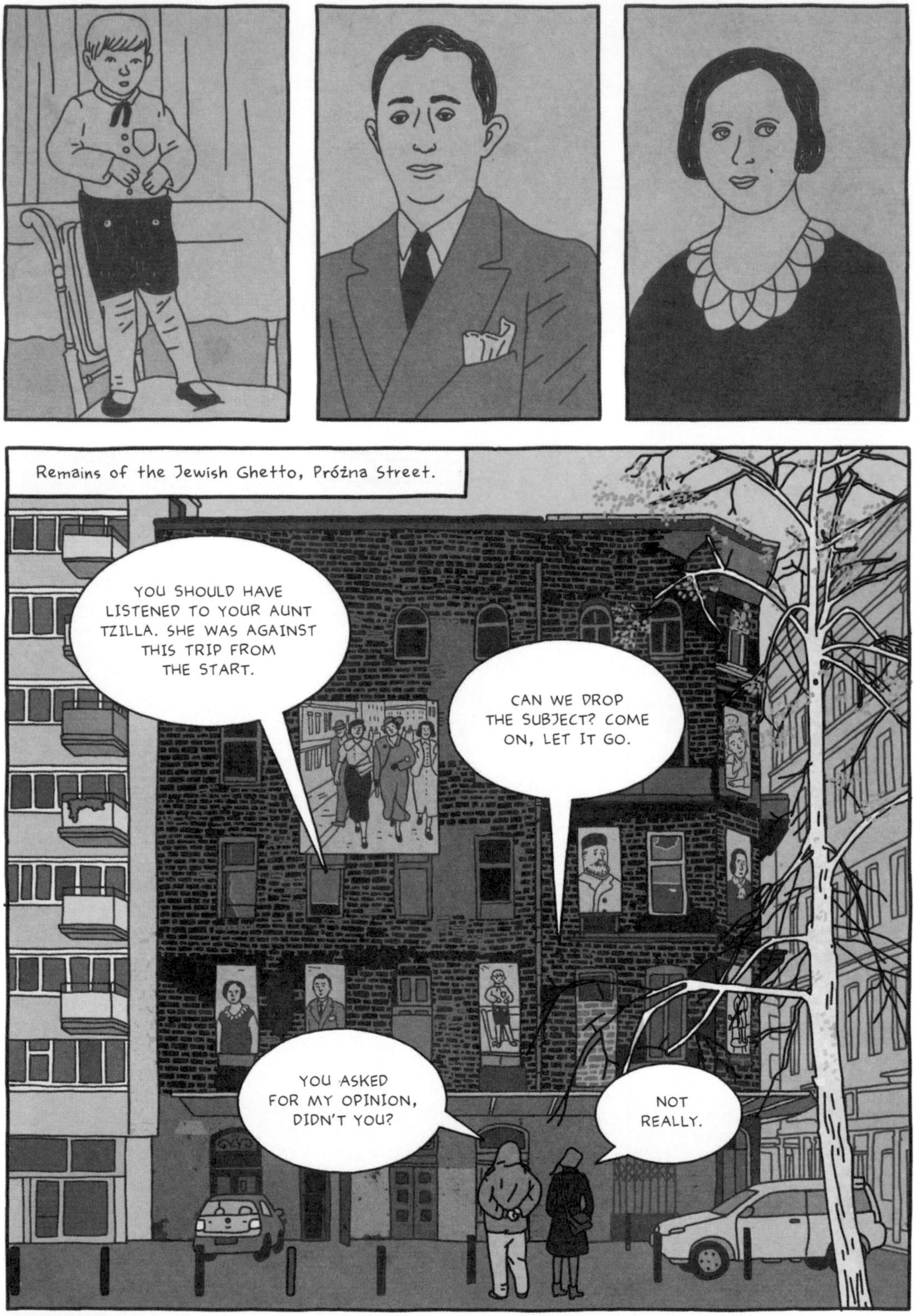
Remains of the Jewish Ghetto, Prózna Street.
YOU SHOULD HAVE LISTENED TO YOUR AUNT TZILLA. SHE WAS AGAINST THIS TRIP FROM THE START.
CAN WE DROP THE SUBJECT? COME ON, LET IT GO.
YOU ASKED FOR MY OPINION, DIDN'T YOU?
NOT REALLY.

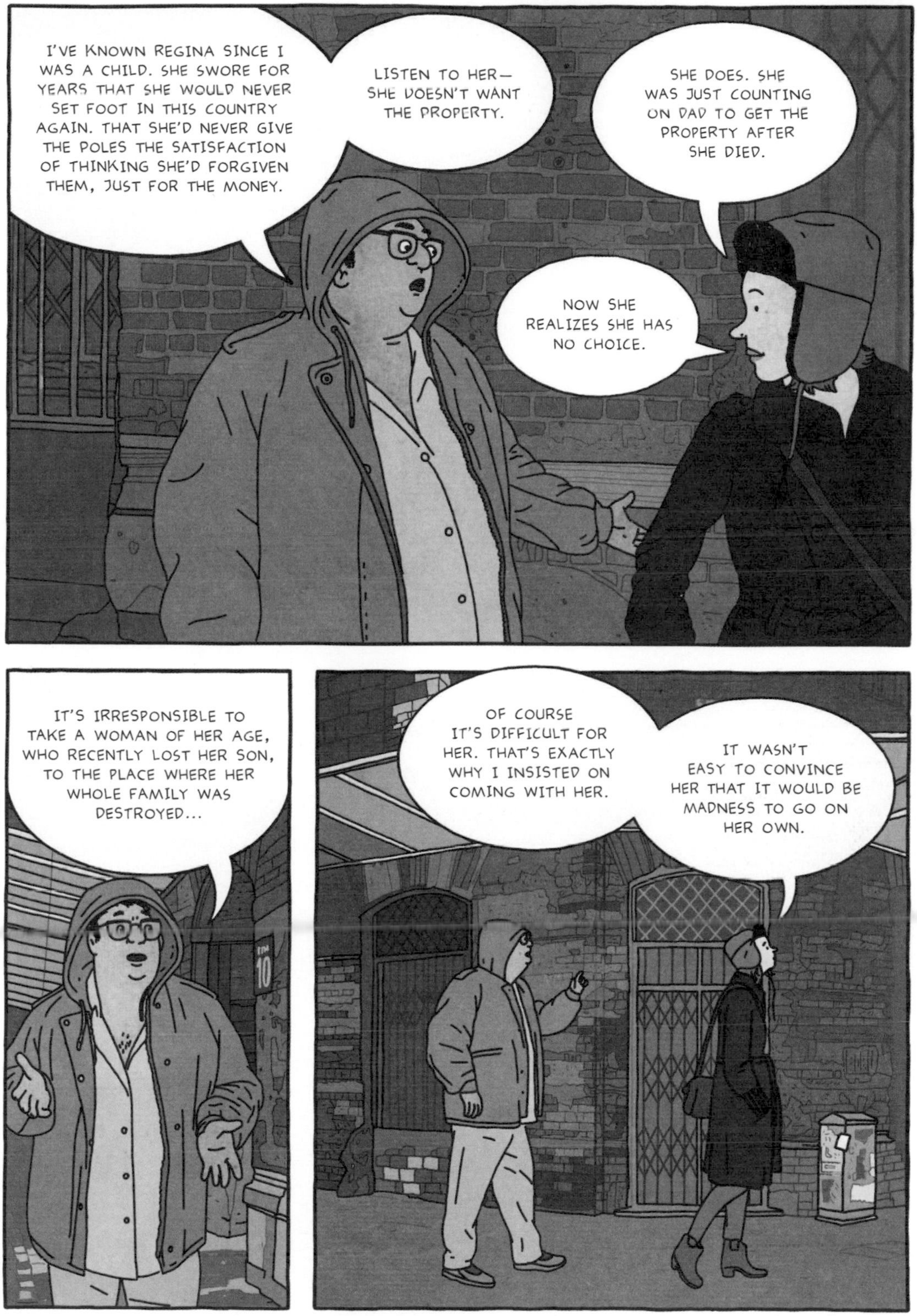
I'VE KNOWN REGINA SINCE I WAS A CHILD. SHE SWORE FOR YEARS THAT SHE WOULD NEVER SET FOOT IN THIS COUNTRY AGAIN. THAT SHE'D NEVER GIVE THE POLES THE SATISFACTION OF THINKING SHE'D FORGIVEN THEM, JUST FOR THE MONEY.
LISTEN TO HER— SHE DOESN'T WANT THE PROPERTY.
SHE DOES. SHE WAS JUST COUNTING ON DAD TO GET THE PROPERTY AFTER SHE DIED.
NOW SHE REALIZES SHE HAS NO CHOICE.
IT'S IRRESPONSIBLE TO TAKE A WOMAN OF HER AGE, WHO RECENTLY LOST HER SON, TO THE PLACE WHERE HER WHOLE FAMILY WAS DESTROYED...
10
OF COURSE IT'S DIFFICULT FOR HER. THAT'S EXACTLY WHY I INSISTED ON COMING WITH HER.
IT WASN'T EASY TO CONVINCE HER THAT IT WOULD BE MADNESS TO GO ON HER OWN.

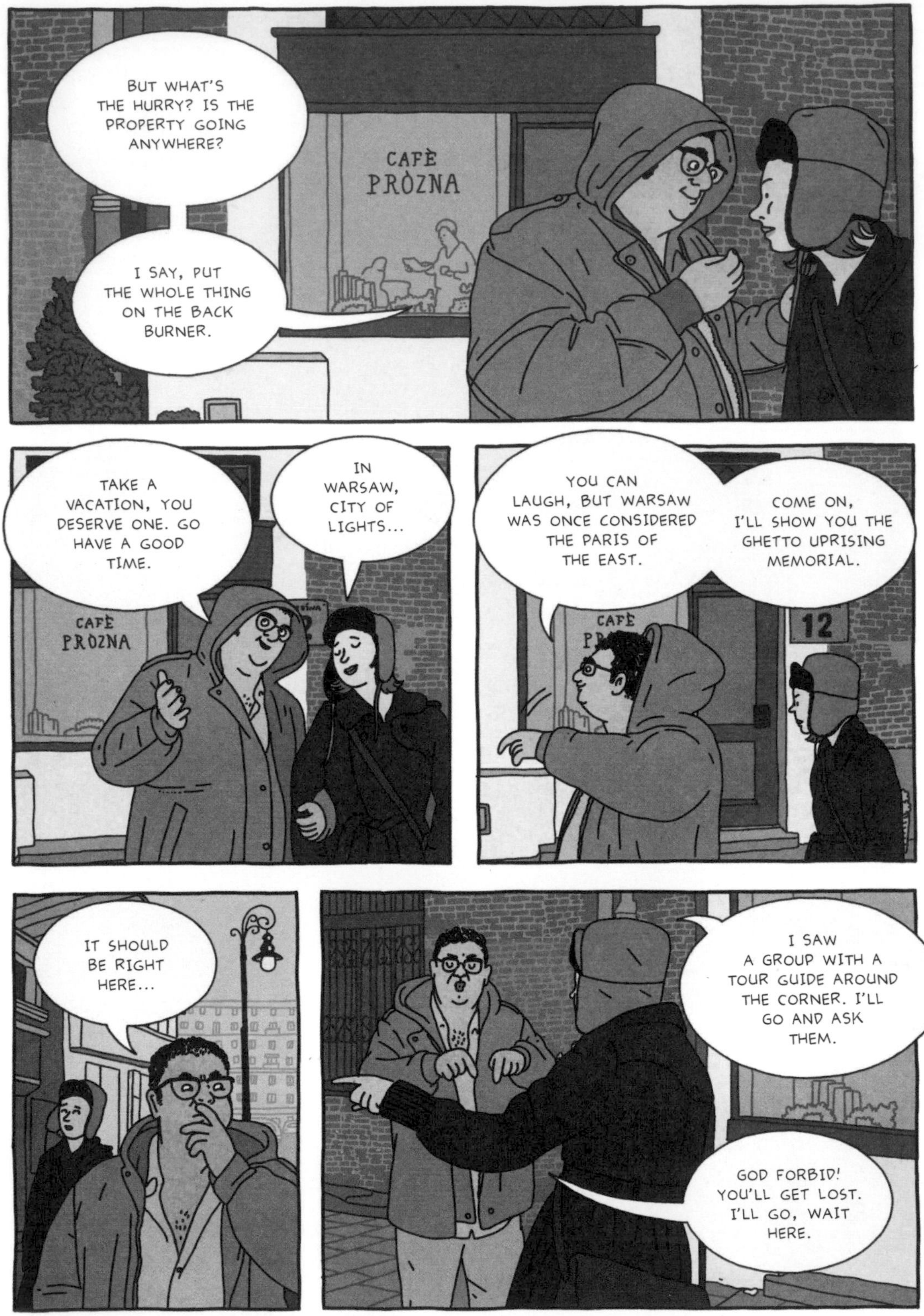
BUT WHAT'S THE HURRY? IS THE PROPERTY GOING ANYWHERE?
CAFÈ PRÒZNA
I SAY, PUT THE WHOLE THING ON THE BACK BURNER.
TAKE A VACATION, YOU DESERVE ONE. GO HAVE A GOOD TIME.
IN WARSAW, CITY OF LIGHTS...
CAFÈ PRÒZNA
YOU CAN LAUGH, BUT WARSAW WAS ONCE CONSIDERED THE PARIS OF THE EAST.
COME ON, I'LL SHOW YOU THE GHETTO UPRISING MEMORIAL.
12
IT SHOULD BE RIGHT HERE...
I SAW A GROUP WITH A TOUR GUIDE AROUND THE CORNER. I'LL GO AND ASK THEM.
GOD FORBID! YOU'LL GET LOST. I'LL GO, WAIT HERE.

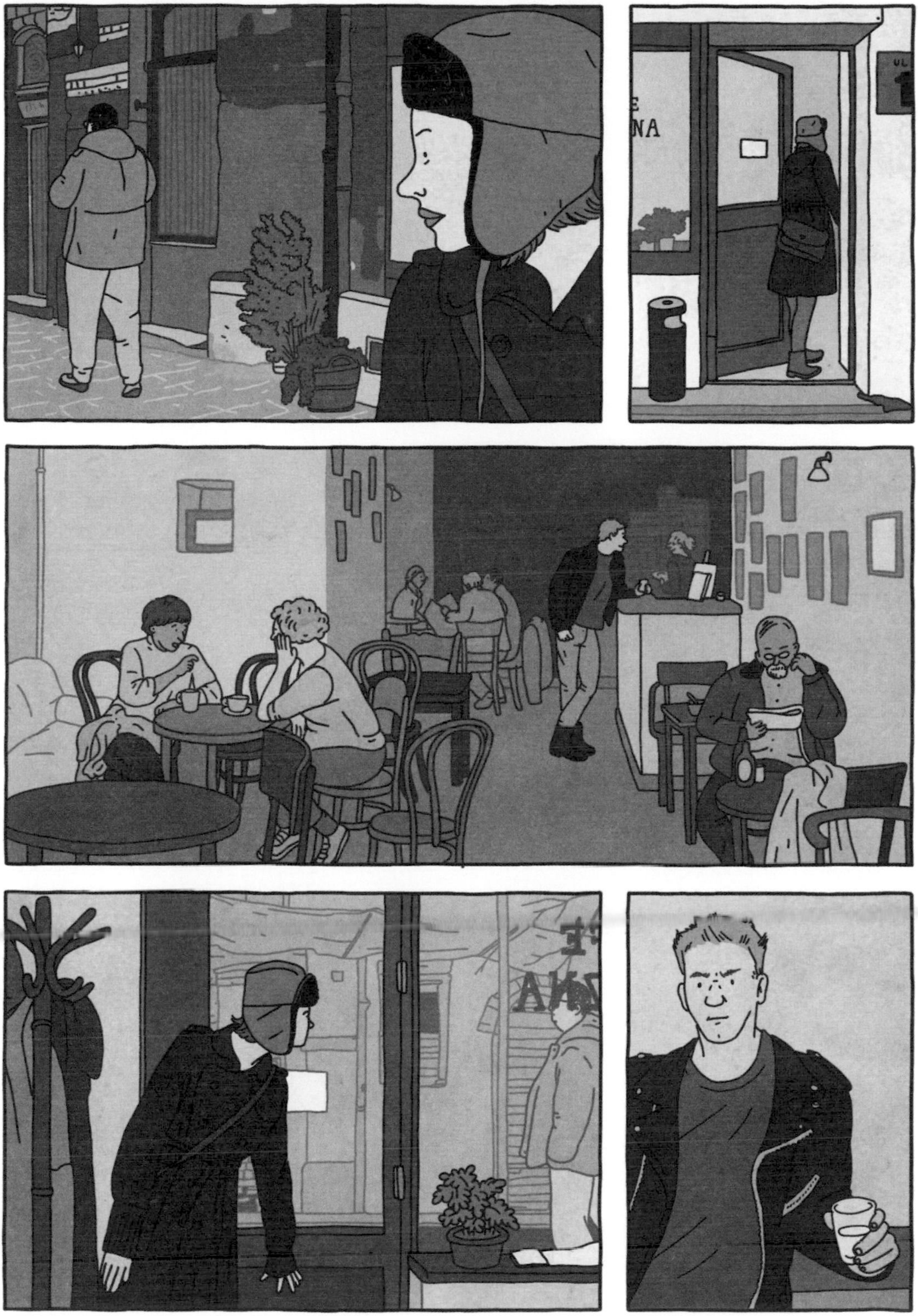

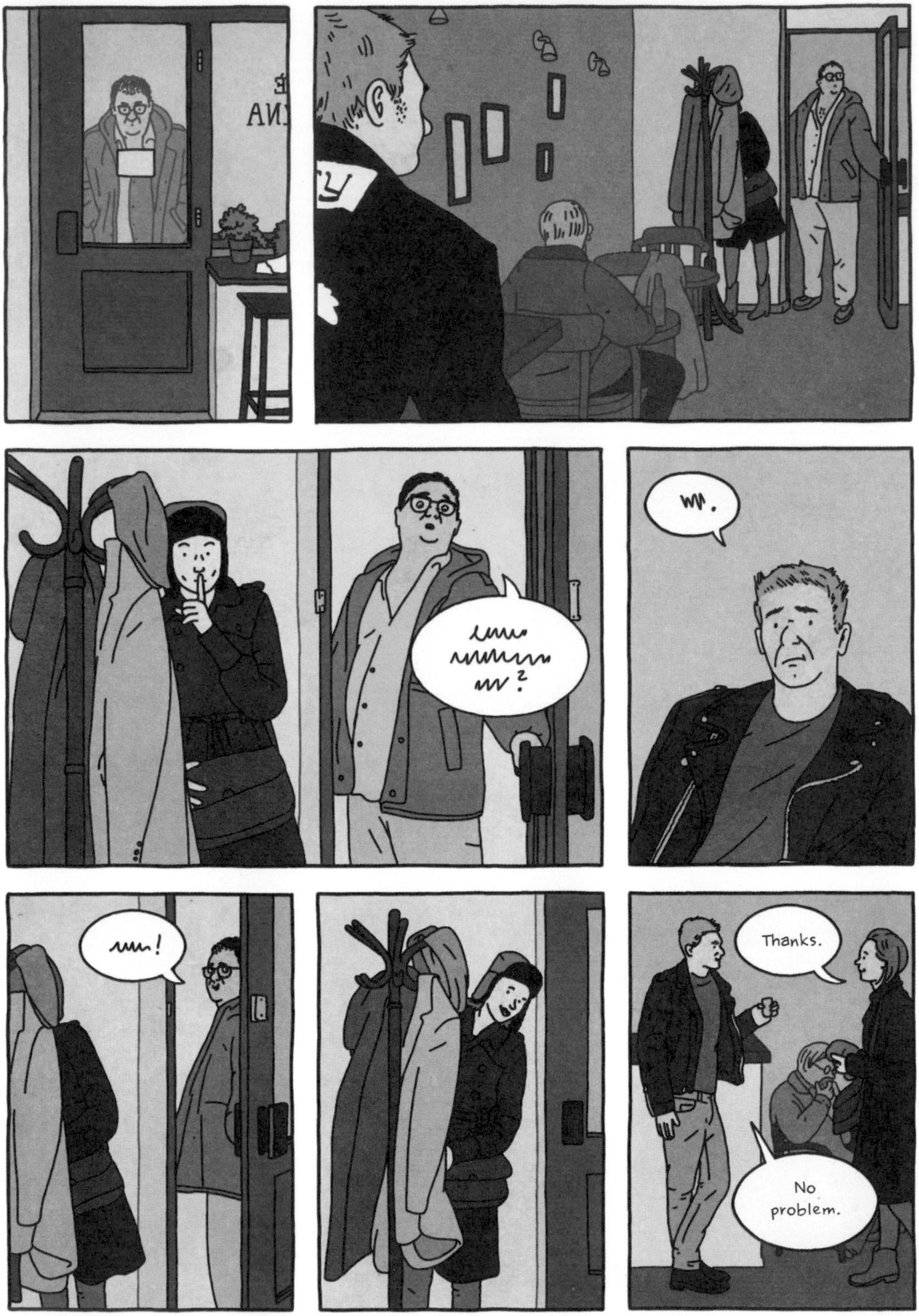
Thanks.
No problem.

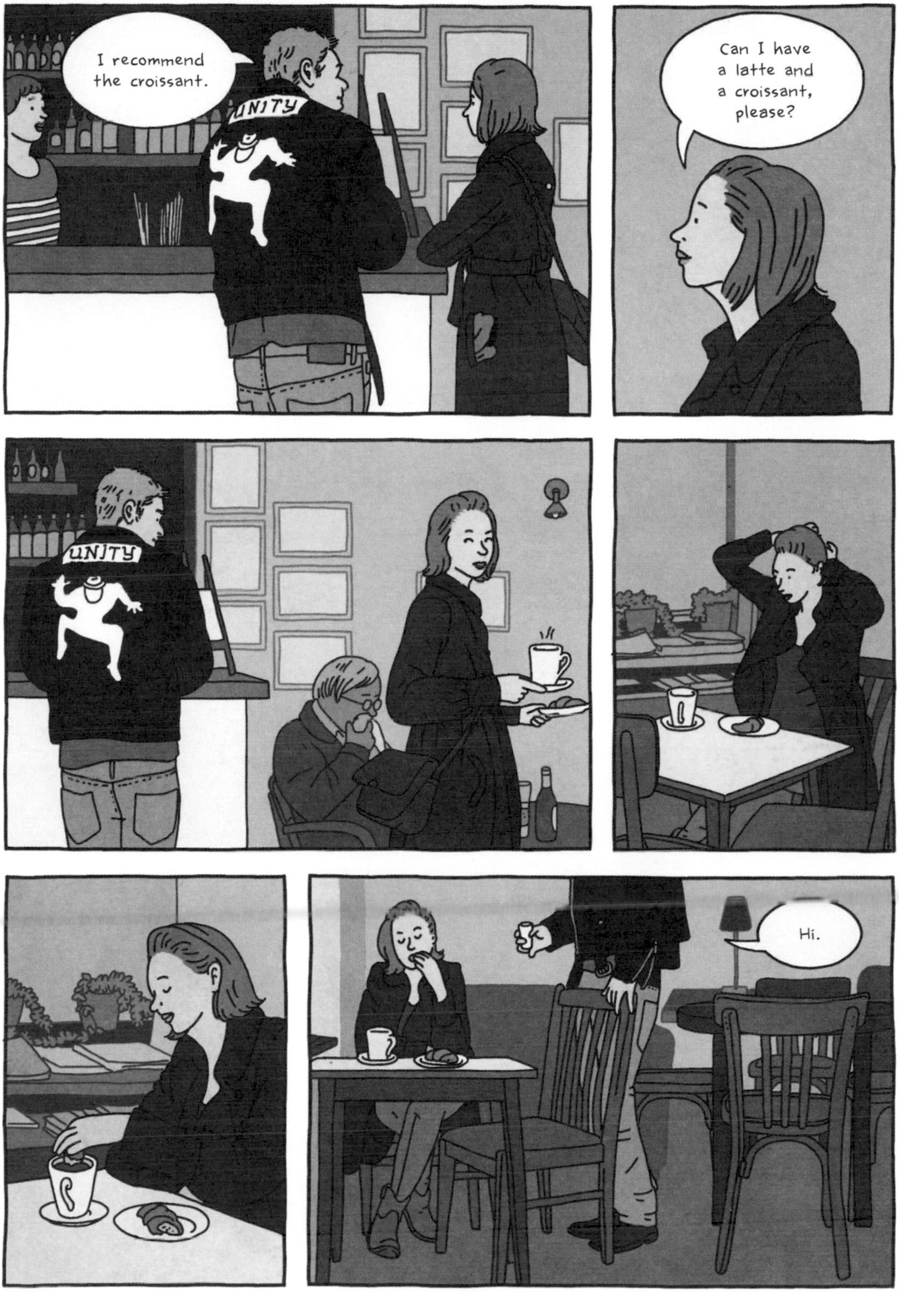
I recommend the croissant.
UNITY
Can I have a latte and a croissant, please?
UNITY
Hi.

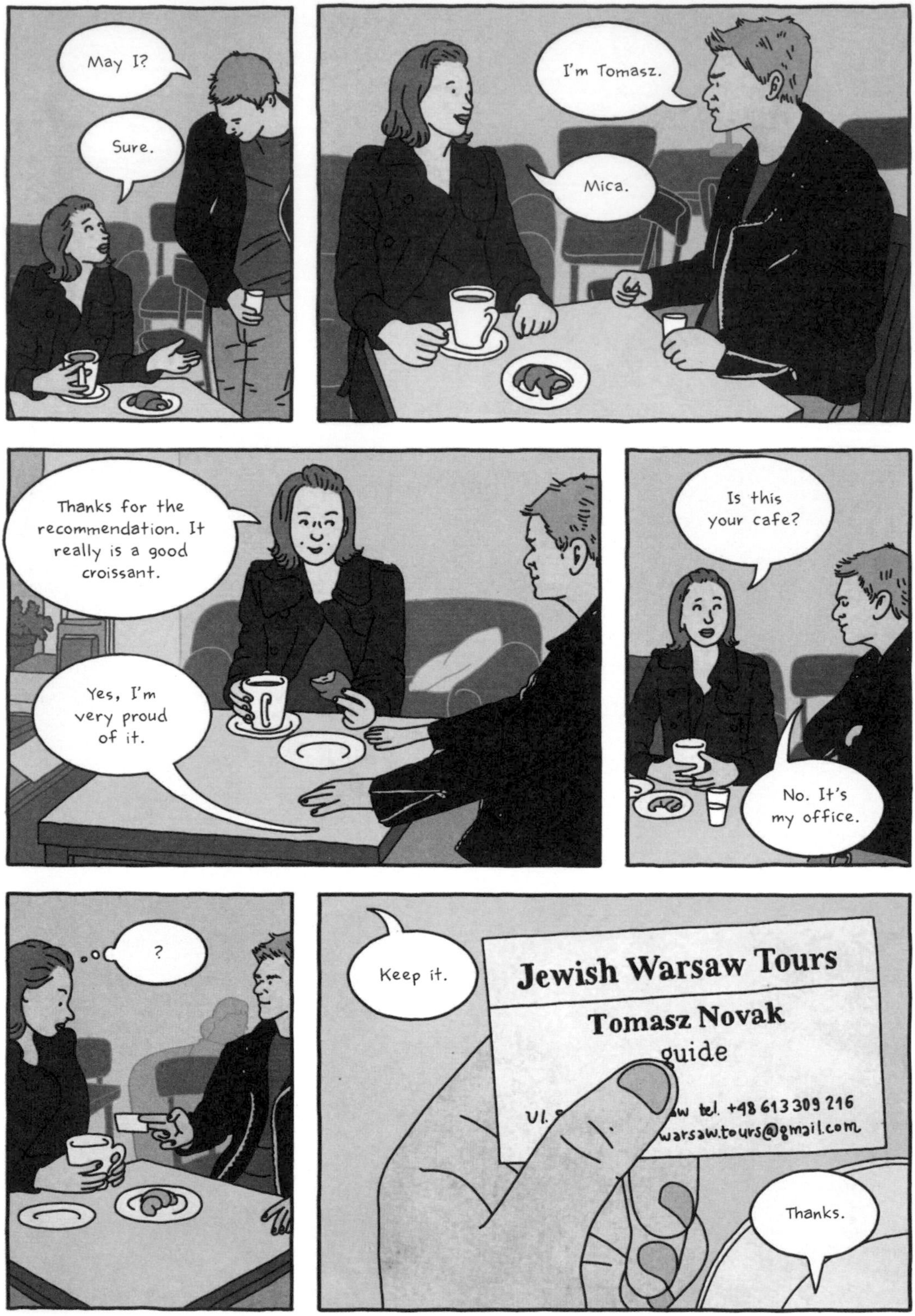
May I?
Sure.
I'm Tomasz.
Mica.
Thanks for the recommendation. It really is a good croissant.
Yes, I'm very proud of it.
Is this your cafe?
No. It's my office.
?
Keep it.
Jewish Warsaw Tours
Tomasz Novak
guide
tel. +48 613 309 216
warsaw.tours@gmail.com
Thanks.

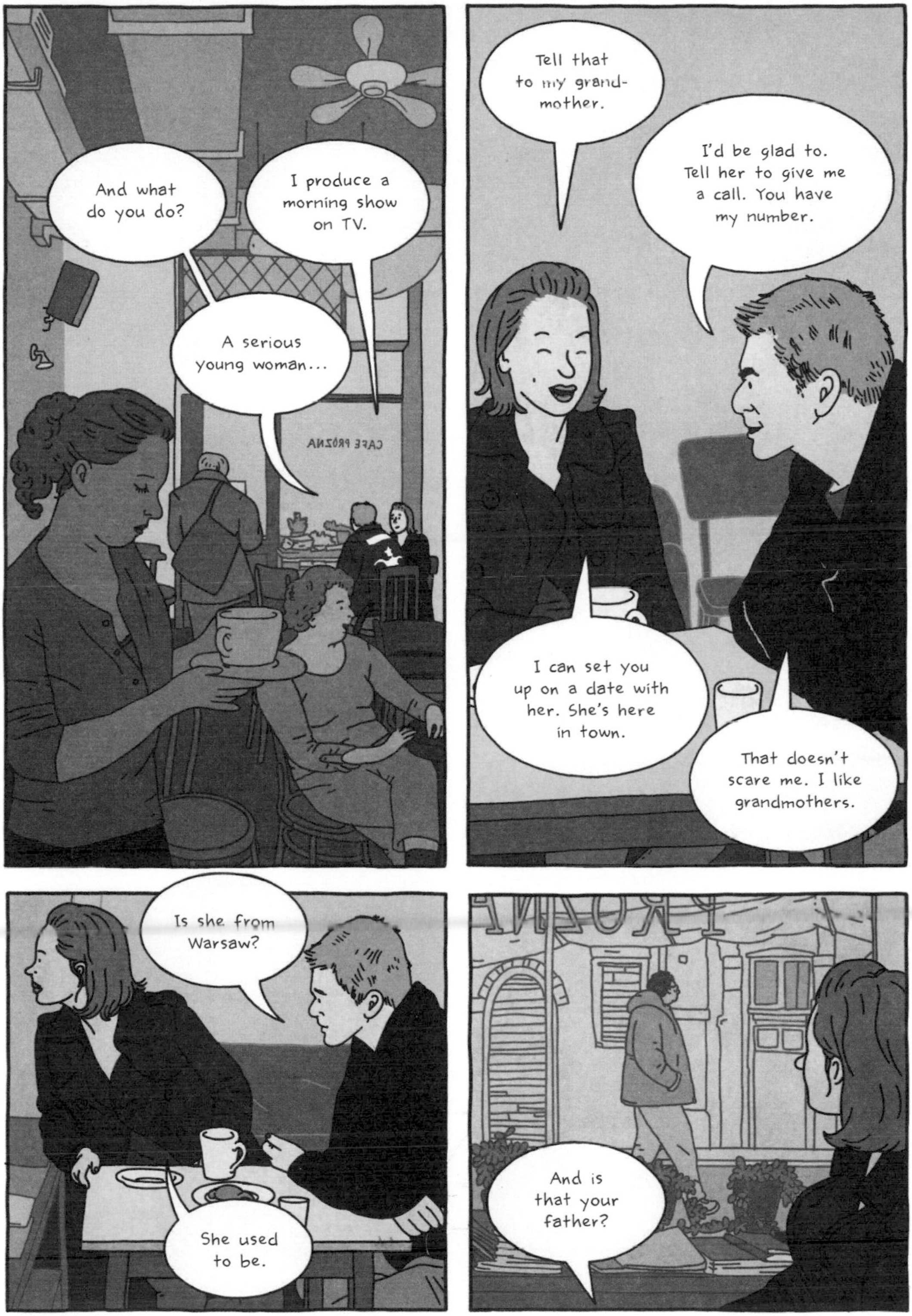
And what do you do?
I produce a morning show on TV.
A serious young woman...
Tell that to my grand-mother.
I'd be glad to. Tell her to give me a call. You have my number.
I can set you up on a date with her. She's here in town.
That doesn't scare me. I like grandmothers.
Is she from Warsaw?
She used to be.
And is that your father?

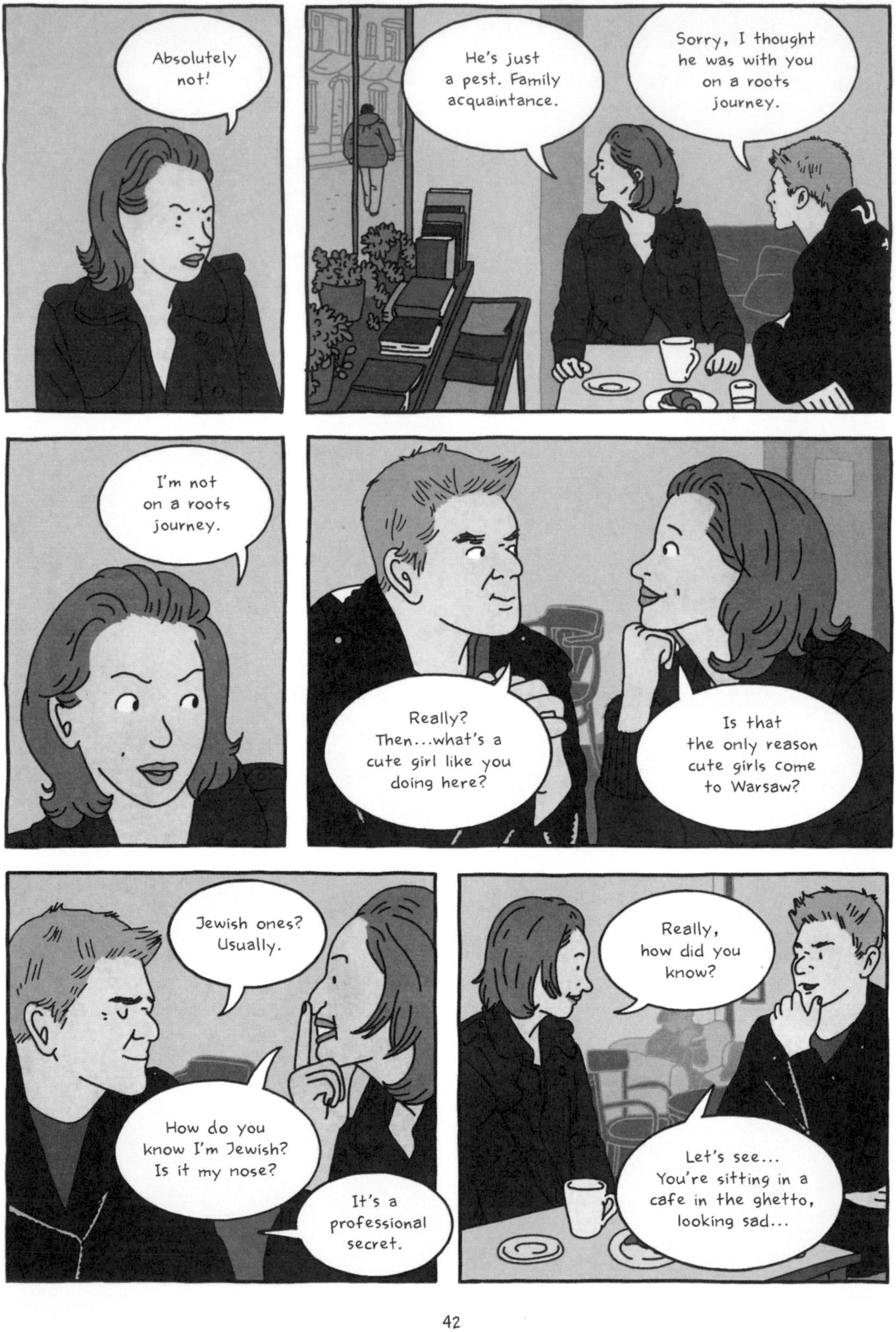
Absolutely not!
He's just a pest. Family acquaintance.
Sorry, I thought he was with you on a roots journey.
I'm not on a roots journey.
Really? Then...what's a cute girl like you doing here?
Is that the only reason cute girls come to Warsaw?
Jewish ones? Usually.
How do you know I'm Jewish? Is it my nose?
It's a professional secret.
Really, how did you know?
Let's see... You're sitting in a cafe in the ghetto, looking sad...

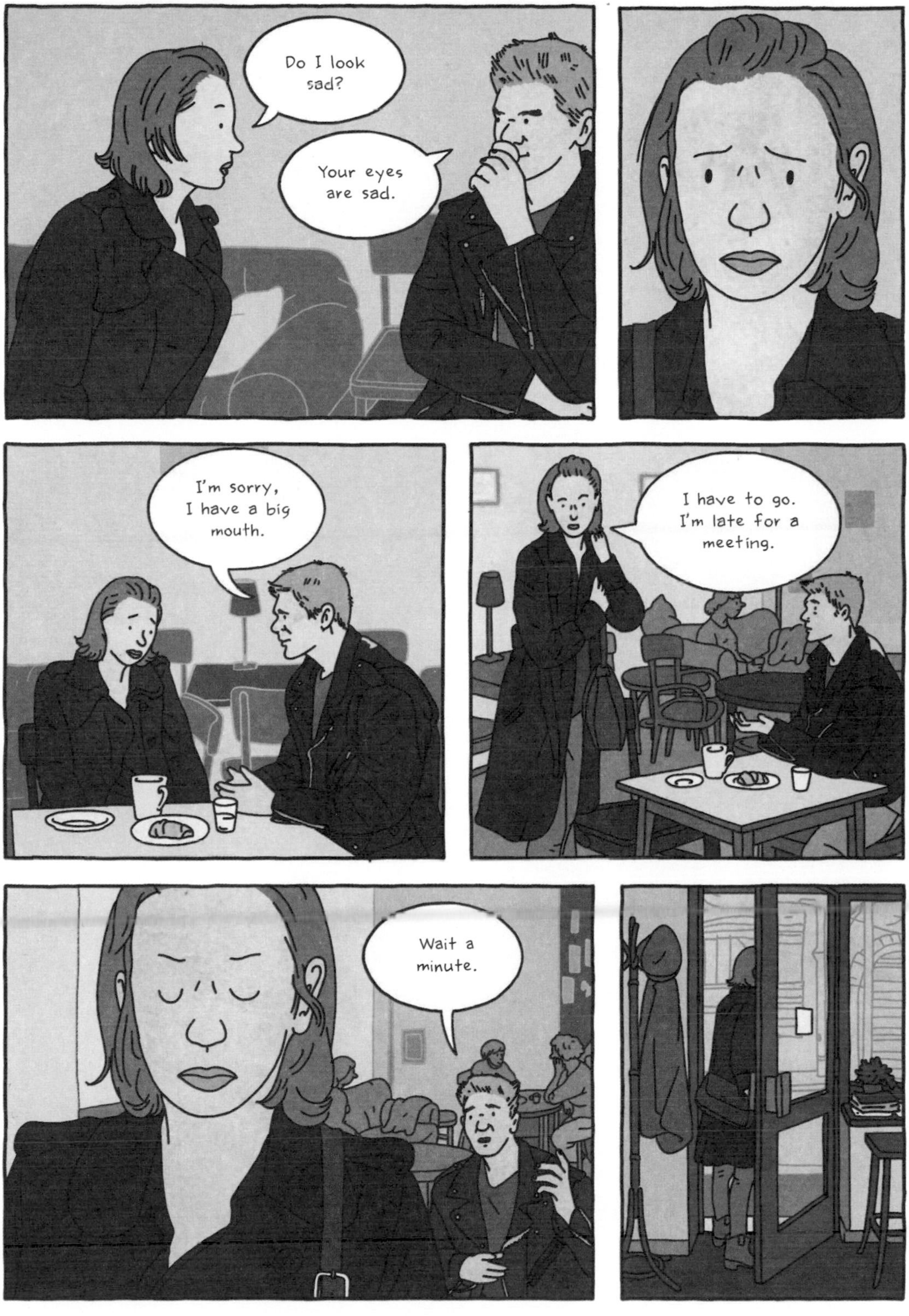
Do I look sad?
Your eyes are sad.
I'm sorry, I have a big mouth.
I have to go. I'm late for a meeting.
Wait a minute.

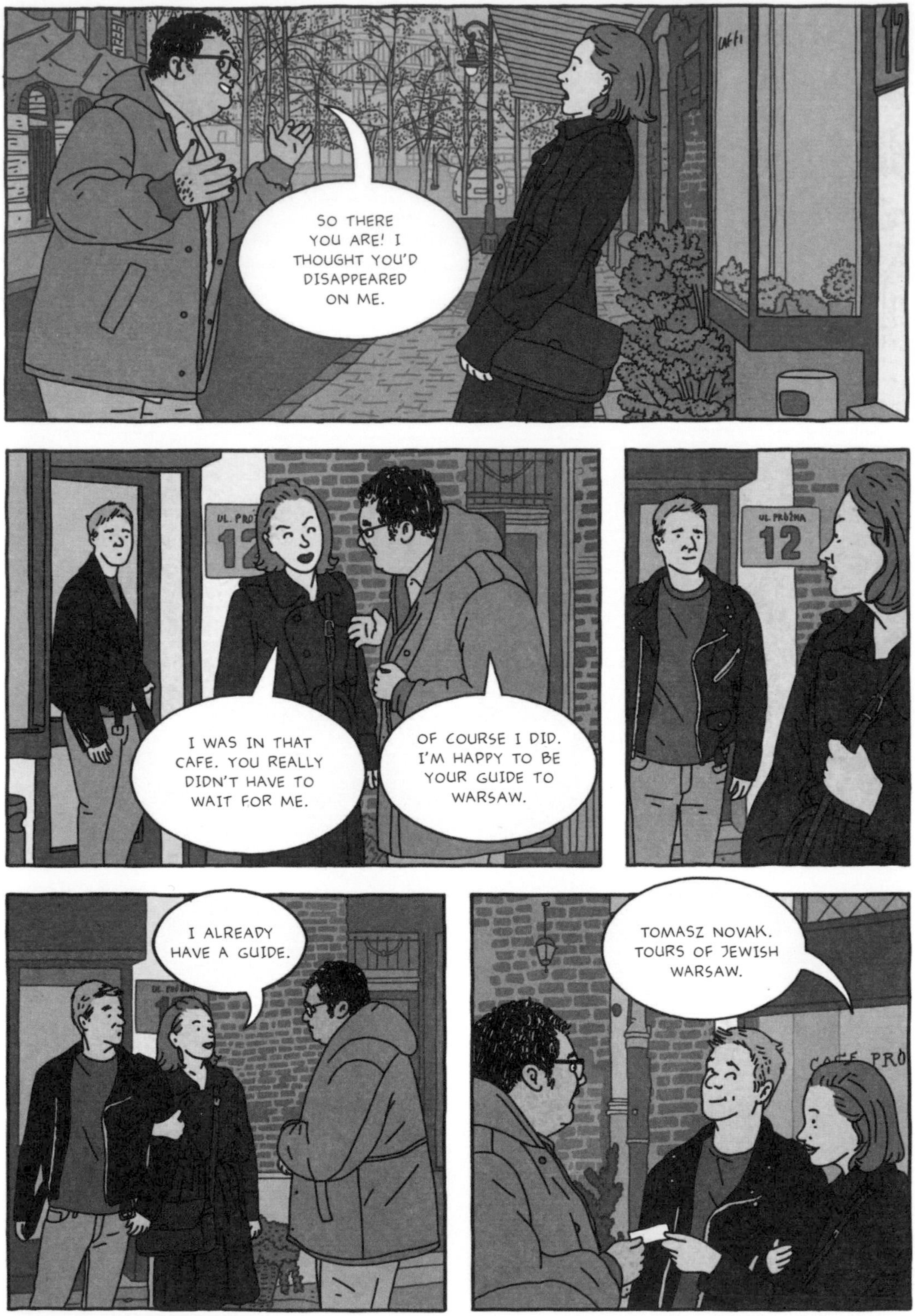
SO THERE YOU ARE! I THOUGHT YOU'D DISAPPEARED ON ME.
CAFFI
UL. PRÓŻNA
12
I WAS IN THAT CAFE. YOU REALLY DIDN'T HAVE TO WAIT FOR ME.
OF COURSE I DID. I'M HAPPY TO BE YOUR GUIDE TO WARSAW.
I ALREADY HAVE A GUIDE.
TOMASZ NOVAK. TOURS OF JEWISH WARSAW.

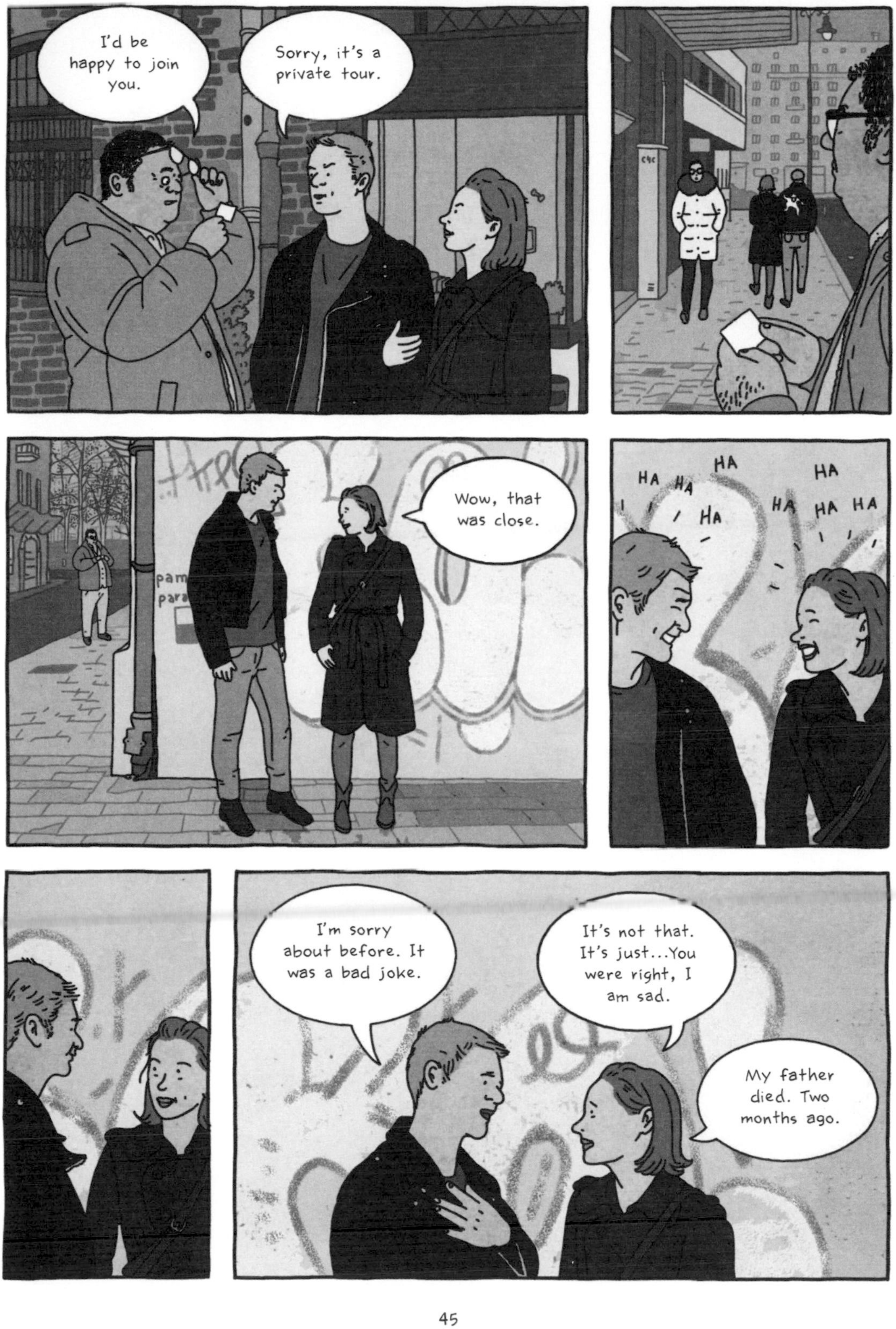
I'd be happy to join you.
Sorry, it's a private tour.
Wow, that was close.
HA HA HA HA HA HA HA
I'm sorry about before. It was a bad joke.
It's not that. It's just...You were right, I am sad.
My father died. Two months ago.

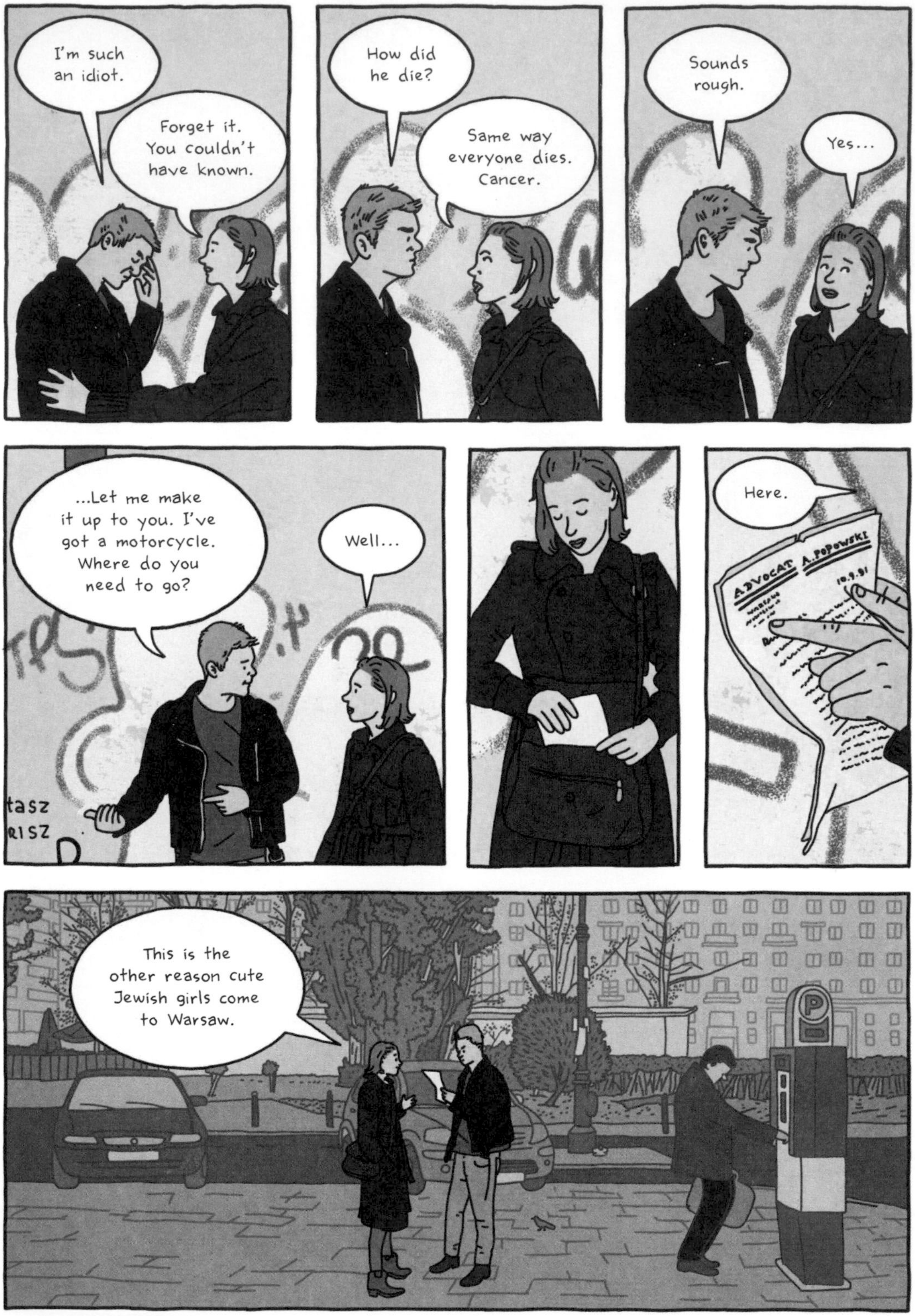
I'm such an idiot.
Forget it. You couldn't have known.
How did he die?
Same way everyone dies. Cancer.
Sounds rough.
Yes...
...Let me make it up to you. I've got a motorcycle. Where do you need to go?
Well...
Here.
ADVOCAT A. POPOWSKI
This is the other reason cute Jewish girls come to Warsaw.

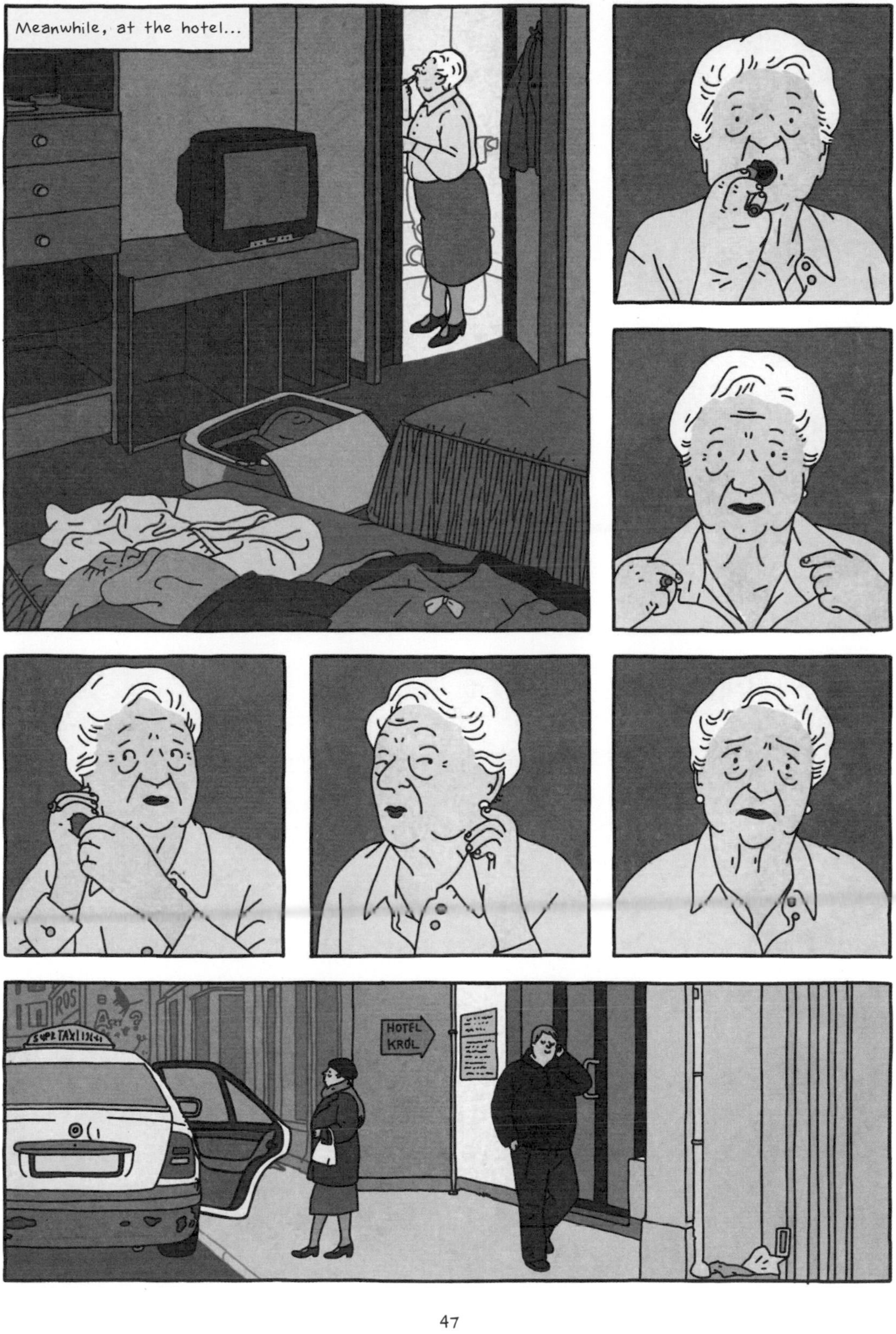
Meanwhile, at the hotel...
HOTEL KRÓL

WÓDKI
LIKIEDY
WINO
Nasza 31, madam.

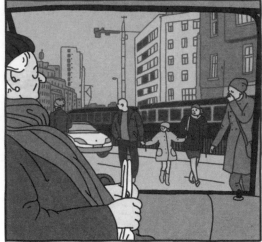

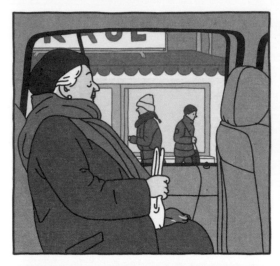

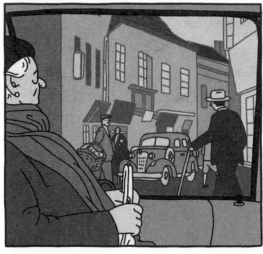

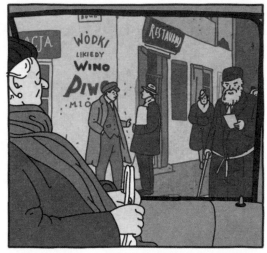

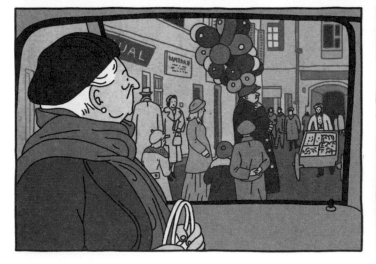

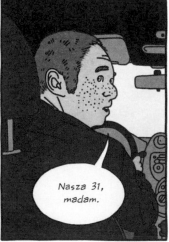

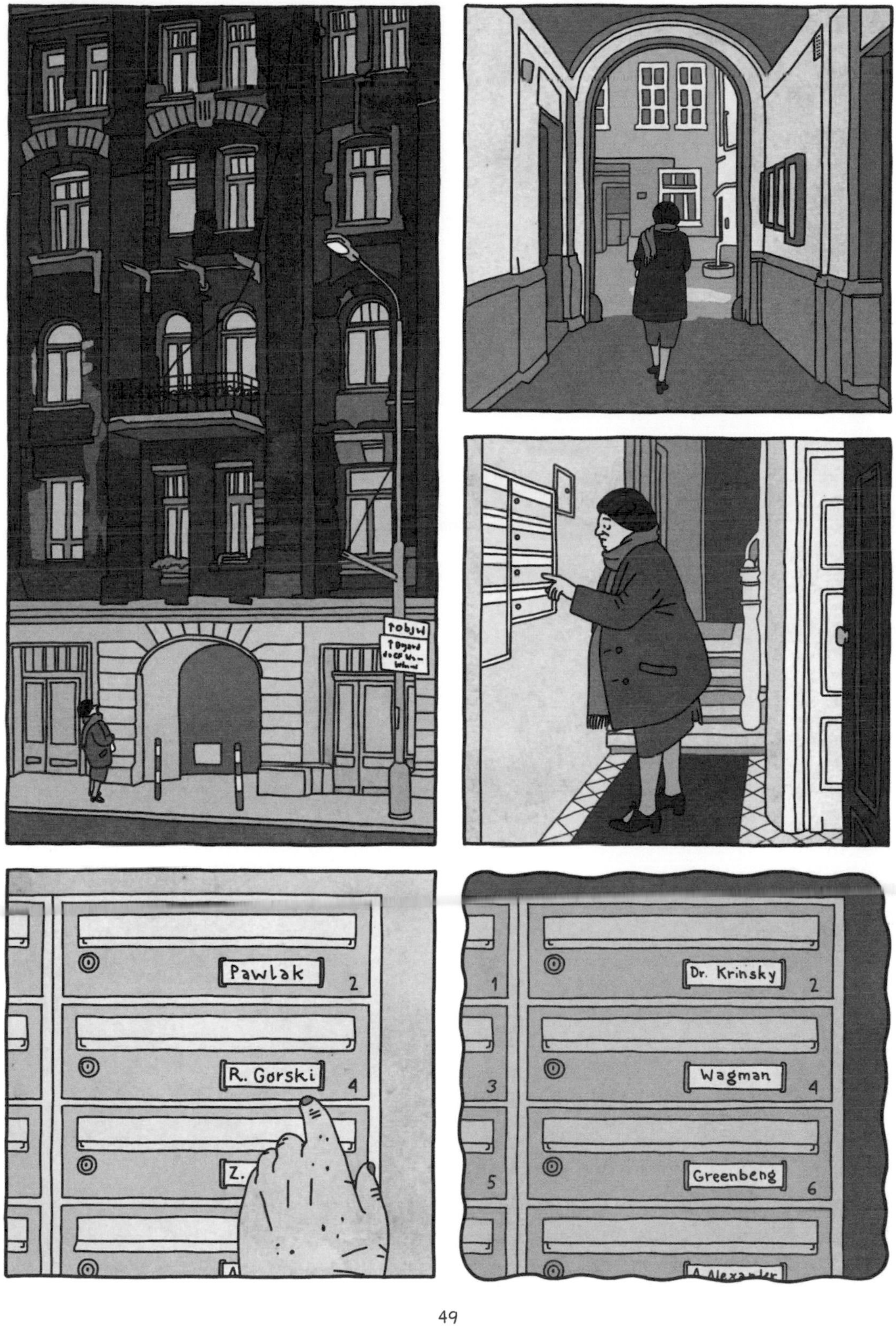
Pawlak
2
R. Gorski
4
1
Dr. Krinsky
2
3
Wagman
4
5
Greenbeng
6

Welcome!

Come in, please.

Make yourself at home.

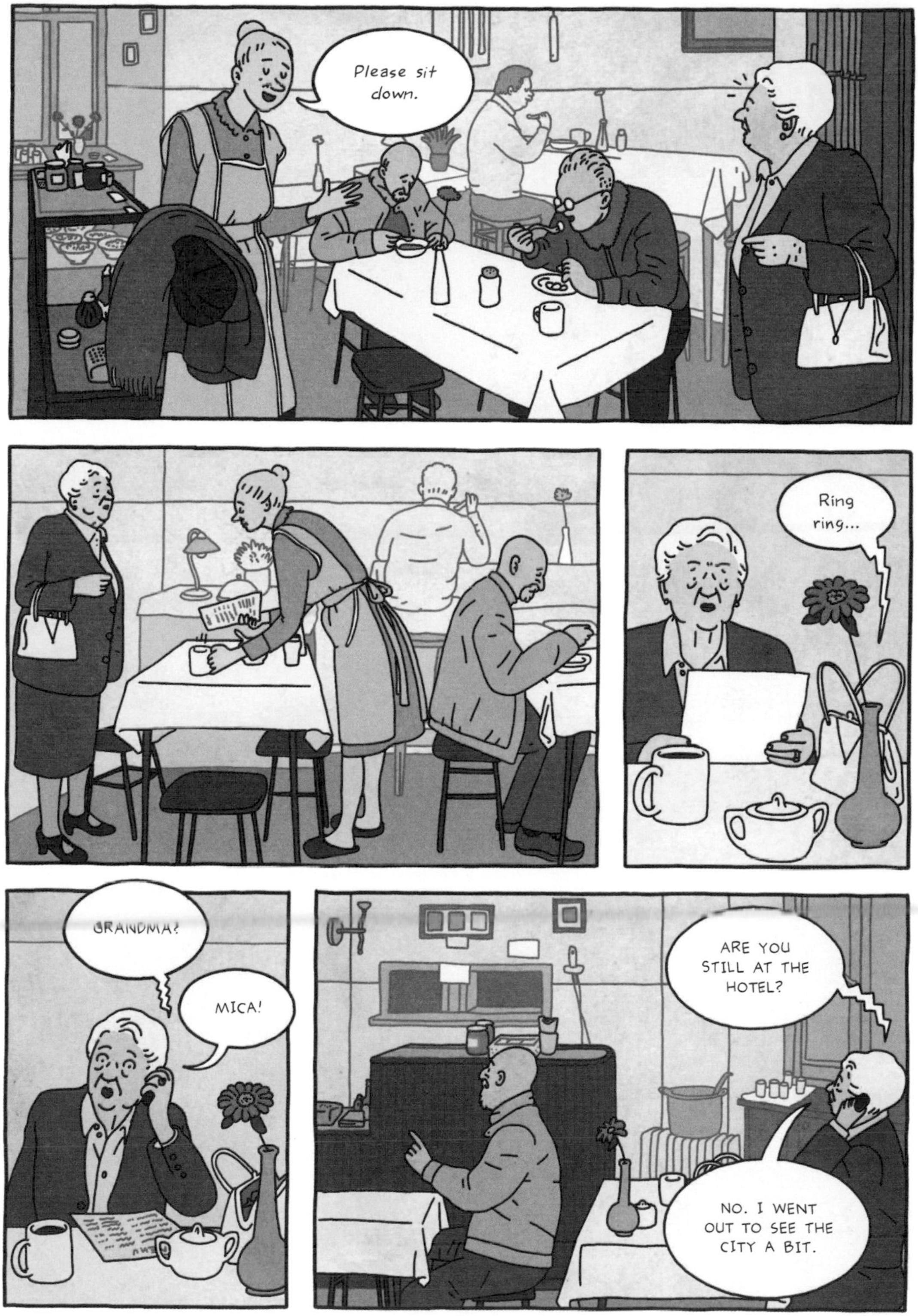
Please sit down.
Ring ring...
GRANDMA?
MICA!
ARE YOU STILL AT THE HOTEL?
NO. I WENT OUT TO SEE THE CITY A BIT.

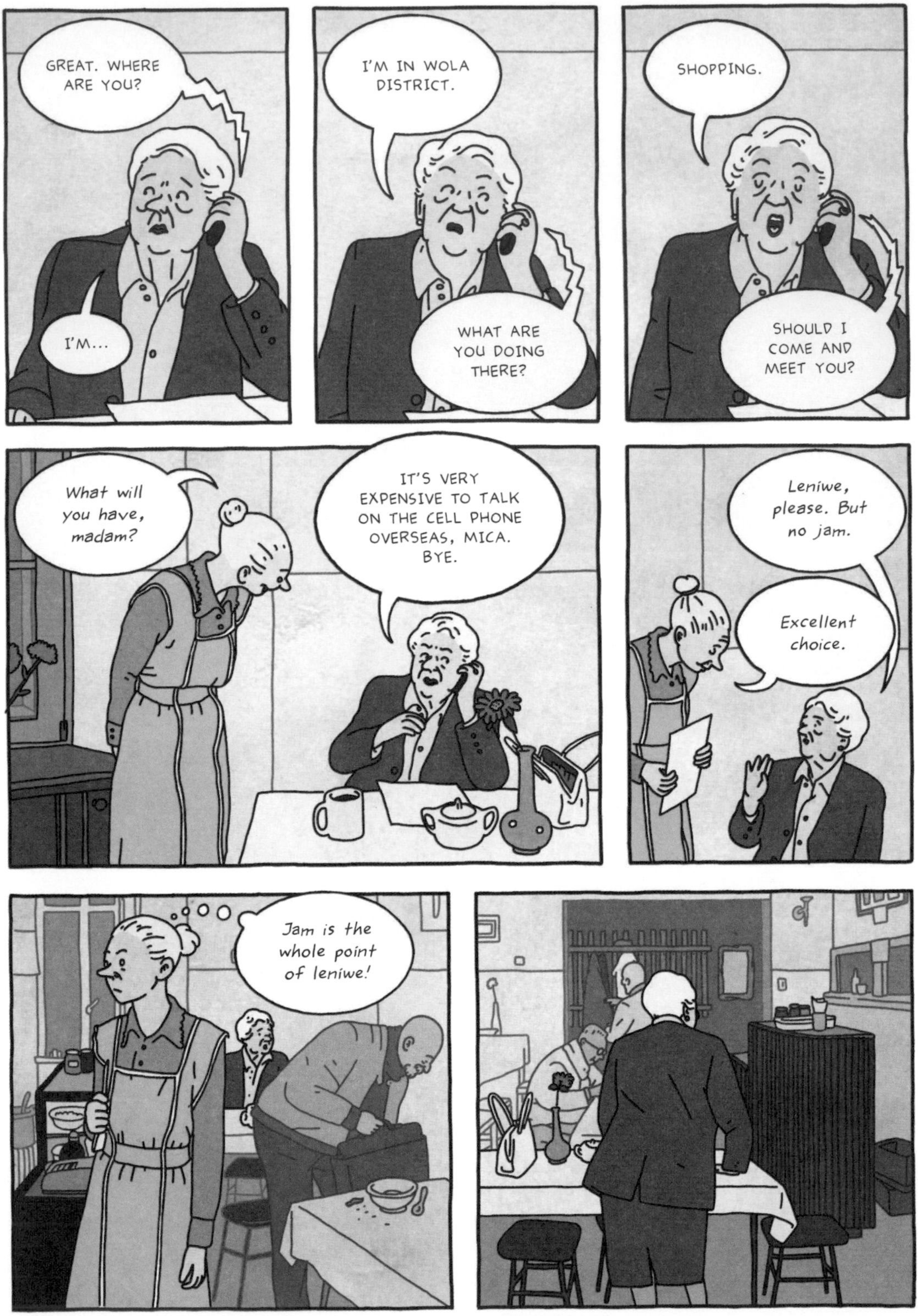
GREAT. WHERE ARE YOU?
I'M...
I'M IN WOLA DISTRICT.
WHAT ARE YOU DOING THERE?
SHOPPING.
SHOULD I COME AND MEET YOU?
What will you have, madam?
IT'S VERY EXPENSIVE TO TALK ON THE CELL PHONE OVERSEAS, MICA. BYE.
Leniwe, please. But no jam.
Excellent choice.
Jam is the whole point of leniwe!

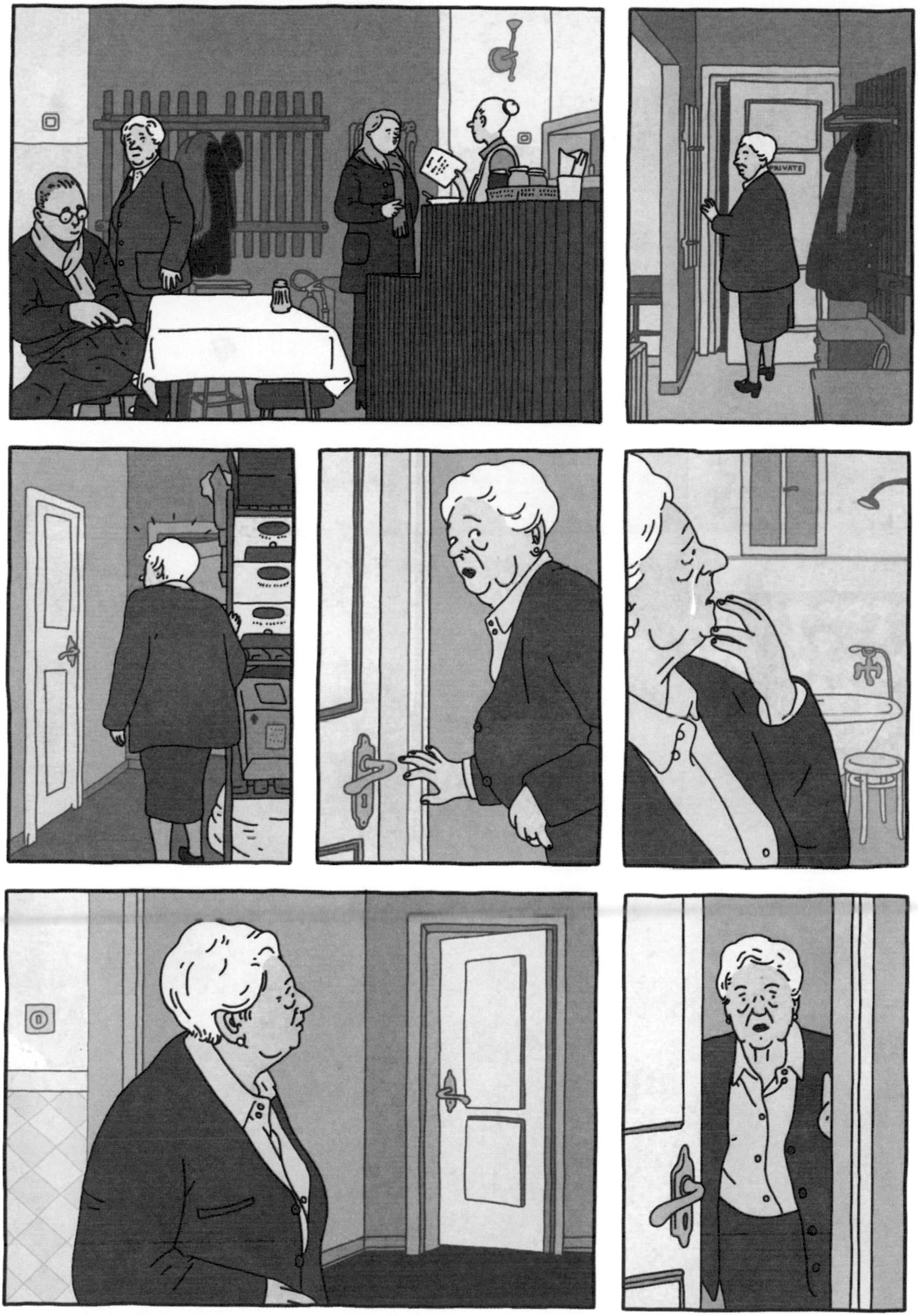
PRIVATE

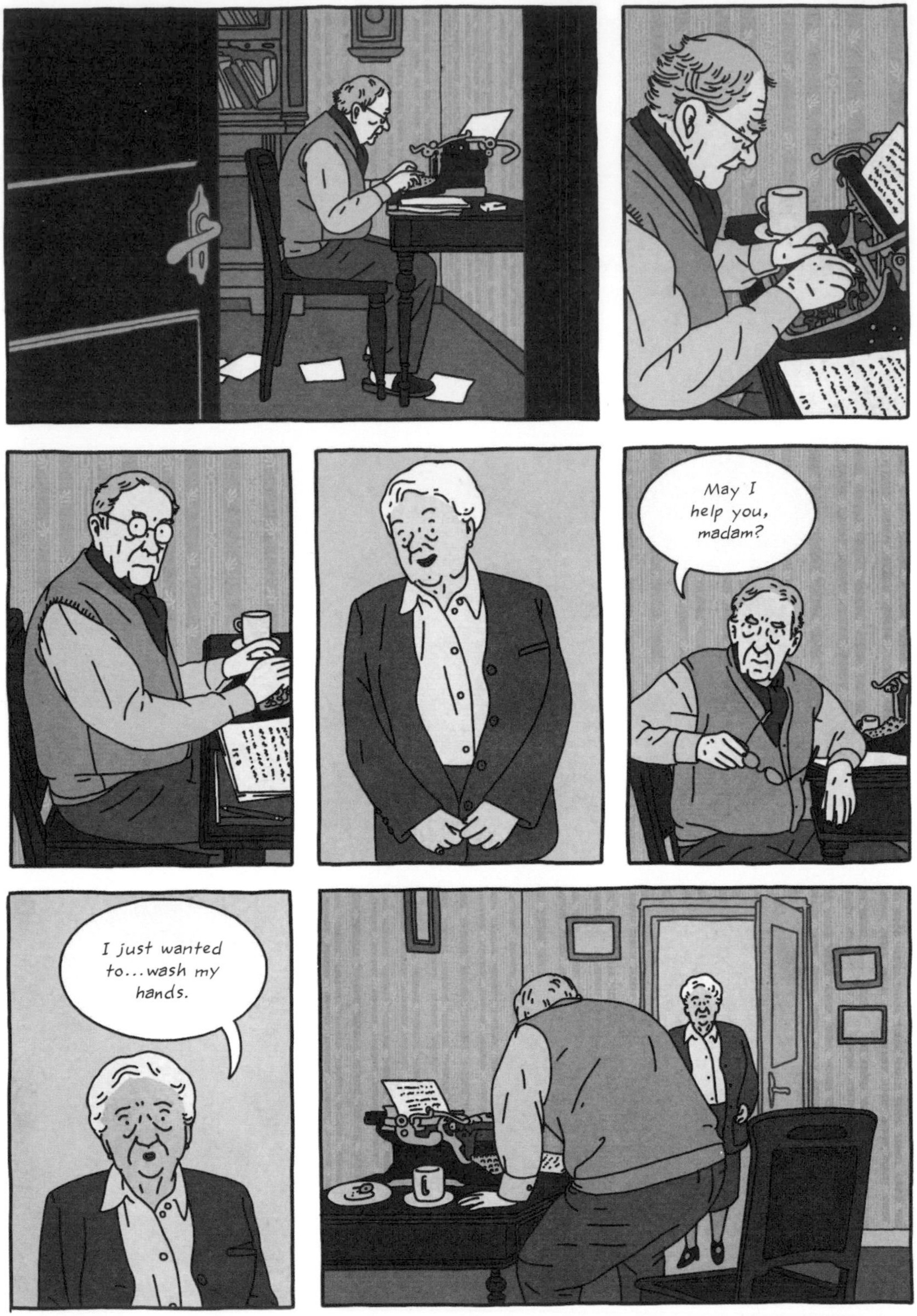
May I help you, madam?
I just wanted to...wash my hands.

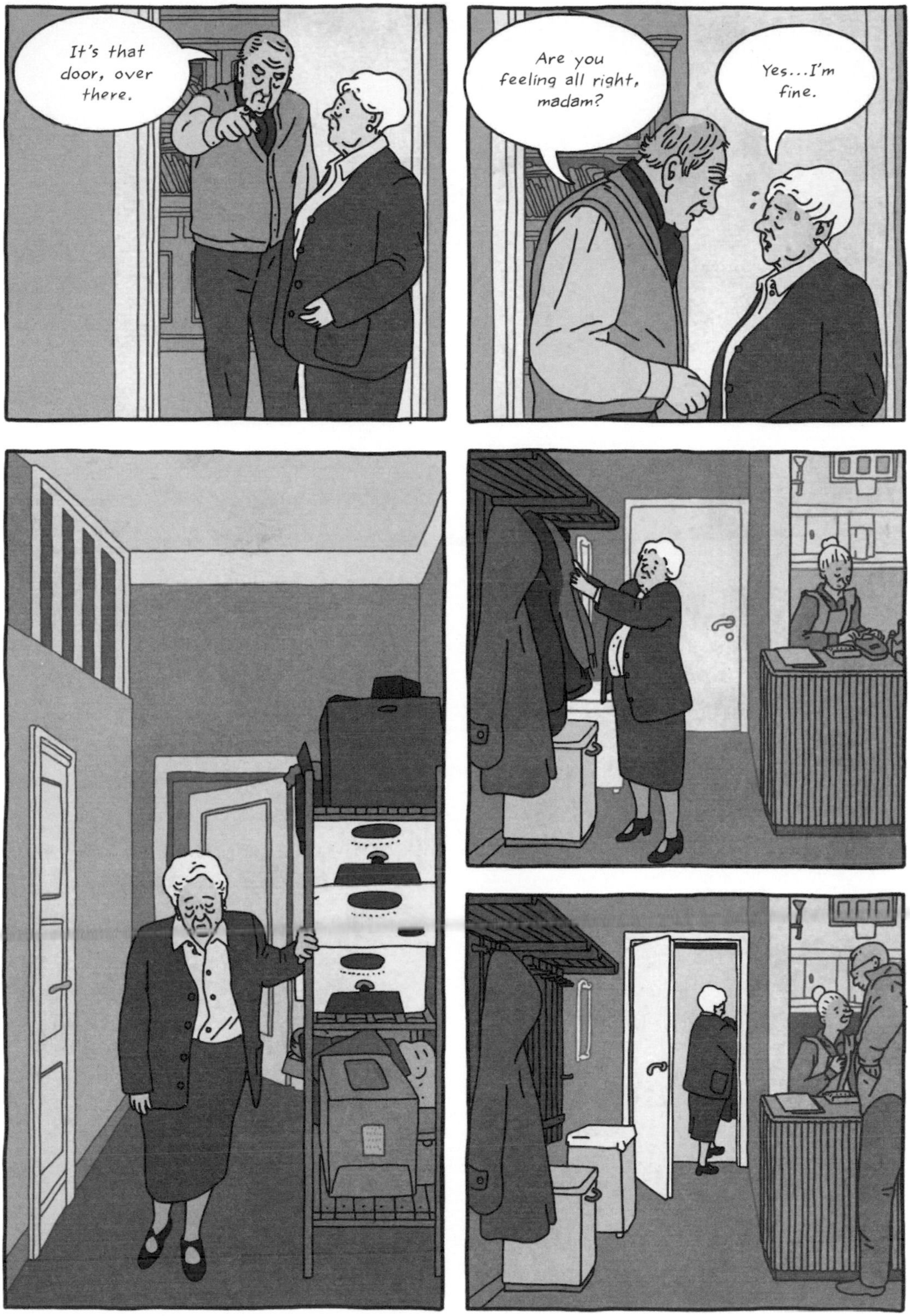
It's that door, over there.
Are you feeling all right, madam?
Yes...I'm fine.

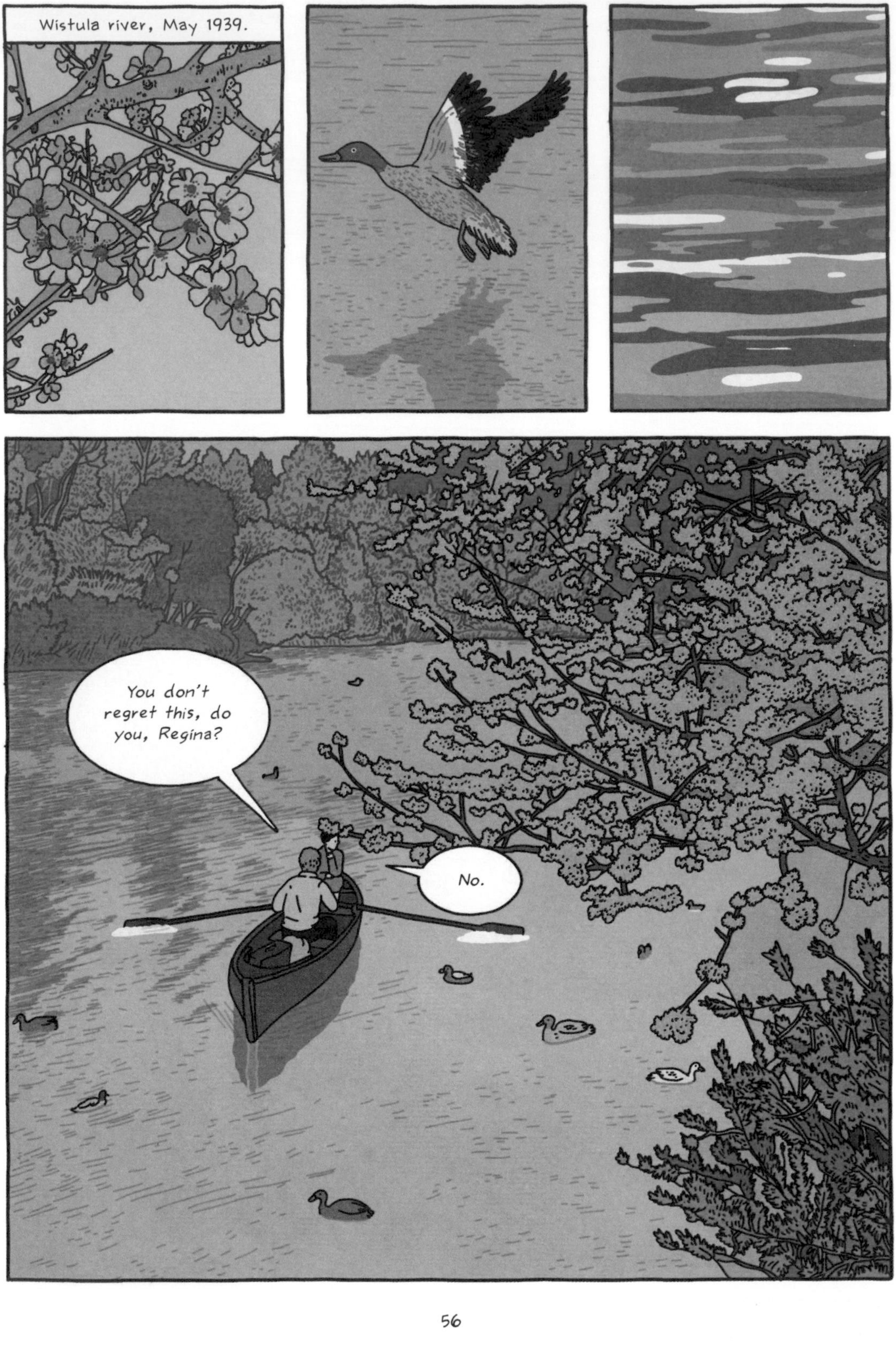
Wistula river, May 1939.
You don't regret this, do you, Regina?
No.

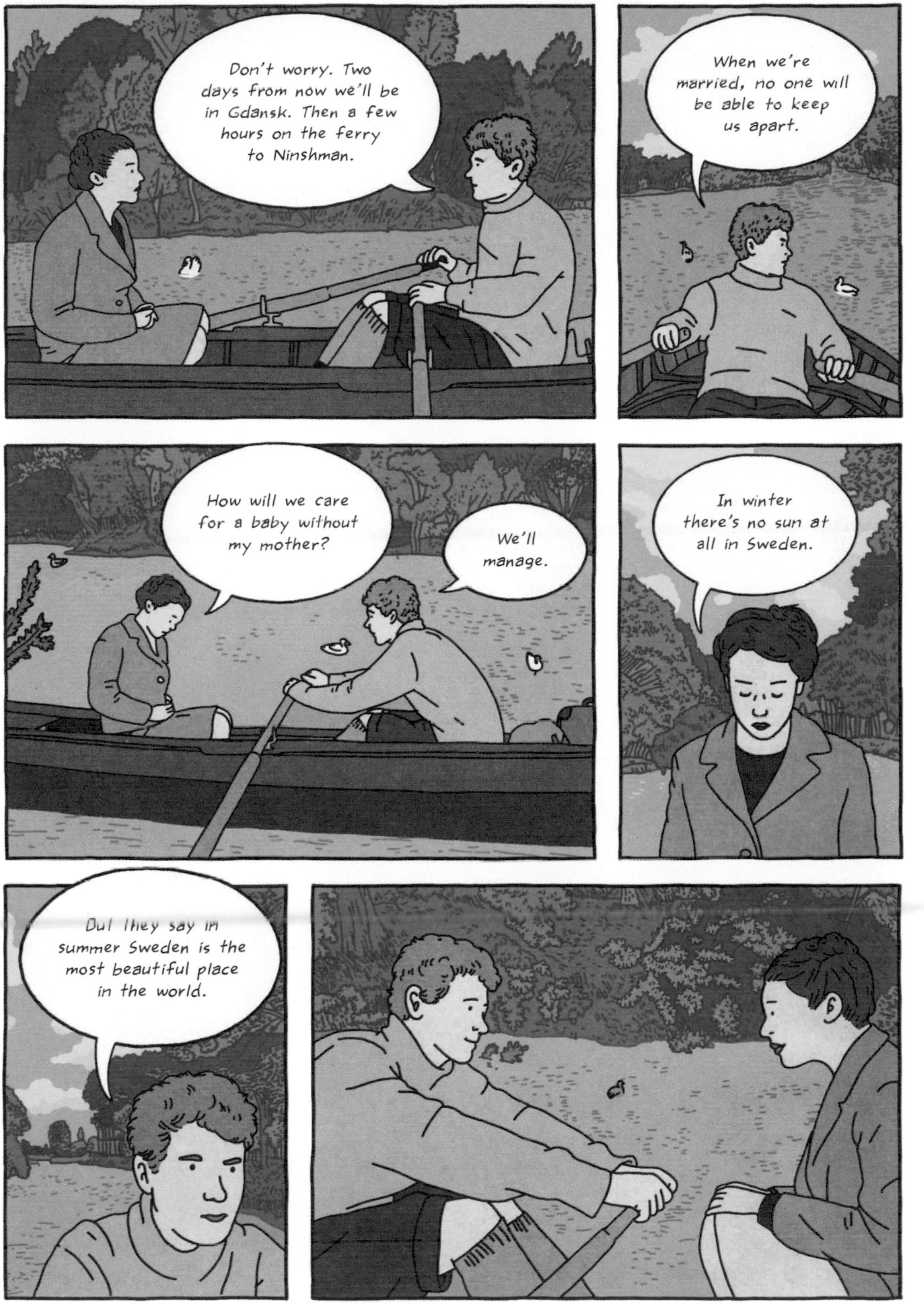
Don't worry. Two days from now we'll be in Gdansk. Then a few hours on the ferry to Ninshman.
When we're married, no one will be able to keep us apart.
How will we care for a baby without my mother?
We'll manage.
In winter there's no sun at all in Sweden.
But they say in summer Sweden is the most beautiful place in the world.

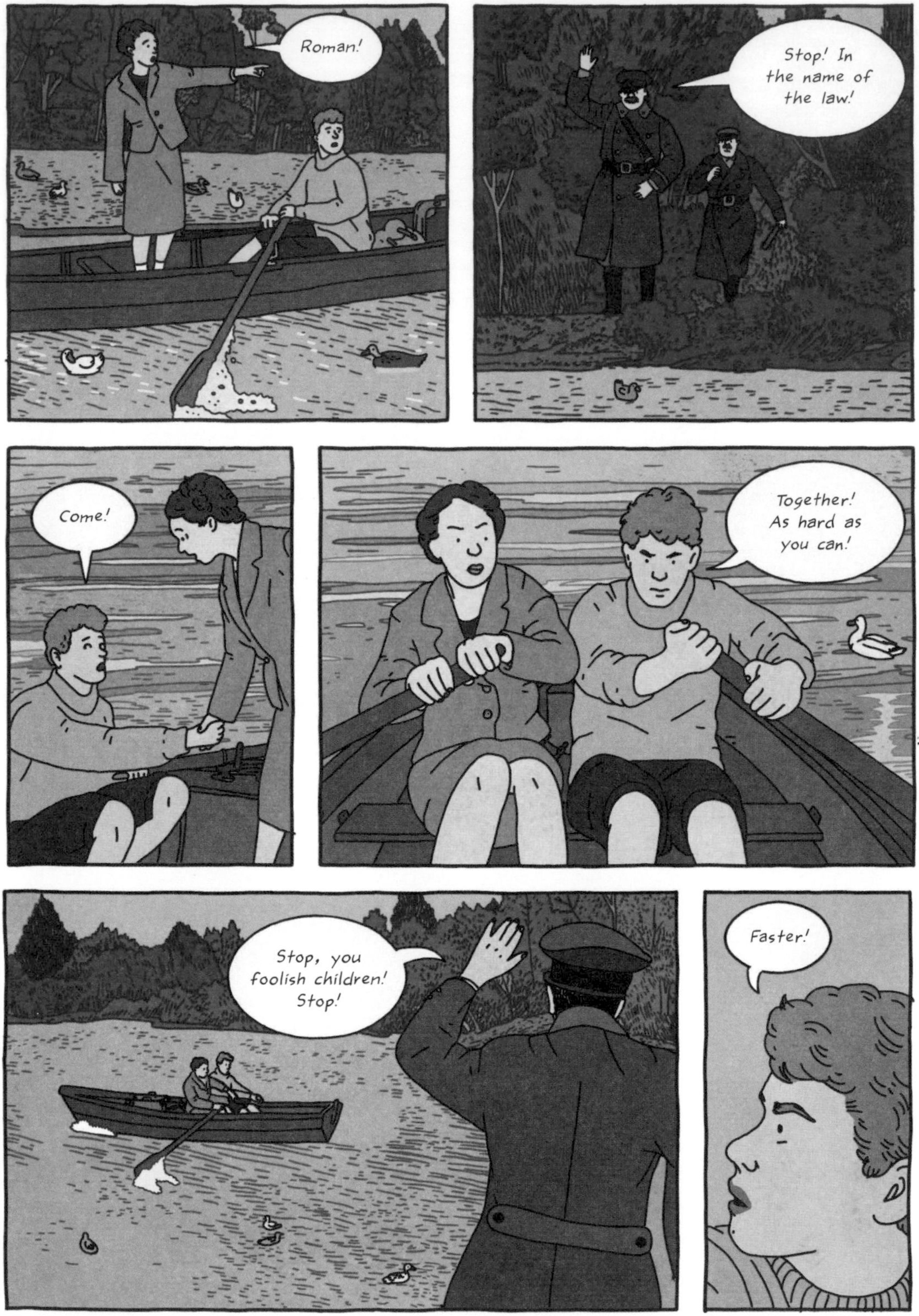
Roman!
Stop! In the name of the law!
Come!
Together! As hard as you can!
Stop, you foolish children! Stop!
Faster!

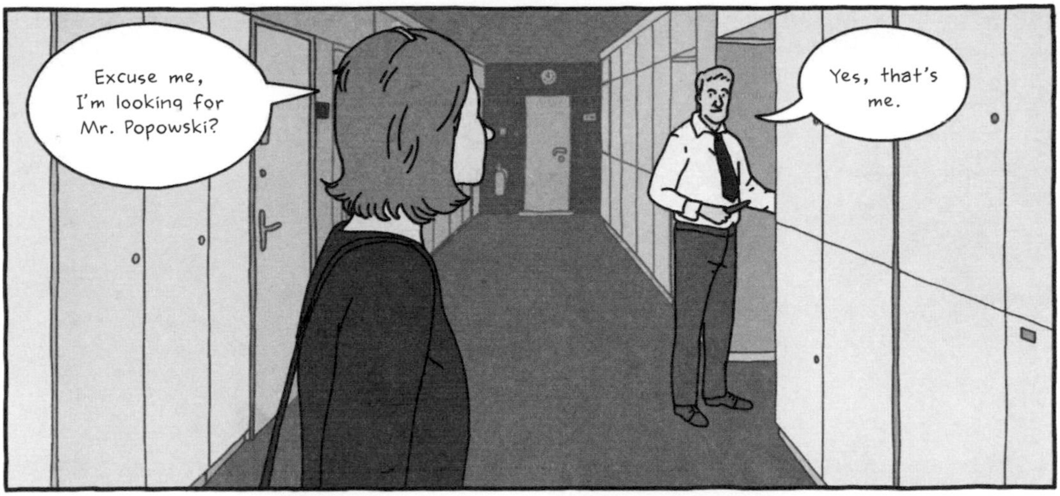
Excuse me, I'm looking for Mr. Popowski?
Yes, that's me.

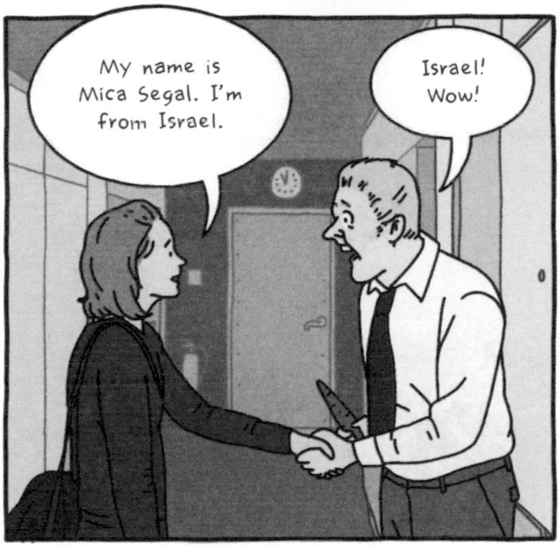
My name is Mica Segal. I'm from Israel.
Israel! Wow!

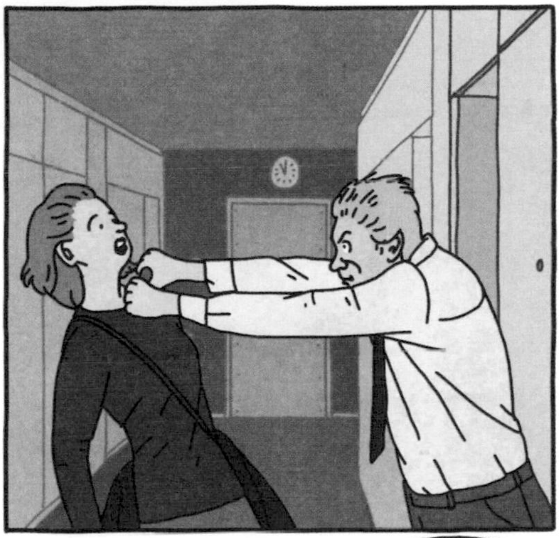

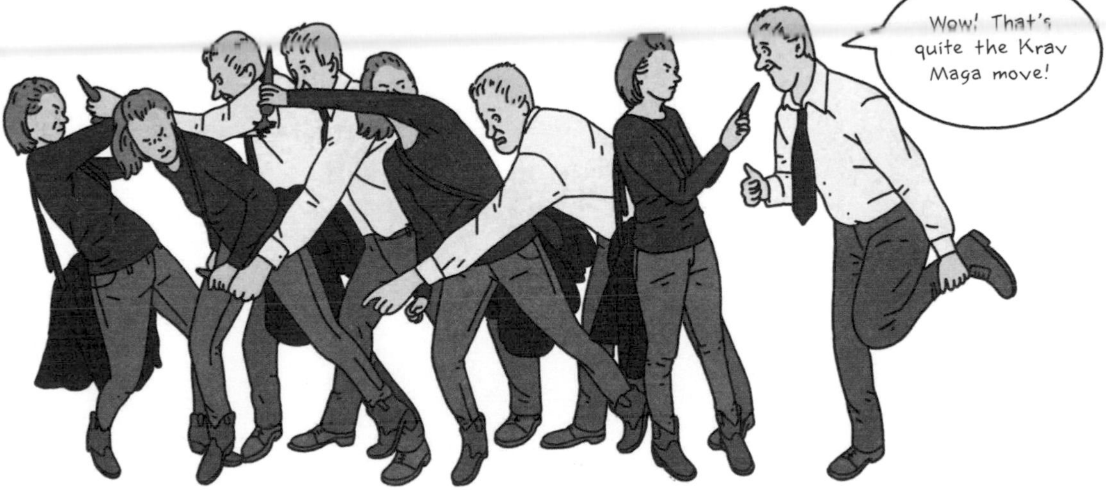
Wow! That's quite the Krav Maga move!

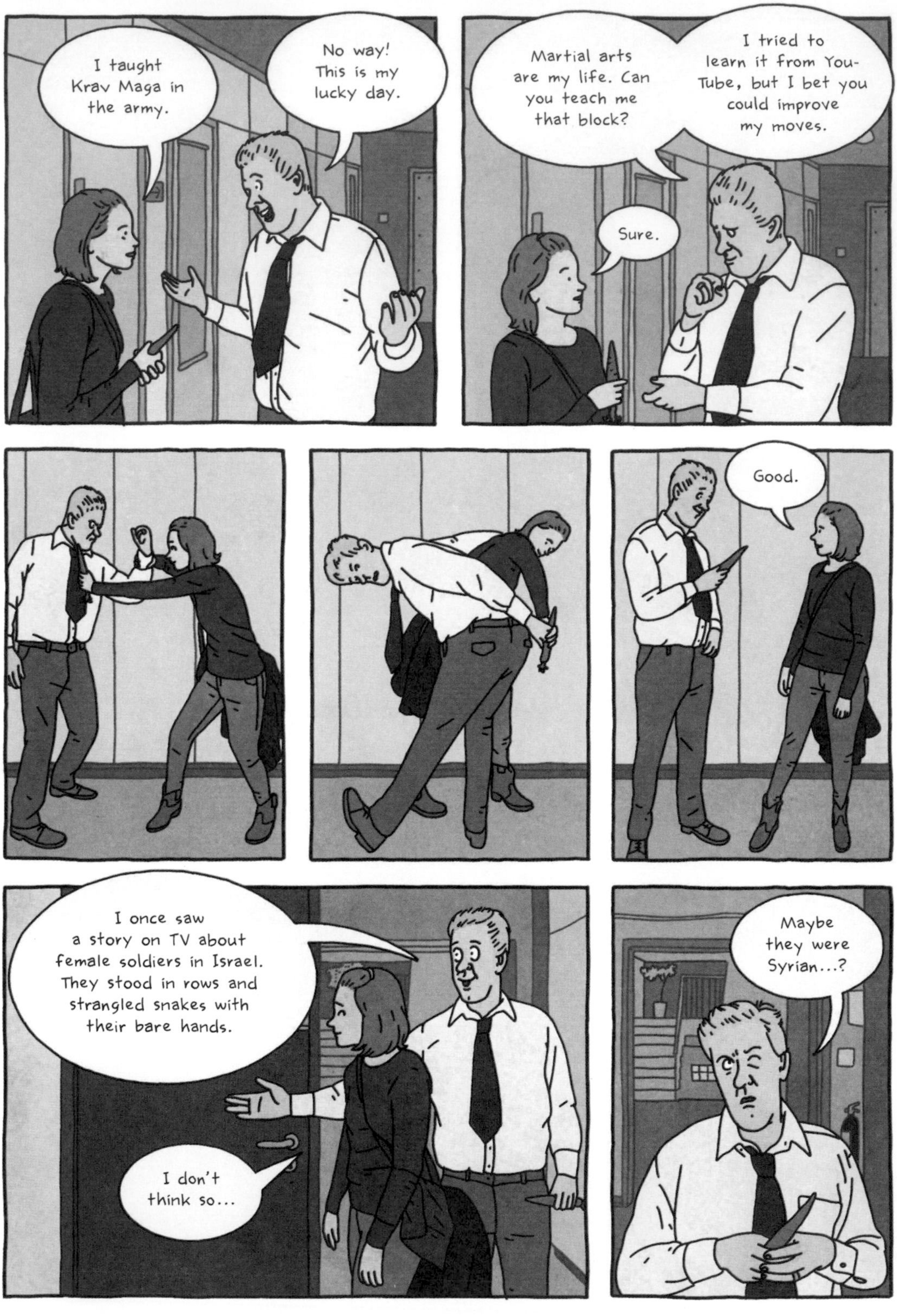
I taught Krav Maga in the army.
No way! This is my lucky day.
Martial arts are my life. Can you teach me that block?
I tried to learn it from You-Tube, but I bet you could improve my moves.
Sure.
Good.
I once saw a story on TV about female soldiers in Israel. They stood in rows and strangled snakes with their bare hands.
I don't think so...
Maybe they were Syrian...?

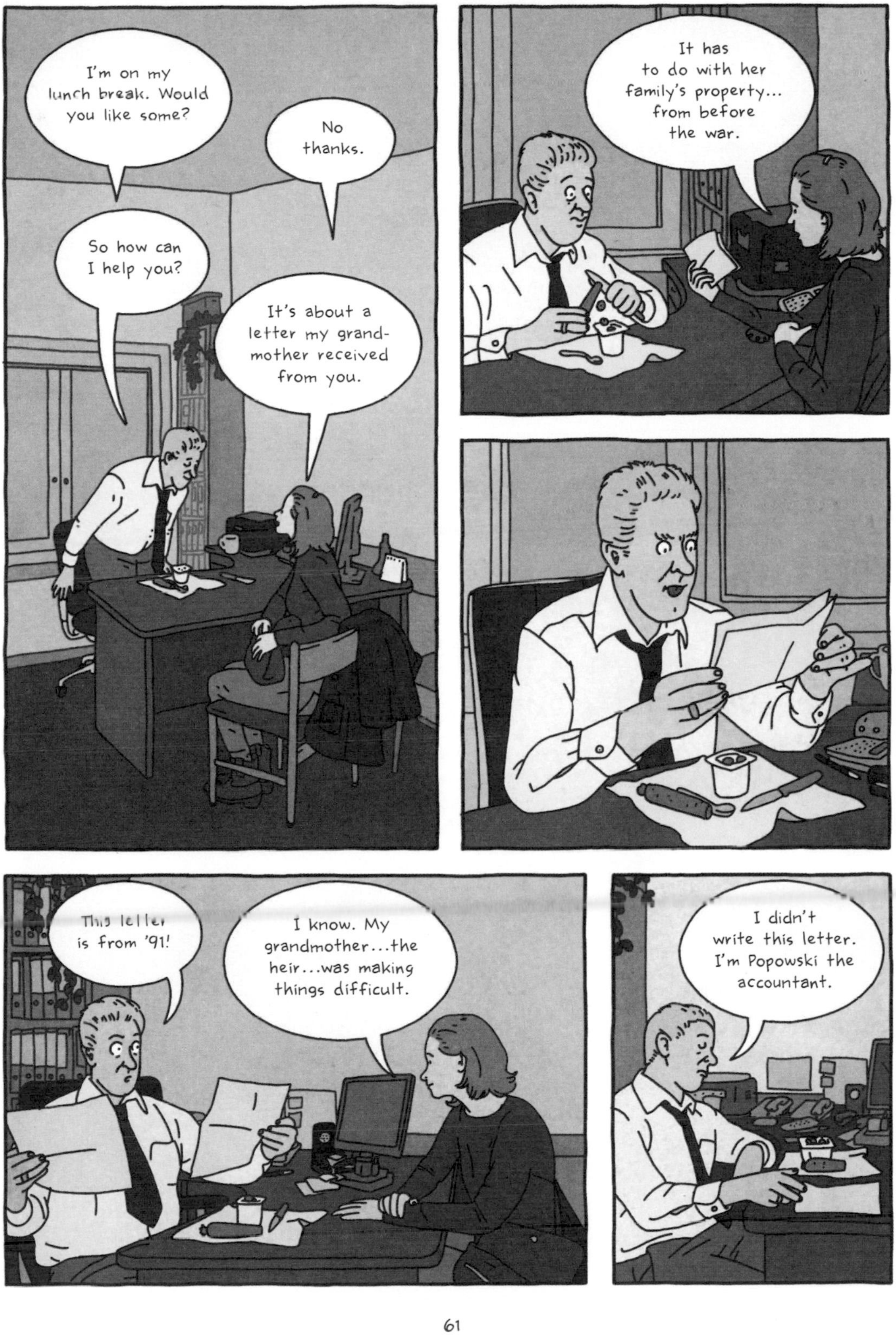
I'm on my lunch break. Would you like some?
No thanks.
So how can I help you?
It's about a letter my grand-mother received from you.
It has to do with her family's property... from before the war.
This letter is from '91!
I know. My grandmother...the heir...was making things difficult.
I didn't write this letter. I'm Popowski the accountant.

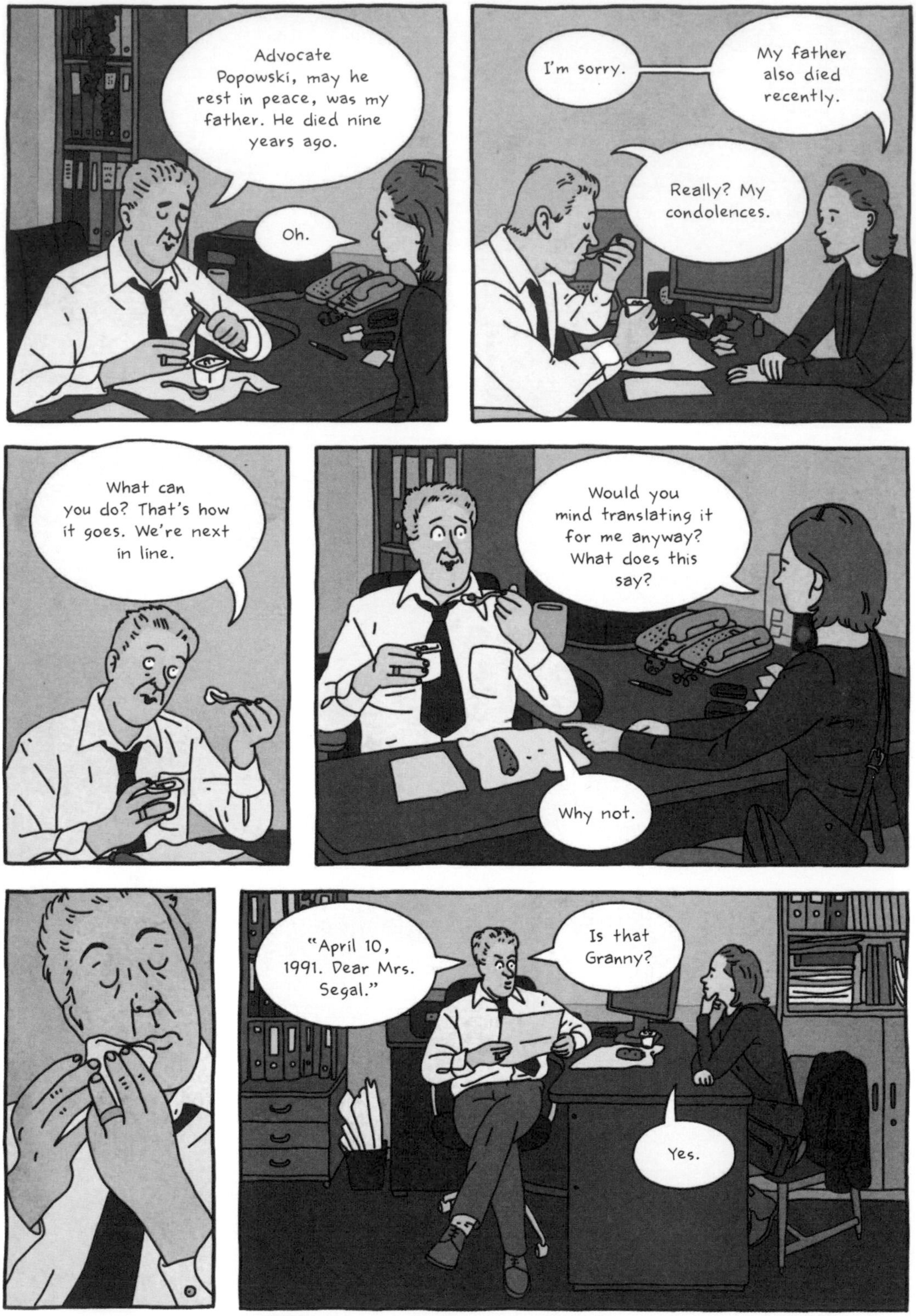
Advocate Popowski, may he rest in peace, was my father. He died nine years ago.
Oh.
I'm sorry.
My father also died recently.
Really? My condolences.
What can you do? That's how it goes. We're next in line.
Would you mind translating it for me anyway? What does this say?
Why not.
"April 10, 1991. Dear Mrs. Segal."
Is that Granny?
Yes.

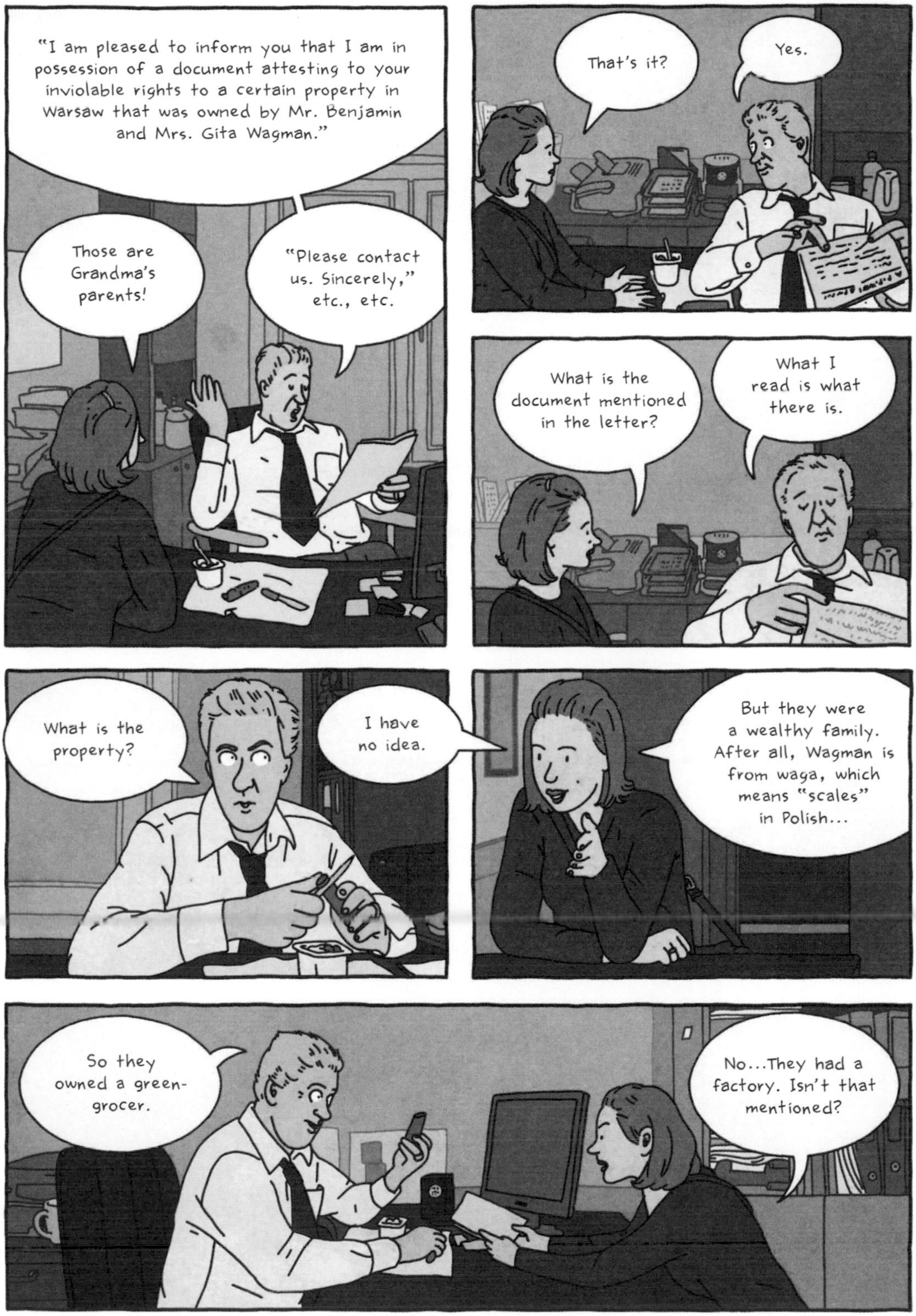
"I am pleased to inform you that I am in possession of a document attesting to your inviolable rights to a certain property in Warsaw that was owned by Mr. Benjamin and Mrs. Gita Wagman."
Those are Grandma's parents!
"Please contact us. Sincerely," etc., etc.
That's it?
Yes.
What is the document mentioned in the letter?
What I read is what there is.
What is the property?
I have no idea.
But they were a wealthy family. After all, Wagman is from waga, which means "scales" in Polish...
So they owned a green-grocer.
No...They had a factory. Isn't that mentioned?

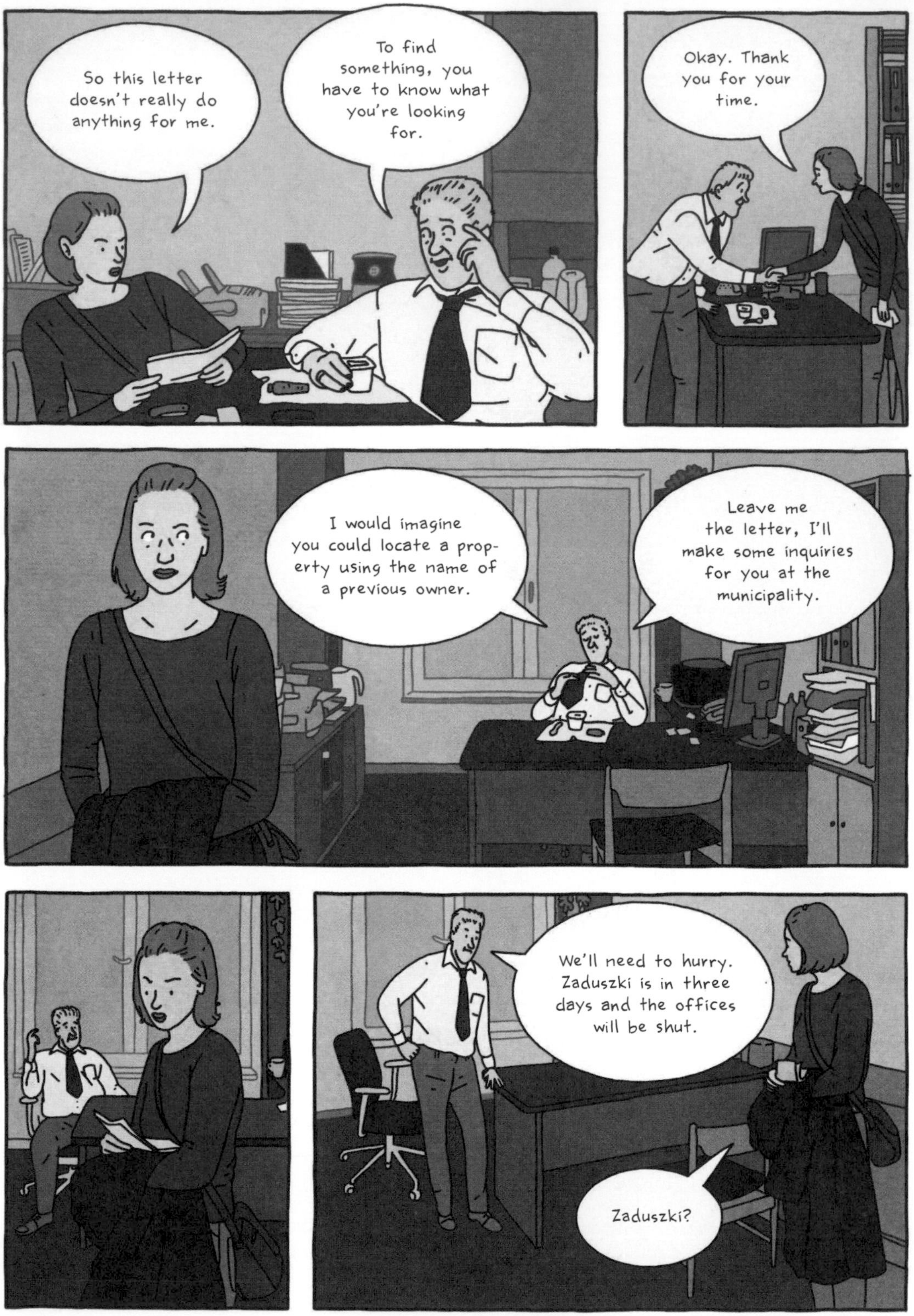
So this letter doesn't really do anything for me.
To find something, you have to know what you're looking for.
Okay. Thank you for your time.
I would imagine you could locate a property using the name of a previous owner.
Leave me the letter, I'll make some inquiries for you at the municipality.
We'll need to hurry. Zaduszki is in three days and the offices will be shut.
Zaduszki?

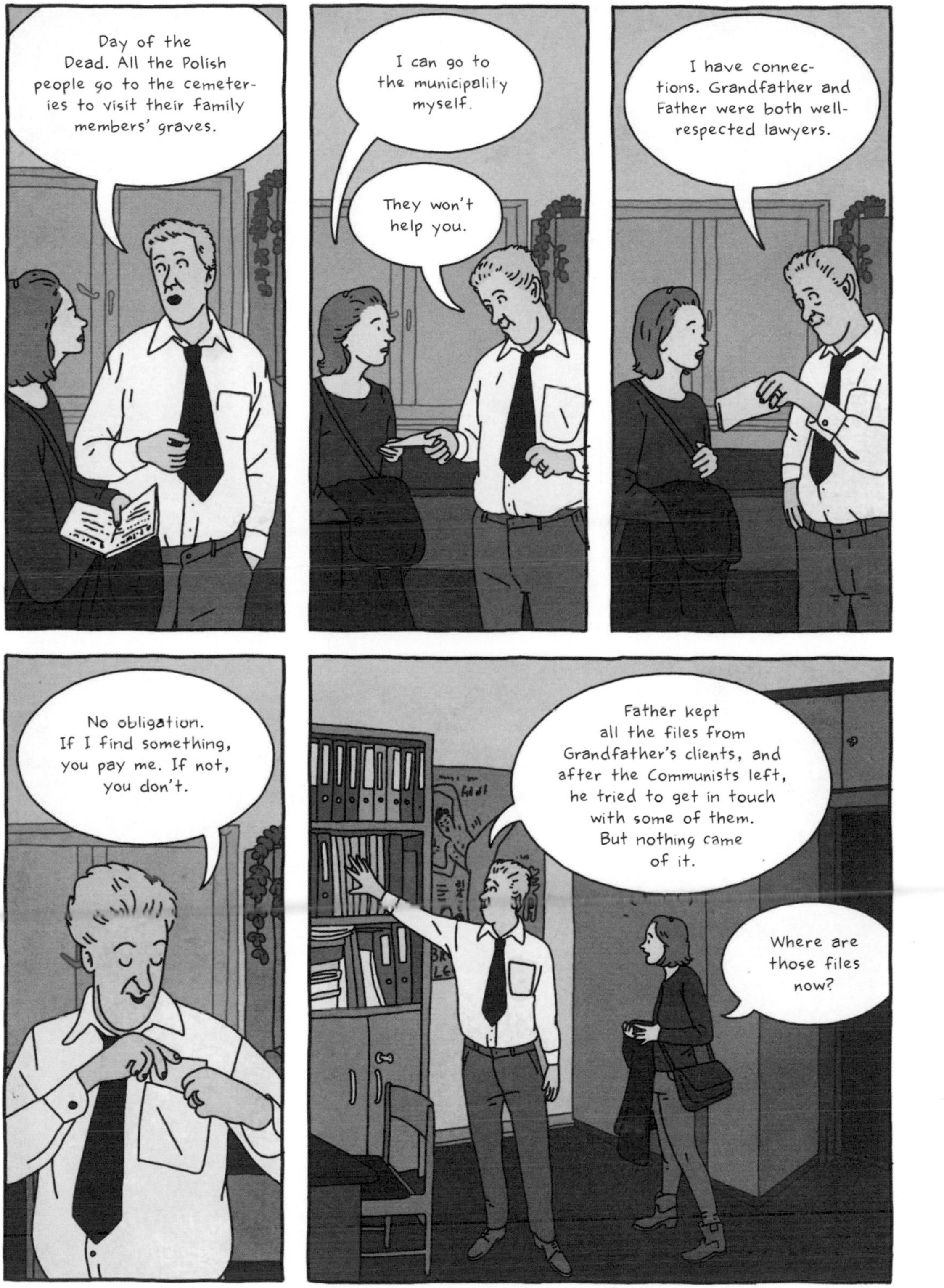
Day of the Dead. All the Polish people go to the cemeteries to visit their family members' graves.
I can go to the municipality myself.
They won't help you.
I have connections. Grandfather and Father were both well-respected lawyers.
No obligation. If I find something, you pay me. If not, you don't.
Father kept all the files from Grandfather's clients, and after the Communists left, he tried to get in touch with some of them. But nothing came of it.
Where are those files now?

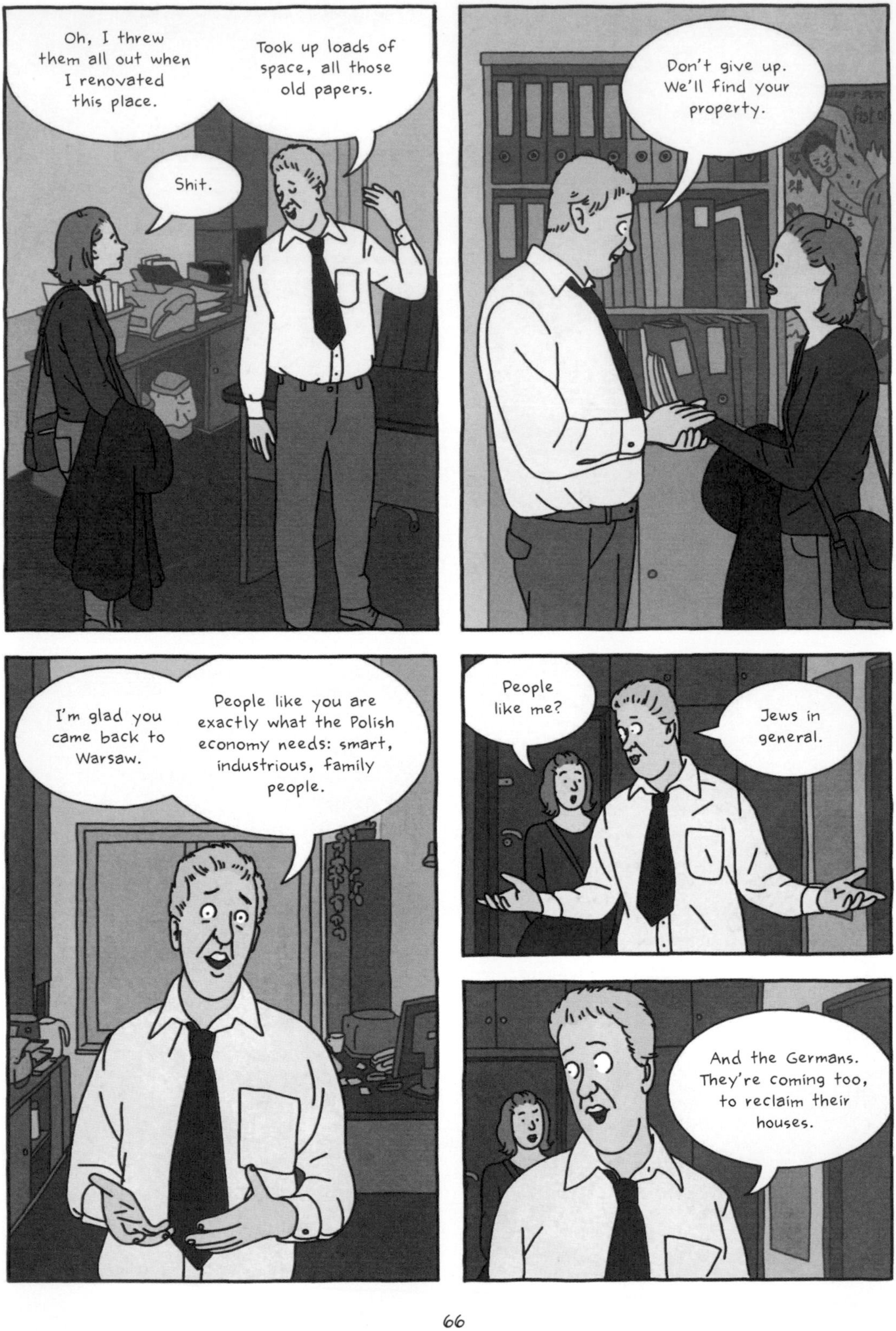
Oh, I threw them all out when I renovated this place.
Took up loads of space, all those old papers.
Shit.
Don't give up. We'll find your property.
I'm glad you came back to Warsaw.
People like you are exactly what the Polish economy needs: smart, industrious, family people.
People like me?
Jews in general.
And the Germans. They're coming too, to reclaim their houses.

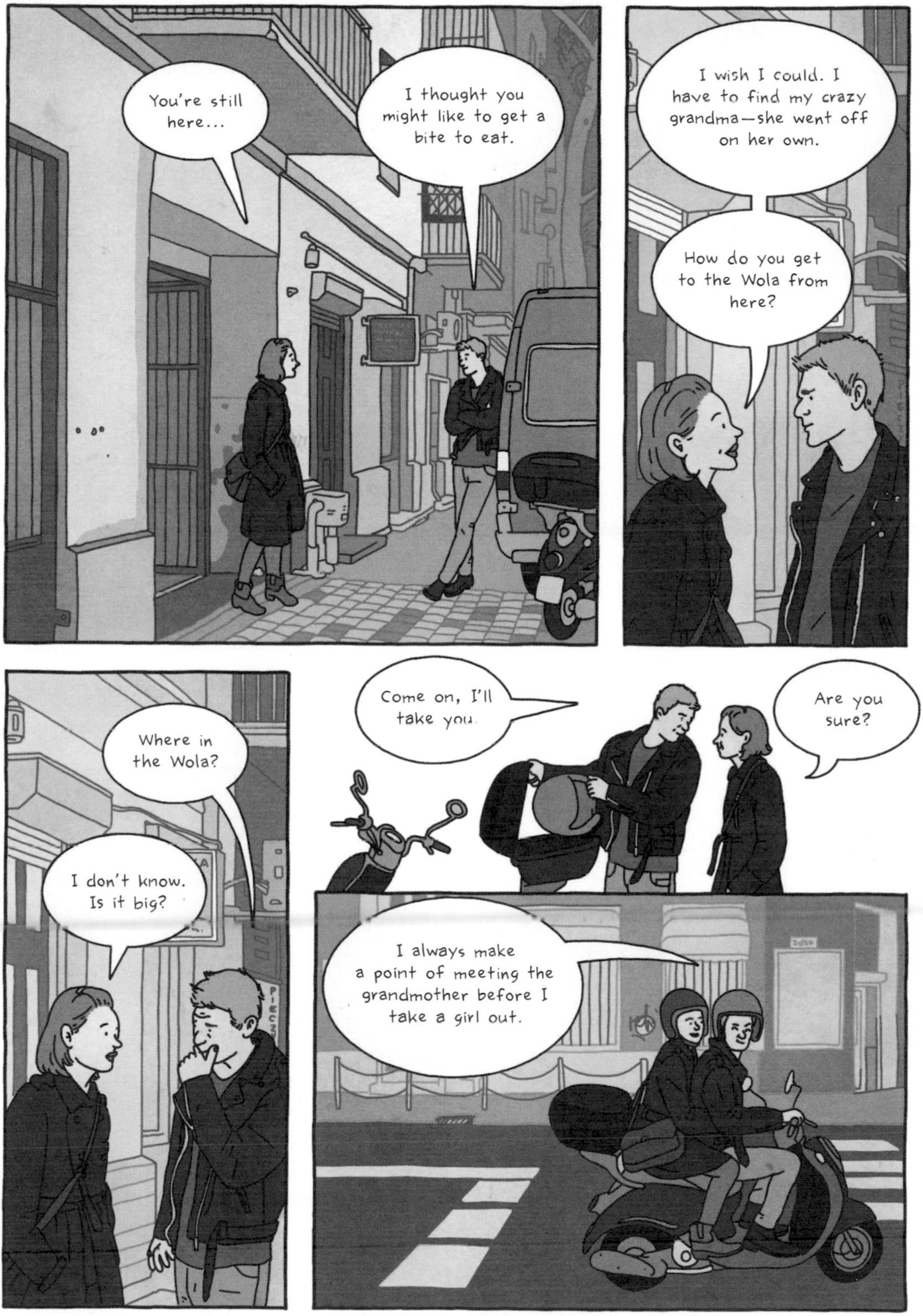
You're still here...
I thought you might like to get a bite to eat.
I wish I could. I have to find my crazy grandma—she went off on her own.
How do you get to the Wola from here?
Where in the Wola?
I don't know. Is it big?
Come on, I'll take you.
Are you sure?
I always make a point of meeting the grandmother before I take a girl out.

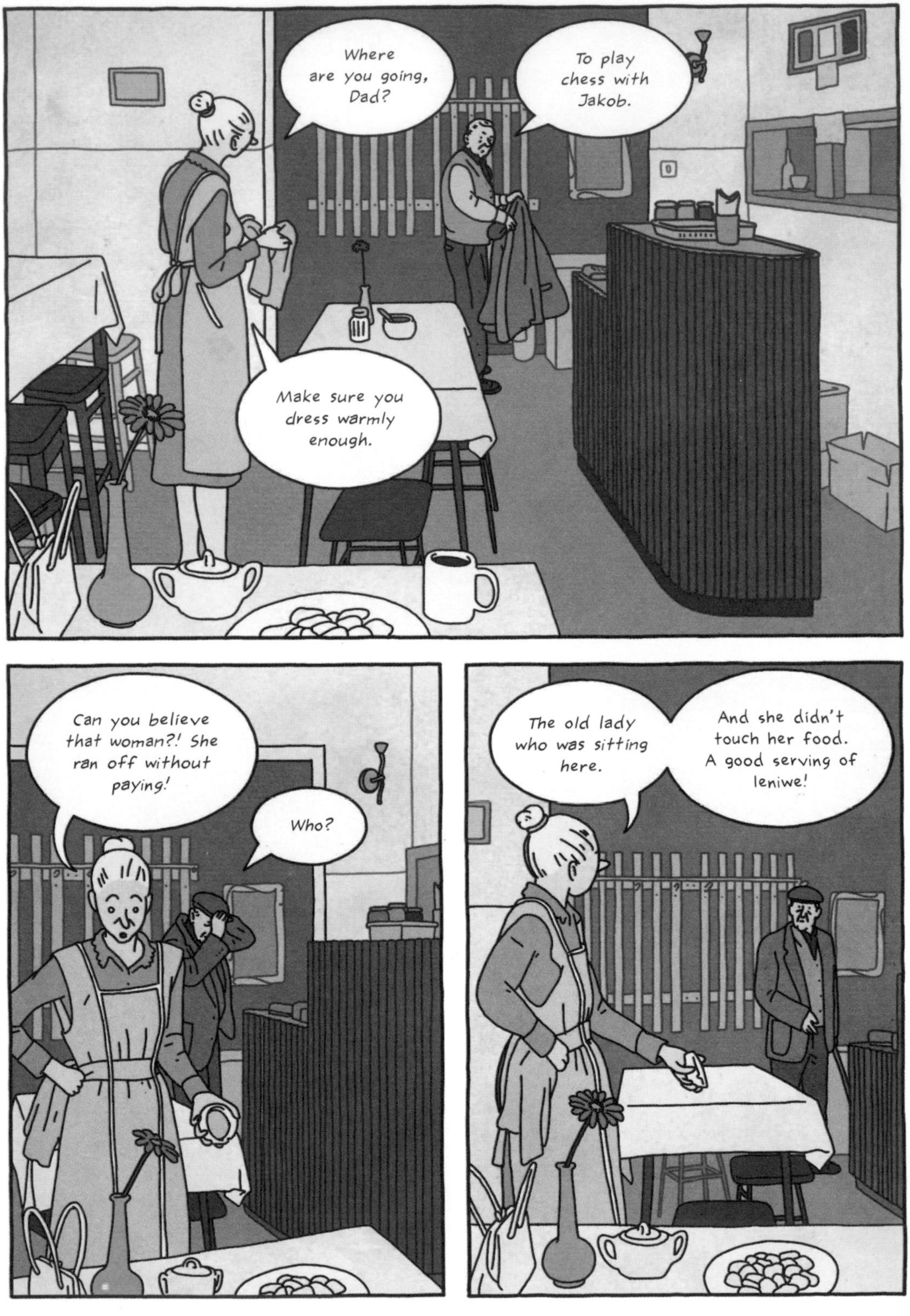
Where are you going, Dad?
To play chess with Jakob.
Make sure you dress warmly enough.
Can you believe that woman?! She ran off without paying!
Who?
The old lady who was sitting here.
And she didn't touch her food. A good serving of leniwe!

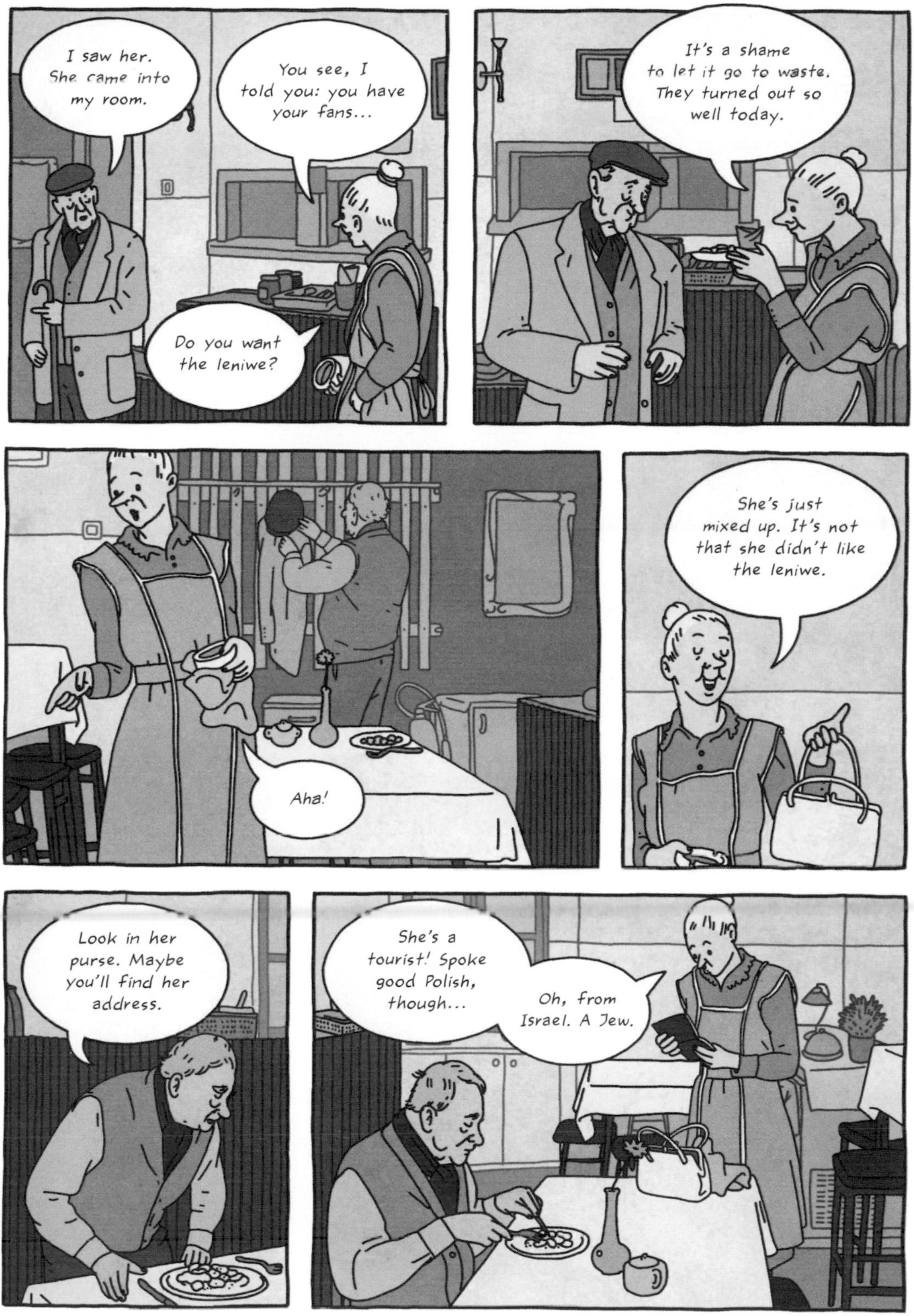
I saw her. She came into my room.
You see, I told you: you have your fans...
Do you want the leniwe?
It's a shame to let it go to waste. They turned out so well today.
Aha!
She's just mixed up. It's not that she didn't like the leniwe.
Look in her purse. Maybe you'll find her address.
She's a tourist! Spoke good Polish, though...
Oh, from Israel. A Jew.

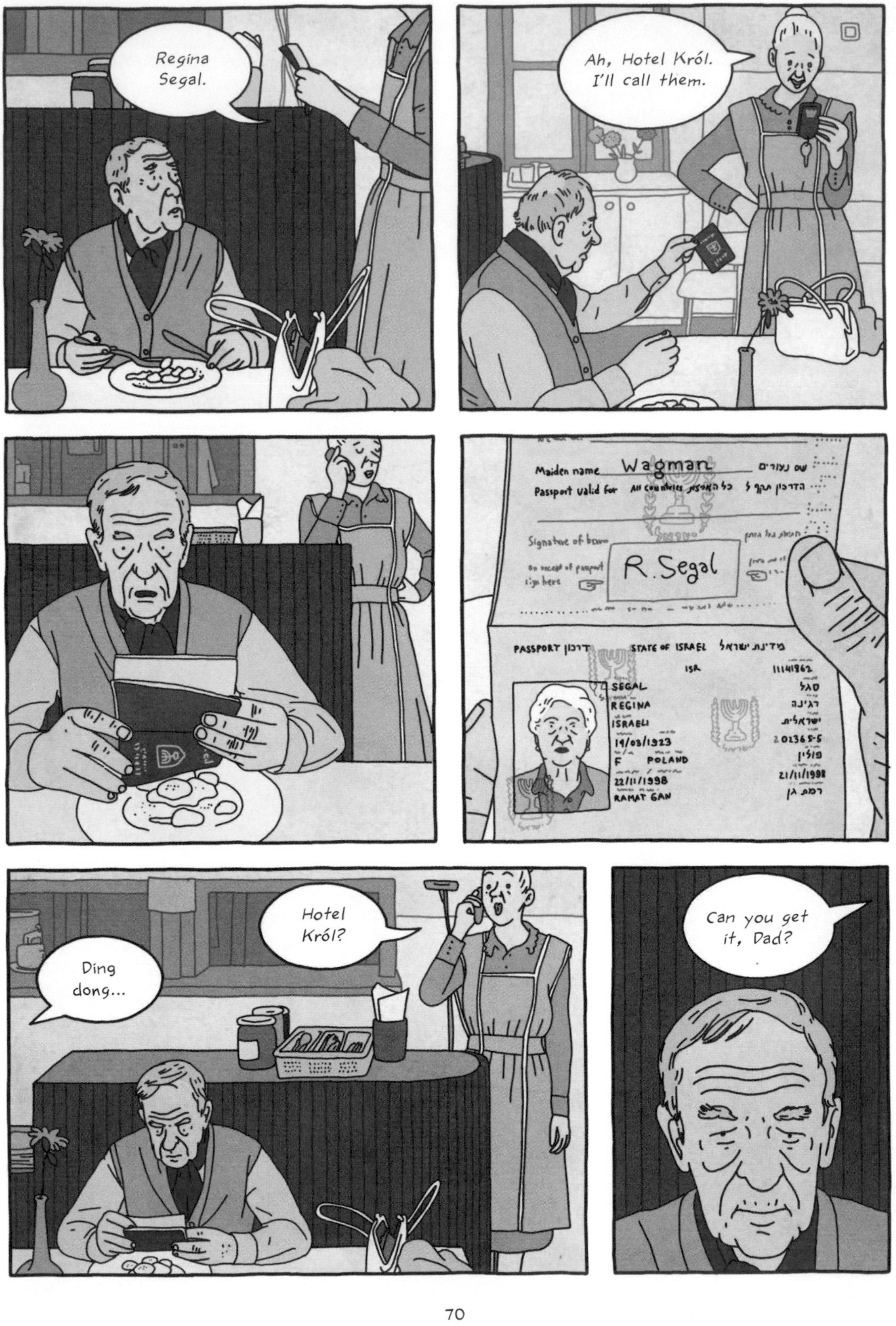
Regina Segal.
Ah, Hotel Król. I'll call them.
Maiden name Wagman
שם נעורים
Passport valid for All countries
Signature of bearer
R. Segal
PASSPORT
דרכון
STATE OF ISRAEL
מדינת ישראל
ISR
11141862
SEGAL
סגל
REGINA
רגינה
ISRAELI
ישראלית
19/03/1923
F POLAND
פולין
22/11/1998
21/11/1998
RAMAT GAN
רמת גן
Hotel Król?
Ding dong...
Can you get it, Dad?

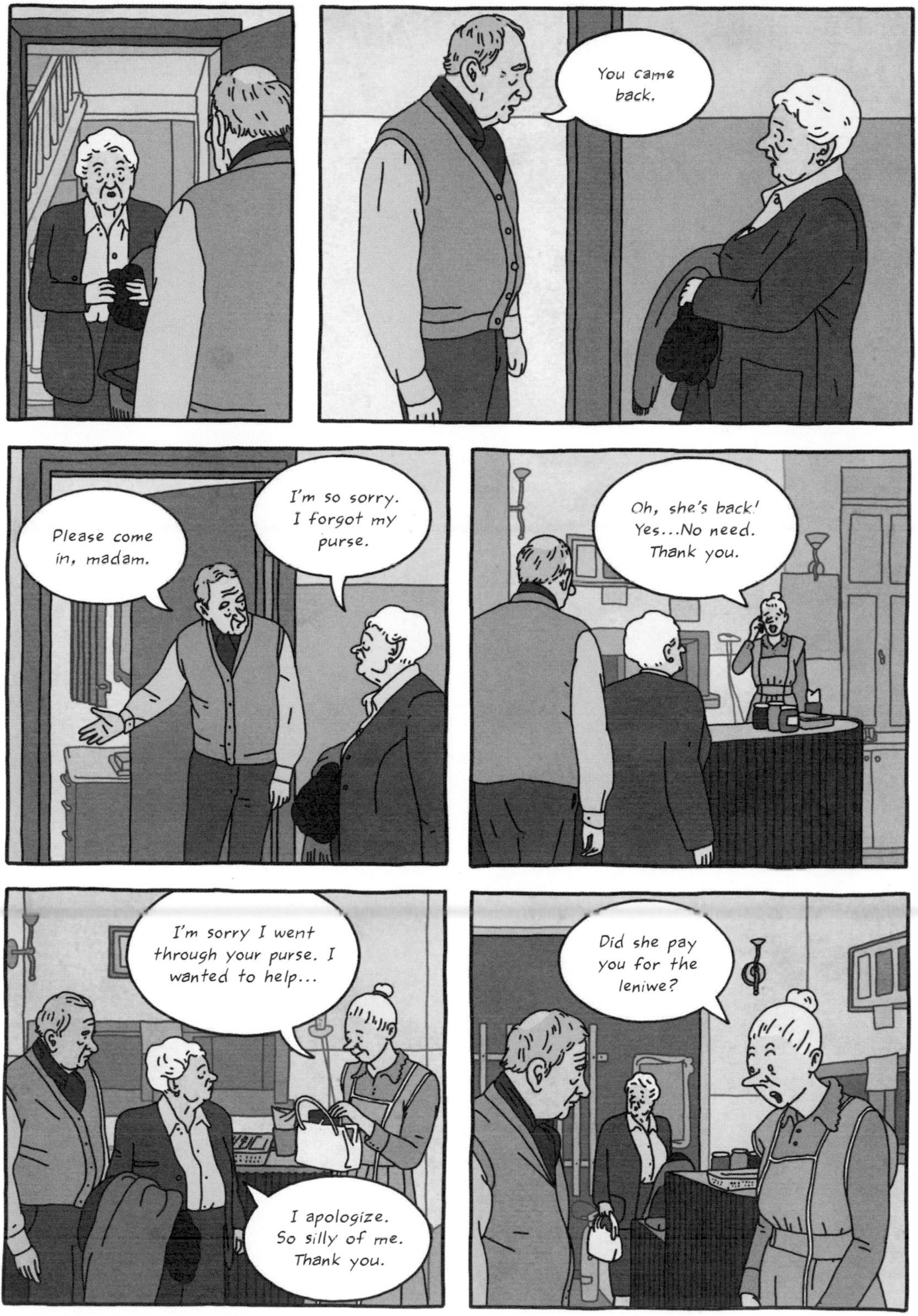
You came back.
Please come in, madam.
I'm so sorry. I forgot my purse.
Oh, she's back! Yes...No need. Thank you.
I'm sorry I went through your purse. I wanted to help...
I apologize. So silly of me. Thank you.
Did she pay you for the leniwe?

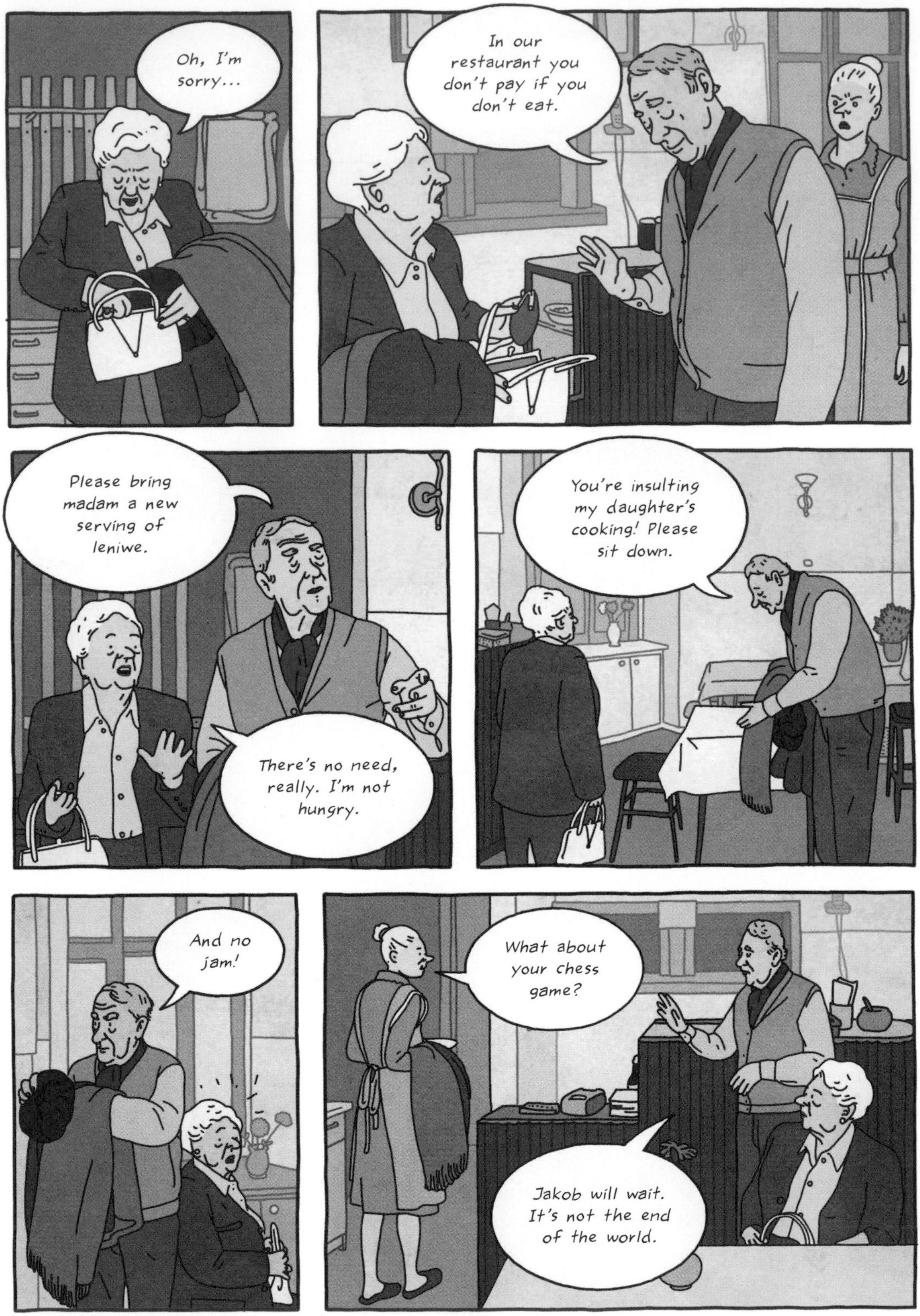
Oh, I'm sorry...
In our restaurant you don't pay if you don't eat.
Please bring madam a new serving of leniwe.
There's no need, really. I'm not hungry.
You're insulting my daughter's cooking! Please sit down.
And no jam!
What about your chess game?
Jakob will wait. It's not the end of the world.

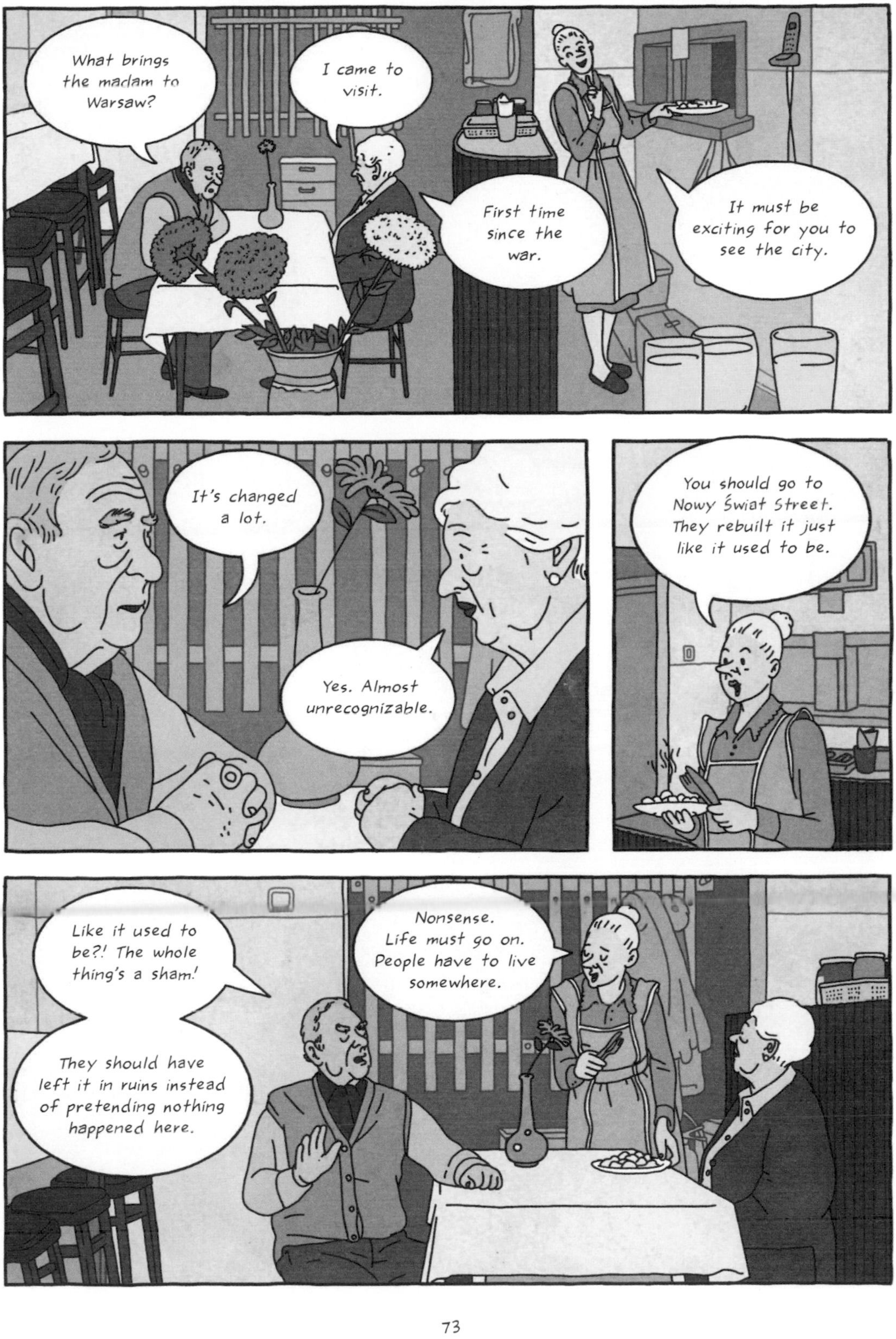
What brings the madam to Warsaw?
I came to visit.
First time since the war.
It must be exciting for you to see the city.
It's changed a lot.
Yes. Almost unrecognizable.
You should go to Nowy Świat Street. They rebuilt it just like it used to be.
Like it used to be?! The whole thing's a sham!
They should have left it in ruins instead of pretending nothing happened here.
Nonsense. Life must go on. People have to live somewhere.

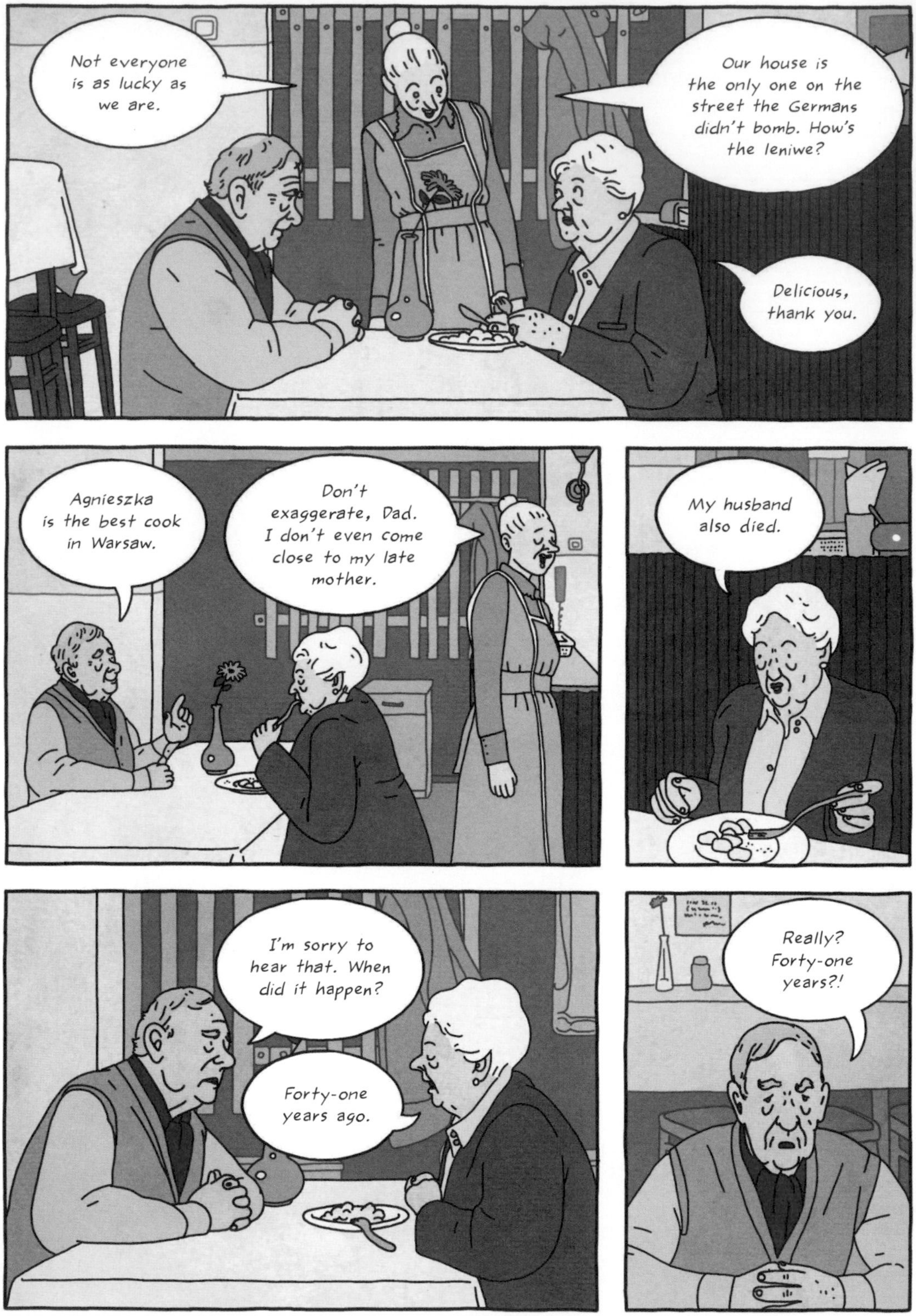
Not everyone is as lucky as we are.
Our house is the only one on the street the Germans didn't bomb. How's the leniwe?
Delicious, thank you.
Agnieszka is the best cook in Warsaw.
Don't exaggerate, Dad. I don't even come close to my late mother.
My husband also died.
I'm sorry to hear that. When did it happen?
Forty-one years ago.
Really? Forty-one years?!

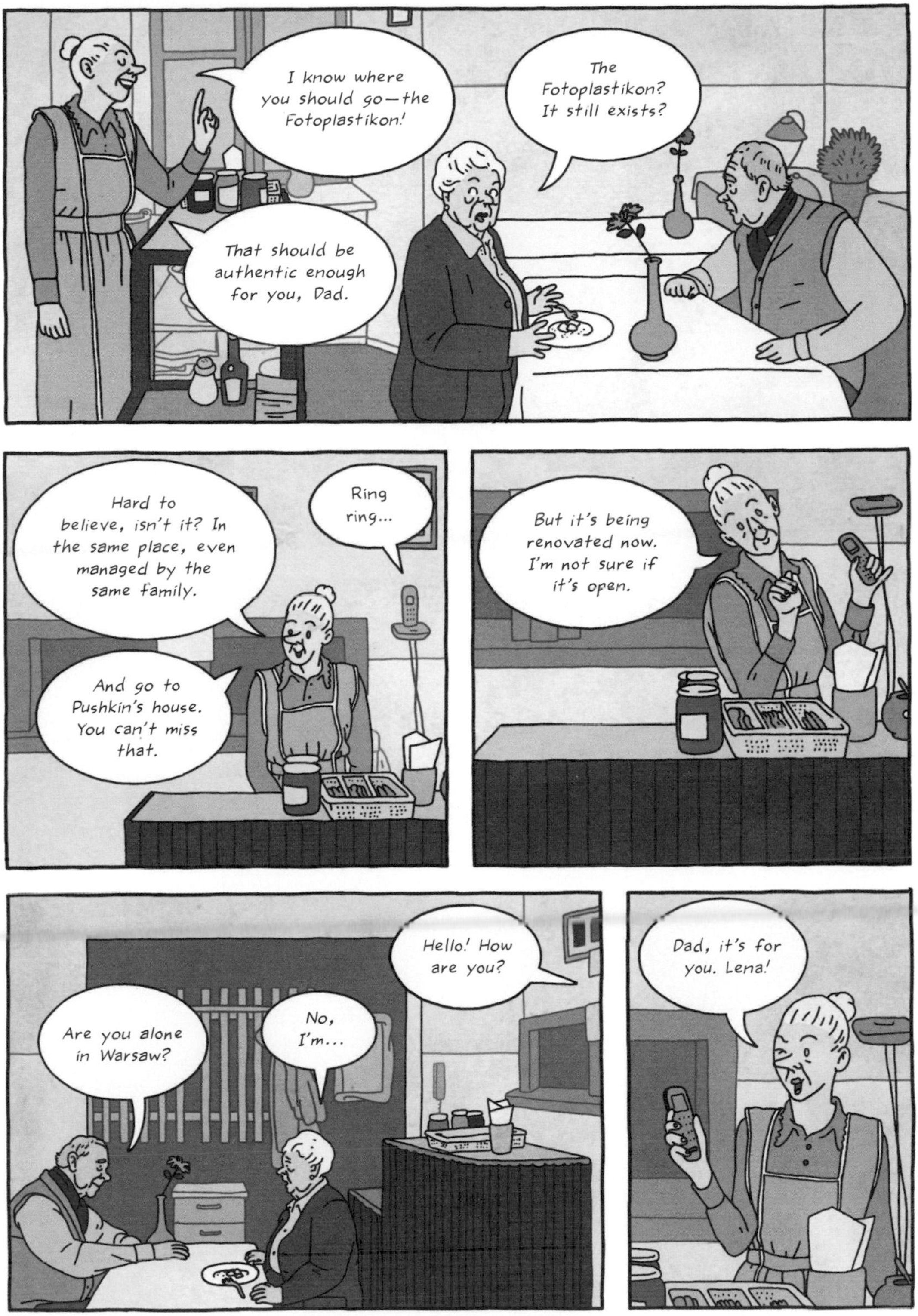
I know where you should go—the Fotoplastikon!
The Fotoplastikon? It still exists?
That should be authentic enough for you, Dad.
Hard to believe, isn't it? In the same place, even managed by the same family.
Ring ring...
And go to Pushkin's house. You can't miss that.
But it's being renovated now. I'm not sure if it's open.
Are you alone in Warsaw?
No, I'm...
Hello! How are you?
Dad, it's for you. Lena!

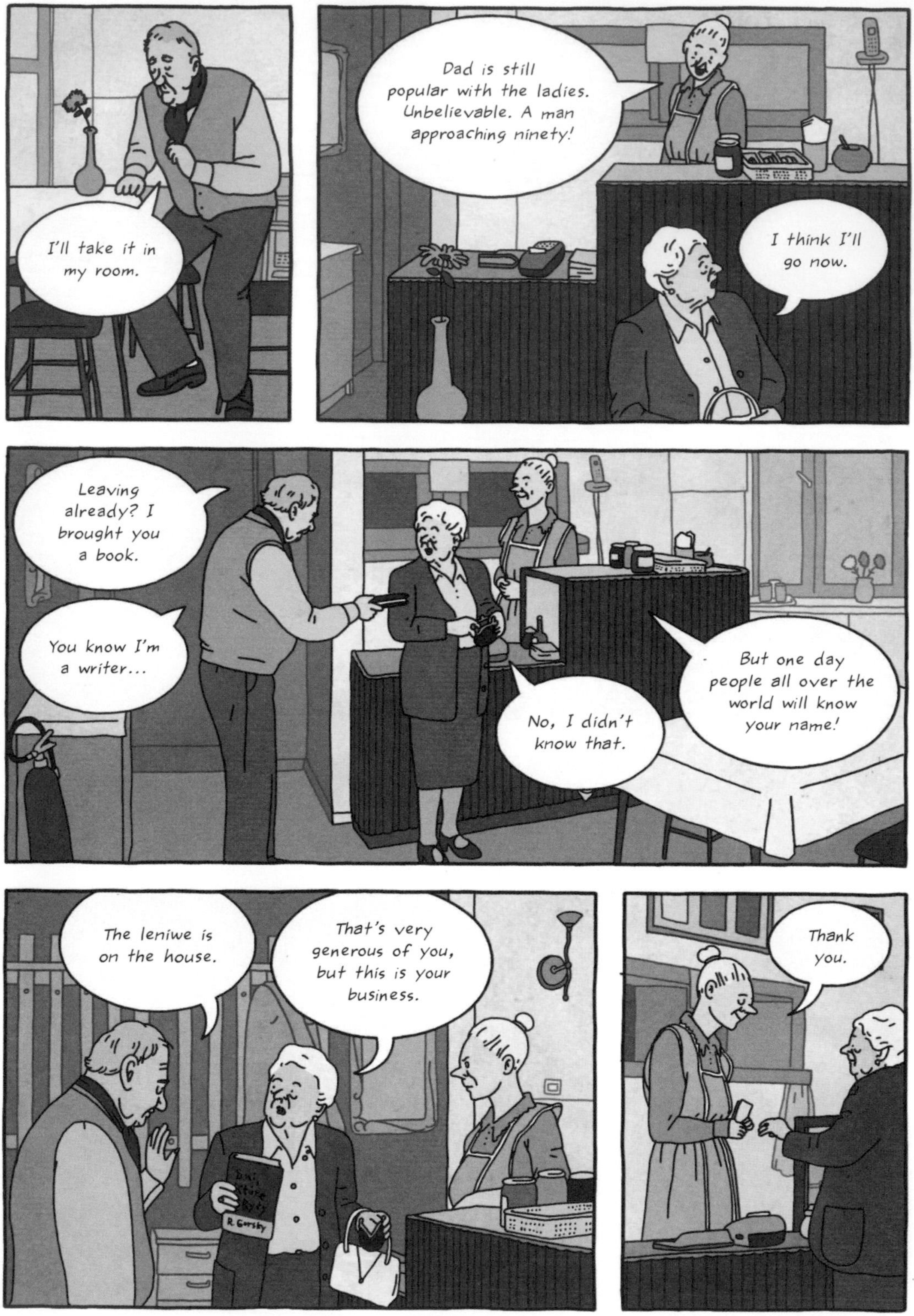
I'll take it in my room.
Dad is still popular with the ladies. Unbelievable. A man approaching ninety!
I think I'll go now.
Leaving already? I brought you a book.
You know I'm a writer...
No, I didn't know that.
But one day people all over the world will know your name!
The leniwe is on the house.
That's very generous of you, but this is your business.
Thank you.

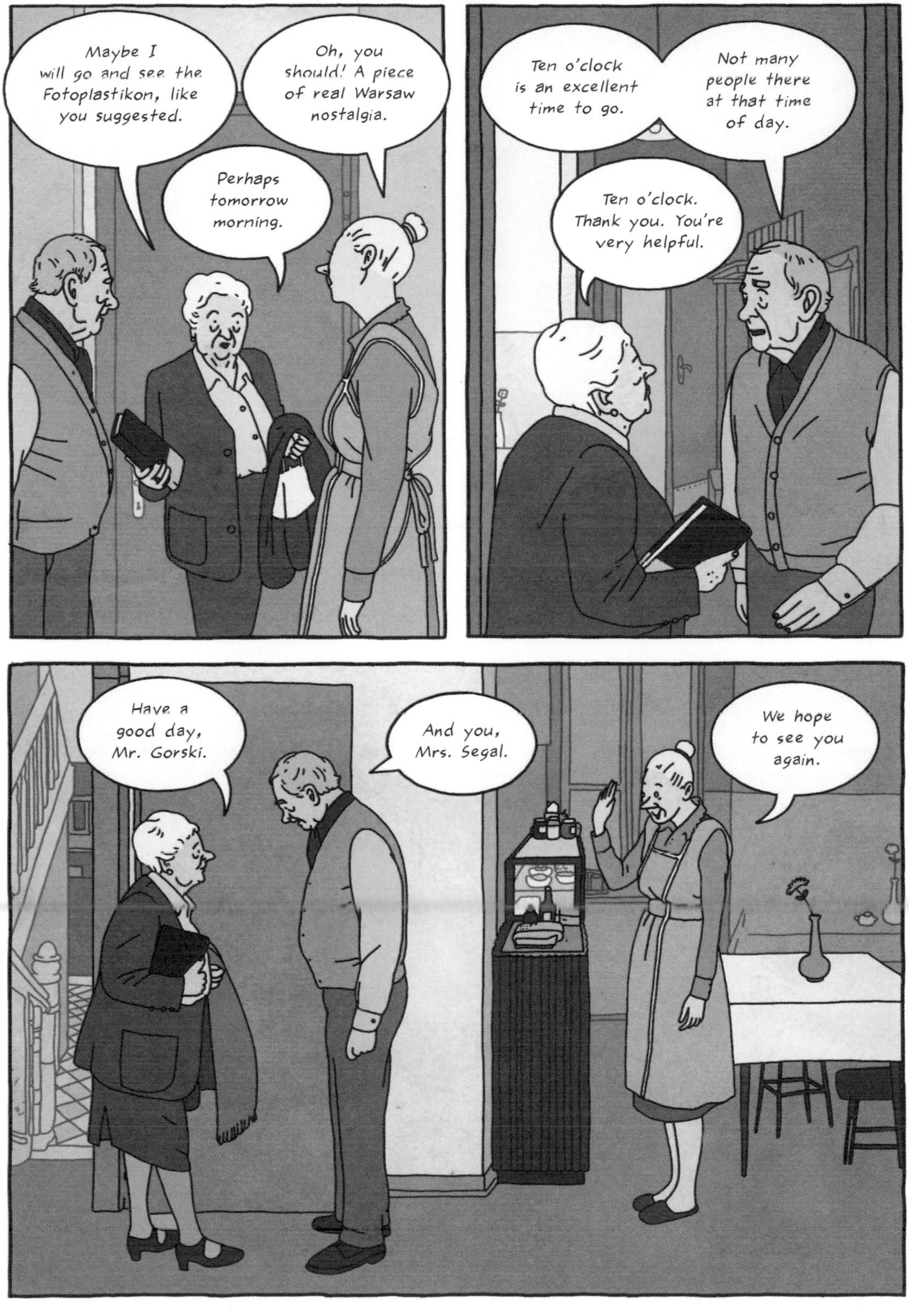
Maybe I will go and see the Fotoplastikon, like you suggested.
Oh, you should! A piece of real Warsaw nostalgia.
Perhaps tomorrow morning.
Ten o'clock is an excellent time to go.
Not many people there at that time of day.
Ten o'clock. Thank you. You're very helpful.
Have a good day, Mr. Gorski.
And you, Mrs. Segal.
We hope to see you again.

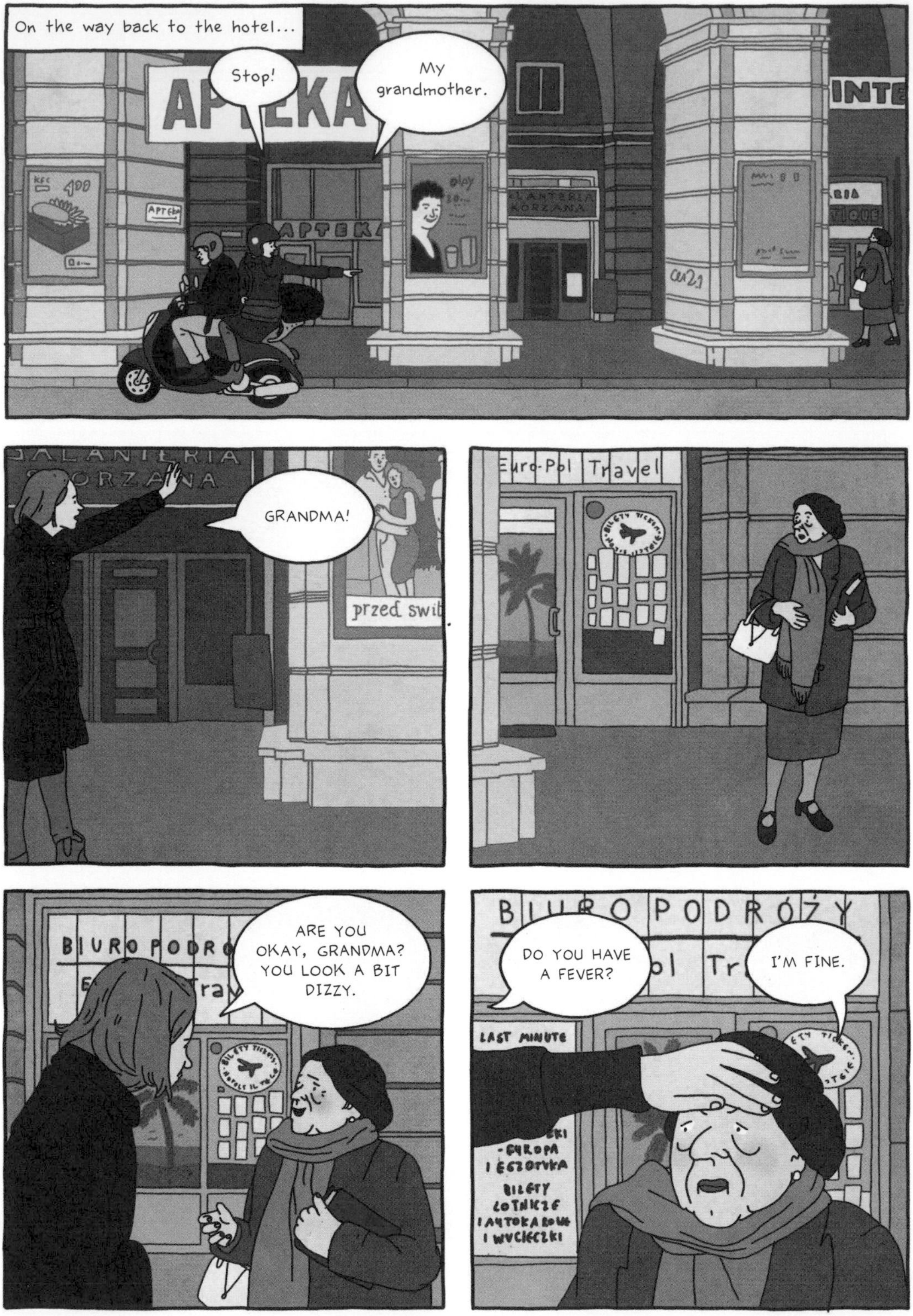

On the way back to the hotel...
APTEKA
Stop!
My grandmother.
GRANDMA!
przed swit
Euro-Pol Travel
BIURO PODRÓŻY
ARE YOU OKAY, GRANDMA? YOU LOOK A BIT DIZZY.
DO YOU HAVE A FEVER?
I'M FINE.
LAST MINUTE

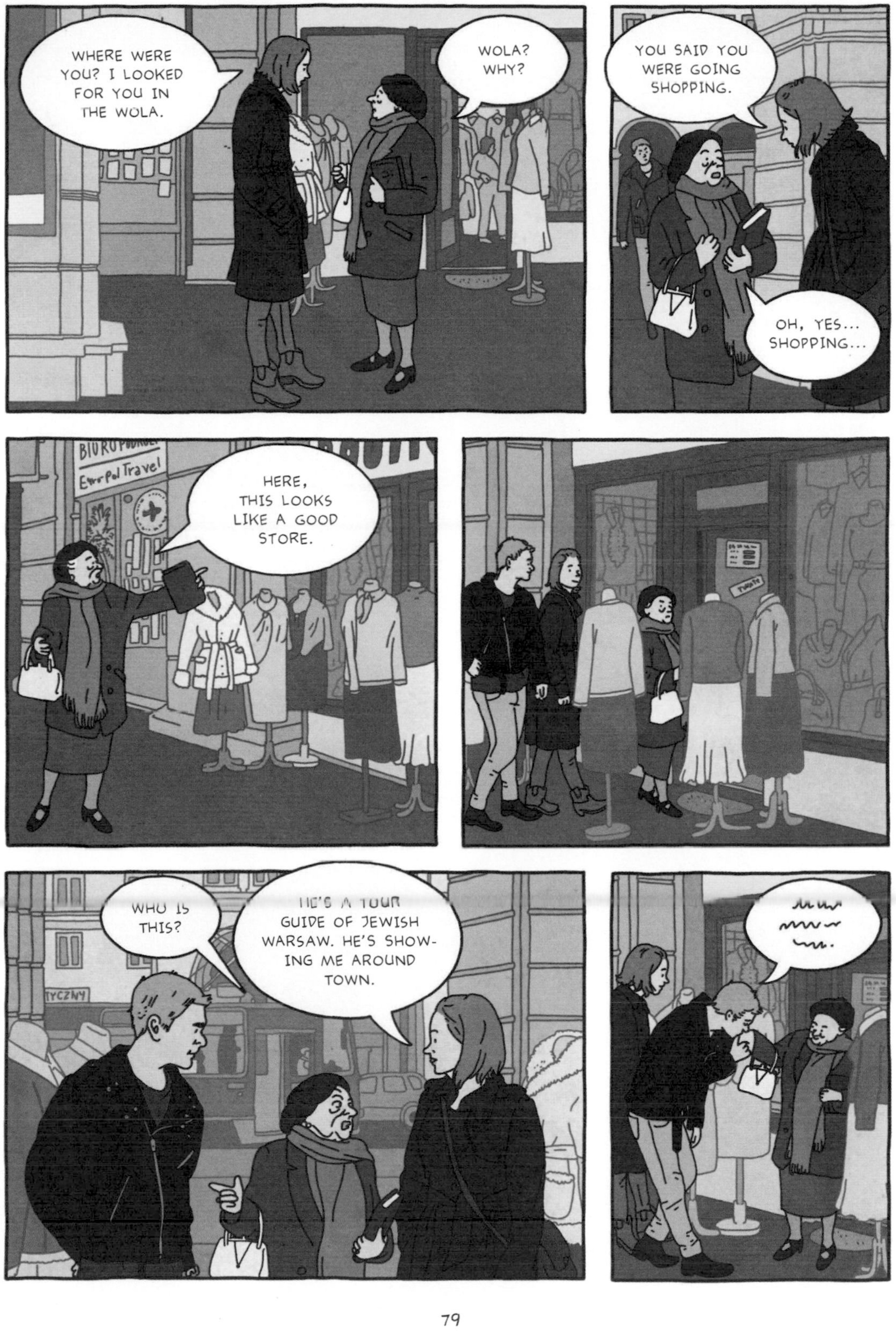
WHERE WERE YOU? I LOOKED FOR YOU IN THE WOLA.
WOLA? WHY?
YOU SAID YOU WERE GOING SHOPPING.
OH, YES... SHOPPING...
HERE, THIS LOOKS LIKE A GOOD STORE.
WHO IS THIS?
HE'S A TOUR GUIDE OF JEWISH WARSAW. HE'S SHOWING ME AROUND TOWN.

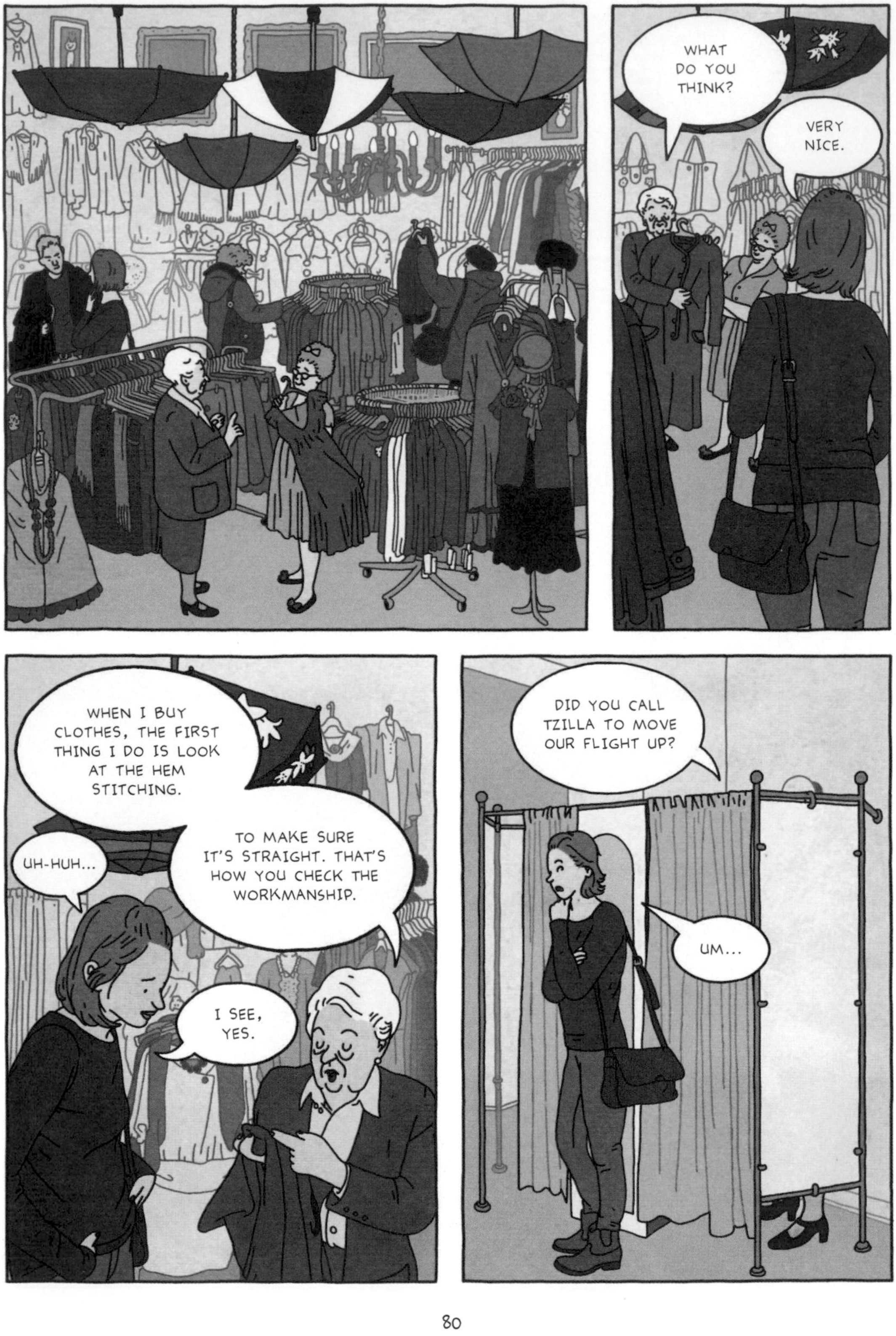

WHAT DO YOU THINK?
VERY NICE.
WHEN I BUY CLOTHES, THE FIRST THING I DO IS LOOK AT THE HEM STITCHING.
UH-HUH...
TO MAKE SURE IT'S STRAIGHT. THAT'S HOW YOU CHECK THE WORKMANSHIP.
I SEE, YES.
DID YOU CALL TZILLA TO MOVE OUR FLIGHT UP?
UM...

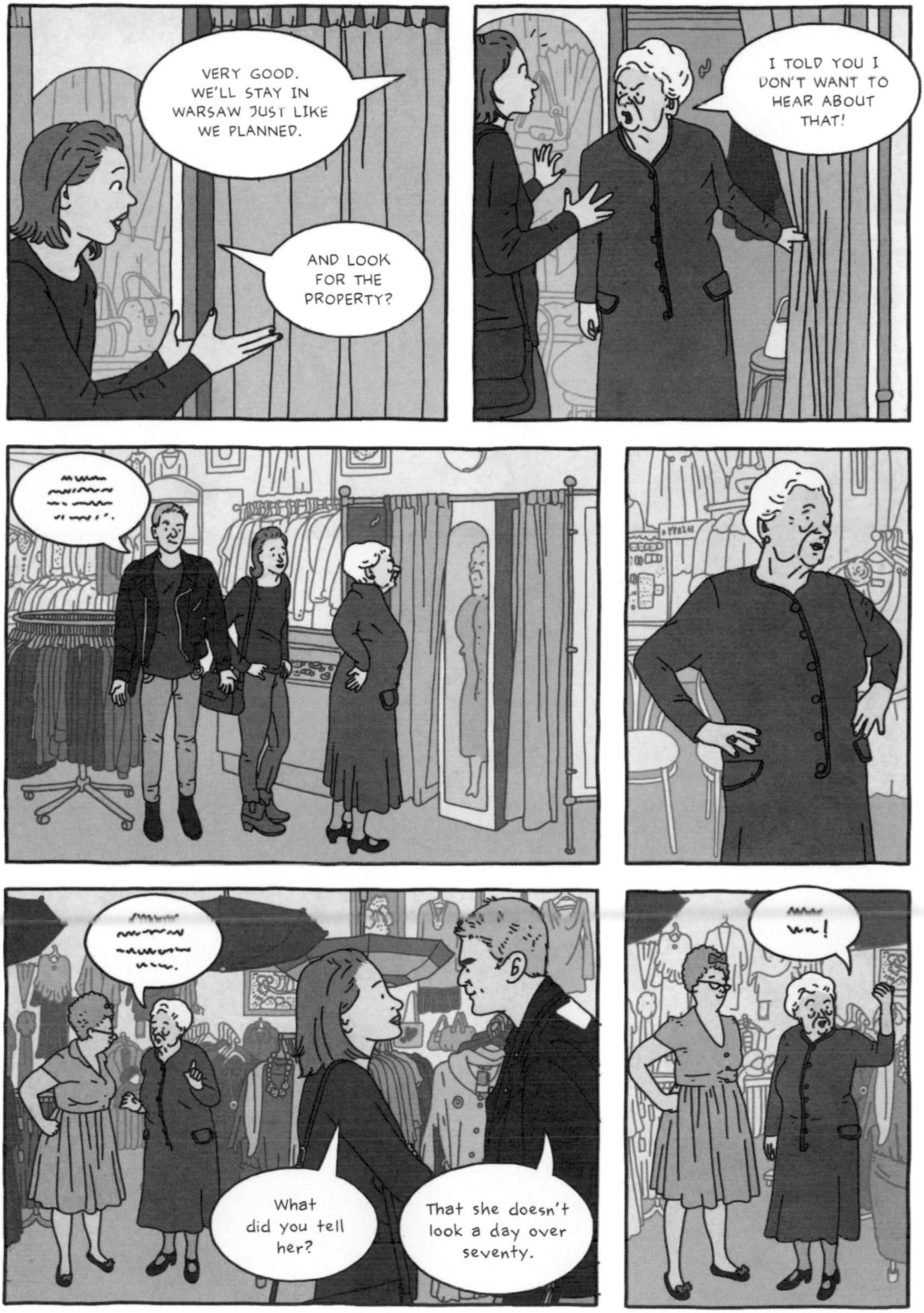
VERY GOOD. WE'LL STAY IN WARSAW JUST LIKE WE PLANNED.
AND LOOK FOR THE PROPERTY?
I TOLD YOU I DON'T WANT TO HEAR ABOUT THAT!
What did you tell her?
That she doesn't look a day over seventy.

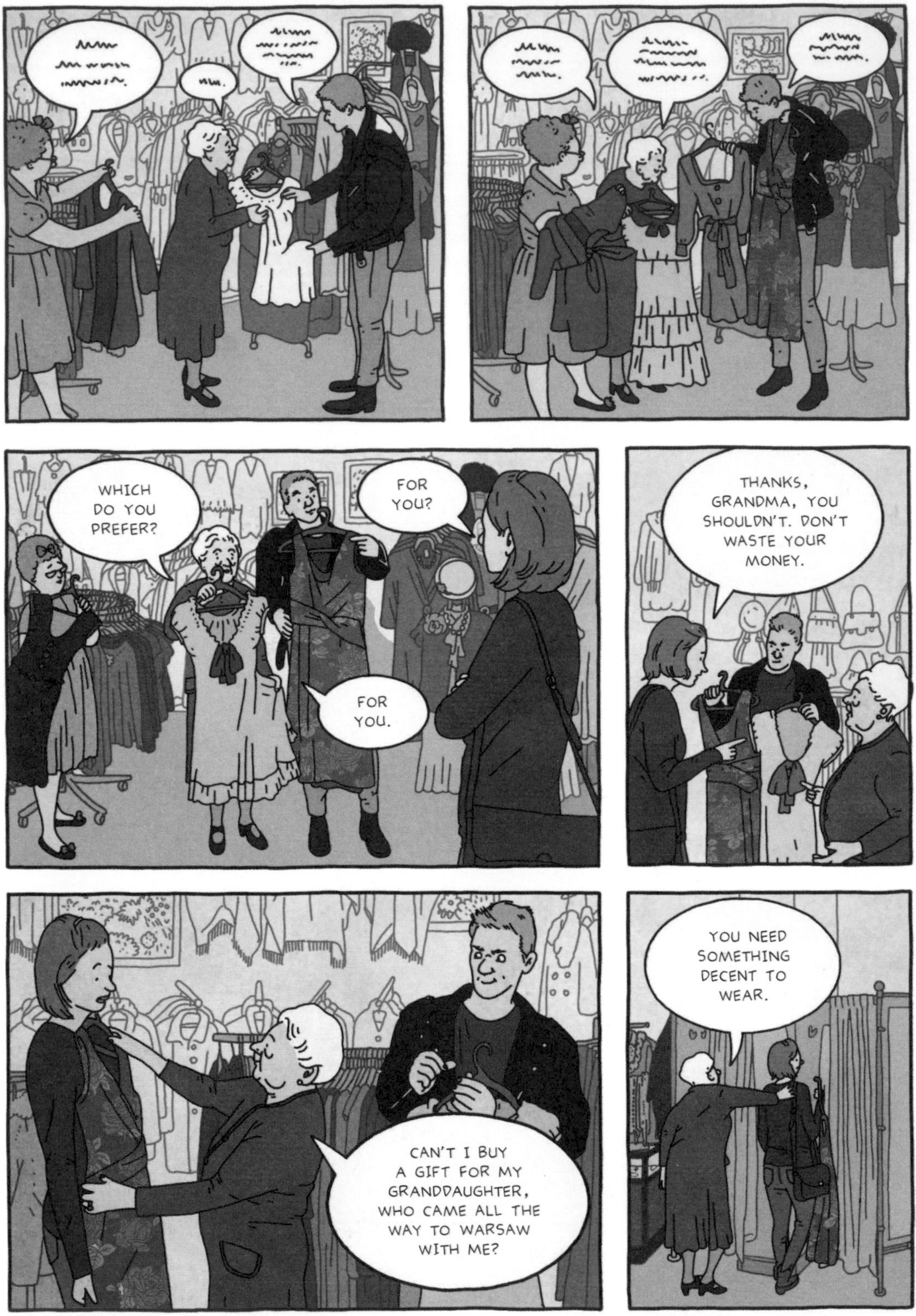
WHICH DO YOU PREFER?
FOR YOU?
FOR YOU.
THANKS, GRANDMA, YOU SHOULDN'T. DON'T WASTE YOUR MONEY.
CAN'T I BUY A GIFT FOR MY GRANDDAUGHTER, WHO CAME ALL THE WAY TO WARSAW WITH ME?
YOU NEED SOMETHING DECENT TO WEAR.

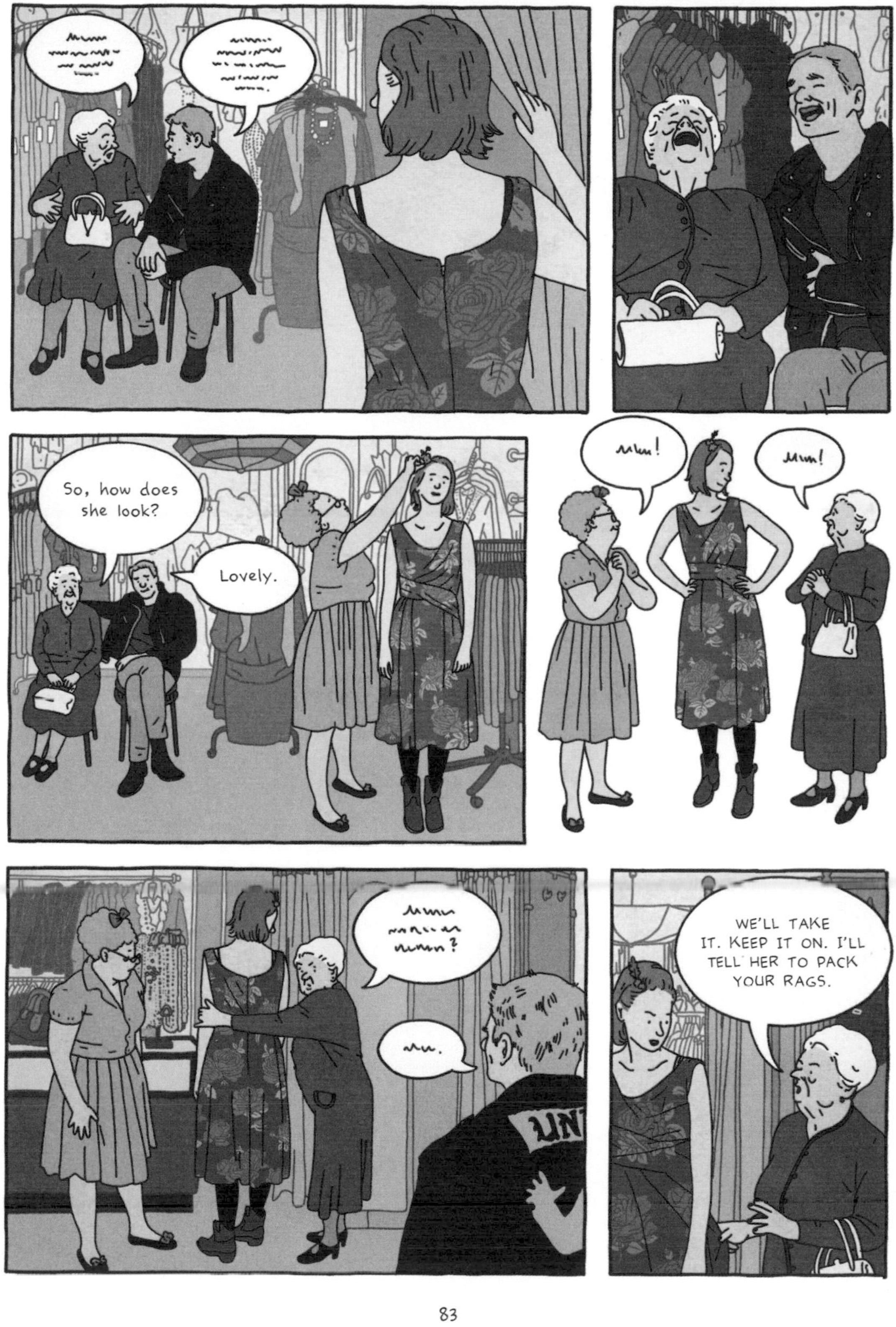
So, how does she look?
Lovely.
WE'LL TAKE IT. KEEP IT ON. I'LL TELL HER TO PACK YOUR RAGS.

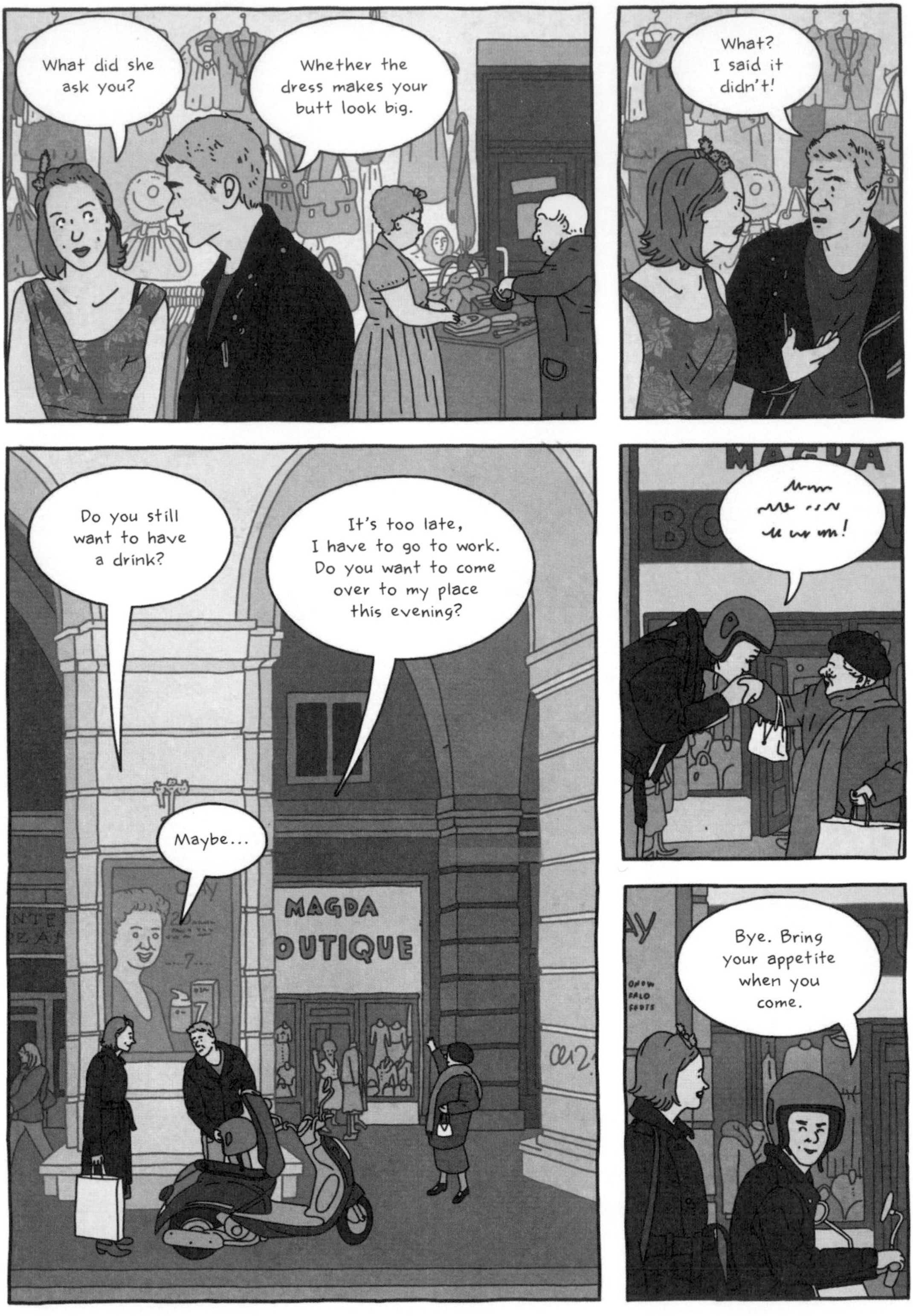
What did she ask you?
Whether the dress makes your butt look big.
What? I said it didn't!
Do you still want to have a drink?
It's too late, I have to go to work. Do you want to come over to my place this evening?
Maybe...
MAGDA
OUTIQUE
MAGDA
Bye. Bring your appetite when you come.

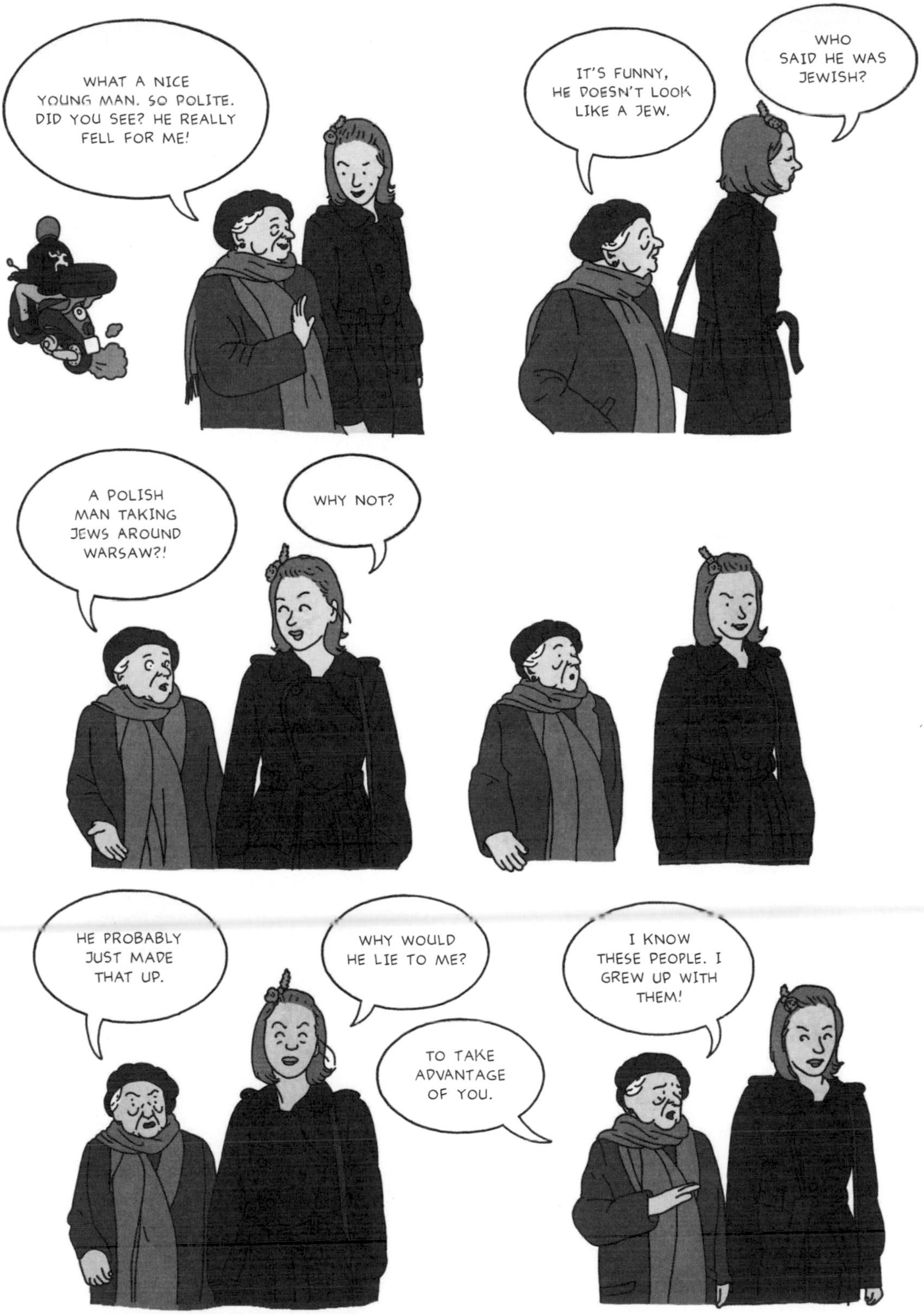
WHAT A NICE YOUNG MAN. SO POLITE. DID YOU SEE? HE REALLY FELL FOR ME!
IT'S FUNNY, HE DOESN'T LOOK LIKE A JEW.
WHO SAID HE WAS JEWISH?
A POLISH MAN TAKING JEWS AROUND WARSAW?!
WHY NOT?
HE PROBABLY JUST MADE THAT UP.
WHY WOULD HE LIE TO ME?
TO TAKE ADVANTAGE OF YOU.
I KNOW THESE PEOPLE. I GREW UP WITH THEM!

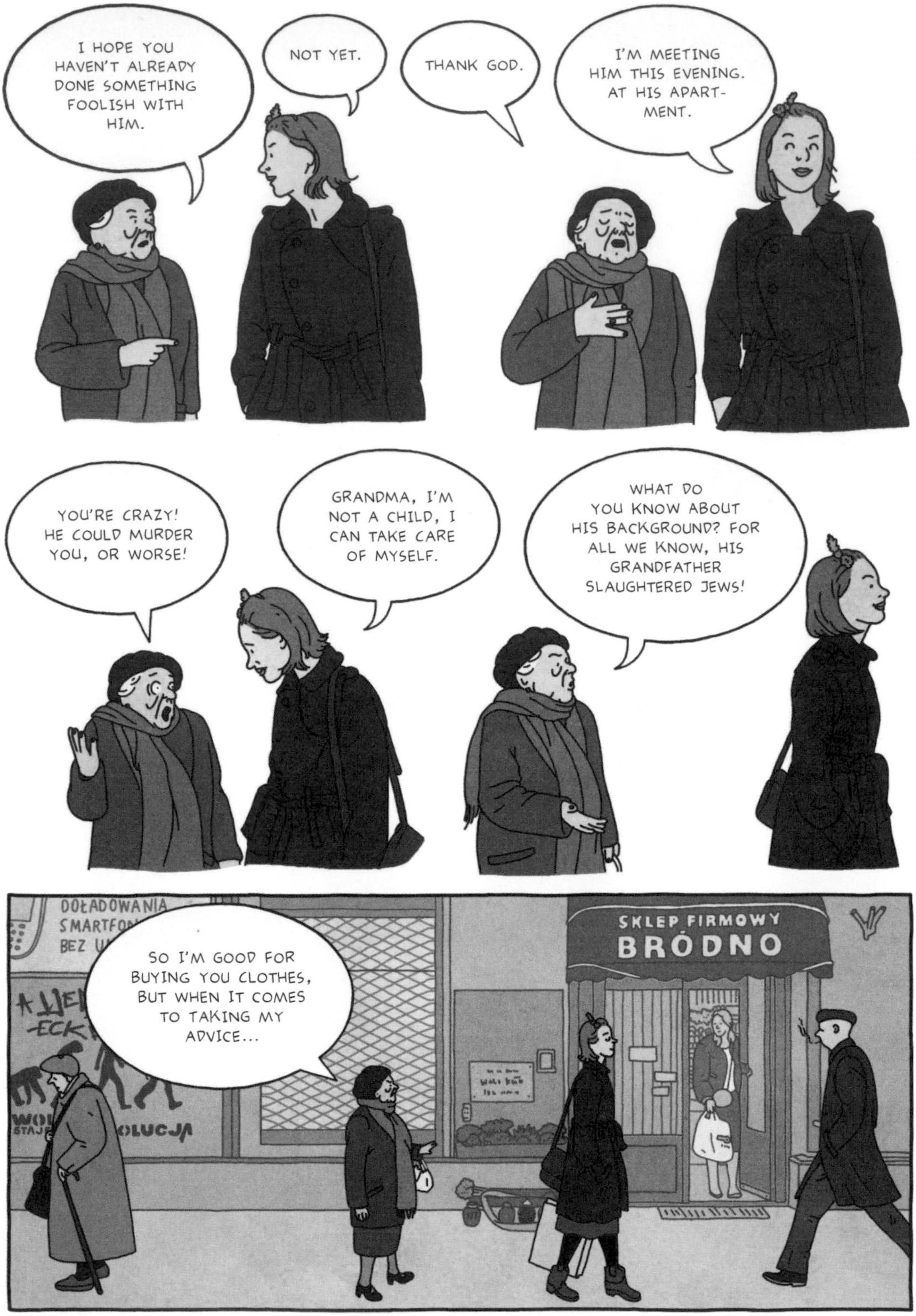
I HOPE YOU HAVEN'T ALREADY DONE SOMETHING FOOLISH WITH HIM.
NOT YET.
THANK GOD.
I'M MEETING HIM THIS EVENING. AT HIS APARTMENT.
YOU'RE CRAZY! HE COULD MURDER YOU, OR WORSE!
GRANDMA, I'M NOT A CHILD, I CAN TAKE CARE OF MYSELF.
WHAT DO YOU KNOW ABOUT HIS BACKGROUND? FOR ALL WE KNOW, HIS GRANDFATHER SLAUGHTERED JEWS!
DOŁADOWANIA
SKLEP FIRMOWY
BRÓDNO
SO I'M GOOD FOR BUYING YOU CLOTHES, BUT WHEN IT COMES TO TAKING MY ADVICE...

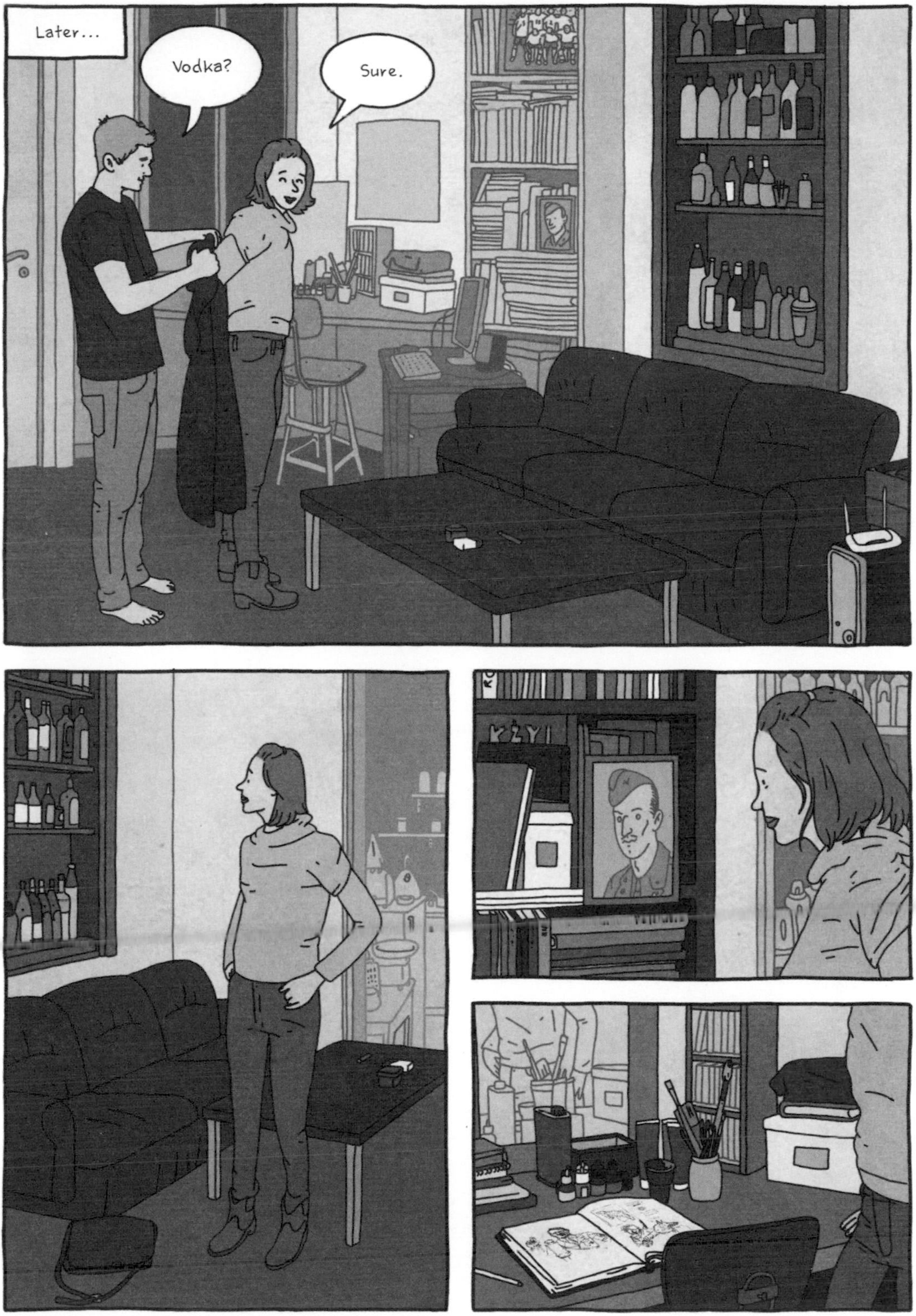
Later...
Vodka?
Sure.

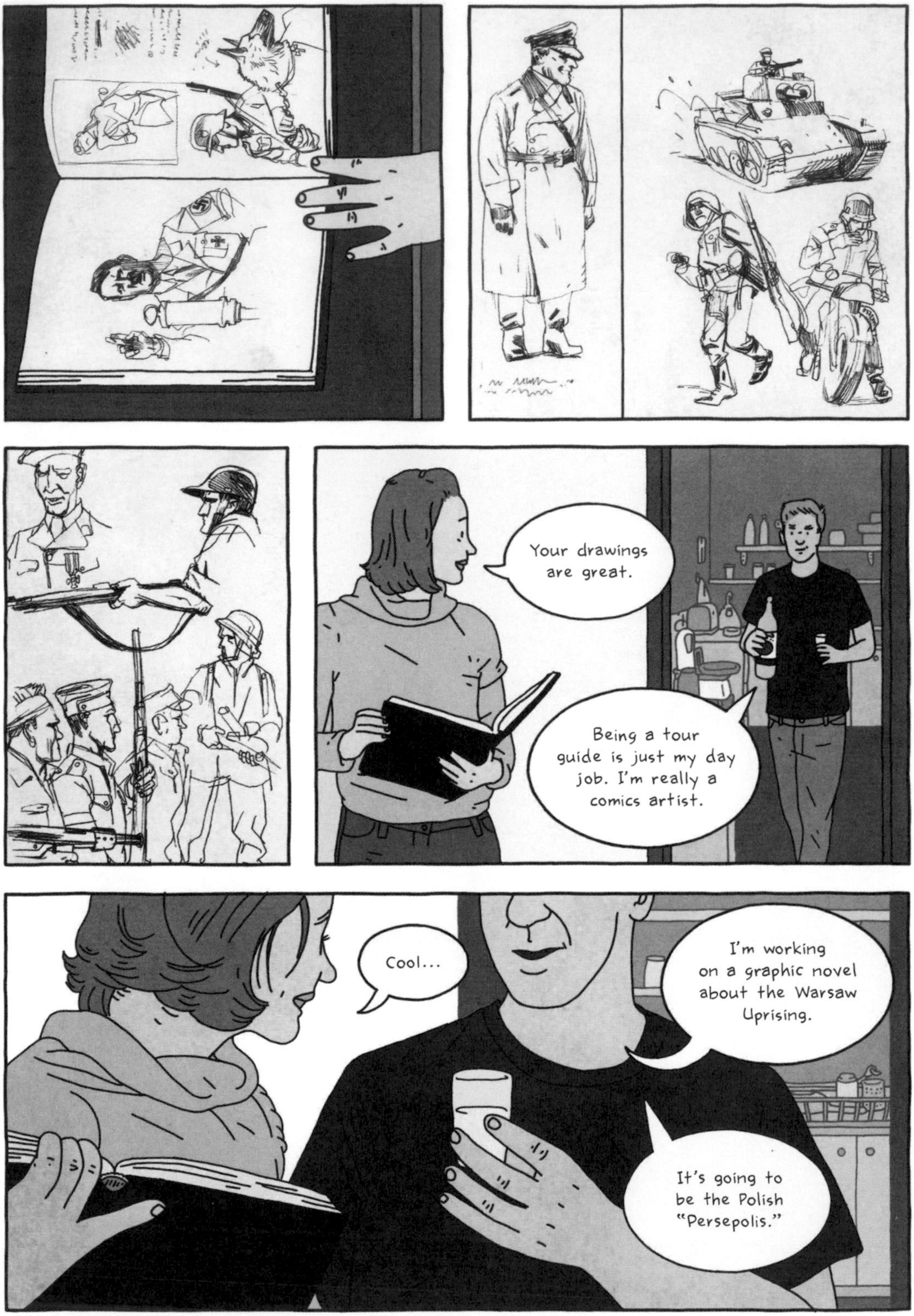
Your drawings are great.
Being a tour guide is just my day job. I'm really a comics artist.
Cool...
I'm working on a graphic novel about the Warsaw Uprising.
It's going to be the Polish "Persepolis."

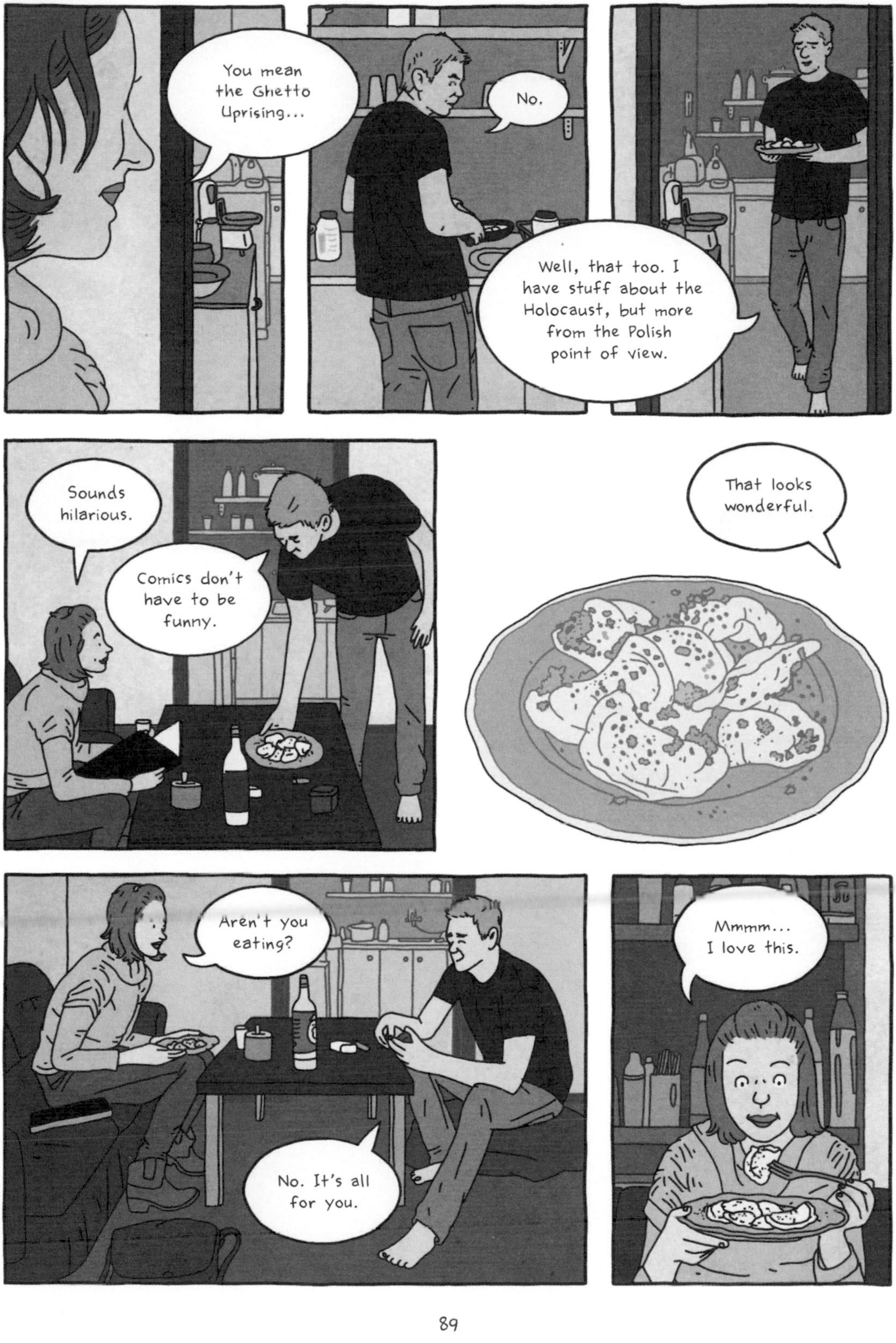
You mean the Ghetto Uprising...
No.
Well, that too. I have stuff about the Holocaust, but more from the Polish point of view.
Sounds hilarious.
Comics don't have to be funny.
That looks wonderful.
Aren't you eating?
No. It's all for you.
Mmmm... I love this.

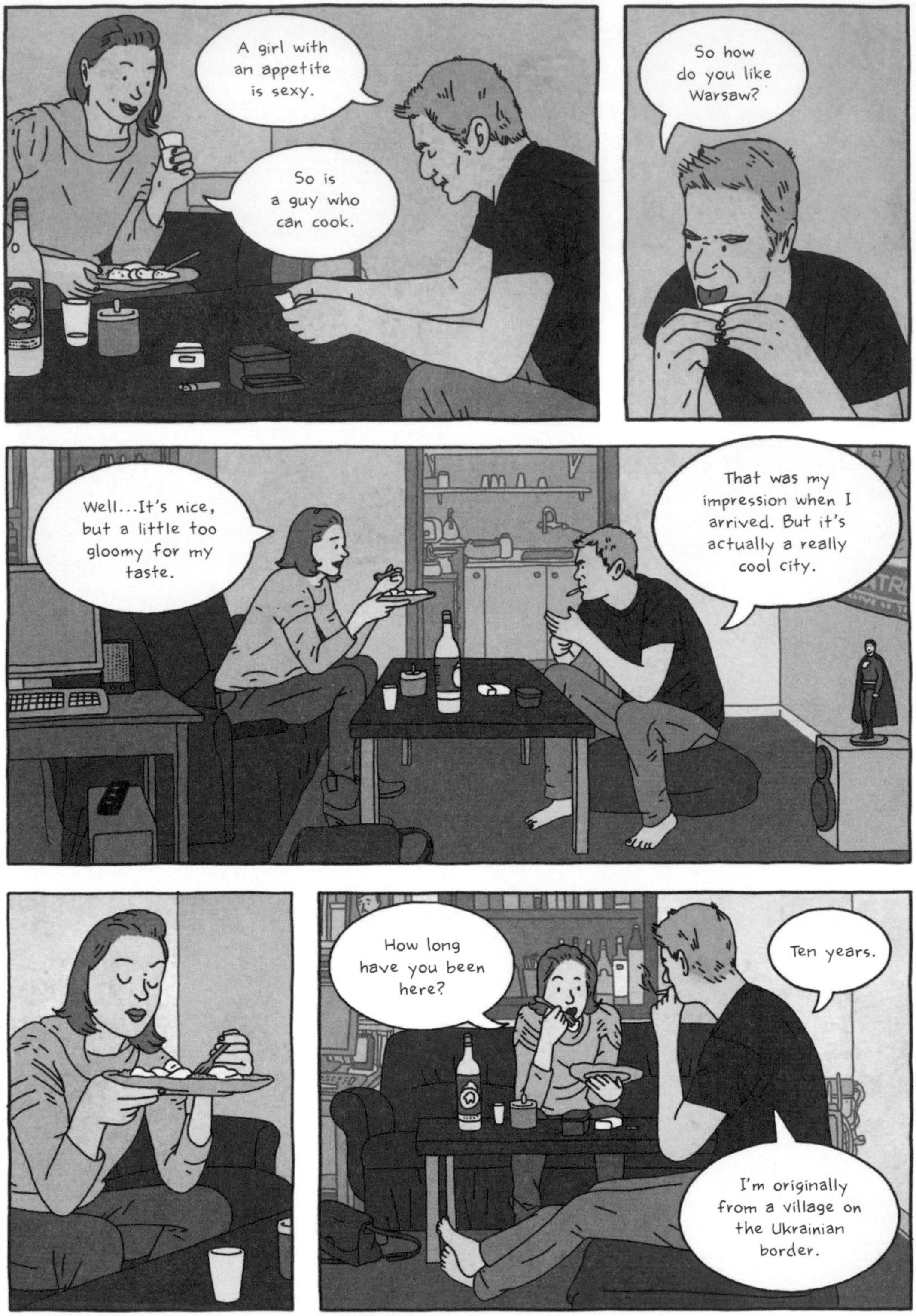
A girl with an appetite is sexy.
So is a guy who can cook.
So how do you like Warsaw?
Well...It's nice, but a little too gloomy for my taste.
That was my impression when I arrived. But it's actually a really cool city.
How long have you been here?
Ten years.
I'm originally from a village on the Ukrainian border.

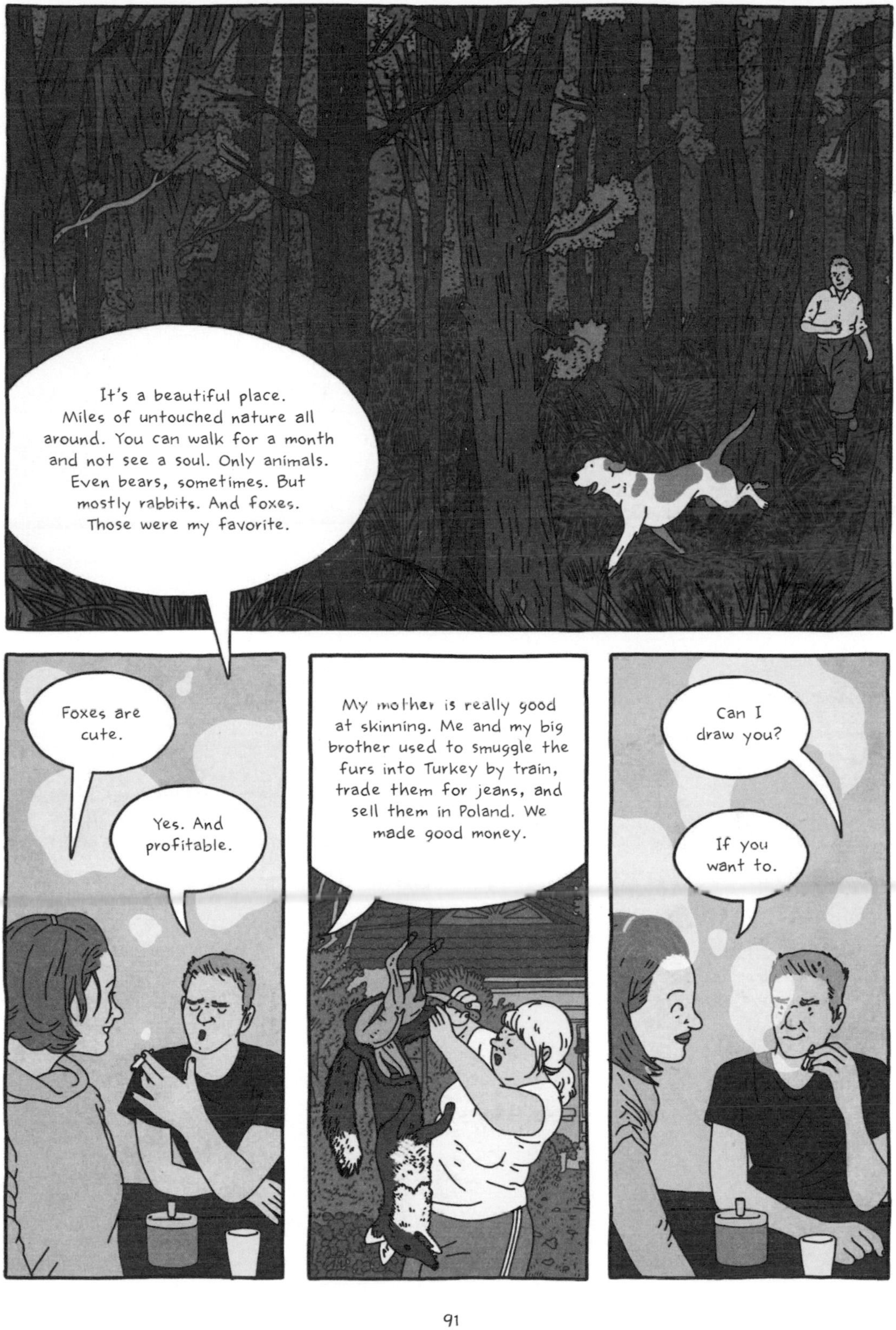
It's a beautiful place. Miles of untouched nature all around. You can walk for a month and not see a soul. Only animals. Even bears, sometimes. But mostly rabbits. And foxes. Those were my favorite.
Foxes are cute.
Yes. And profitable.
My mother is really good at skinning. Me and my big brother used to smuggle the furs into Turkey by train, trade them for jeans, and sell them in Poland. We made good money.
Can I draw you?
If you want to.

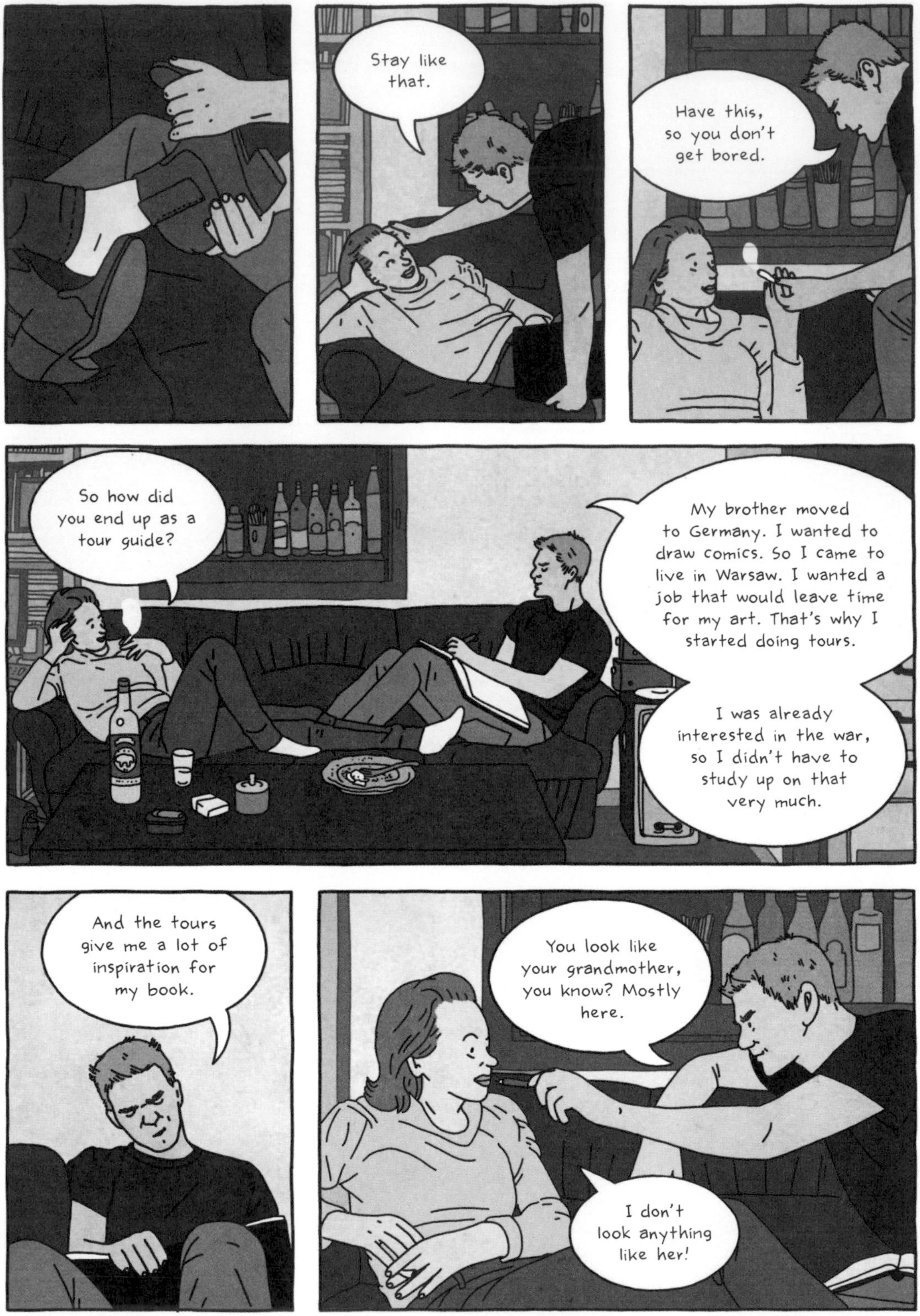
Stay like that.
Have this, so you don't get bored.
So how did you end up as a tour guide?
My brother moved to Germany. I wanted to draw comics. So I came to live in Warsaw. I wanted a job that would leave time for my art. That's why I started doing tours.
I was already interested in the war, so I didn't have to study up on that very much.
And the tours give me a lot of inspiration for my book.
You look like your grandmother, you know? Mostly here.
I don't look anything like her!

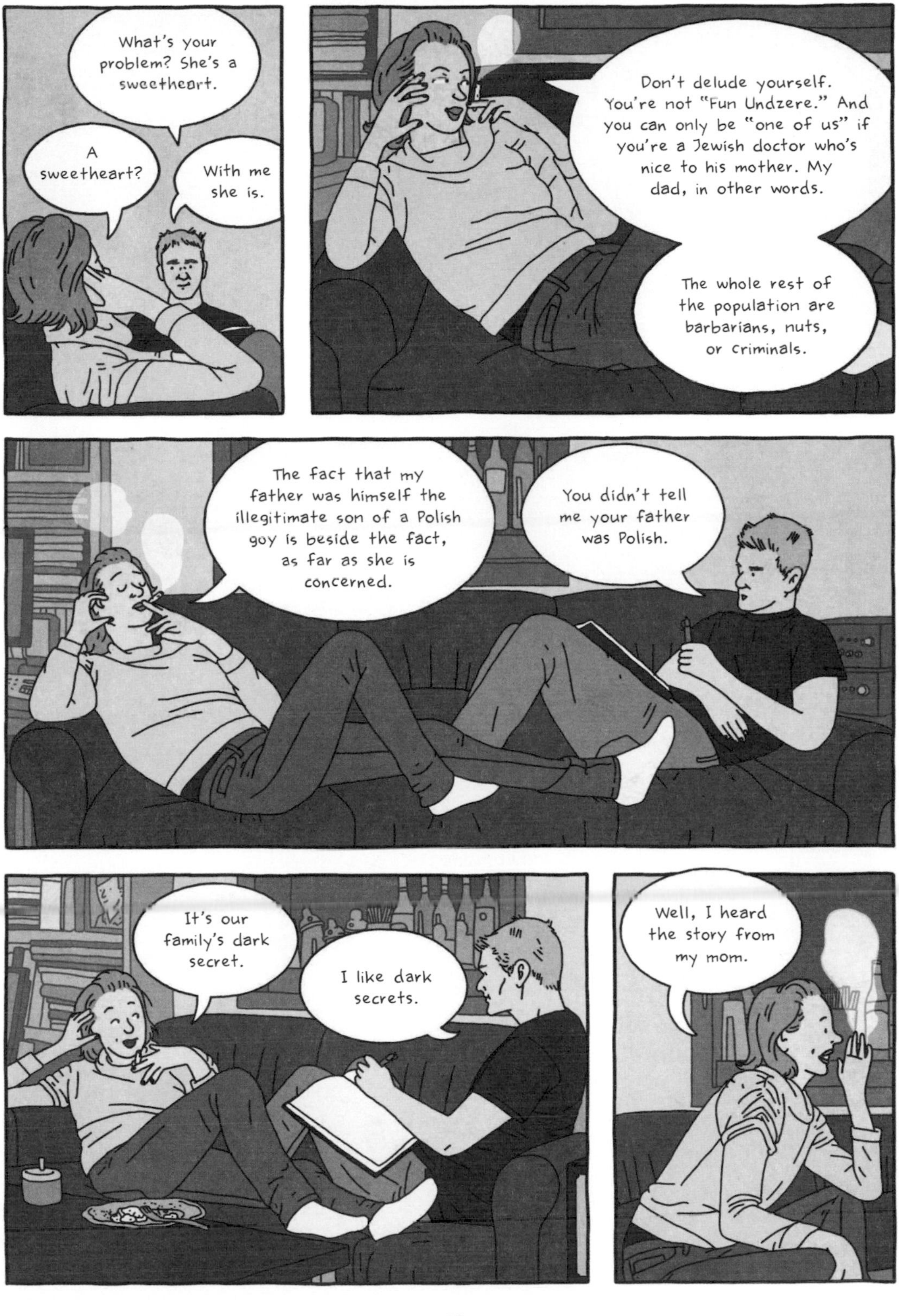
What's your problem? She's a sweetheart.
A sweetheart?
With me she is.
Don't delude yourself. You're not "Fun Undzere." And you can only be "one of us" if you're a Jewish doctor who's nice to his mother. My dad, in other words.
The whole rest of the population are barbarians, nuts, or criminals.
The fact that my father was himself the illegitimate son of a Polish goy is beside the fact, as far as she is concerned.
You didn't tell me your father was Polish.
It's our family's dark secret.
I like dark secrets.
Well, I heard the story from my mom.

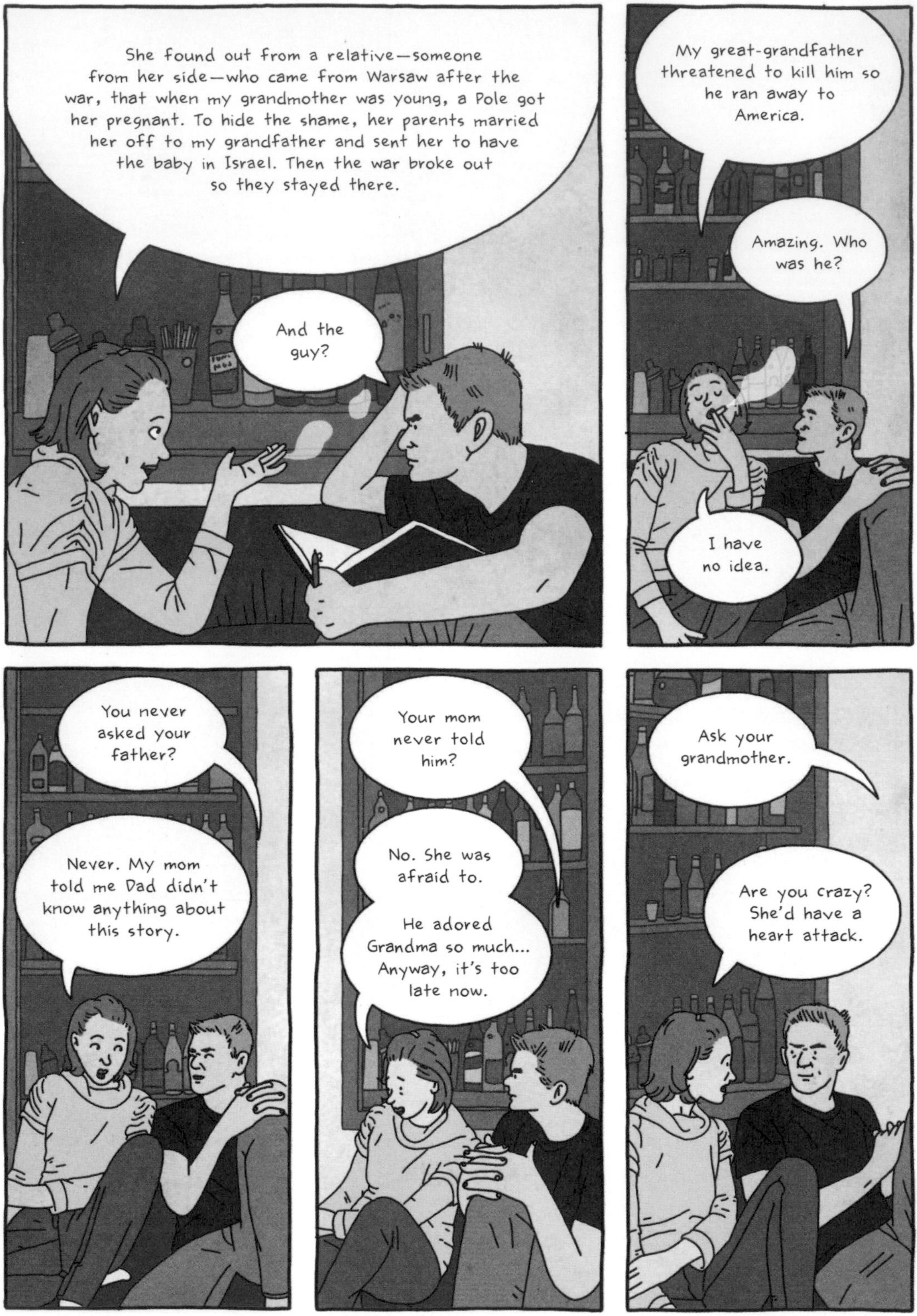
She found out from a relative—someone from her side—who came from Warsaw after the war, that when my grandmother was young, a Pole got her pregnant. To hide the shame, her parents married her off to my grandfather and sent her to have the baby in Israel. Then the war broke out so they stayed there.
And the guy?
My great-grandfather threatened to kill him so he ran away to America.
Amazing. Who was he?
I have no idea.
You never asked your father?
Never. My mom told me Dad didn't know anything about this story.
Your mom never told him?
No. She was afraid to.
He adored Grandma so much... Anyway, it's too late now.
Ask your grandmother.
Are you crazy? She'd have a heart attack.

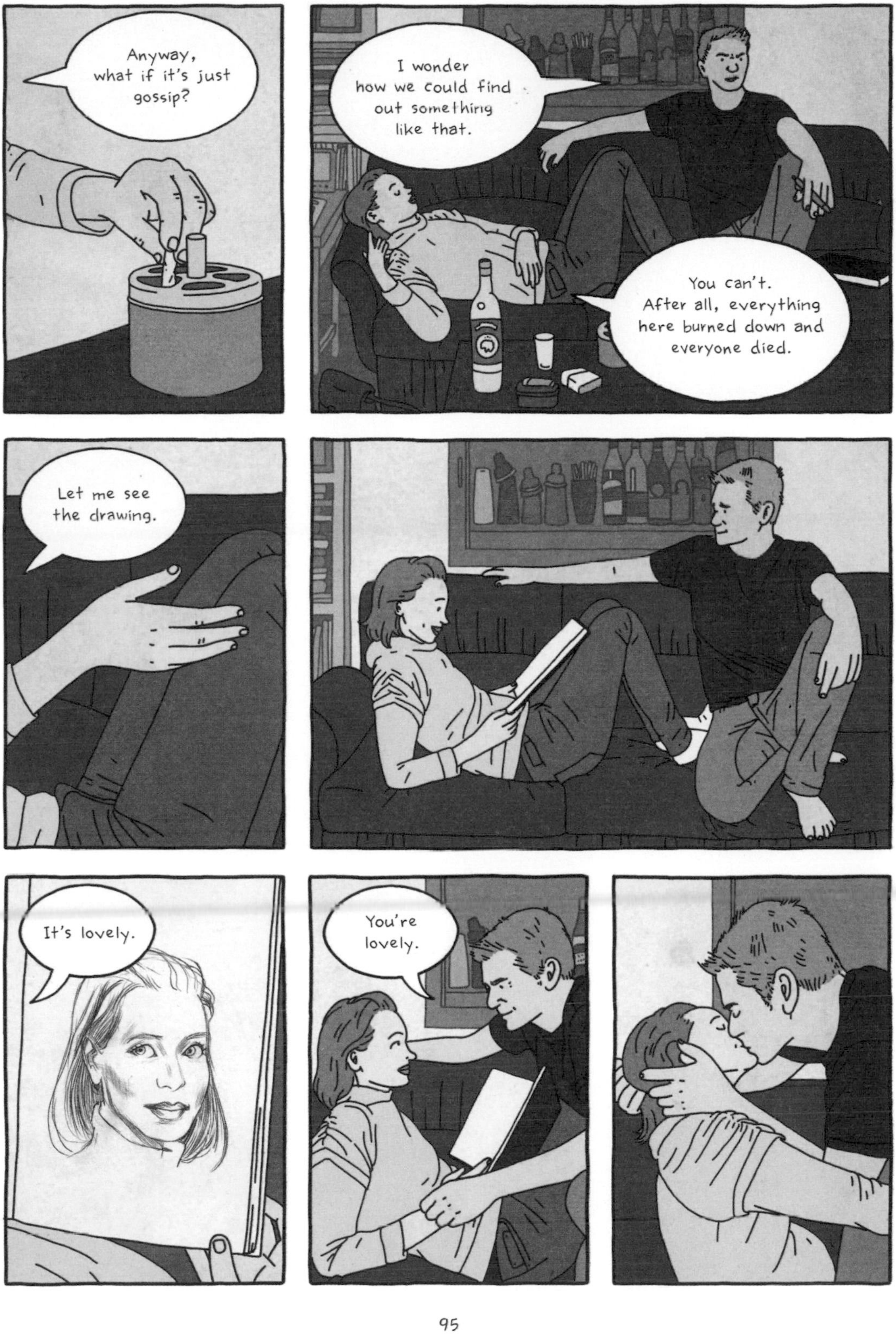
Anyway, what if it's just gossip?
I wonder how we could find out something like that.
You can't. After all, everything here burned down and everyone died.
Let me see the drawing.
It's lovely.
You're lovely.

You are definitely the best guide to Jewish Warsaw.

I know...

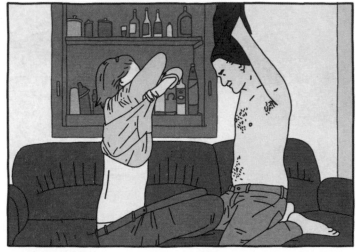

Ring ring...

Ring ring...

Ugh!

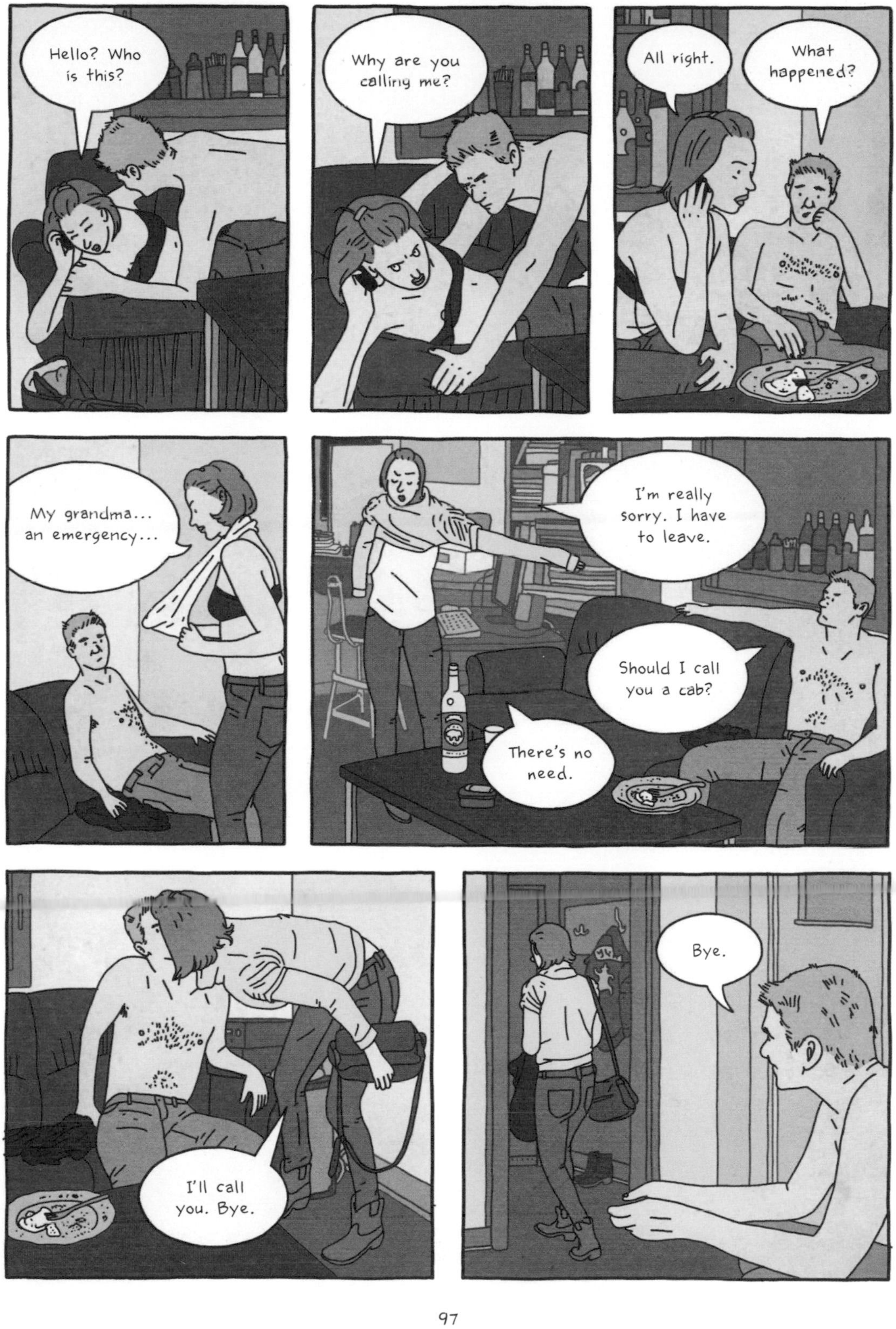

Hello? Who is this?
Why are you calling me?
All right.
What happened?
My grandma... an emergency...
I'm really sorry. I have to leave.
Should I call you a cab?
There's no need.
I'll call you. Bye.
Bye.

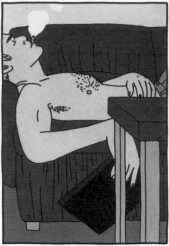

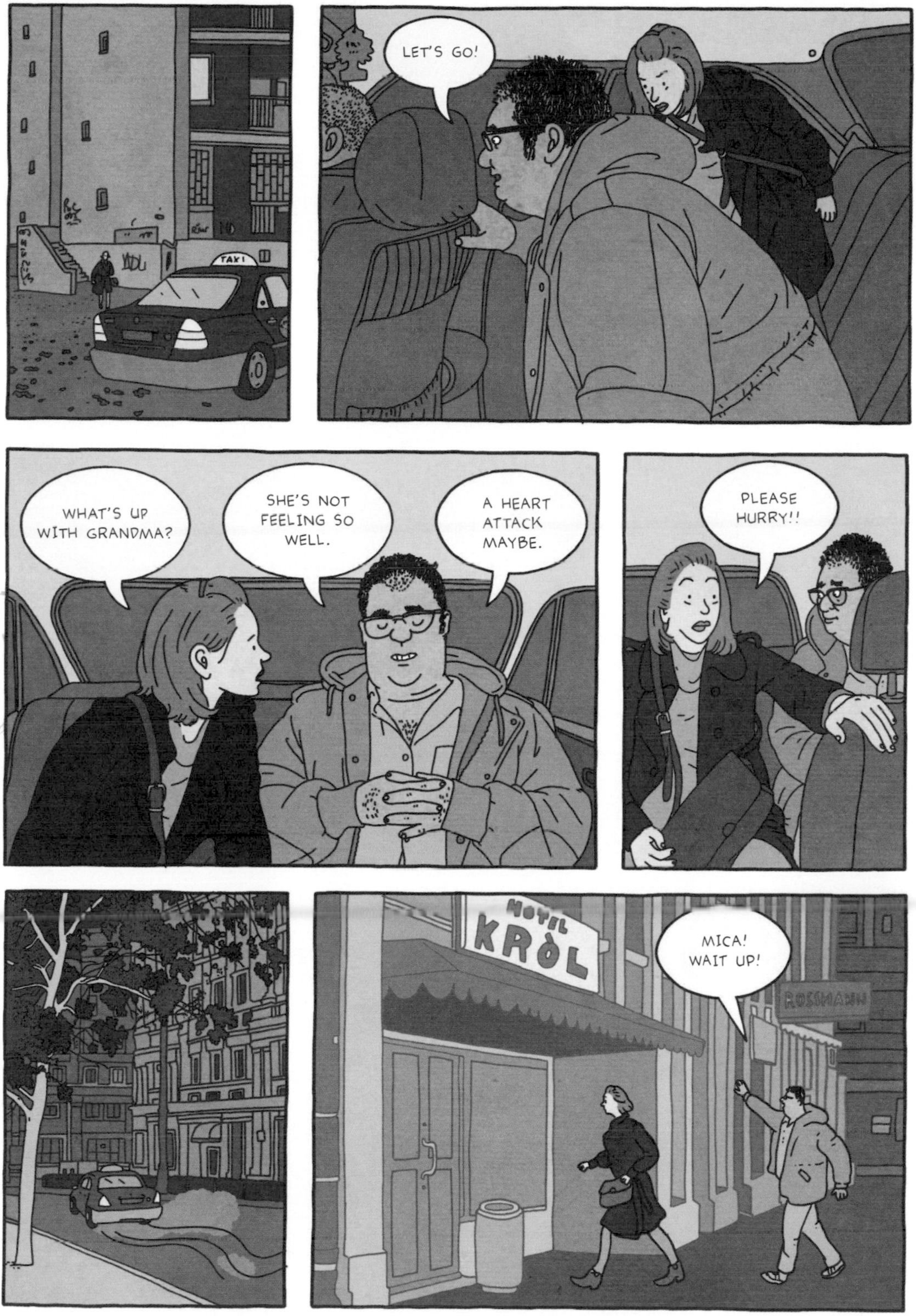
TAXI
LET'S GO!
WHAT'S UP WITH GRANDMA?
SHE'S NOT FEELING SO WELL.
A HEART ATTACK MAYBE.
PLEASE HURRY!!
HOTEL KRÒL
ROSSMANN
MICA! WAIT UP!

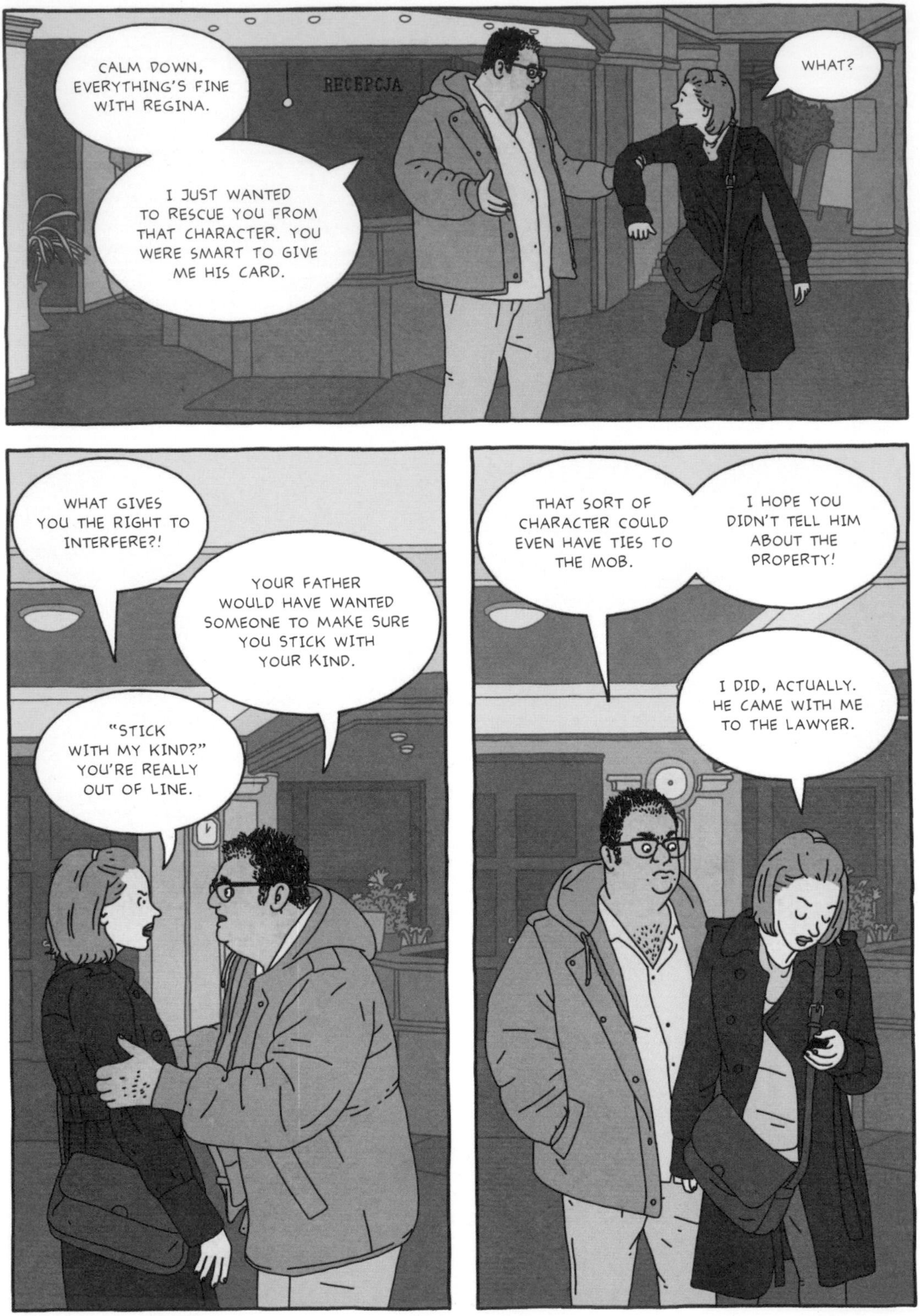
RECEPCJA
CALM DOWN, EVERYTHING'S FINE WITH REGINA.
I JUST WANTED TO RESCUE YOU FROM THAT CHARACTER. YOU WERE SMART TO GIVE ME HIS CARD.
WHAT?
WHAT GIVES YOU THE RIGHT TO INTERFERE?!
YOUR FATHER WOULD HAVE WANTED SOMEONE TO MAKE SURE YOU STICK WITH YOUR KIND.
"STICK WITH MY KIND?" YOU'RE REALLY OUT OF LINE.
THAT SORT OF CHARACTER COULD EVEN HAVE TIES TO THE MOB.
I HOPE YOU DIDN'T TELL HIM ABOUT THE PROPERTY!
I DID, ACTUALLY. HE CAME WITH ME TO THE LAWYER.

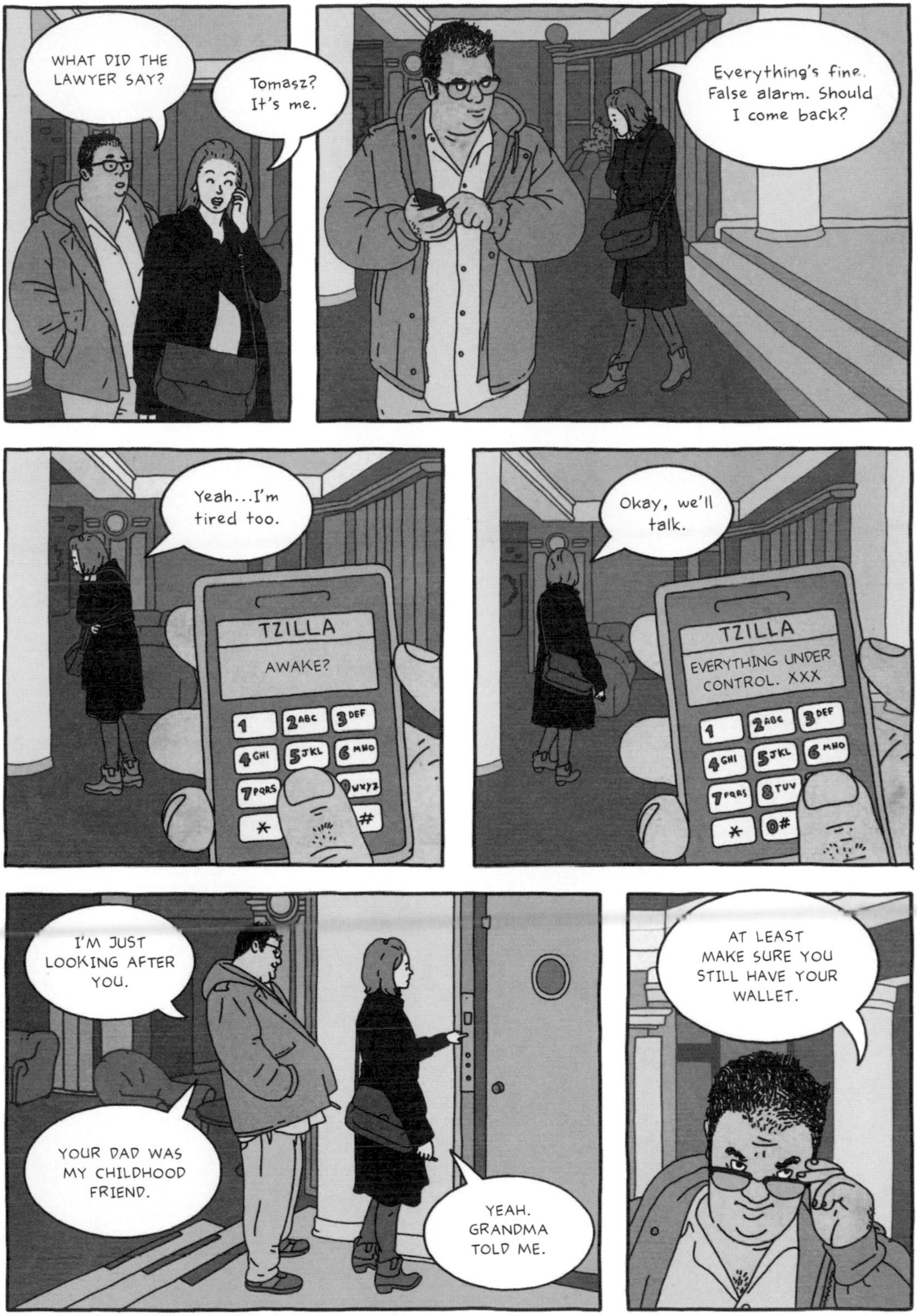
WHAT DID THE LAWYER SAY?
Tomasz? It's me.
Everything's fine. False alarm. Should I come back?
Yeah...I'm tired too.
TZILLA
AWAKE?
Okay, we'll talk.
TZILLA
EVERYTHING UNDER CONTROL. XXX
I'M JUST LOOKING AFTER YOU.
YOUR DAD WAS MY CHILDHOOD FRIEND.
YEAH. GRANDMA TOLD ME.
AT LEAST MAKE SURE YOU STILL HAVE YOUR WALLET.

DAY THREE

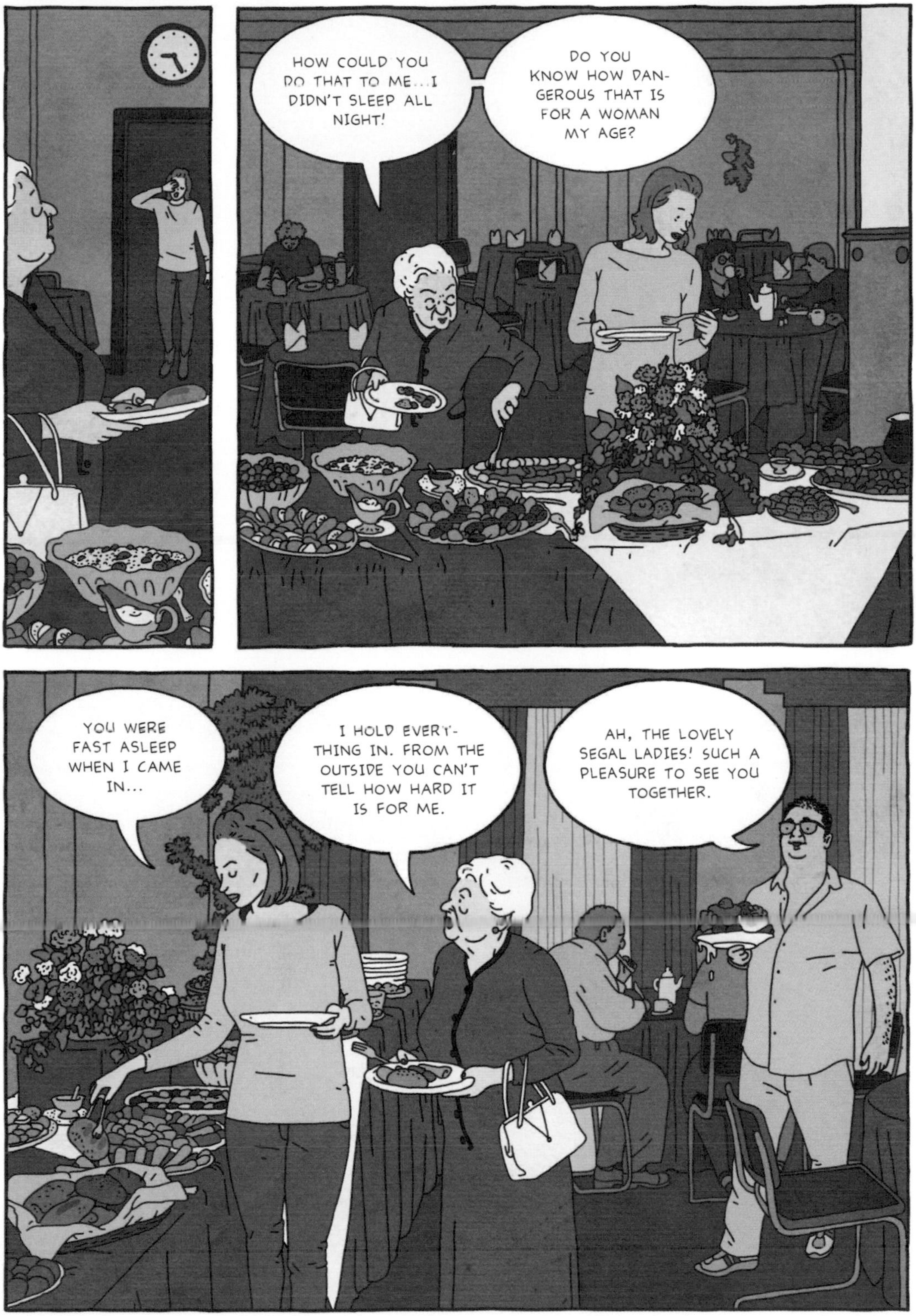
HOW COULD YOU DO THAT TO ME...I DIDN'T SLEEP ALL NIGHT!
DO YOU KNOW HOW DANGEROUS THAT IS FOR A WOMAN MY AGE?
YOU WERE FAST ASLEEP WHEN I CAME IN...
I HOLD EVERYTHING IN. FROM THE OUTSIDE YOU CAN'T TELL HOW HARD IT IS FOR ME.
AH, THE LOVELY SEGAL LADIES! SUCH A PLEASURE TO SEE YOU TOGETHER.

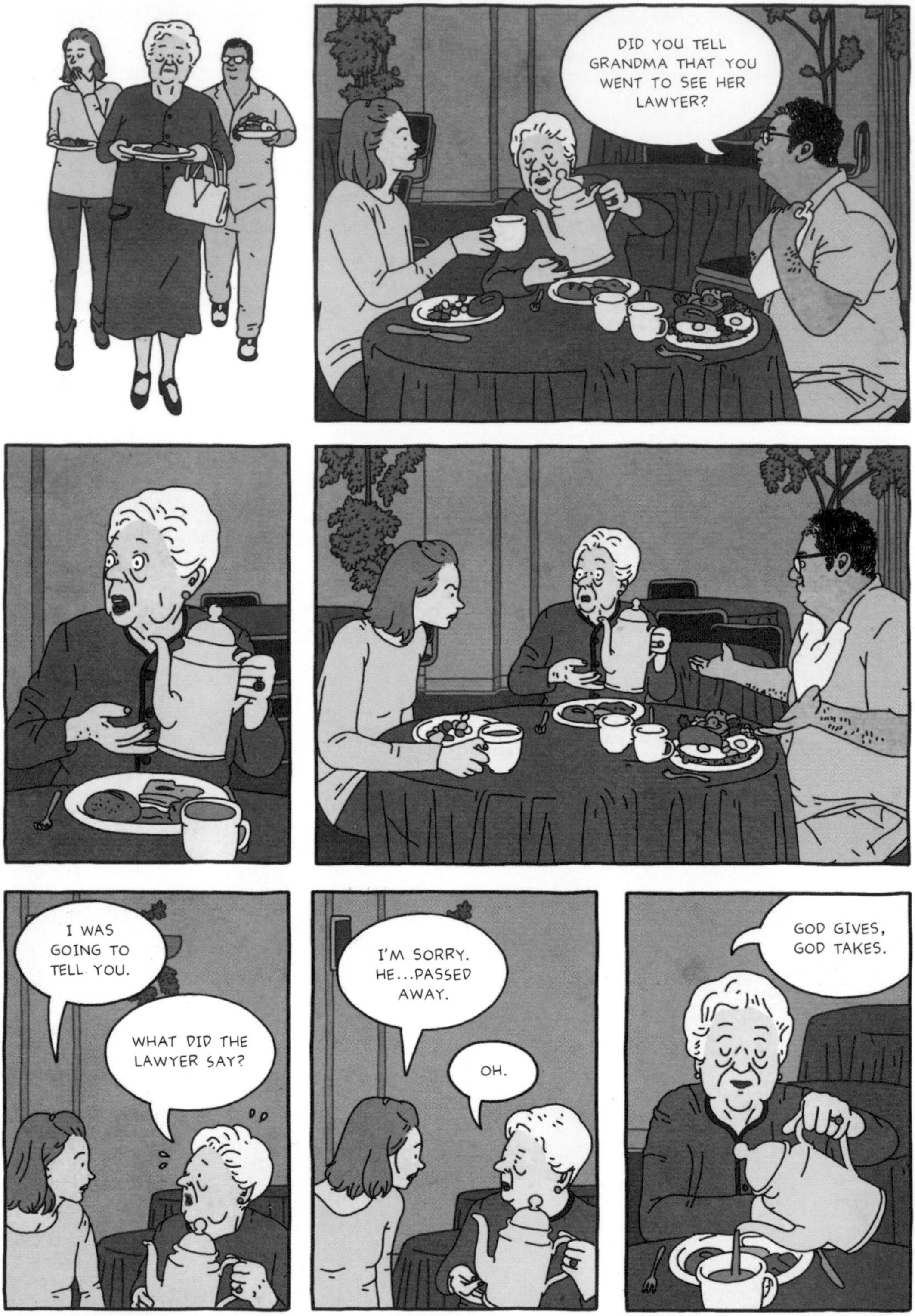
DID YOU TELL GRANDMA THAT YOU WENT TO SEE HER LAWYER?
I WAS GOING TO TELL YOU.
WHAT DID THE LAWYER SAY?
I'M SORRY. HE...PASSED AWAY.
OH.
GOD GIVES, GOD TAKES.

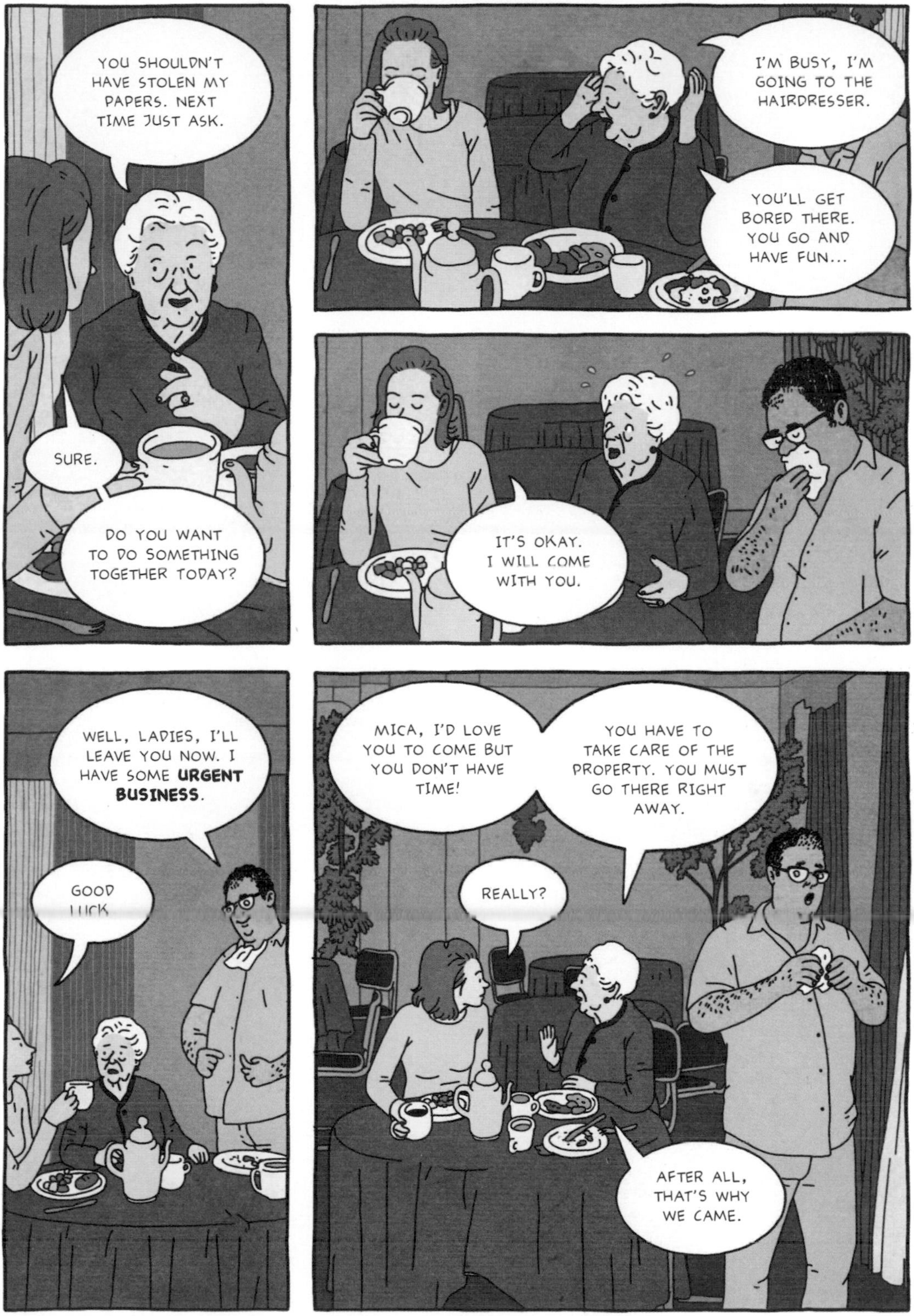

YOU SHOULDN'T HAVE STOLEN MY PAPERS. NEXT TIME JUST ASK.
SURE.
DO YOU WANT TO DO SOMETHING TOGETHER TODAY?
I'M BUSY, I'M GOING TO THE HAIRDRESSER.
YOU'LL GET BORED THERE. YOU GO AND HAVE FUN...
IT'S OKAY. I WILL COME WITH YOU.
WELL, LADIES, I'LL LEAVE YOU NOW. I HAVE SOME **URGENT BUSINESS**.
GOOD LUCK.
MICA, I'D LOVE YOU TO COME BUT YOU DON'T HAVE TIME!
YOU HAVE TO TAKE CARE OF THE PROPERTY. YOU MUST GO THERE RIGHT AWAY.
REALLY?
AFTER ALL, THAT'S WHY WE CAME.

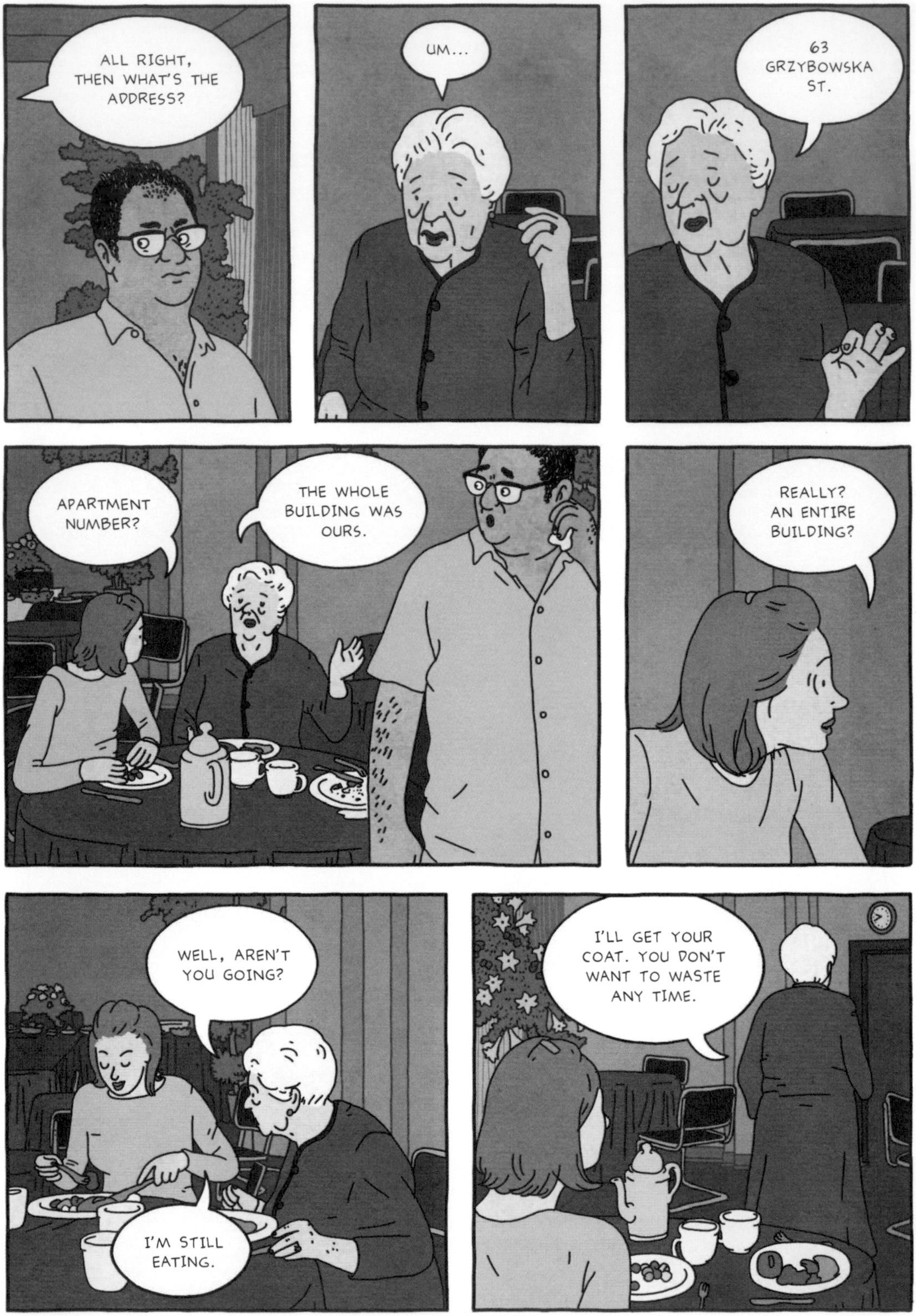
ALL RIGHT, THEN WHAT'S THE ADDRESS?
UM...
63 GRZYBOWSKA ST.
APARTMENT NUMBER?
THE WHOLE BUILDING WAS OURS.
REALLY? AN ENTIRE BUILDING?
WELL, AREN'T YOU GOING?
I'M STILL EATING.
I'LL GET YOUR COAT. YOU DON'T WANT TO WASTE ANY TIME.

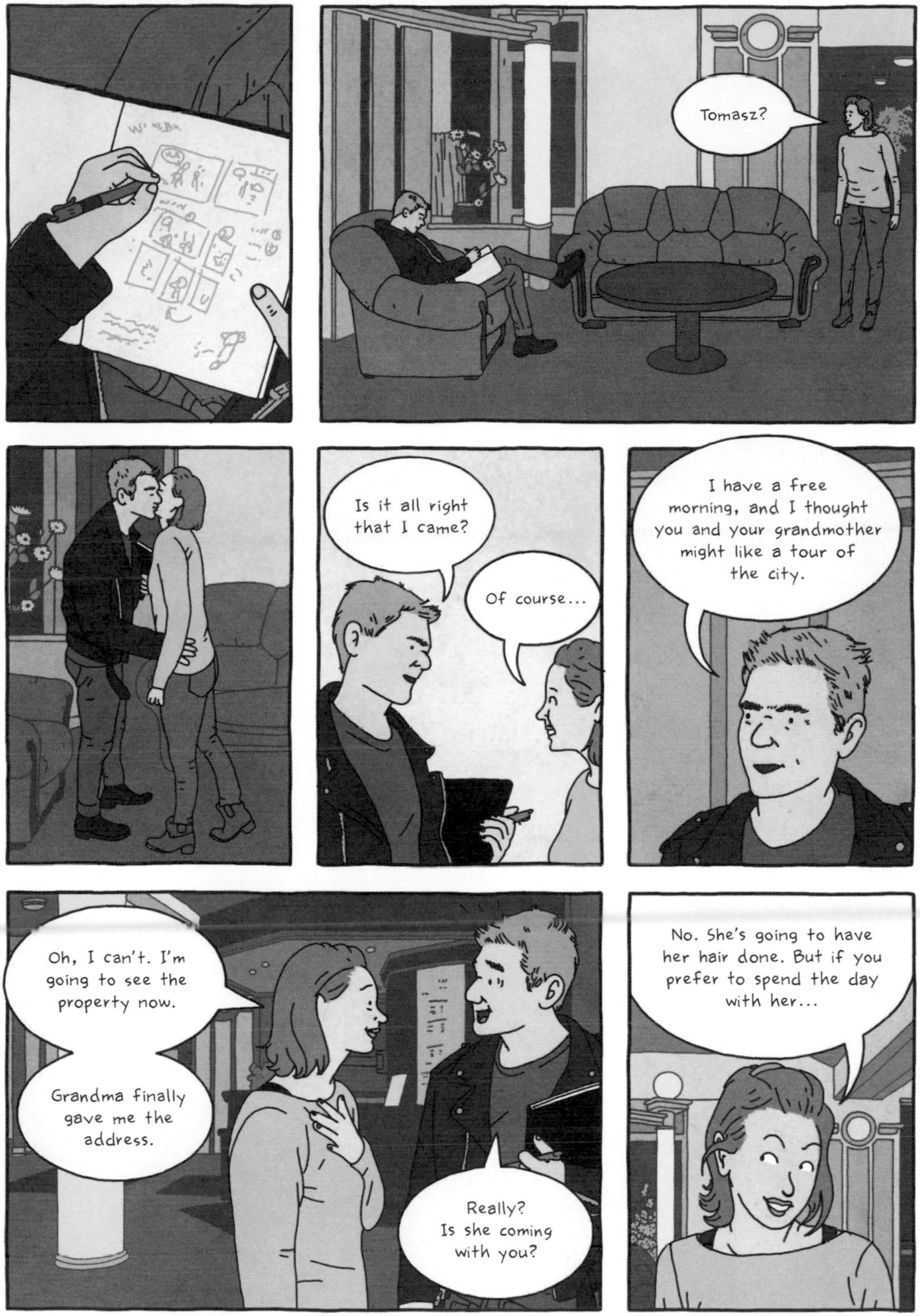

Tomasz?
Is it all right that I came?
Of course...
I have a free morning, and I thought you and your grandmother might like a tour of the city.
Oh, I can't. I'm going to see the property now.
Grandma finally gave me the address.
Really? Is she coming with you?
No. She's going to have her hair done. But if you prefer to spend the day with her...

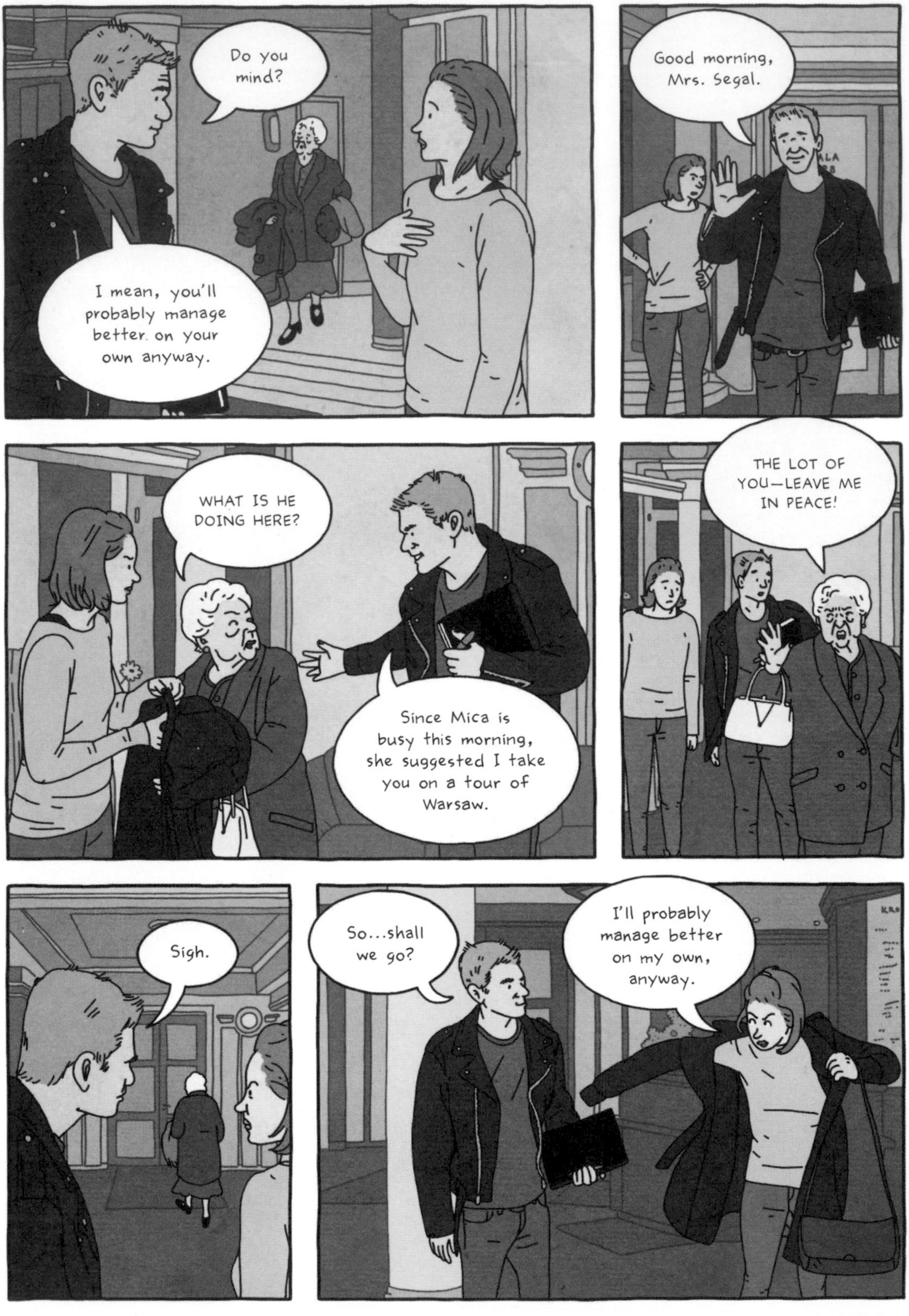
Do you mind?
I mean, you'll probably manage better on your own anyway.
Good morning, Mrs. Segal.
WHAT IS HE DOING HERE?
Since Mica is busy this morning, she suggested I take you on a tour of Warsaw.
THE LOT OF YOU—LEAVE ME IN PEACE!
Sigh.
So...shall we go?
I'll probably manage better on my own, anyway.

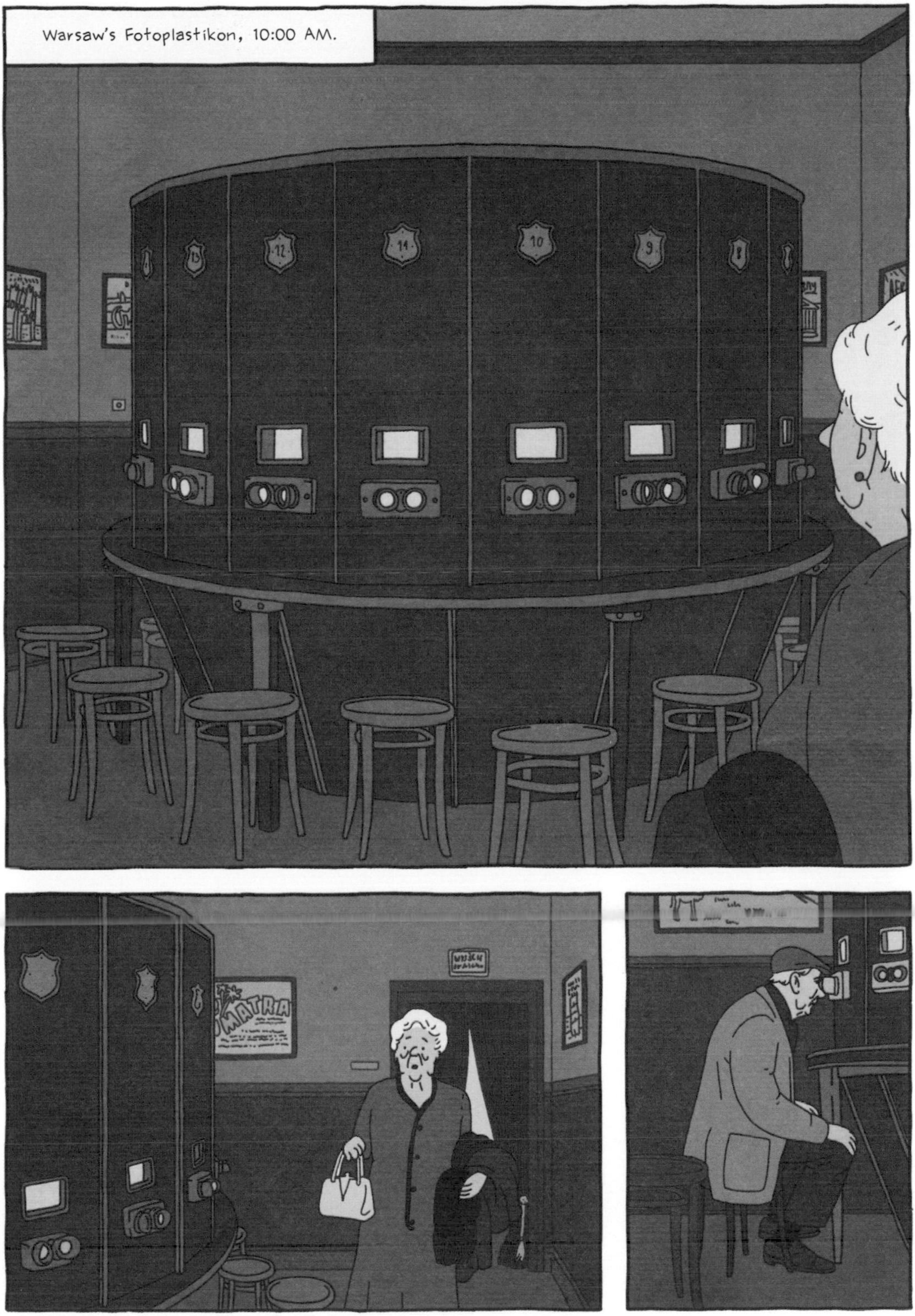
Warsaw's Fotoplastikon, 10:00 AM.

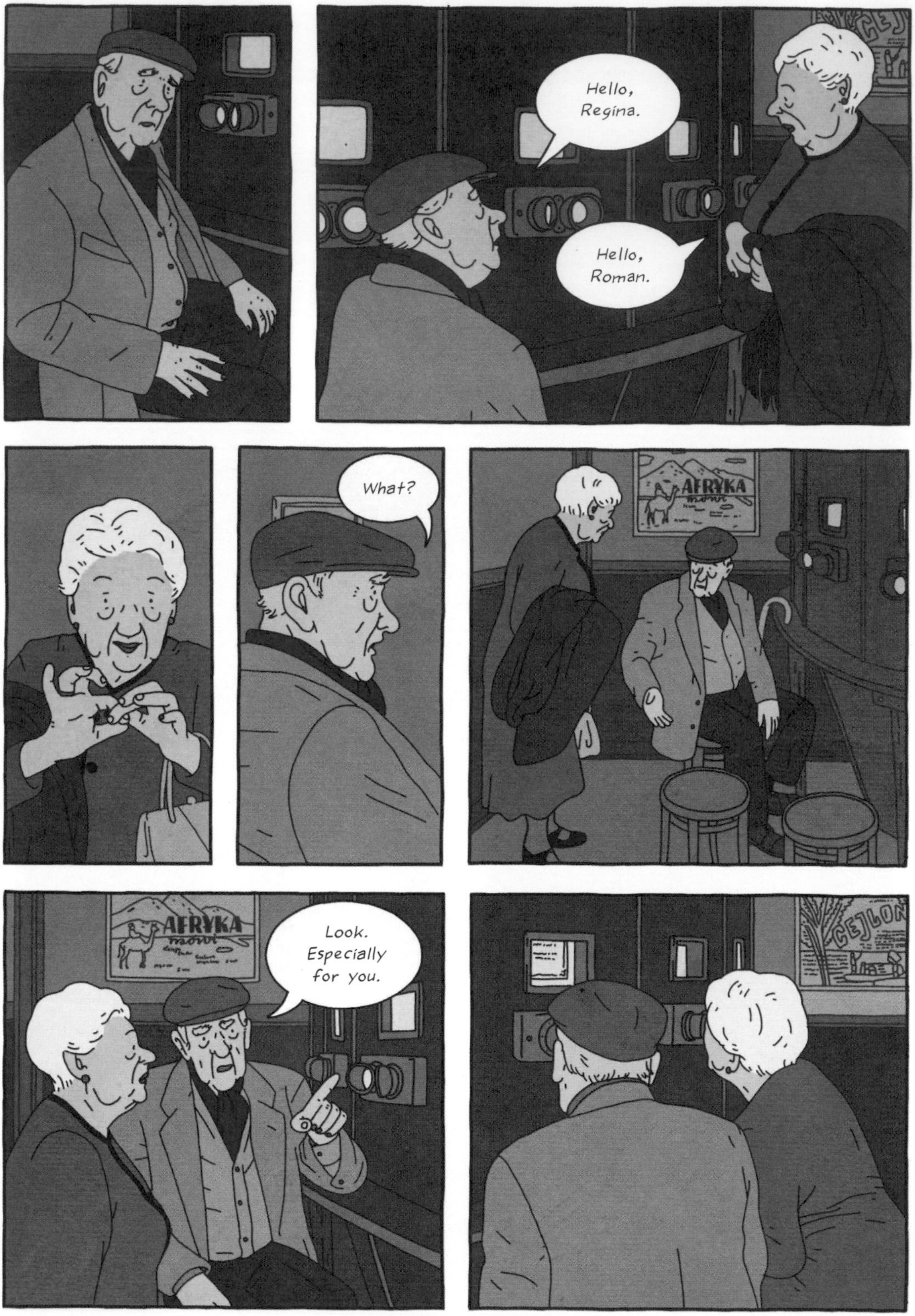
Hello, Regina.
Hello, Roman.
What?
AFRYKA
AFRYKA
Look. Especially for you.
CEJLON

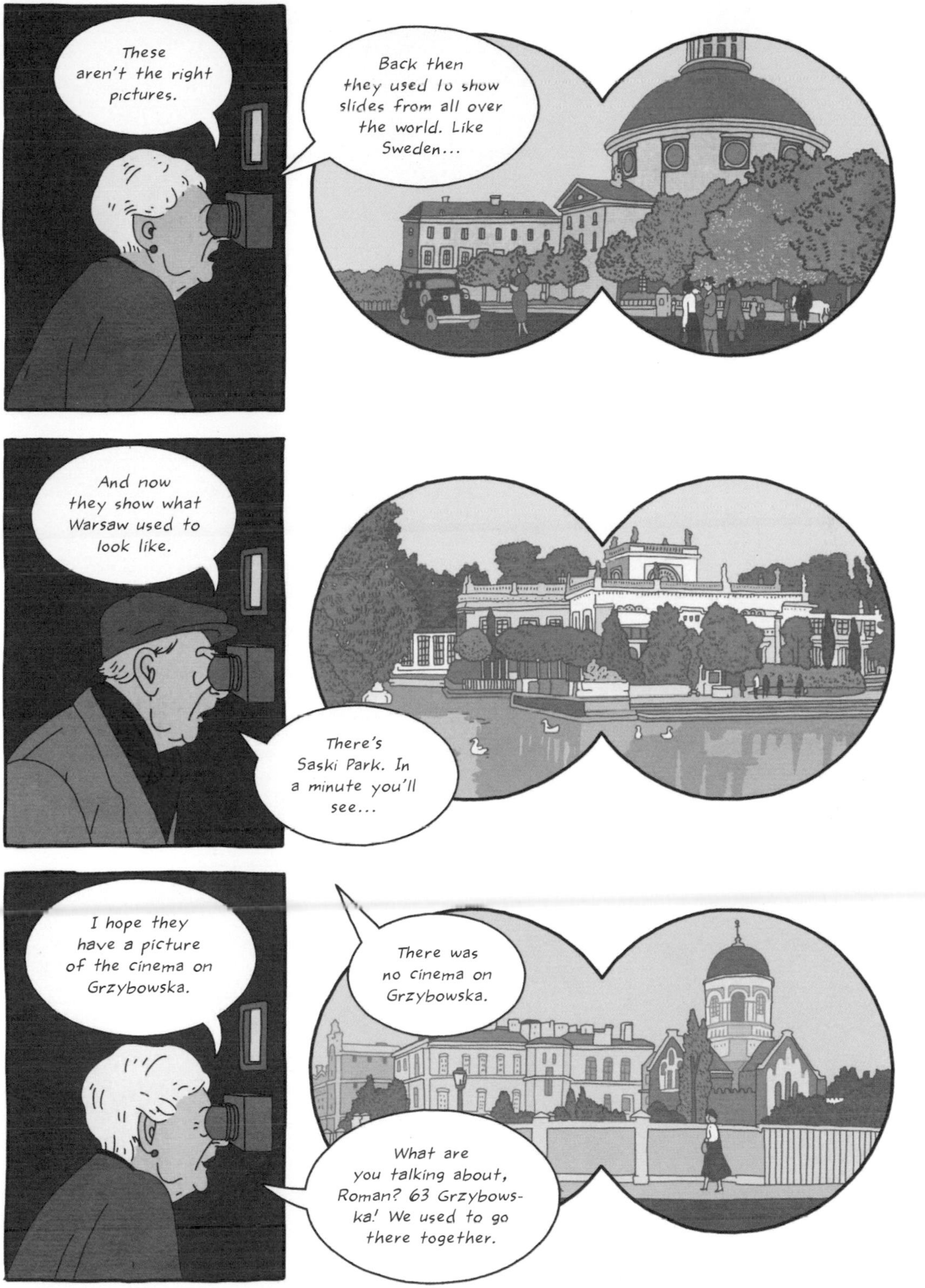
These aren't the right pictures.
Back then they used to show slides from all over the world. Like Sweden...
And now they show what Warsaw used to look like.
There's Saski Park. In a minute you'll see...
I hope they have a picture of the cinema on Grzybowska.
There was no cinema on Grzybowska.
What are you talking about, Roman? 63 Grzybowska! We used to go there together.

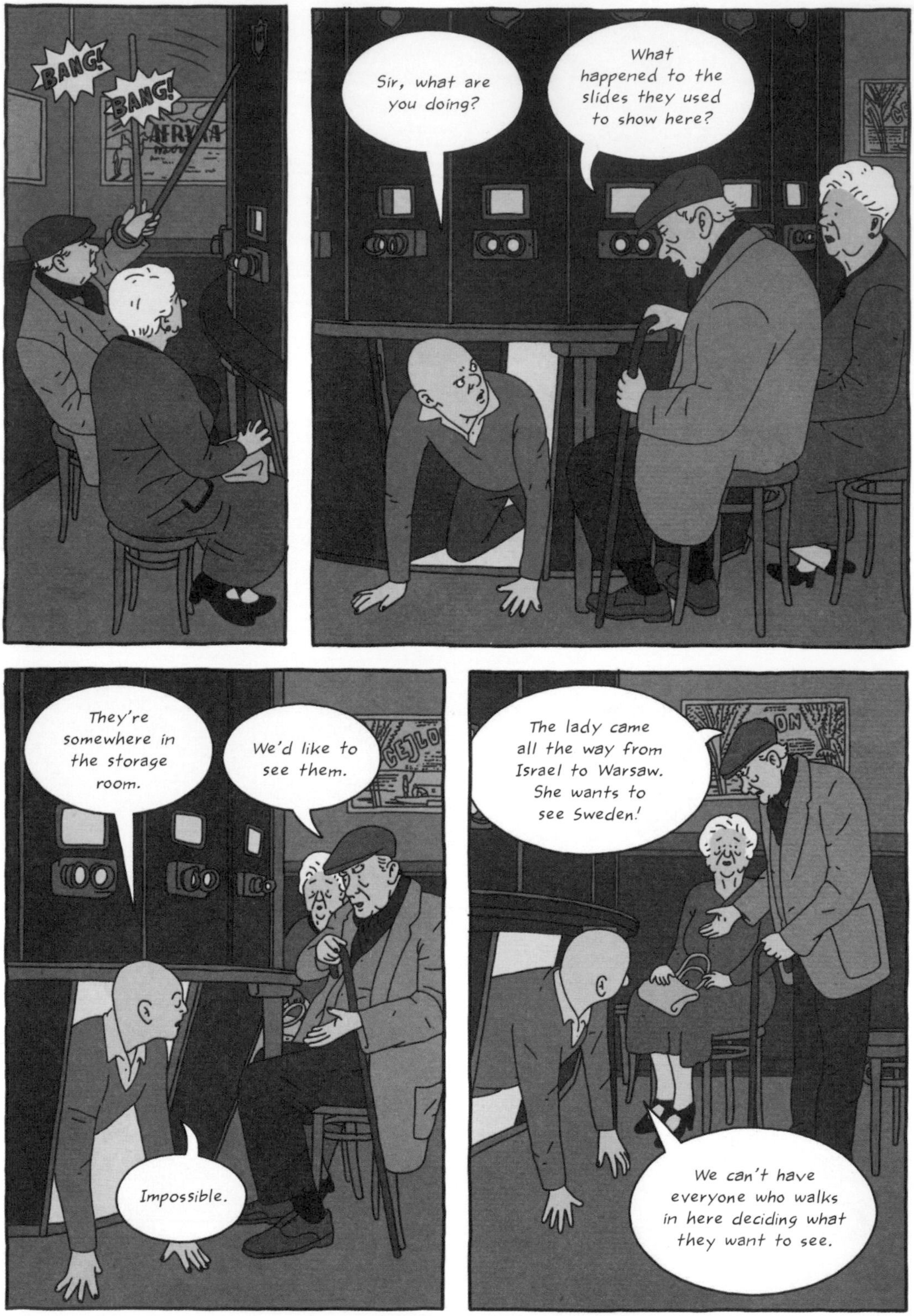
BANG!
BANG!
Sir, what are you doing?
What happened to the slides they used to show here?
They're somewhere in the storage room.
We'd like to see them.
Impossible.
The lady came all the way from Israel to Warsaw. She wants to see Sweden!
We can't have everyone who walks in here deciding what they want to see.

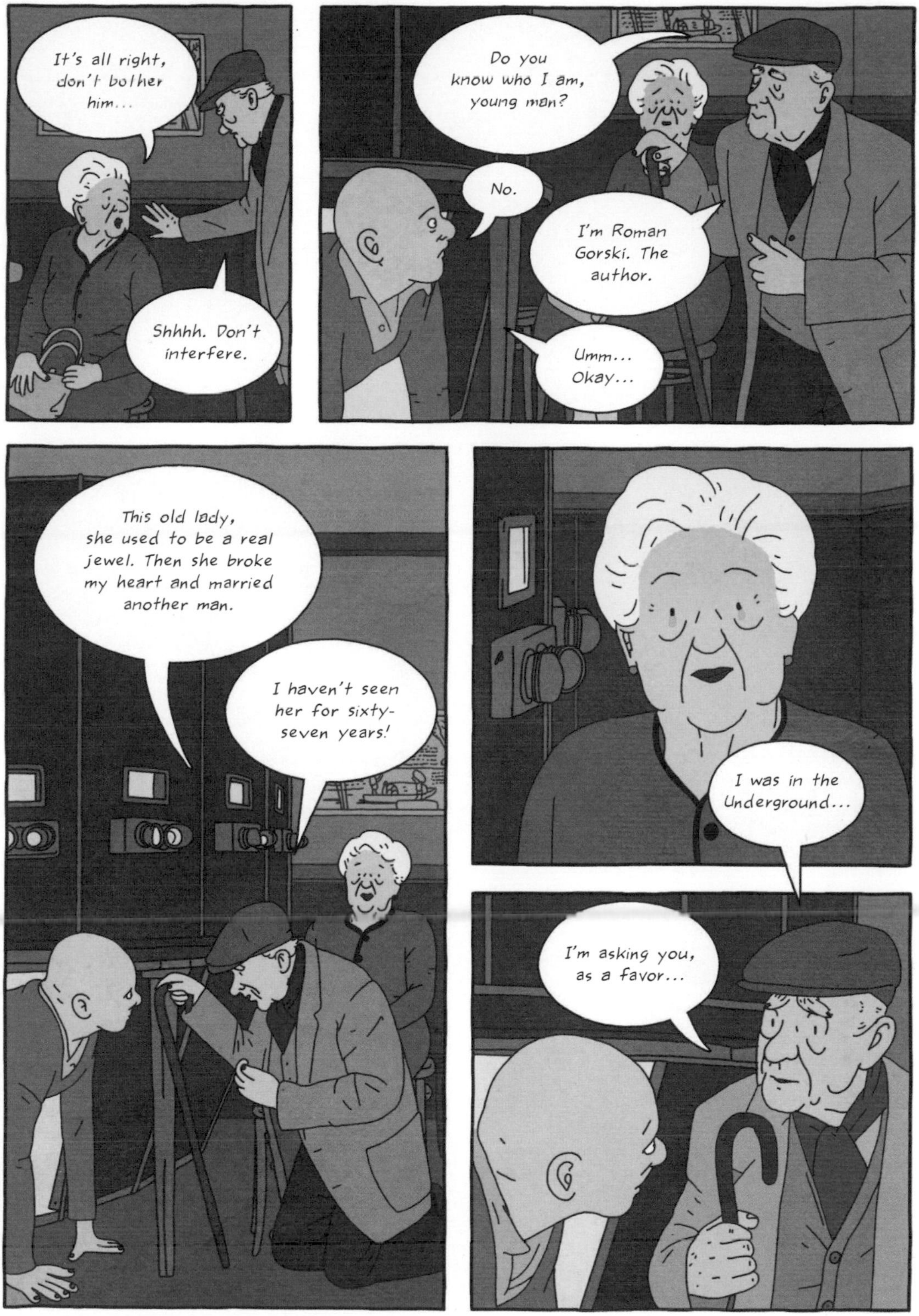
It's all right, don't bother him...
Shhhh. Don't interfere.
Do you know who I am, young man?
No.
I'm Roman Gorski. The author.
Umm... Okay...
This old lady, she used to be a real jewel. Then she broke my heart and married another man.
I haven't seen her for sixty-seven years!
I was in the Underground...
I'm asking you, as a favor...

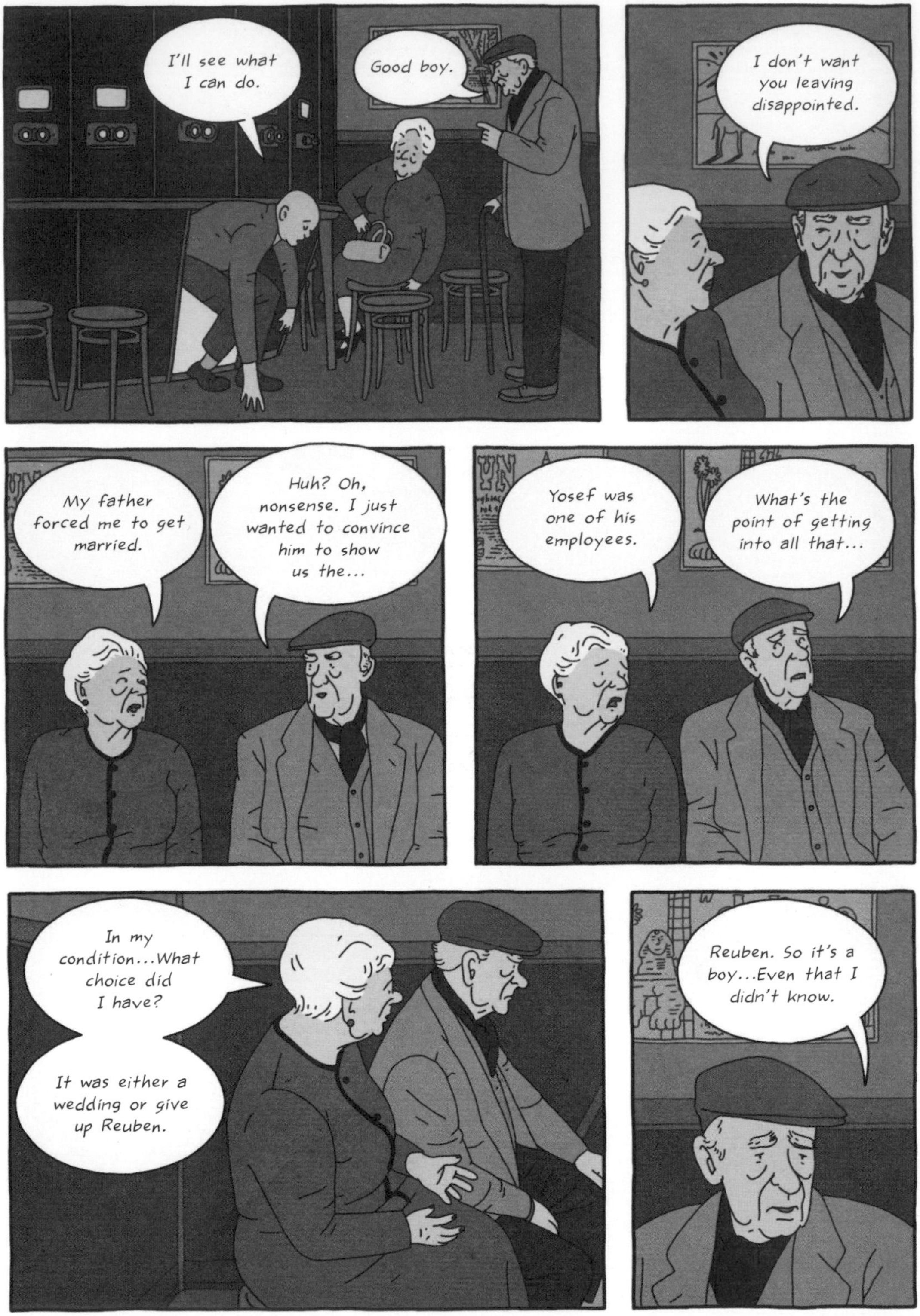
I'll see what I can do.
Good boy.
I don't want you leaving disappointed.
My father forced me to get married.
Huh? Oh, nonsense. I just wanted to convince him to show us the...
Yosef was one of his employees.
What's the point of getting into all that...
In my condition...What choice did I have?
It was either a wedding or give up Reuben.
Reuben. So it's a boy...Even that I didn't know.

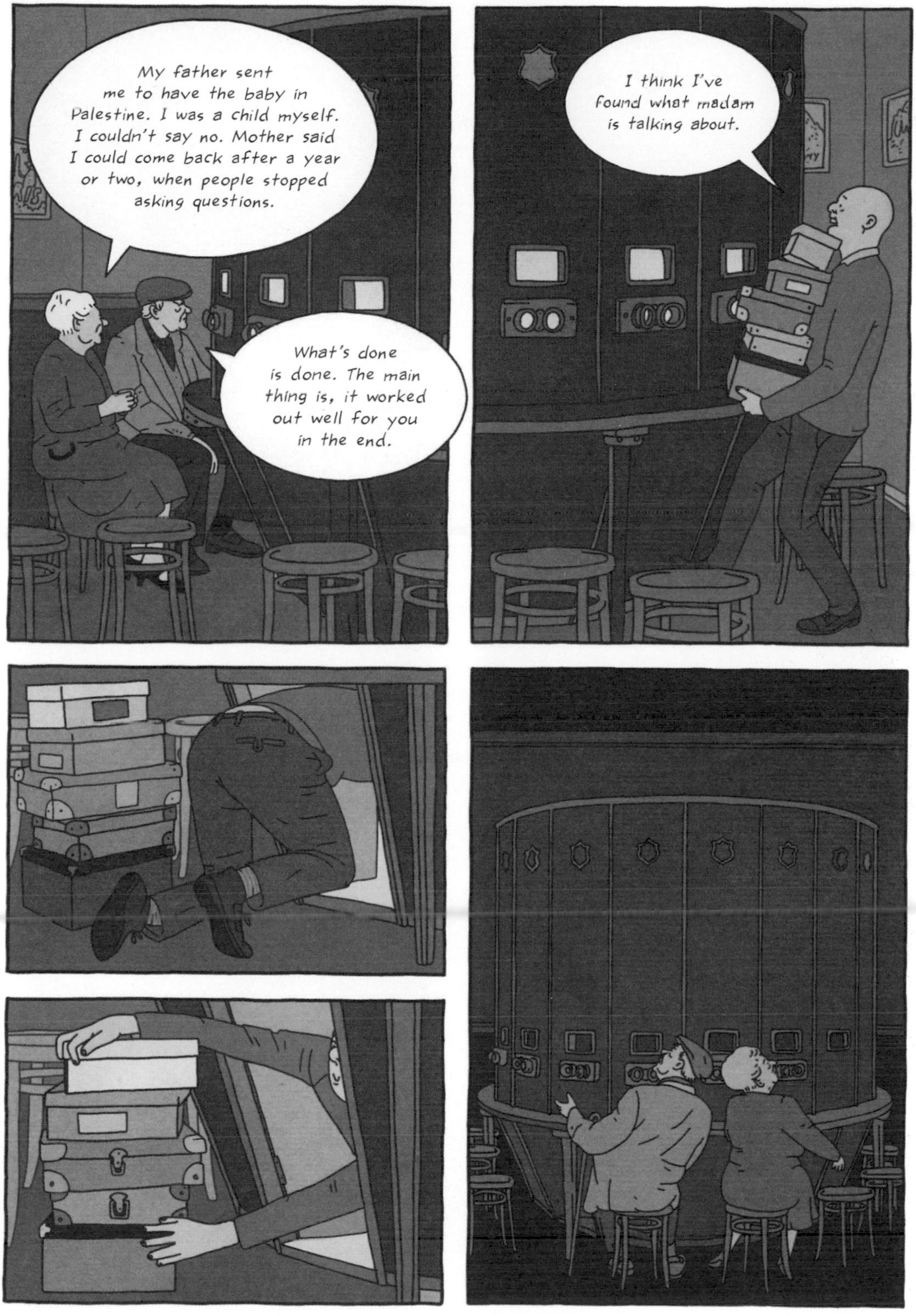
My father sent me to have the baby in Palestine. I was a child myself. I couldn't say no. Mother said I could come back after a year or two, when people stopped asking questions.
What's done is done. The main thing is, it worked out well for you in the end.
I think I've found what madam is talking about.

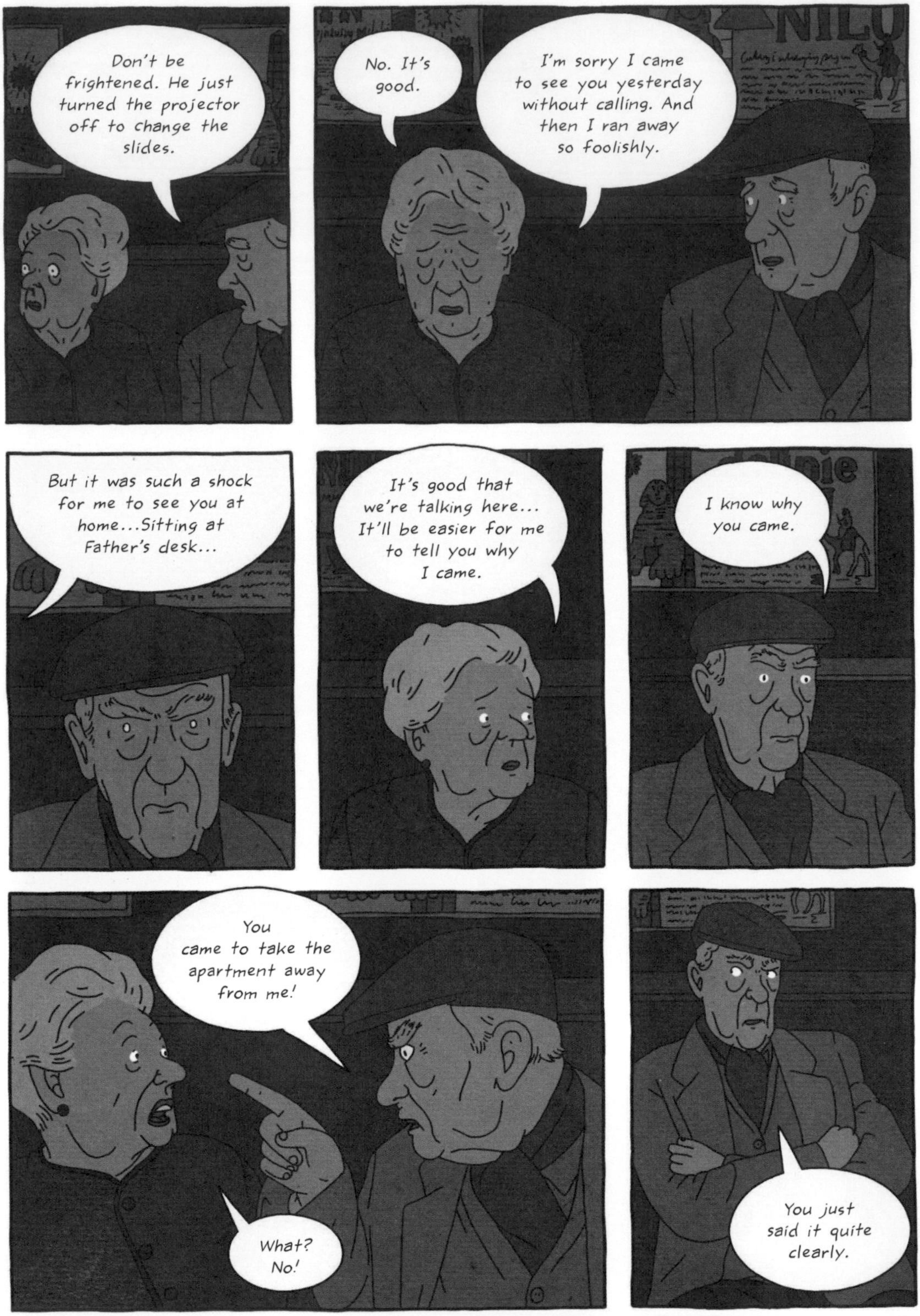
Don't be frightened. He just turned the projector off to change the slides.
No. It's good.
I'm sorry I came to see you yesterday without calling. And then I ran away so foolishly.
But it was such a shock for me to see you at home...Sitting at Father's desk...
It's good that we're talking here... It'll be easier for me to tell you why I came.
I know why you came.
You came to take the apartment away from me!
What? No!
You just said it quite clearly.

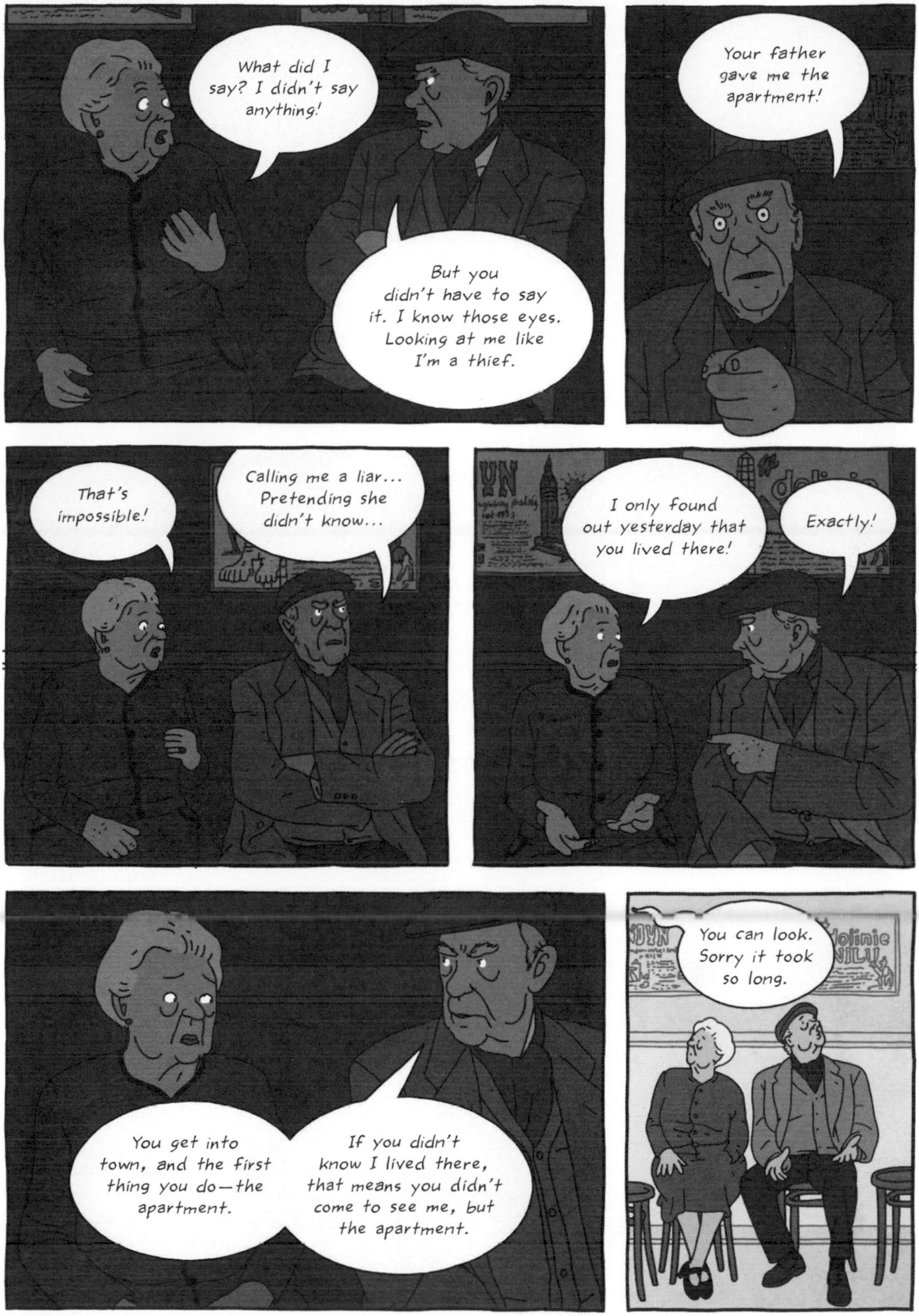
What did I say? I didn't say anything!
But you didn't have to say it. I know those eyes. Looking at me like I'm a thief.
Your father gave me the apartment!
That's impossible!
Calling me a liar... Pretending she didn't know...
I only found out yesterday that you lived there!
Exactly!
You get into town, and the first thing you do—the apartment.
If you didn't know I lived there, that means you didn't come to see me, but the apartment.
You can look. Sorry it took so long.

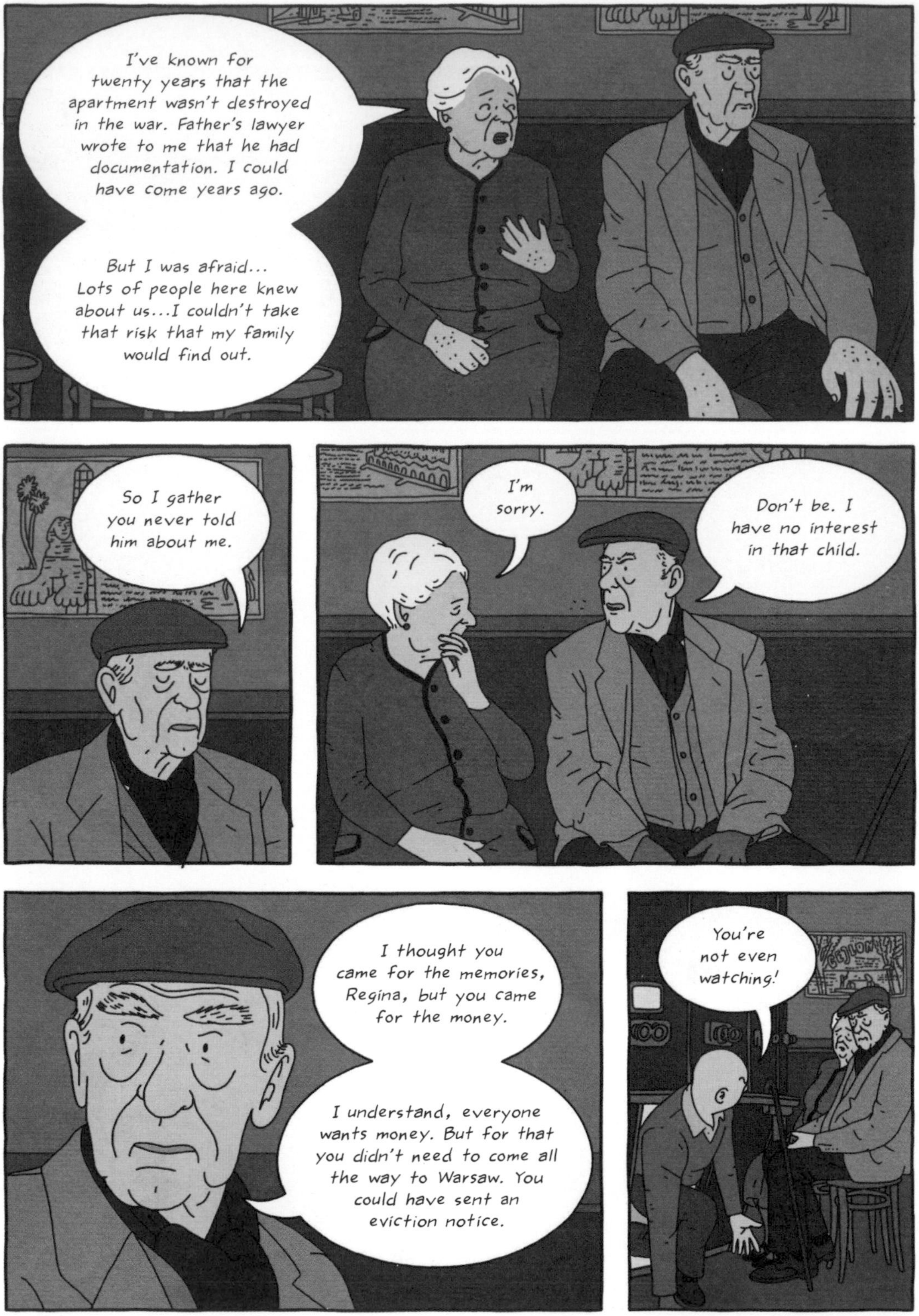
I've known for twenty years that the apartment wasn't destroyed in the war. Father's lawyer wrote to me that he had documentation. I could have come years ago.
But I was afraid... Lots of people here knew about us...I couldn't take that risk that my family would find out.
So I gather you never told him about me.
I'm sorry.
Don't be. I have no interest in that child.
I thought you came for the memories, Regina, but you came for the money.
I understand, everyone wants money. But for that you didn't need to come all the way to Warsaw. You could have sent an eviction notice.
You're not even watching!

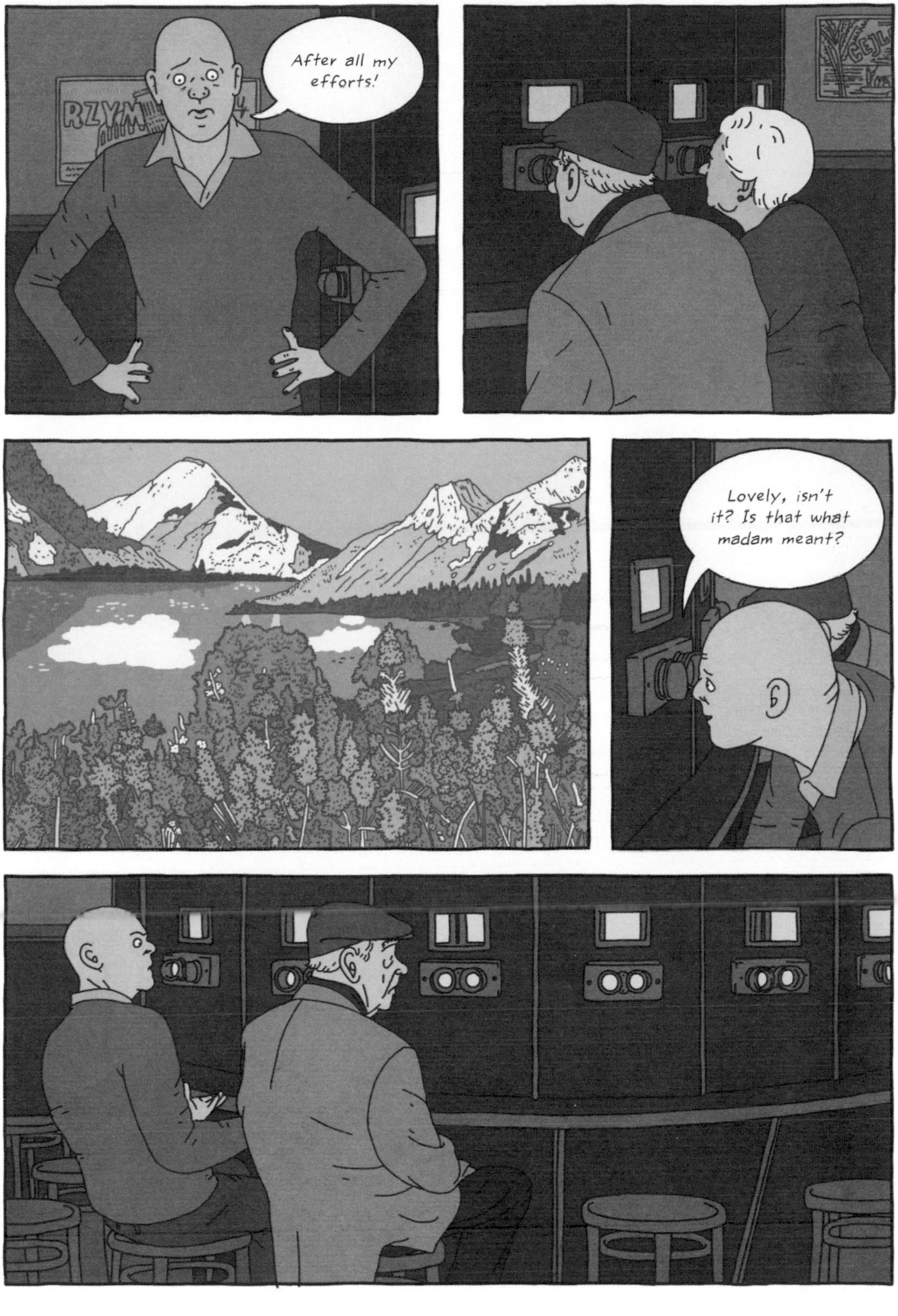
RZYM
After all my efforts!
Lovely, isn't it? Is that what madam meant?

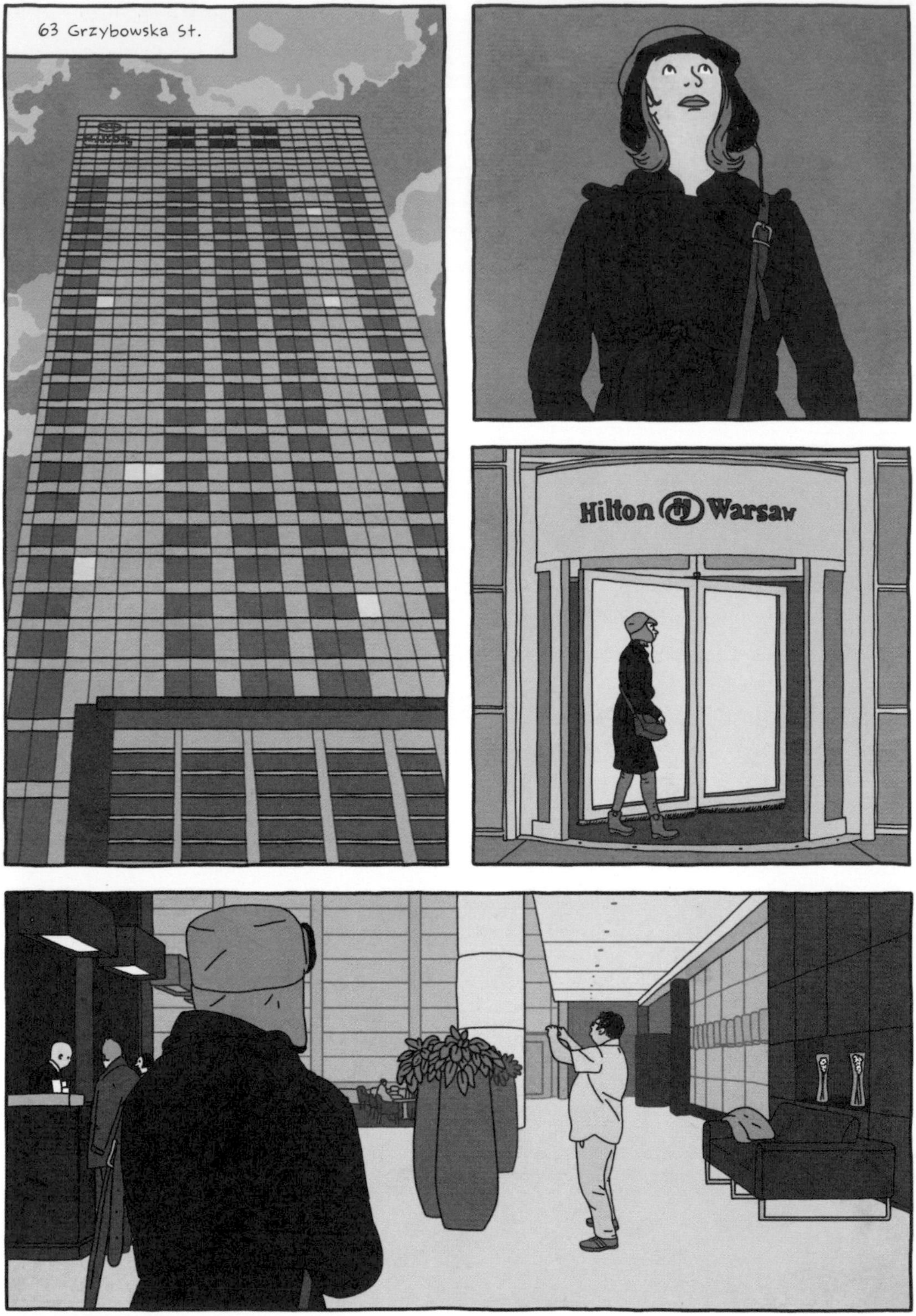
63 Grzybowska St.
Hilton Warsaw

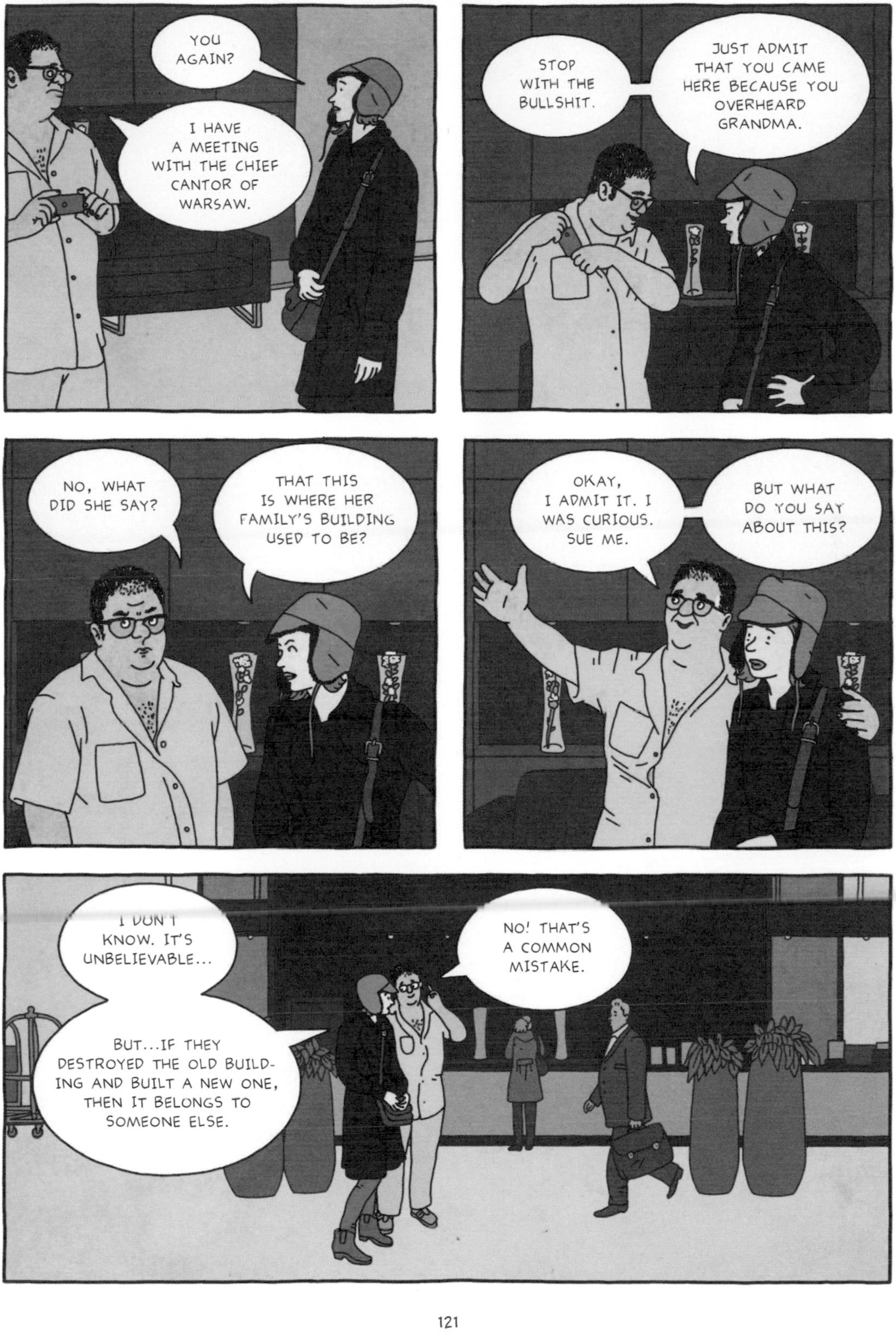
YOU AGAIN?
I HAVE A MEETING WITH THE CHIEF CANTOR OF WARSAW.
STOP WITH THE BULLSHIT.
JUST ADMIT THAT YOU CAME HERE BECAUSE YOU OVERHEARD GRANDMA.
NO, WHAT DID SHE SAY?
THAT THIS IS WHERE HER FAMILY'S BUILDING USED TO BE?
OKAY, I ADMIT IT. I WAS CURIOUS. SUE ME.
BUT WHAT DO YOU SAY ABOUT THIS?
I DON'T KNOW. IT'S UNBELIEVABLE...
BUT...IF THEY DESTROYED THE OLD BUILD-ING AND BUILT A NEW ONE, THEN IT BELONGS TO SOMEONE ELSE.
NO! THAT'S A COMMON MISTAKE.

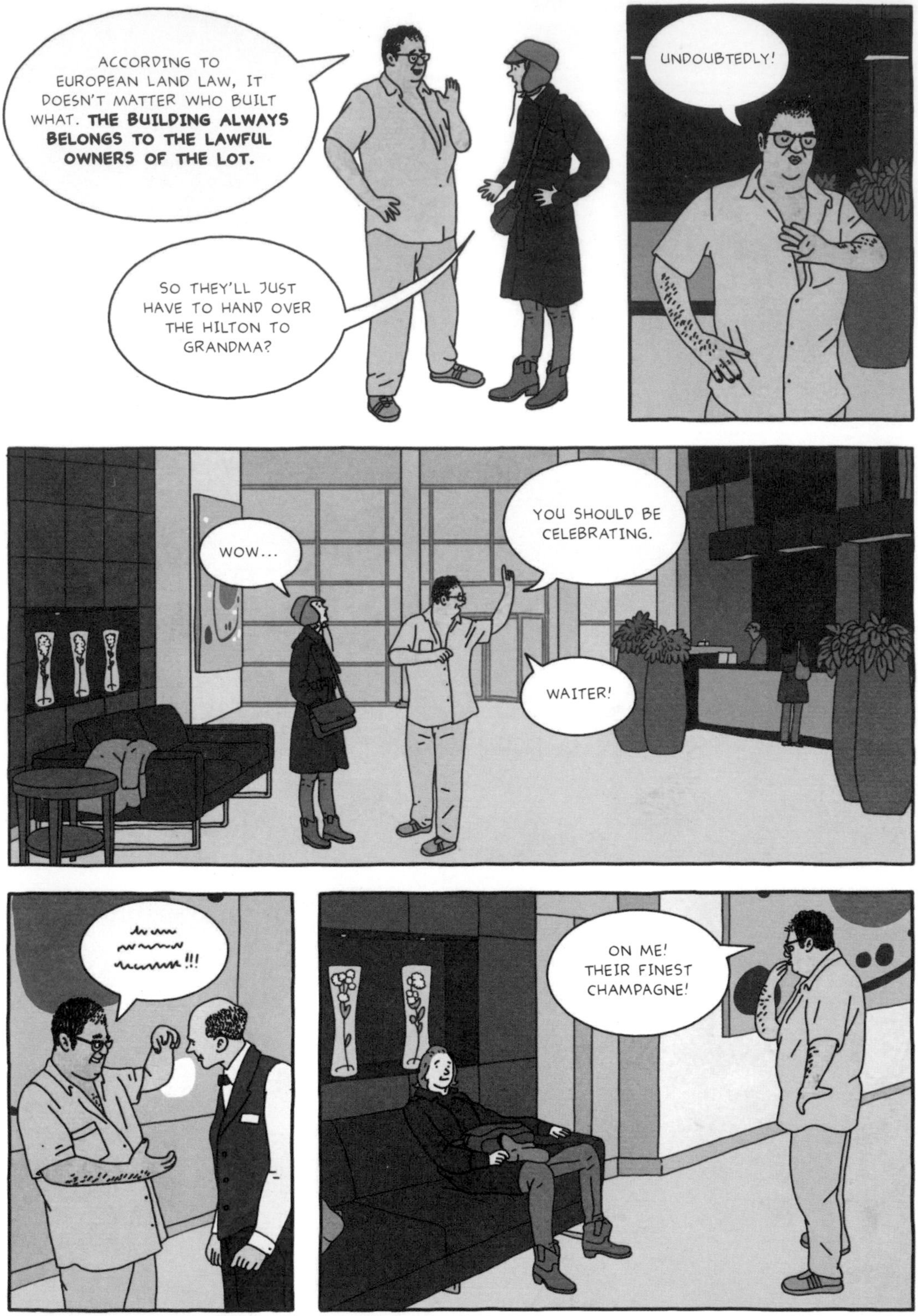
ACCORDING TO EUROPEAN LAND LAW, IT DOESN'T MATTER WHO BUILT WHAT. **THE BUILDING ALWAYS BELONGS TO THE LAWFUL OWNERS OF THE LOT.**
SO THEY'LL JUST HAVE TO HAND OVER THE HILTON TO GRANDMA?
UNDOUBTEDLY!
WOW...
YOU SHOULD BE CELEBRATING.
WAITER!
ON ME! THEIR FINEST CHAMPAGNE!

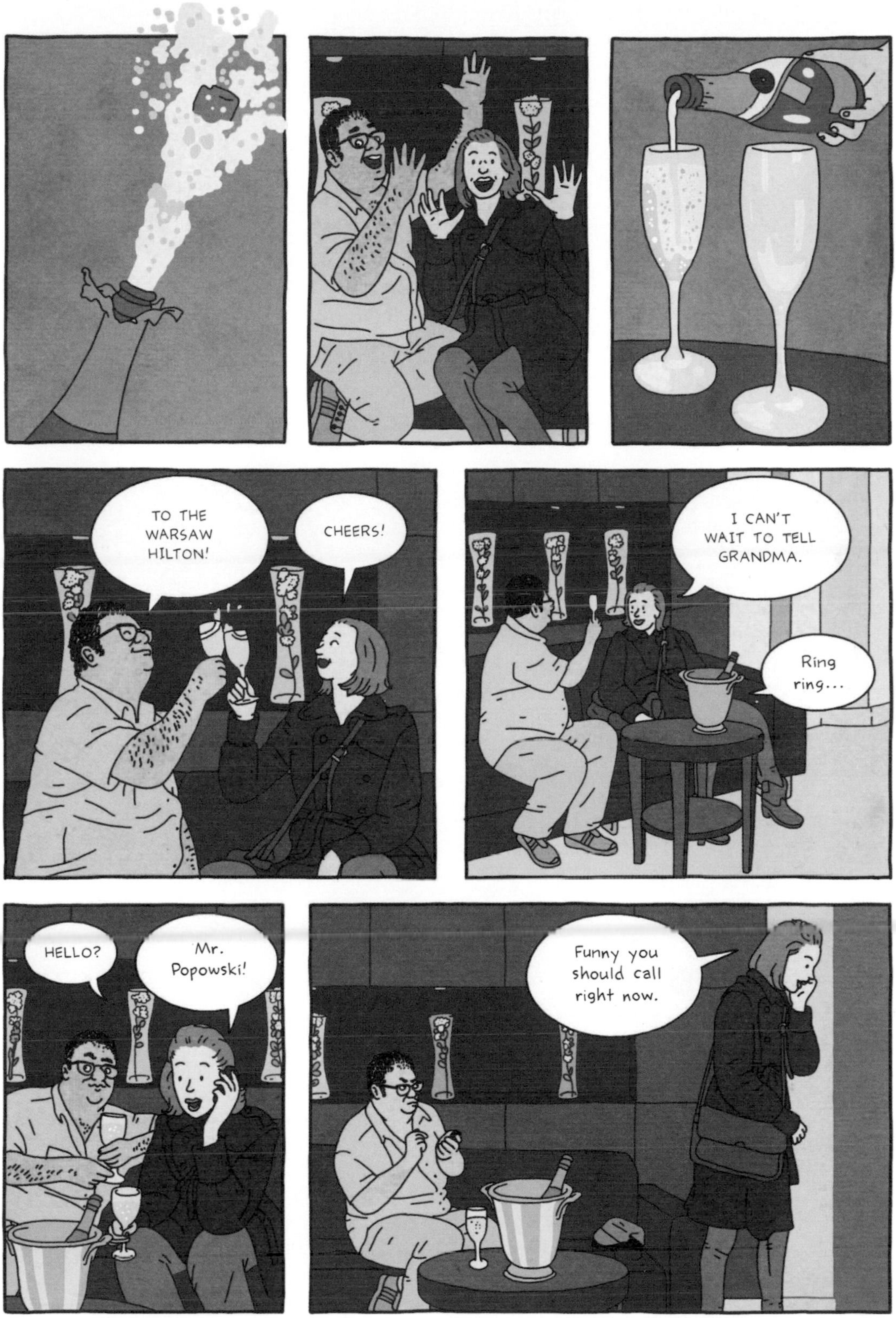
TO THE WARSAW HILTON!
CHEERS!
I CAN'T WAIT TO TELL GRANDMA.
Ring ring...
HELLO?
Mr. Popowski!
Funny you should call right now.

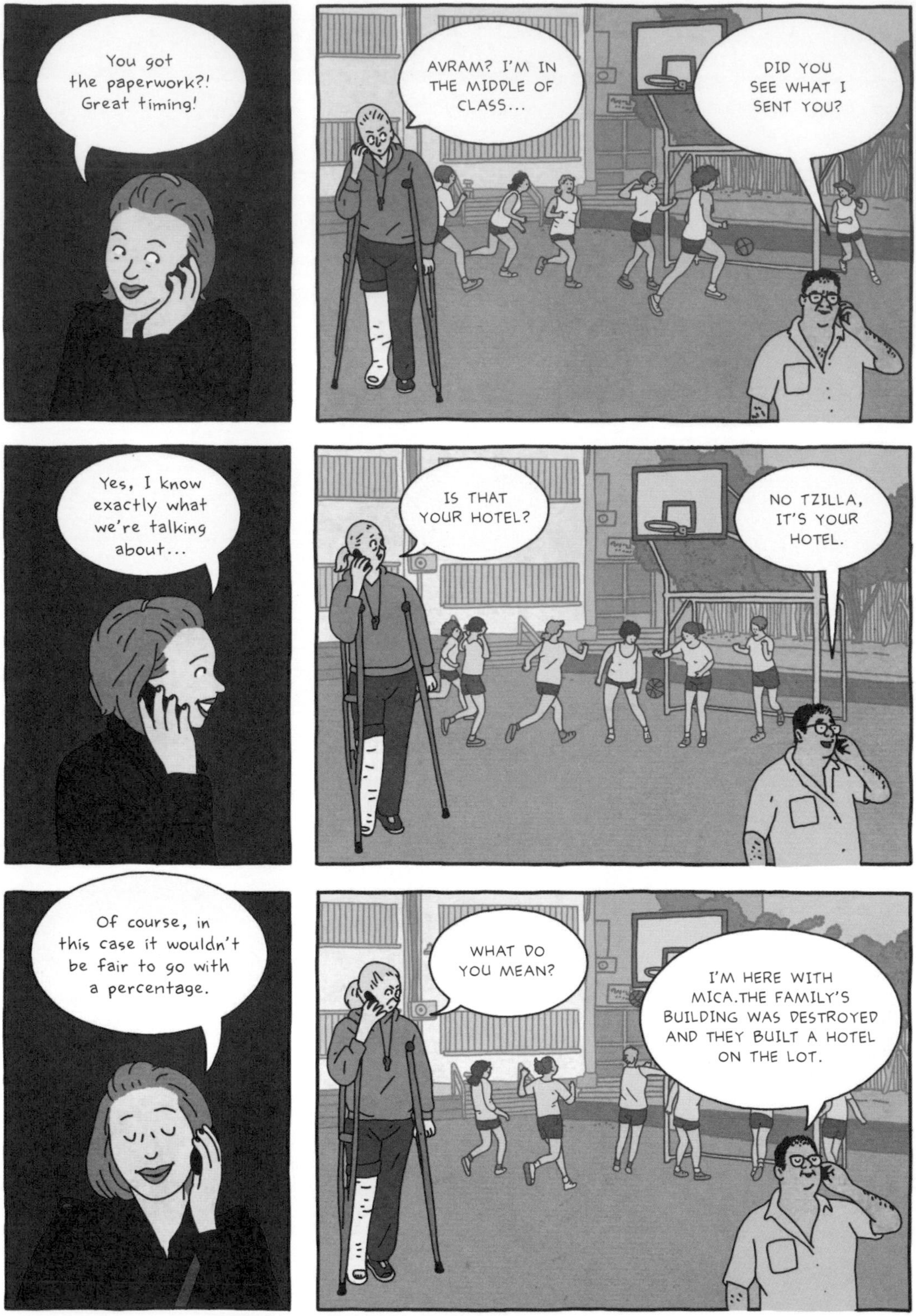
You got the paperwork?! Great timing!
AVRAM? I'M IN THE MIDDLE OF CLASS...
DID YOU SEE WHAT I SENT YOU?
Yes, I know exactly what we're talking about...
IS THAT YOUR HOTEL?
NO TZILLA, IT'S YOUR HOTEL.
Of course, in this case it wouldn't be fair to go with a percentage.
WHAT DO YOU MEAN?
I'M HERE WITH MICA.THE FAMILY'S BUILDING WAS DESTROYED AND THEY BUILT A HOTEL ON THE LOT.

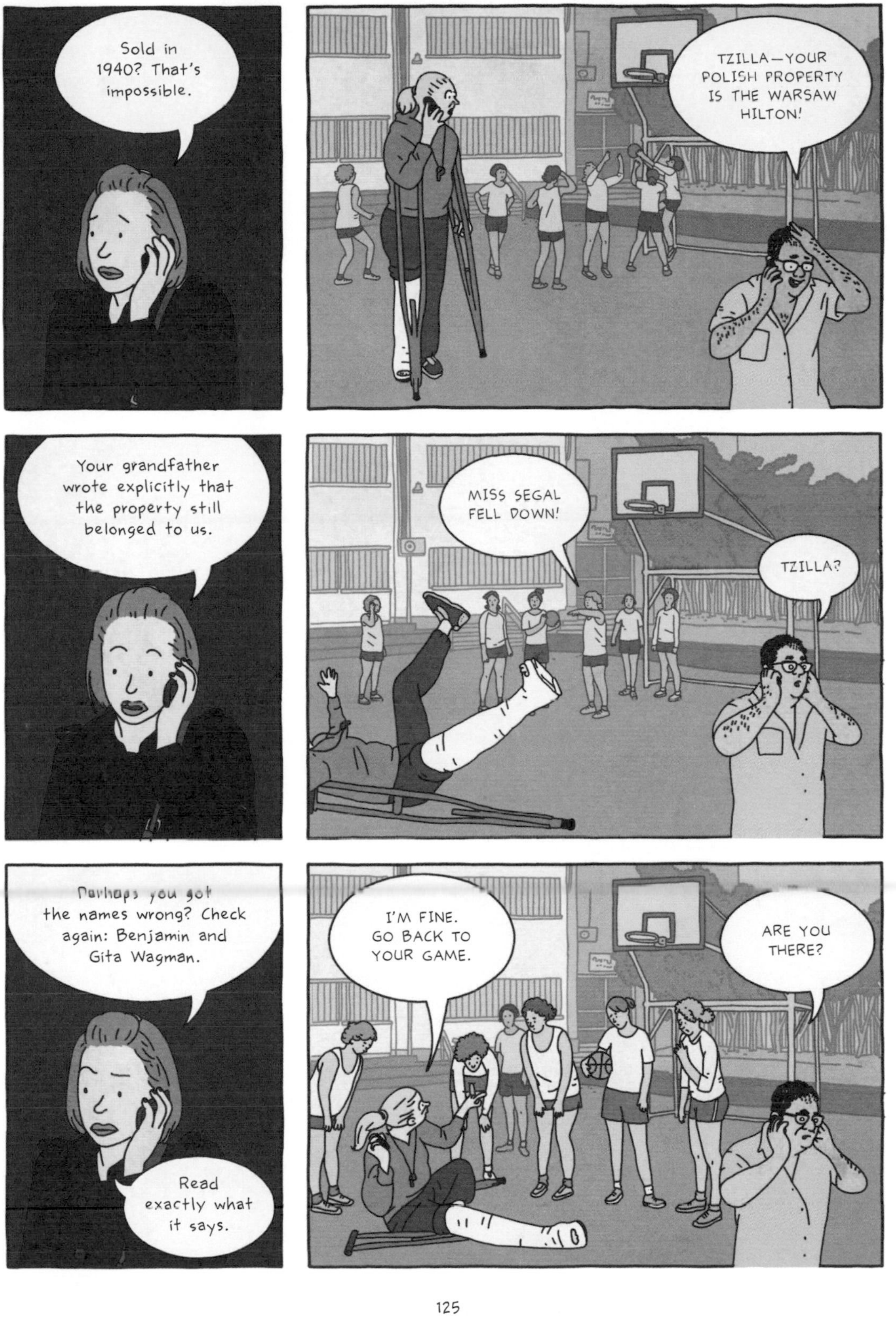
Sold in 1940? That's impossible.
TZILLA—YOUR POLISH PROPERTY IS THE WARSAW HILTON!
Your grandfather wrote explicitly that the property still belonged to us.
MISS SEGAL FELL DOWN!
TZILLA?
Perhaps you got the names wrong? Check again: Benjamin and Gita Wagman.
Read exactly what it says.
I'M FINE. GO BACK TO YOUR GAME.
ARE YOU THERE?

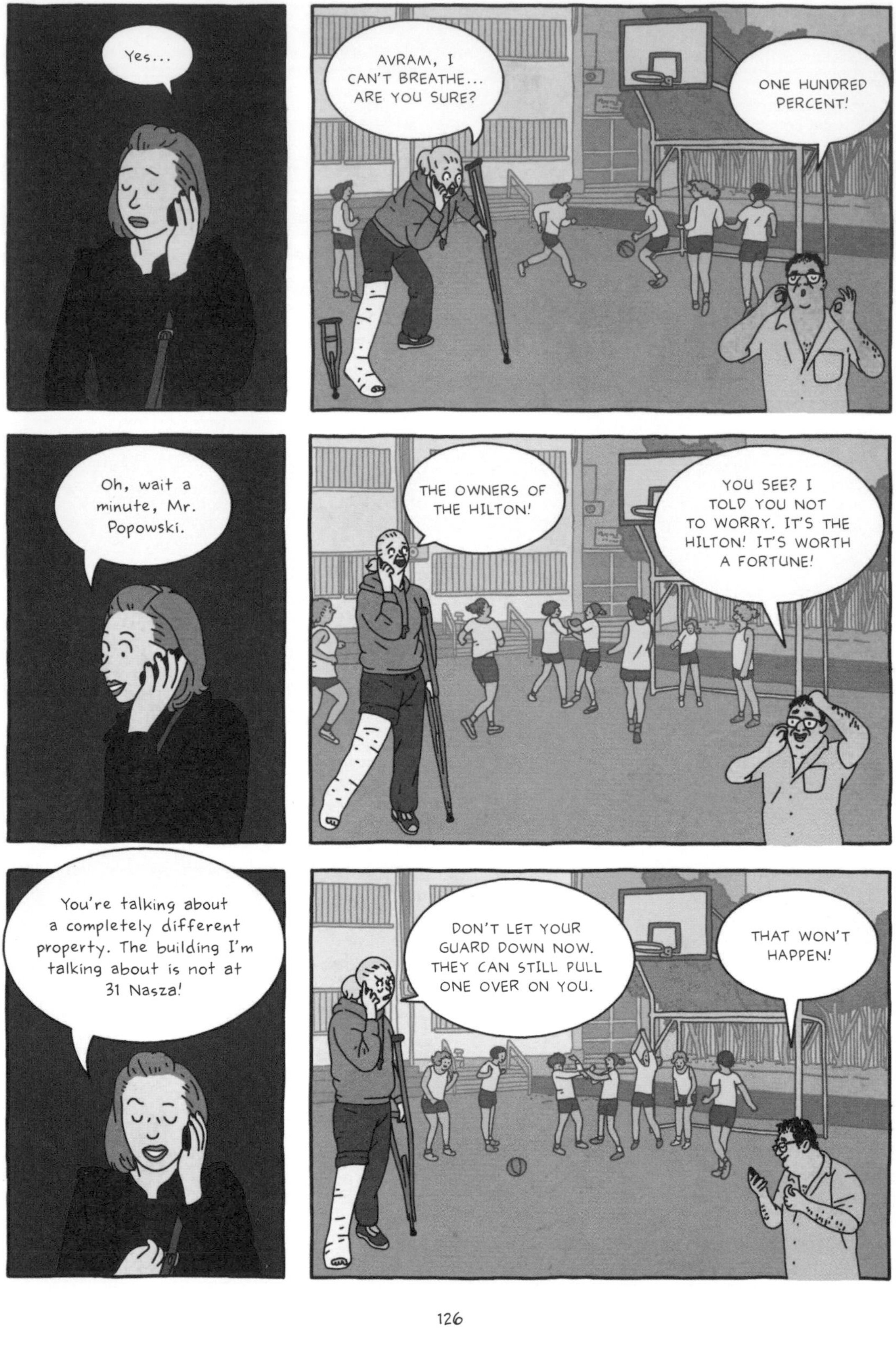
Yes...
AVRAM, I CAN'T BREATHE... ARE YOU SURE?
ONE HUNDRED PERCENT!
Oh, wait a minute, Mr. Popowski.
THE OWNERS OF THE HILTON!
YOU SEE? I TOLD YOU NOT TO WORRY. IT'S THE HILTON! IT'S WORTH A FORTUNE!
You're talking about a completely different property. The building I'm talking about is not at 31 Nasza!
DON'T LET YOUR GUARD DOWN NOW. THEY CAN STILL PULL ONE OVER ON YOU.
THAT WON'T HAPPEN!

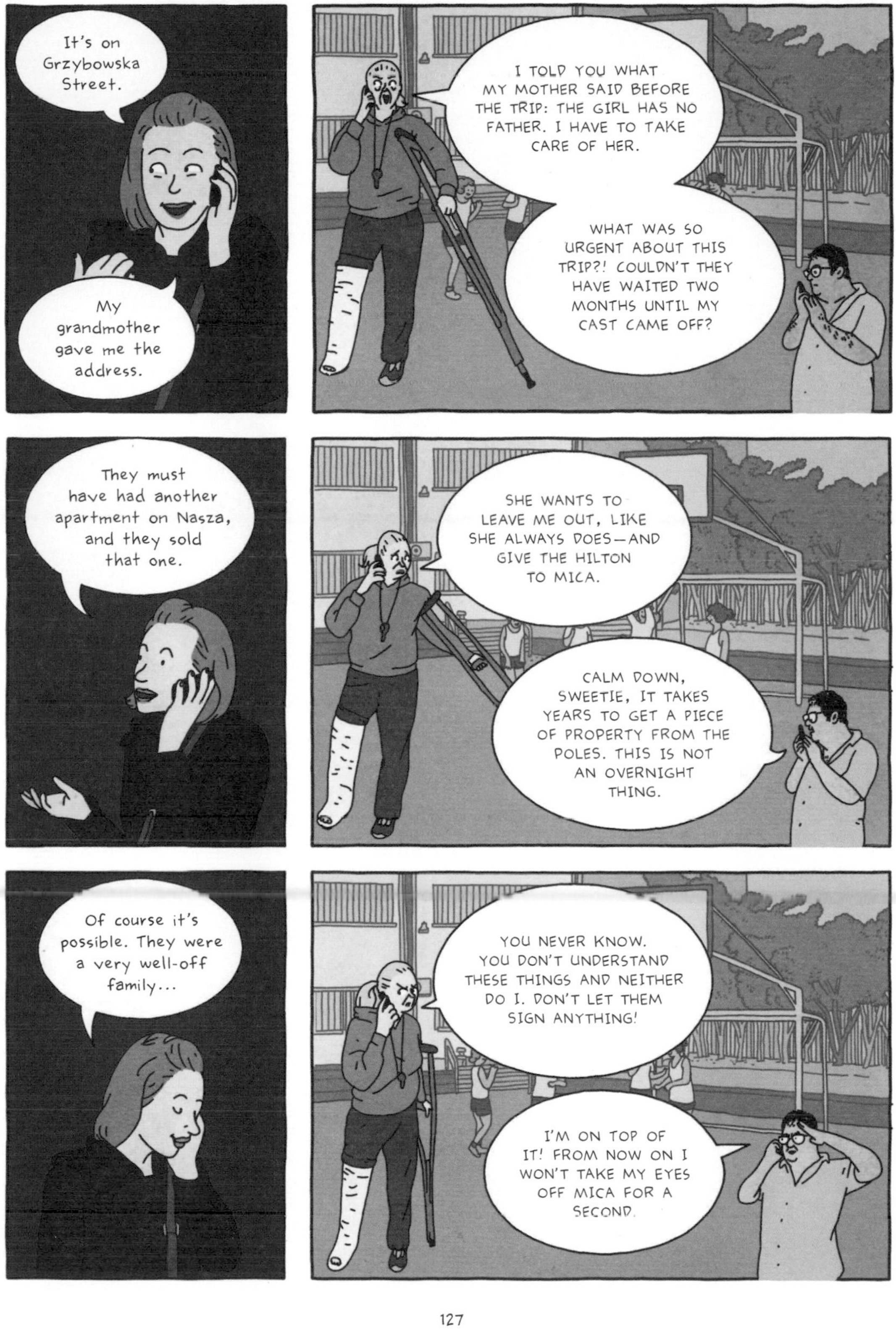
It's on Grzybowska Street.
My grandmother gave me the address.
I TOLD YOU WHAT MY MOTHER SAID BEFORE THE TRIP: THE GIRL HAS NO FATHER. I HAVE TO TAKE CARE OF HER.
WHAT WAS SO URGENT ABOUT THIS TRIP?! COULDN'T THEY HAVE WAITED TWO MONTHS UNTIL MY CAST CAME OFF?
They must have had another apartment on Nasza, and they sold that one.
SHE WANTS TO LEAVE ME OUT, LIKE SHE ALWAYS DOES—AND GIVE THE HILTON TO MICA.
CALM DOWN, SWEETIE, IT TAKES YEARS TO GET A PIECE OF PROPERTY FROM THE POLES. THIS IS NOT AN OVERNIGHT THING.
Of course it's possible. They were a very well-off family...
YOU NEVER KNOW. YOU DON'T UNDERSTAND THESE THINGS AND NEITHER DO I. DON'T LET THEM SIGN ANYTHING!
I'M ON TOP OF IT! FROM NOW ON I WON'T TAKE MY EYES OFF MICA FOR A SECOND.

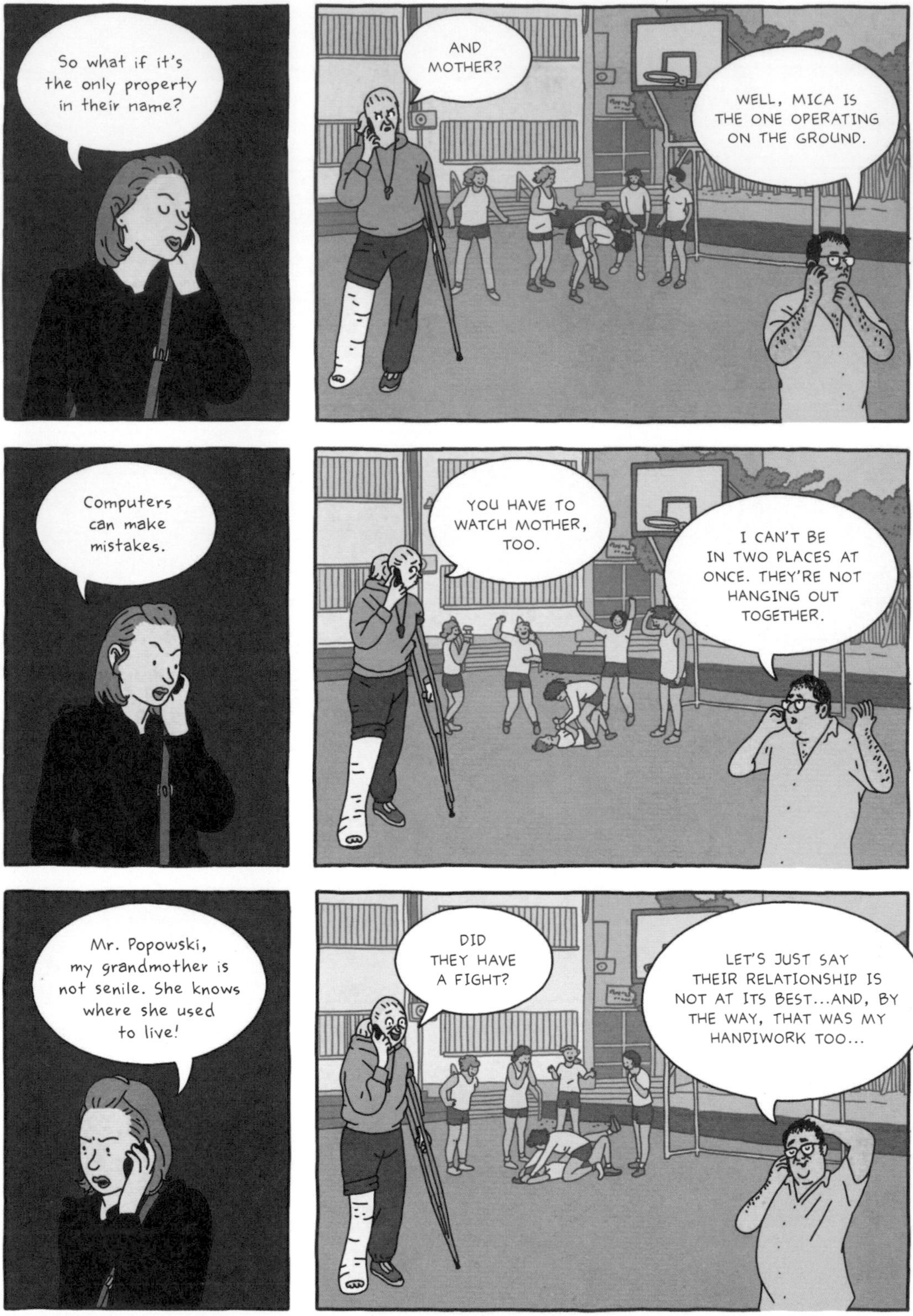
So what if it's the only property in their name?
AND MOTHER?
WELL, MICA IS THE ONE OPERATING ON THE GROUND.
Computers can make mistakes.
YOU HAVE TO WATCH MOTHER, TOO.
I CAN'T BE IN TWO PLACES AT ONCE. THEY'RE NOT HANGING OUT TOGETHER.
Mr. Popowski, my grandmother is not senile. She knows where she used to live!
DID THEY HAVE A FIGHT?
LET'S JUST SAY THEIR RELATIONSHIP IS NOT AT ITS BEST...AND, BY THE WAY, THAT WAS MY HANDIWORK TOO...

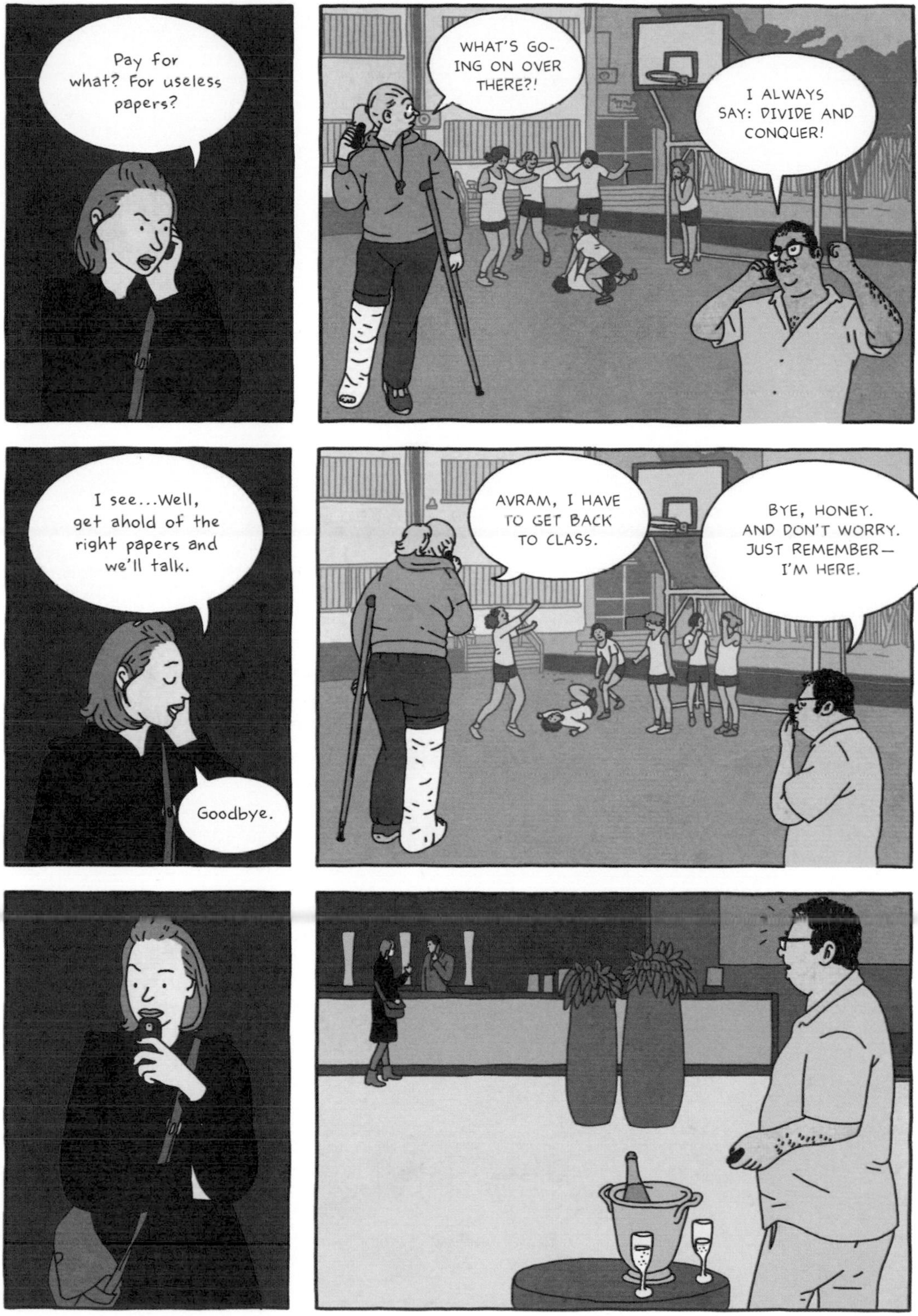
Pay for what? For useless papers?
WHAT'S GOING ON OVER THERE?!
I ALWAYS SAY: DIVIDE AND CONQUER!
I see...Well, get ahold of the right papers and we'll talk.
Goodbye.
AVRAM, I HAVE TO GET BACK TO CLASS.
BYE, HONEY. AND DON'T WORRY. JUST REMEMBER— I'M HERE.

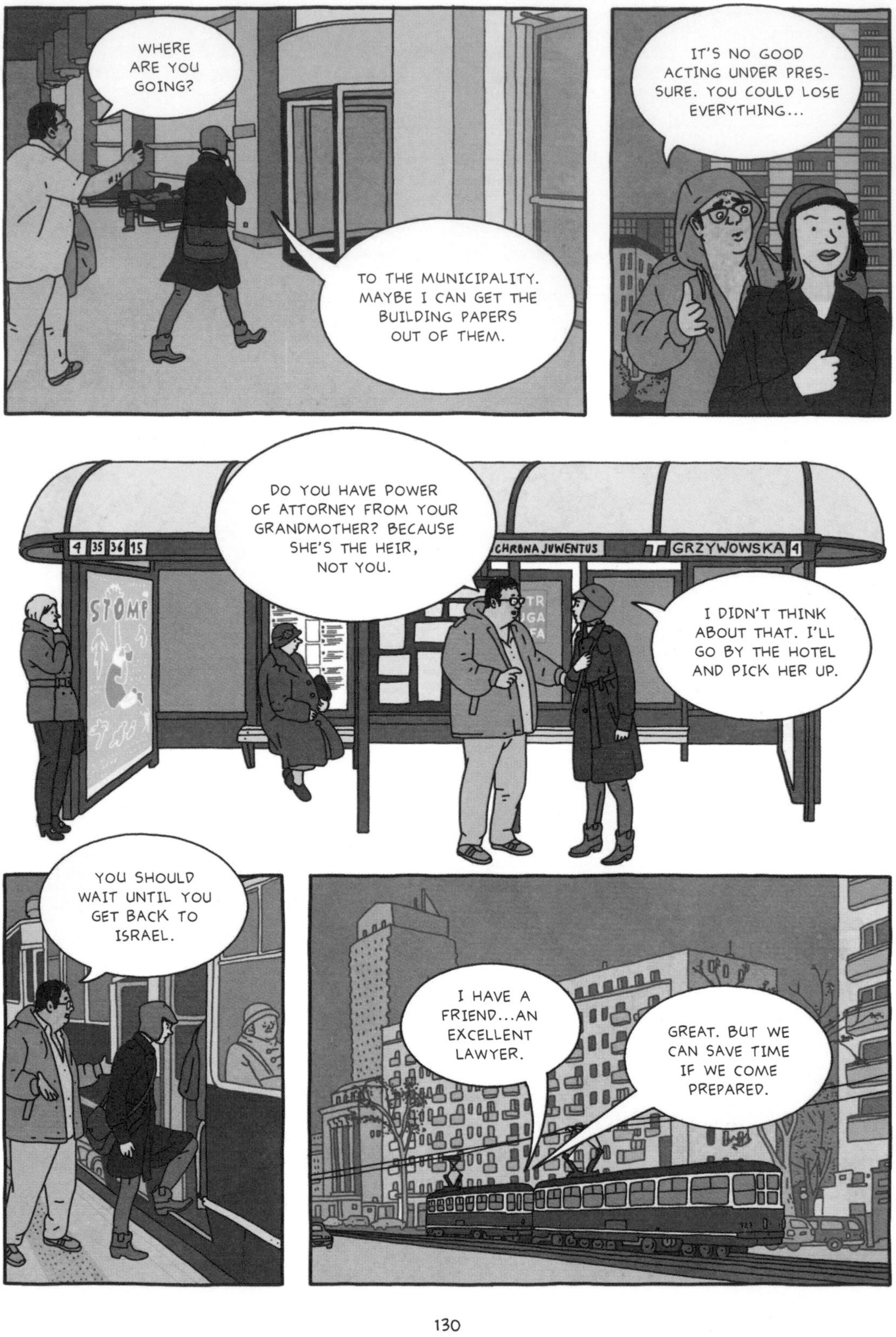
WHERE ARE YOU GOING?
TO THE MUNICIPALITY. MAYBE I CAN GET THE BUILDING PAPERS OUT OF THEM.
IT'S NO GOOD ACTING UNDER PRES-SURE. YOU COULD LOSE EVERYTHING...
4 35 36 15
CHRONA JUWENTUS
GRZYWOWSKA 4
STOMP
DO YOU HAVE POWER OF ATTORNEY FROM YOUR GRANDMOTHER? BECAUSE SHE'S THE HEIR, NOT YOU.
I DIDN'T THINK ABOUT THAT. I'LL GO BY THE HOTEL AND PICK HER UP.
YOU SHOULD WAIT UNTIL YOU GET BACK TO ISRAEL.
I HAVE A FRIEND...AN EXCELLENT LAWYER.
GREAT. BUT WE CAN SAVE TIME IF WE COME PREPARED.

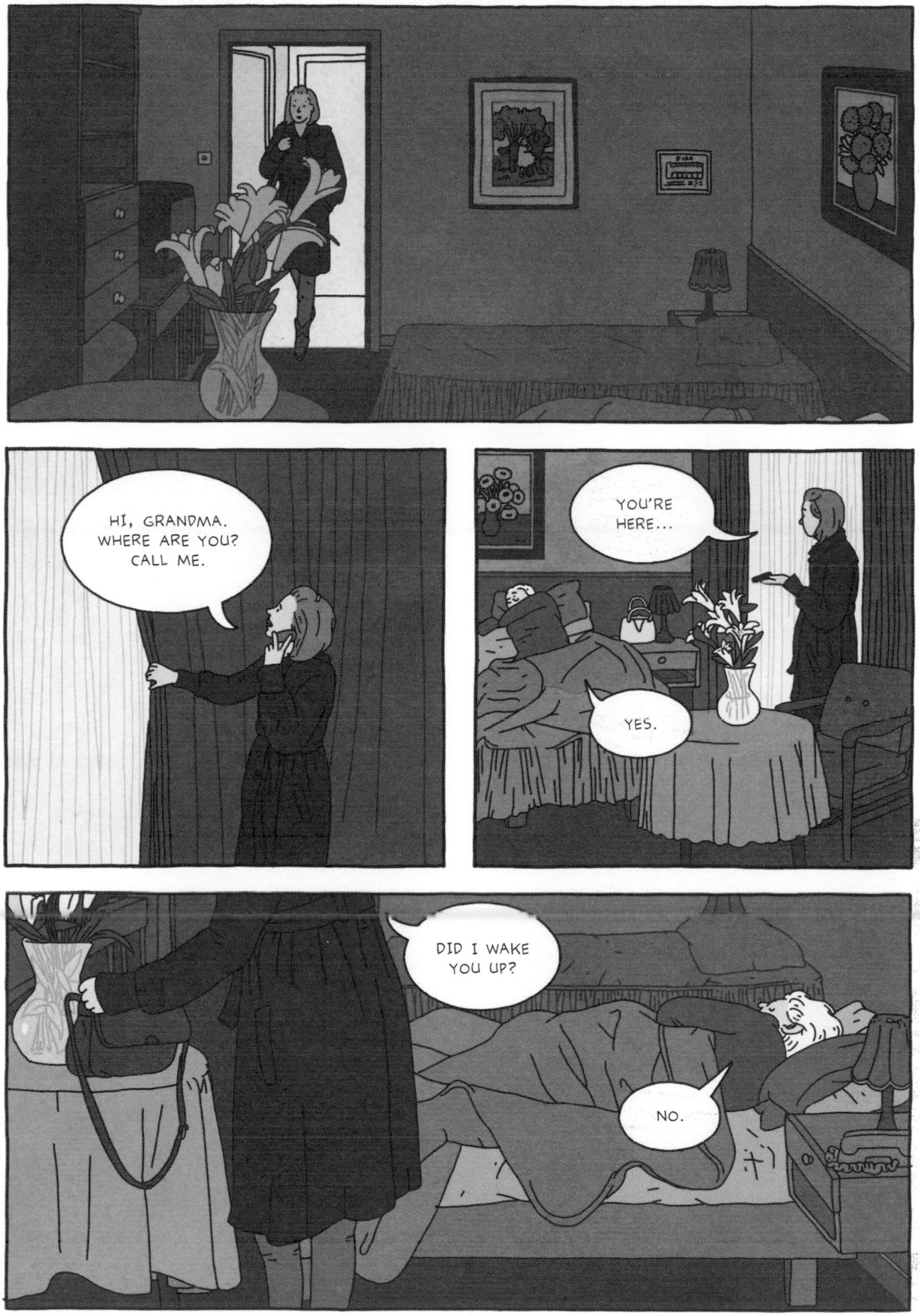
HI, GRANDMA. WHERE ARE YOU? CALL ME.
YOU'RE HERE...
YES.
DID I WAKE YOU UP?
NO.

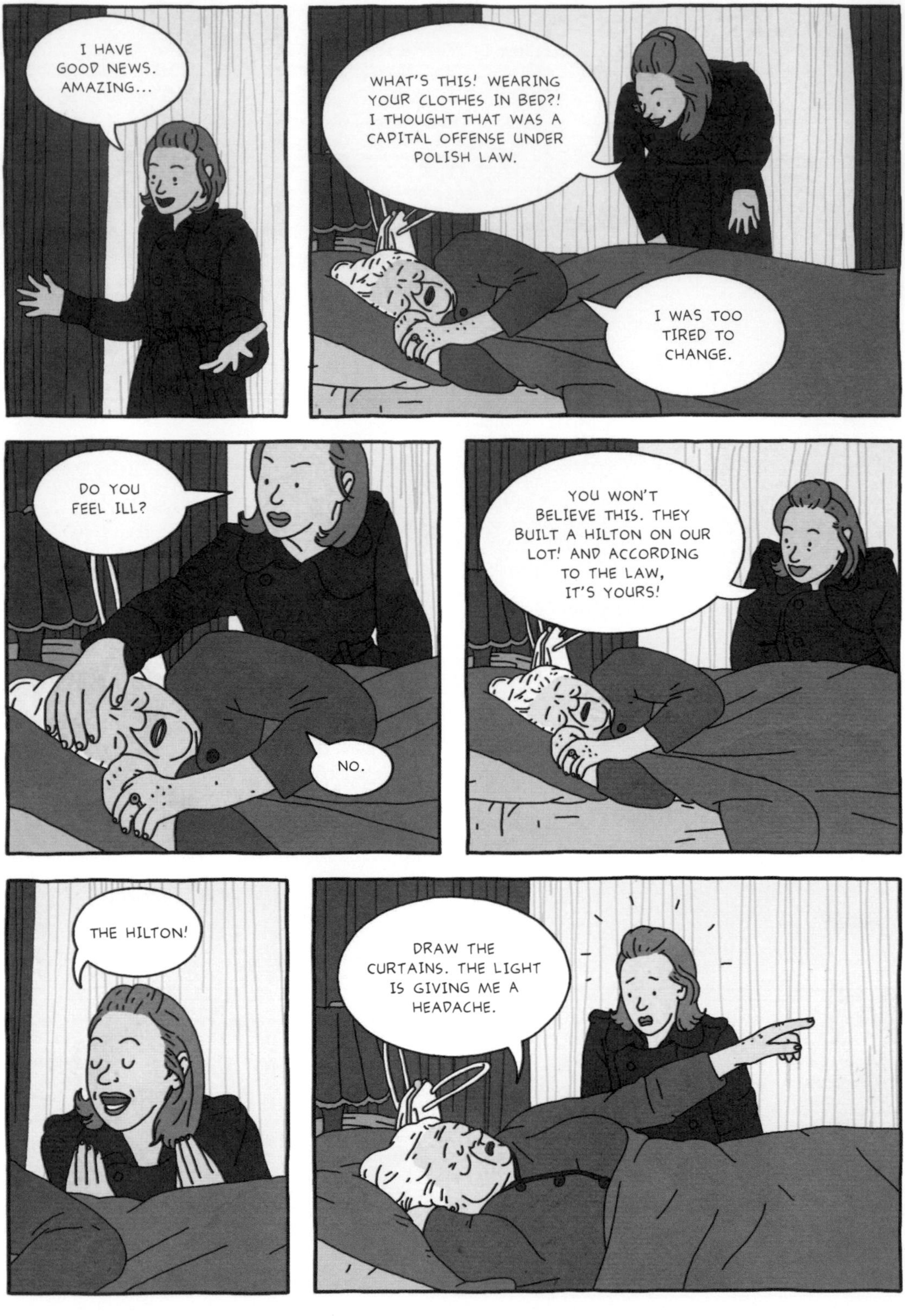
I HAVE GOOD NEWS. AMAZING...
WHAT'S THIS! WEARING YOUR CLOTHES IN BED?! I THOUGHT THAT WAS A CAPITAL OFFENSE UNDER POLISH LAW.
I WAS TOO TIRED TO CHANGE.
DO YOU FEEL ILL?
NO.
YOU WON'T BELIEVE THIS. THEY BUILT A HILTON ON OUR LOT! AND ACCORDING TO THE LAW, IT'S YOURS!
THE HILTON!
DRAW THE CURTAINS. THE LIGHT IS GIVING ME A HEADACHE.

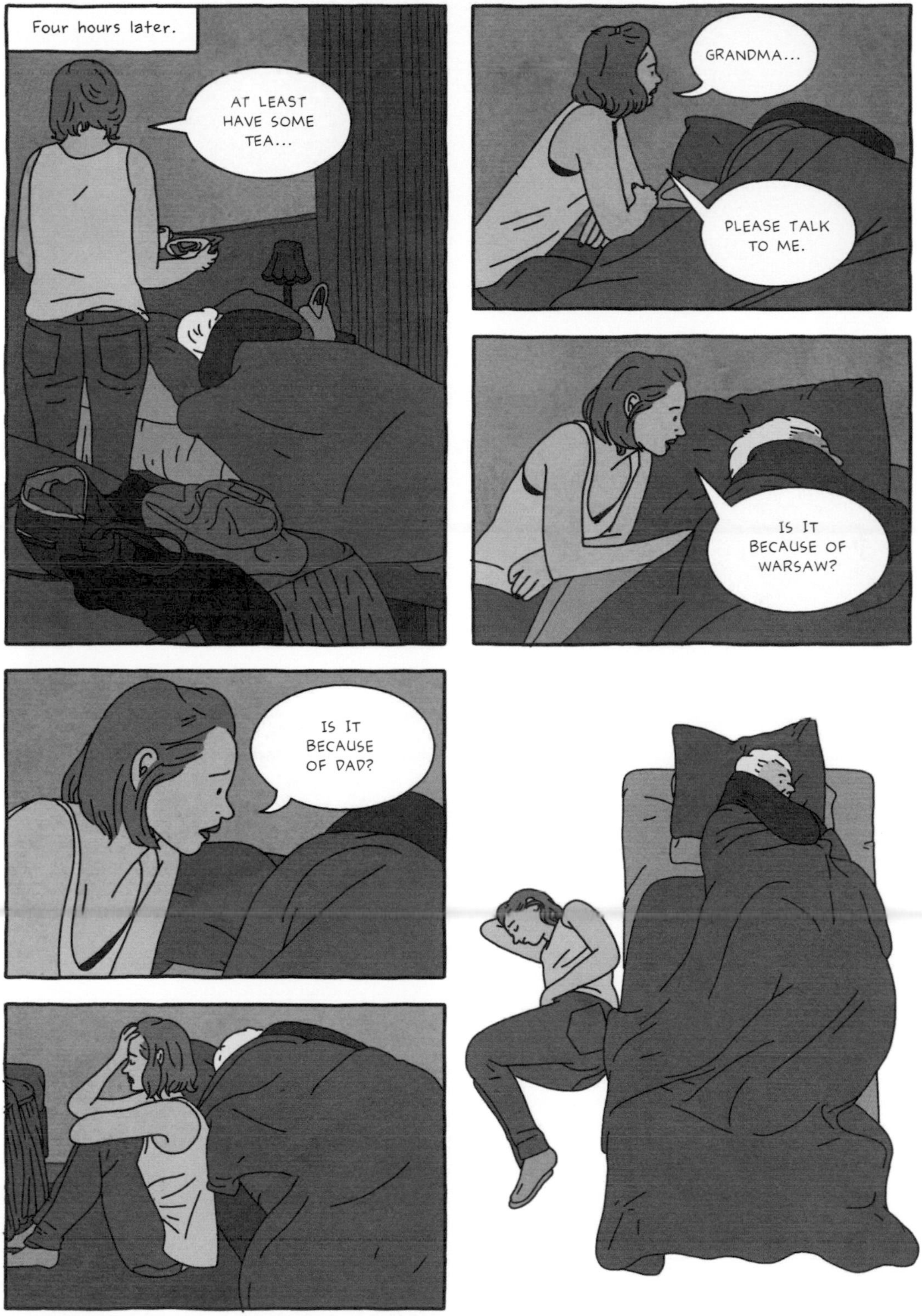
Four hours later.
AT LEAST HAVE SOME TEA...
GRANDMA...
PLEASE TALK TO ME.
IS IT BECAUSE OF WARSAW?
IS IT BECAUSE OF DAD?

DAY FOUR

The next evening.

Ring ring...

Hello? Mica?

Tomasz!

You promised you'd call.

I...I'm...My grandmother is ill.

Oh.. sorry...anything serious?

o..yes....I don't know..The doctor was here.. said
he's all right but what does he know and I called
aunt Tzilla, she said we are going back anyway in
ays so it is better not to schlep her to a hospital
he doesn't speak she didn't drink a sip since yeste
ay I'm afraid she's gonna dehydrate and the only
round is this awful man Yagodnik who keeps tellin
e all these ___ tories about his mother's frie
ho sudden ___ stopped eating because she
s decid ___ she wanted to die and
e DID ___ die two weeks later I
___ n this i can't decid
___ hat to do didn
___ ing to ma
___ he

I'm coming right away.

135

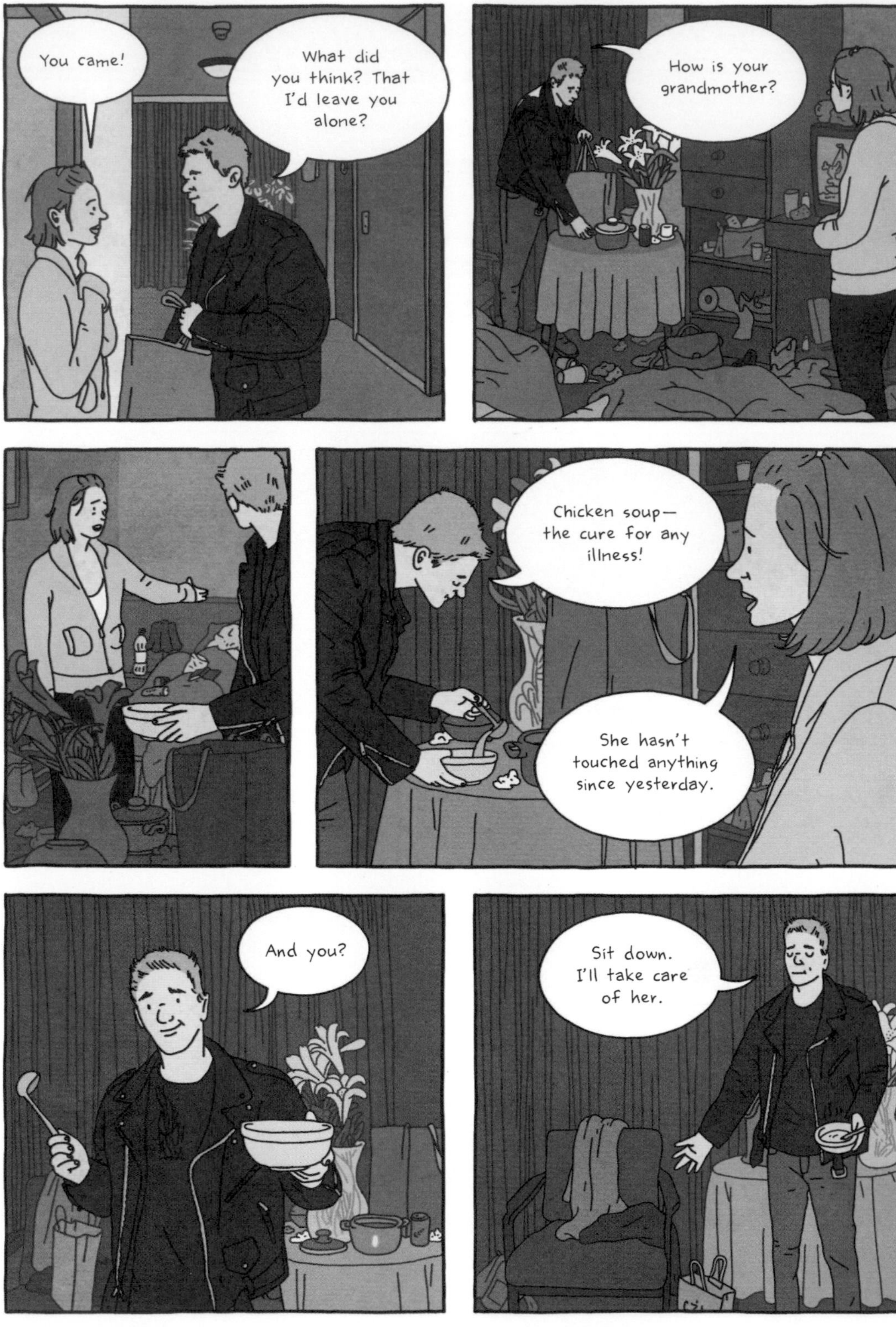
You came!
What did you think? That I'd leave you alone?
How is your grandmother?
Chicken soup— the cure for any illness!
She hasn't touched anything since yesterday.
And you?
Sit down. I'll take care of her.

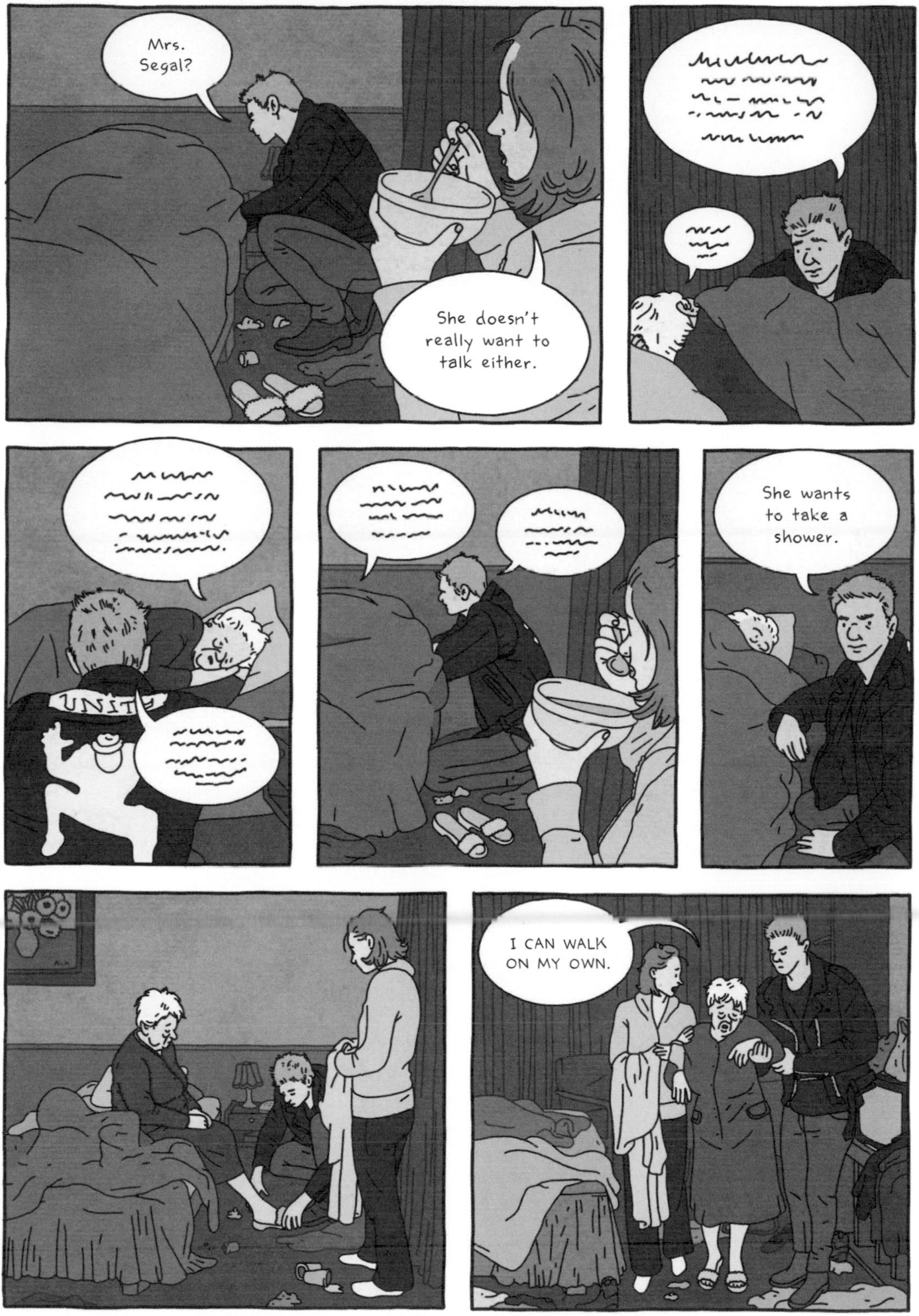
Mrs. Segal?
She doesn't really want to talk either.
She wants to take a shower.
I CAN WALK ON MY OWN.

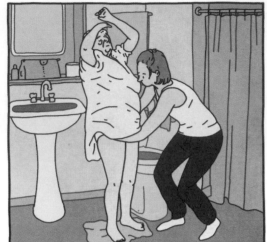

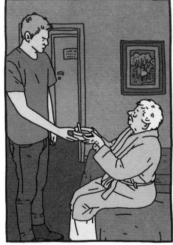

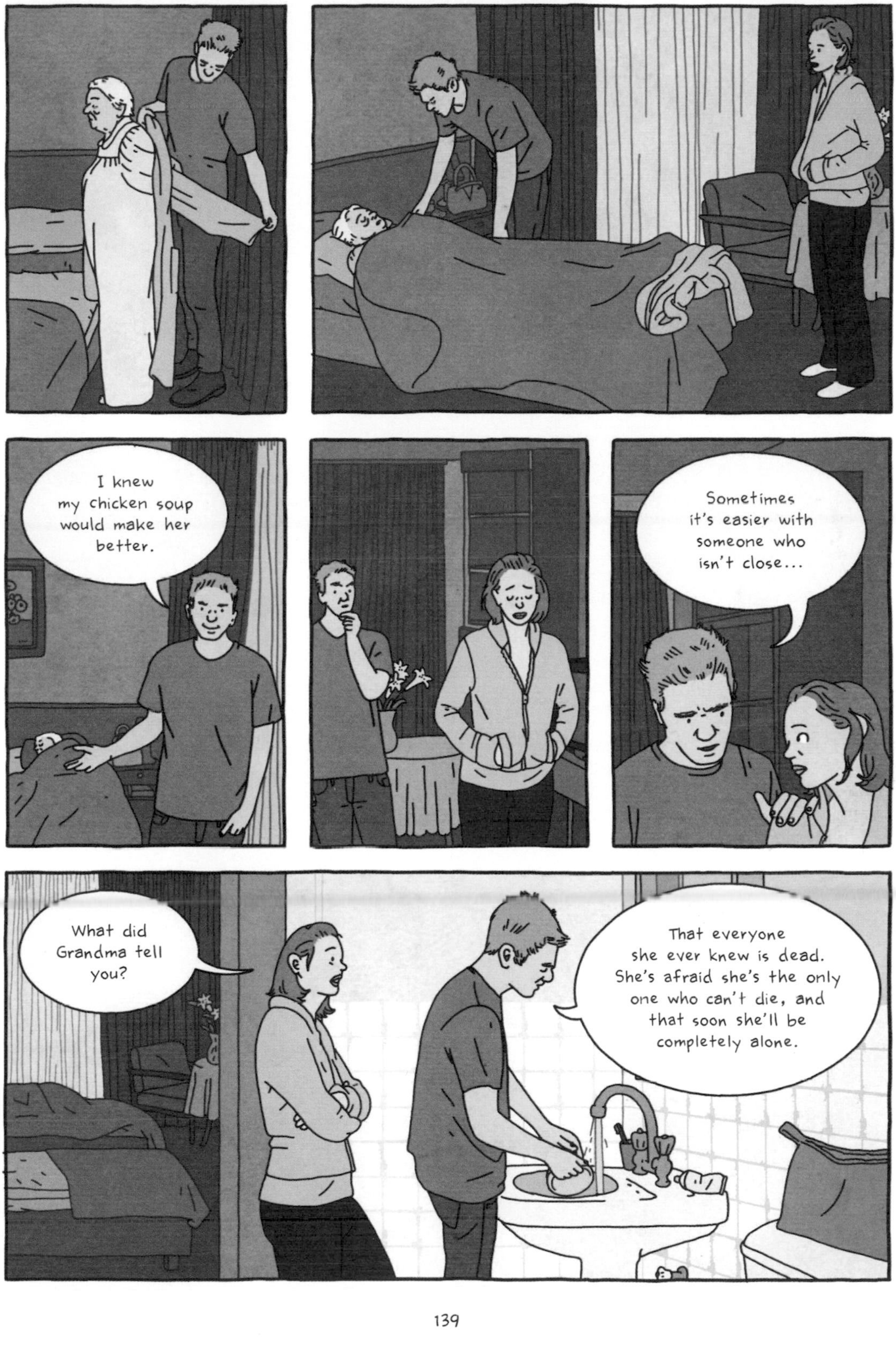
I knew my chicken soup would make her better.
Sometimes it's easier with someone who isn't close...
What did Grandma tell you?
That everyone she ever knew is dead. She's afraid she's the only one who can't die, and that soon she'll be completely alone.

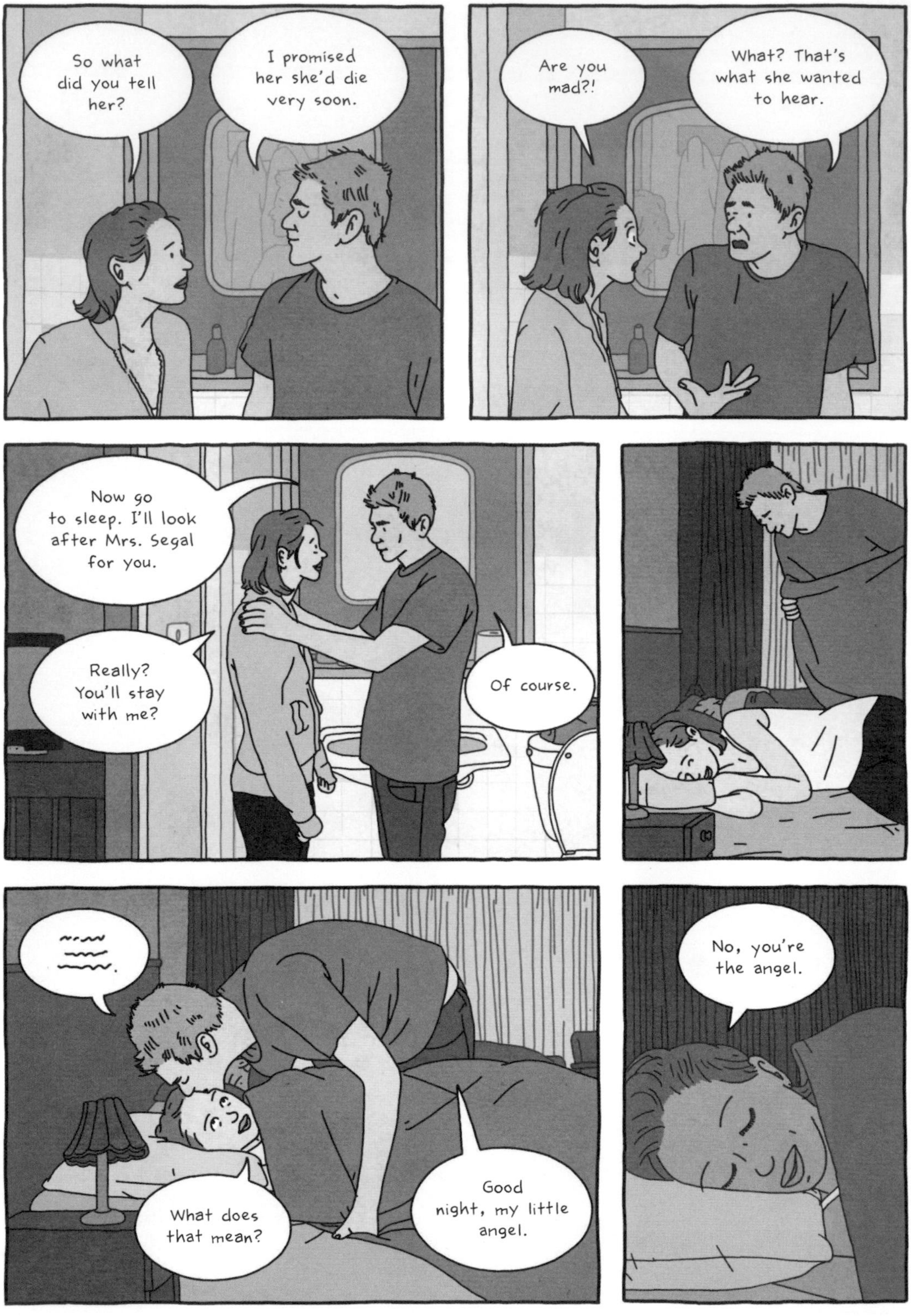
So what did you tell her?
I promised her she'd die very soon.
Are you mad?!
What? That's what she wanted to hear.
Now go to sleep. I'll look after Mrs. Segal for you.
Really? You'll stay with me?
Of course.
What does that mean?
Good night, my little angel.
No, you're the angel.

DAY FIVE

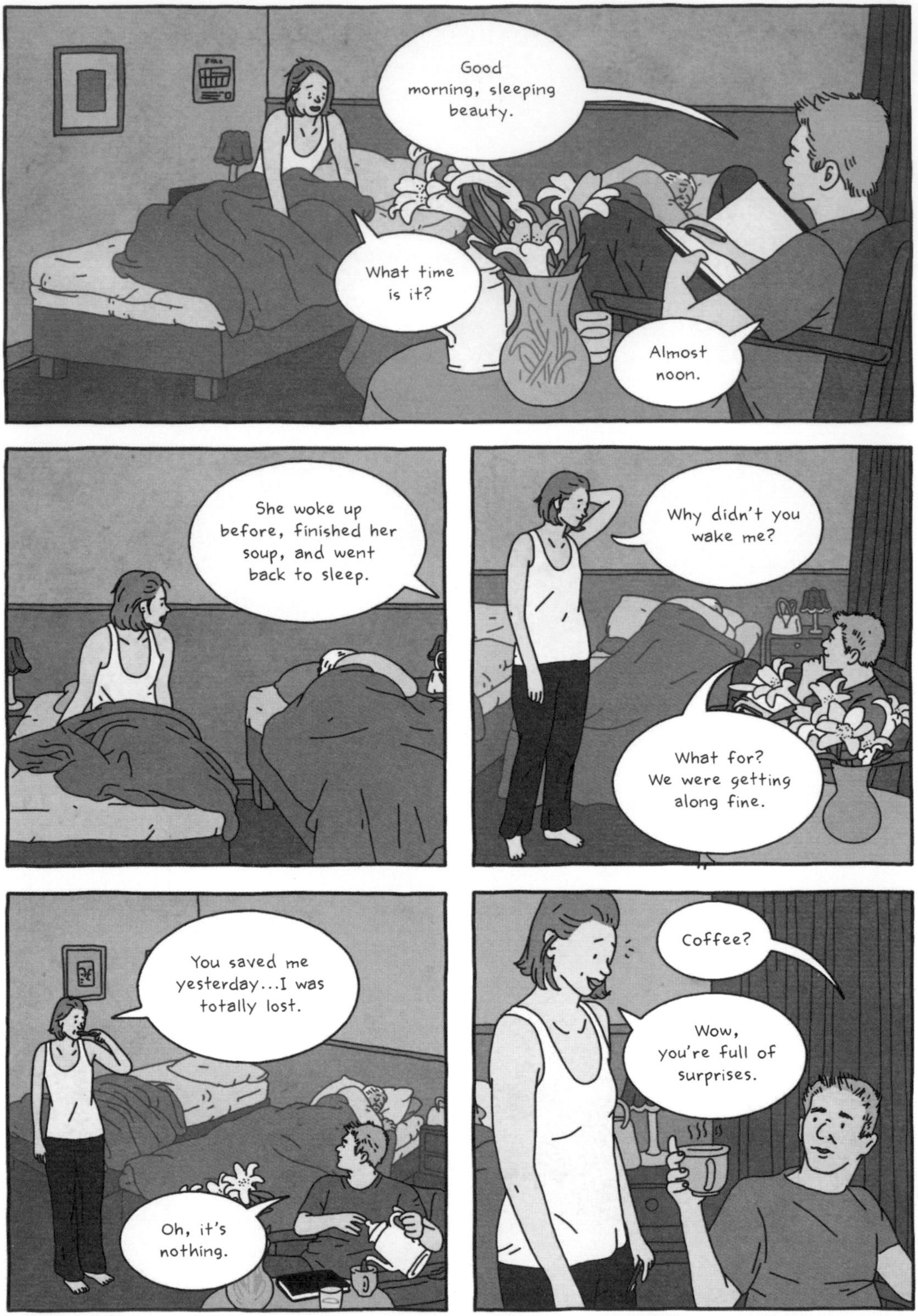
Good morning, sleeping beauty.
What time is it?
Almost noon.
She woke up before, finished her soup, and went back to sleep.
Why didn't you wake me?
What for? We were getting along fine.
You saved me yesterday...I was totally lost.
Oh, it's nothing.
Coffee?
Wow, you're full of surprises.

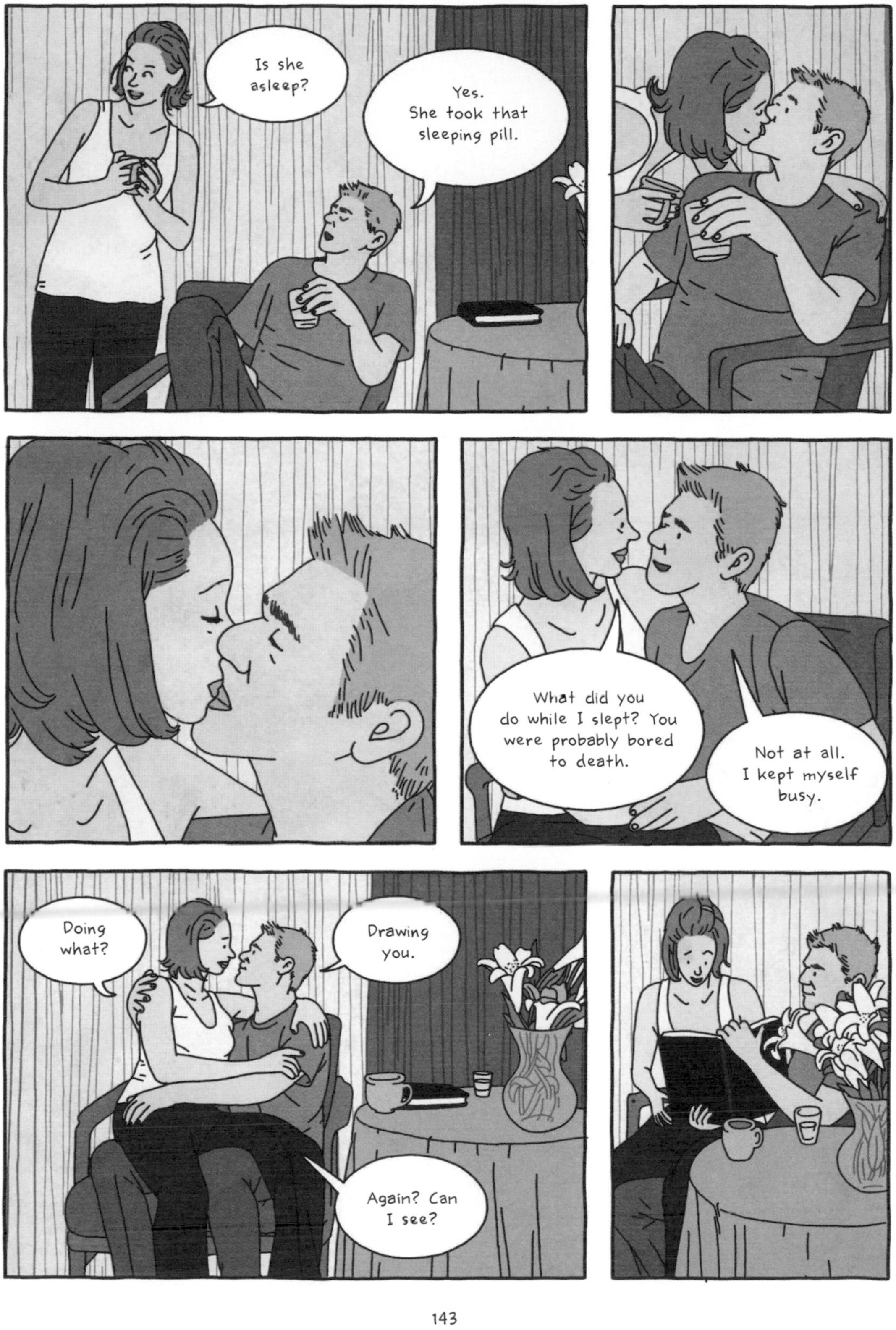
Is she asleep?
Yes. She took that sleeping pill.
What did you do while I slept? You were probably bored to death.
Not at all. I kept myself busy.
Doing what?
Drawing you.
Again? Can I see?

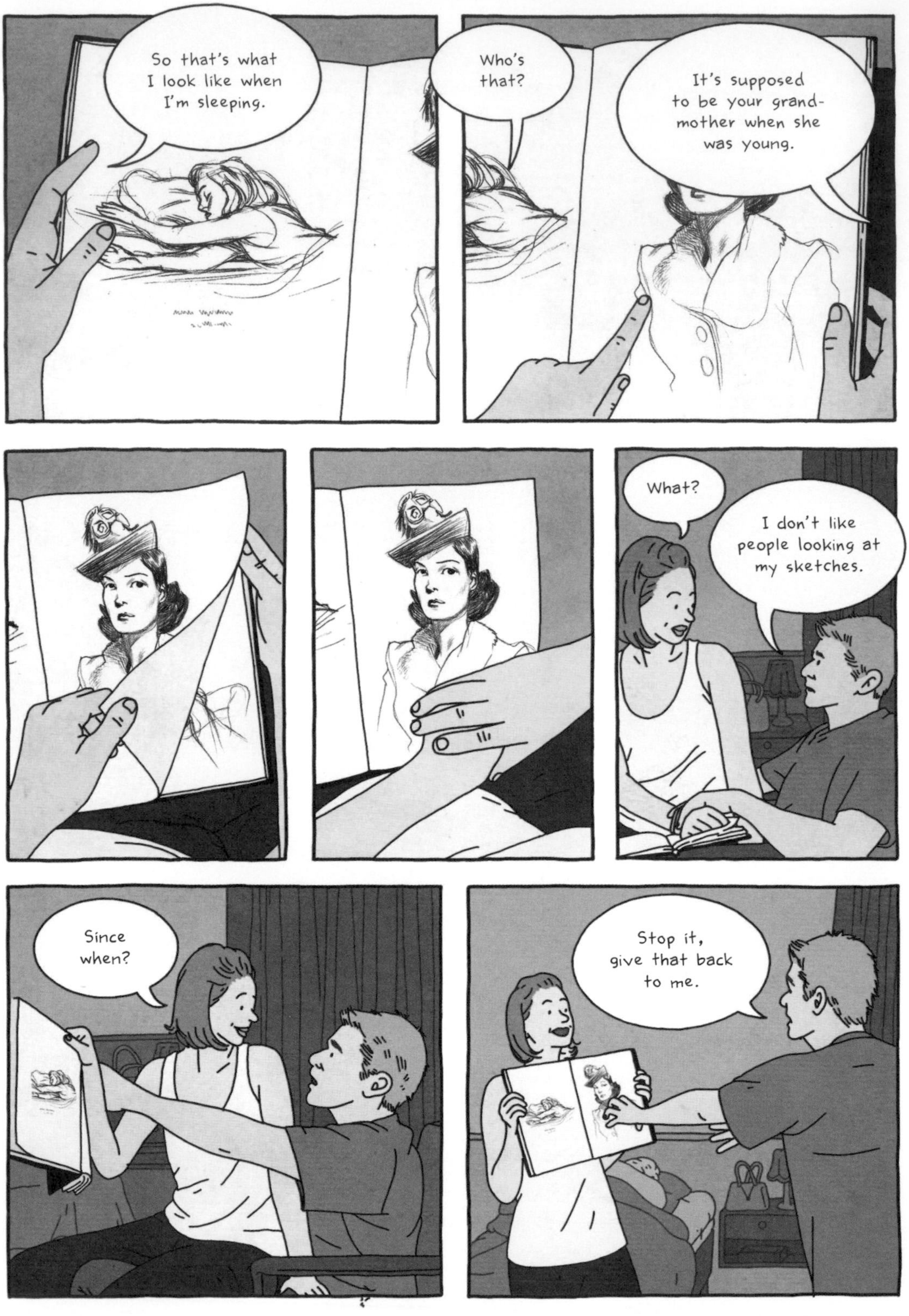
So that's what I look like when I'm sleeping.
Who's that?
It's supposed to be your grand-mother when she was young.
What?
I don't like people looking at my sketches.
Since when?
Stop it, give that back to me.

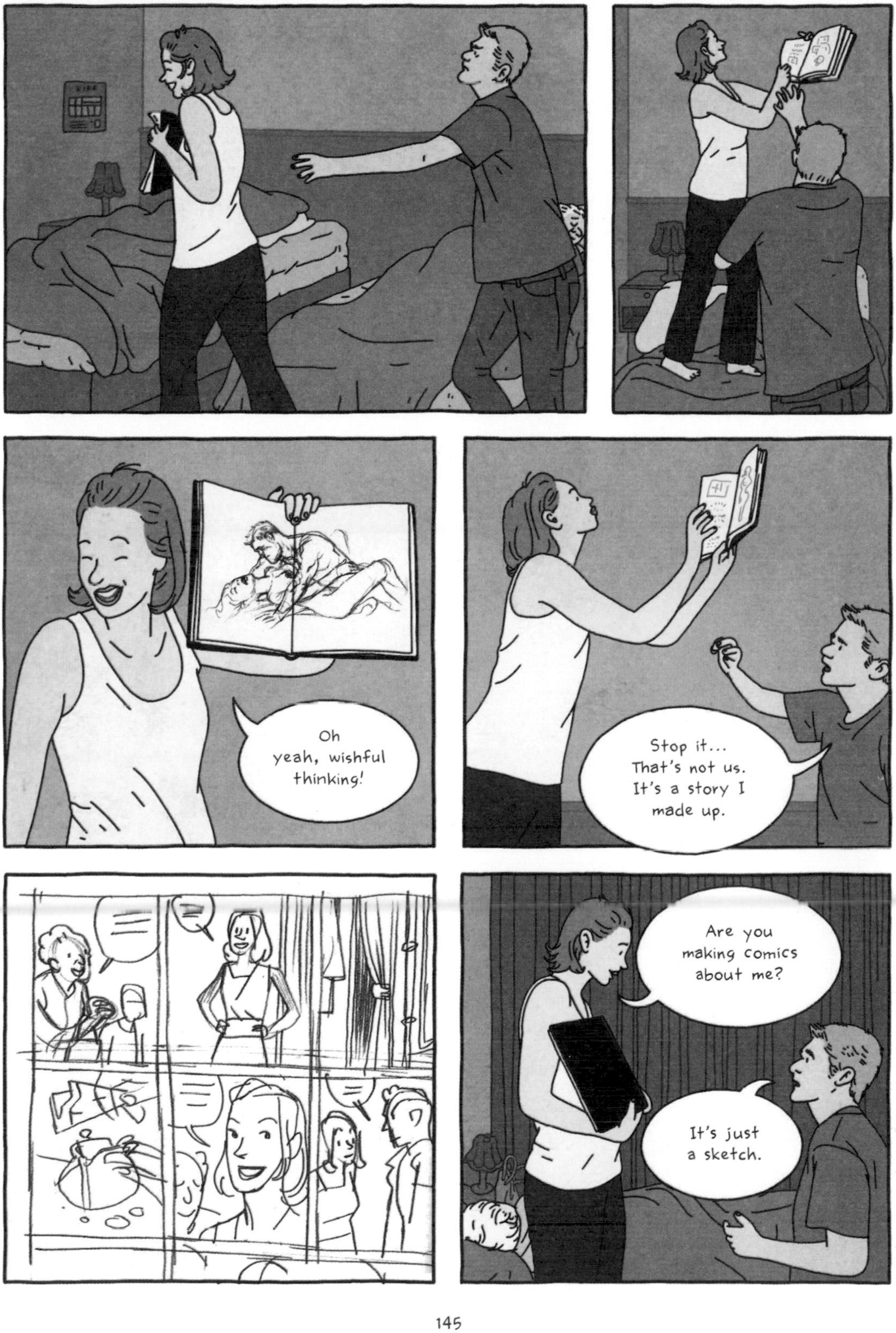
Oh yeah, wishful thinking!
Stop it... That's not us. It's a story I made up.
Are you making comics about me?
It's just a sketch.

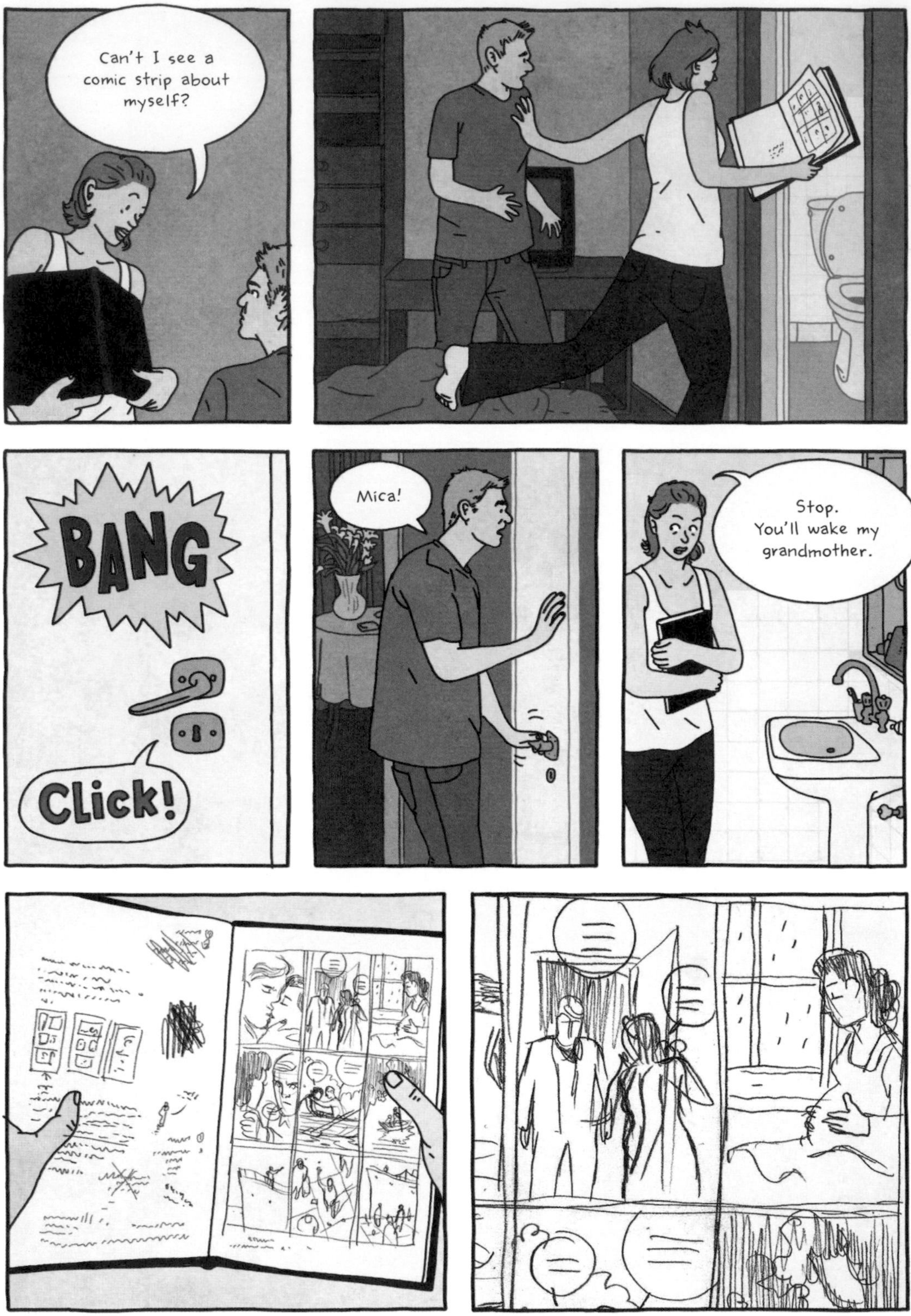
Can't I see a comic strip about myself?
BANG
Click!
Mica!
Stop. You'll wake my grandmother.

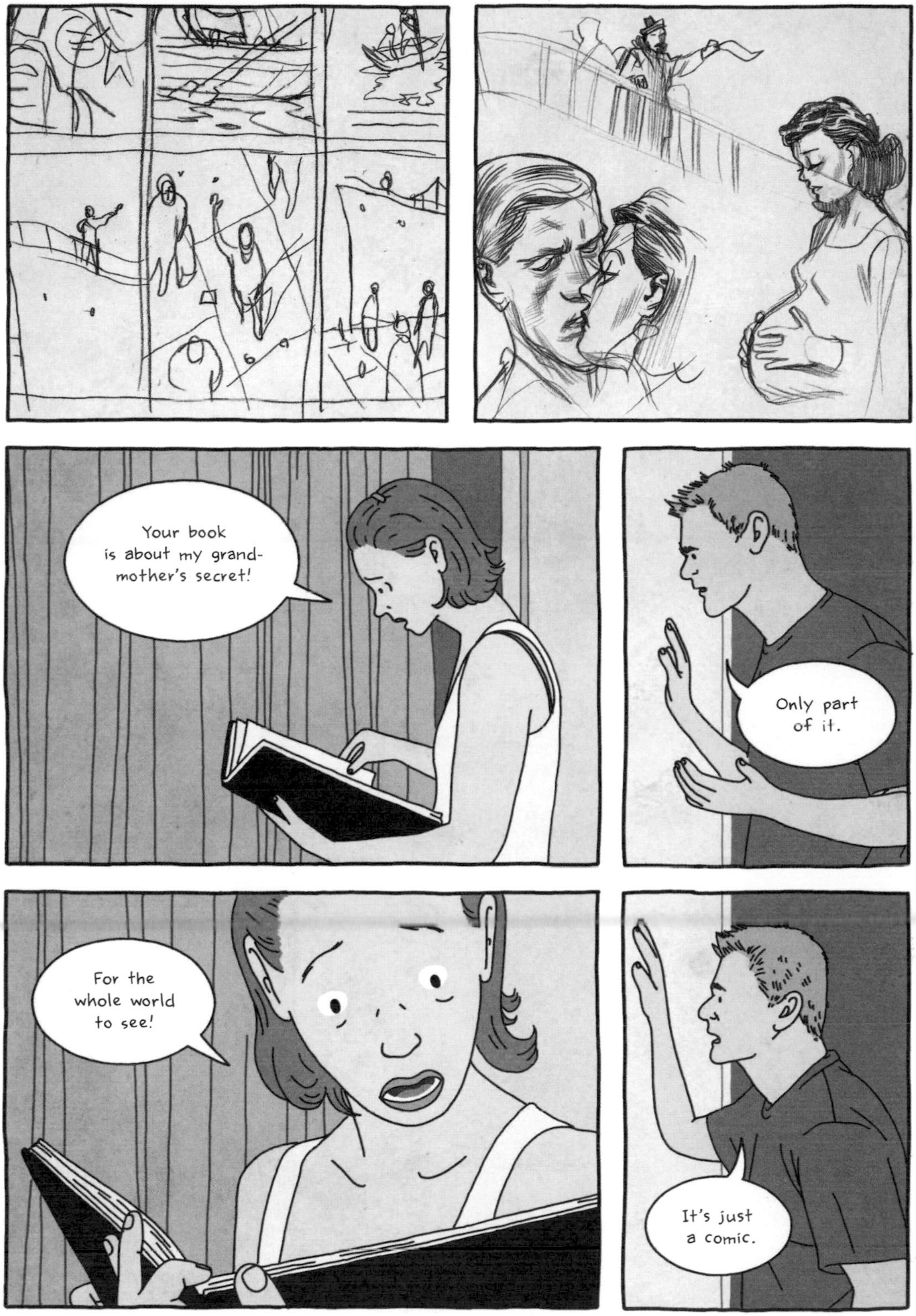
Your book is about my grand-mother's secret!
Only part of it.
For the whole world to see!
It's just a comic.

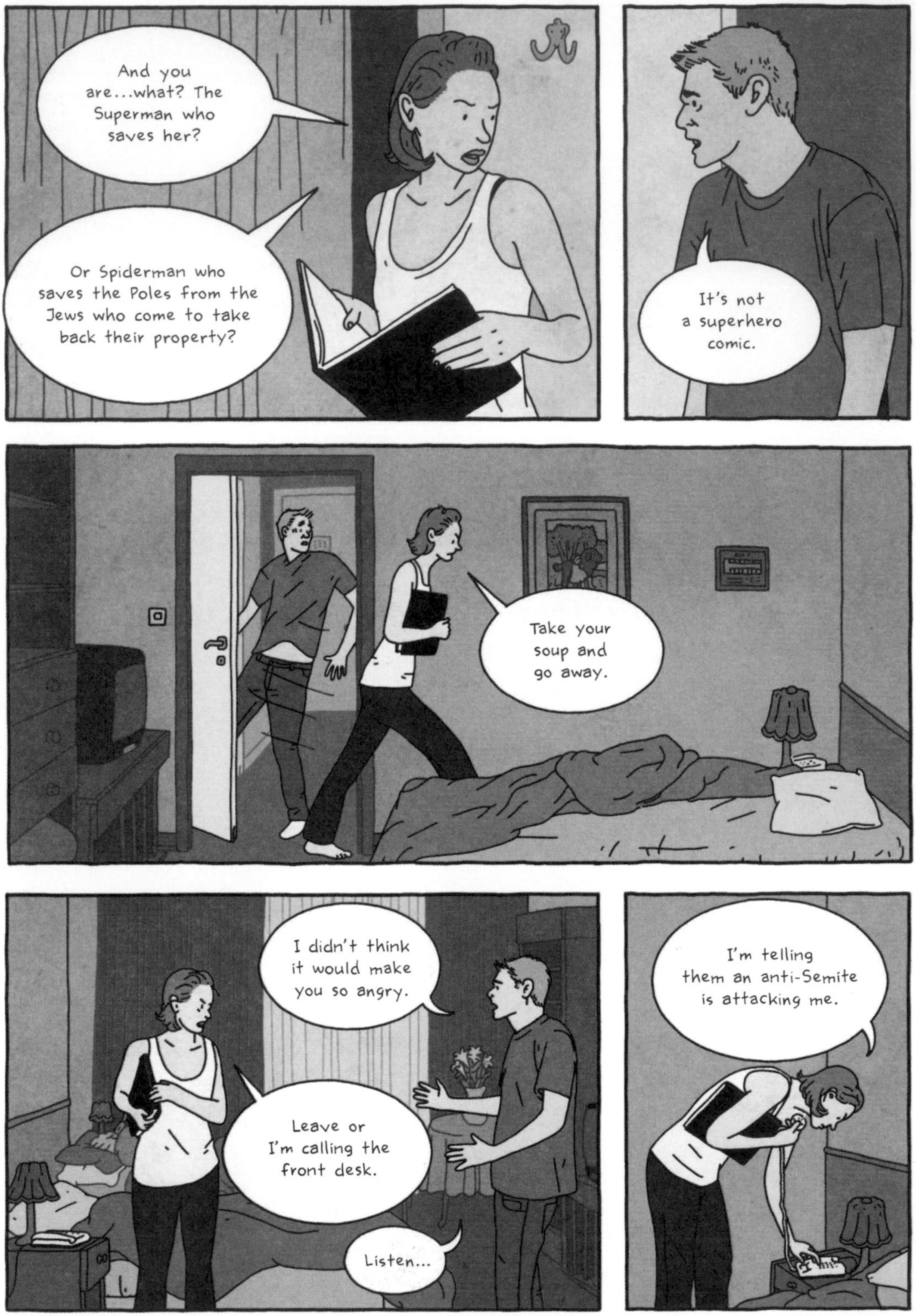
And you are...what? The Superman who saves her?
Or Spiderman who saves the Poles from the Jews who come to take back their property?
It's not a superhero comic.
Take your soup and go away.
I didn't think it would make you so angry.
Leave or I'm calling the front desk.
Listen...
I'm telling them an anti-Semite is attacking me.

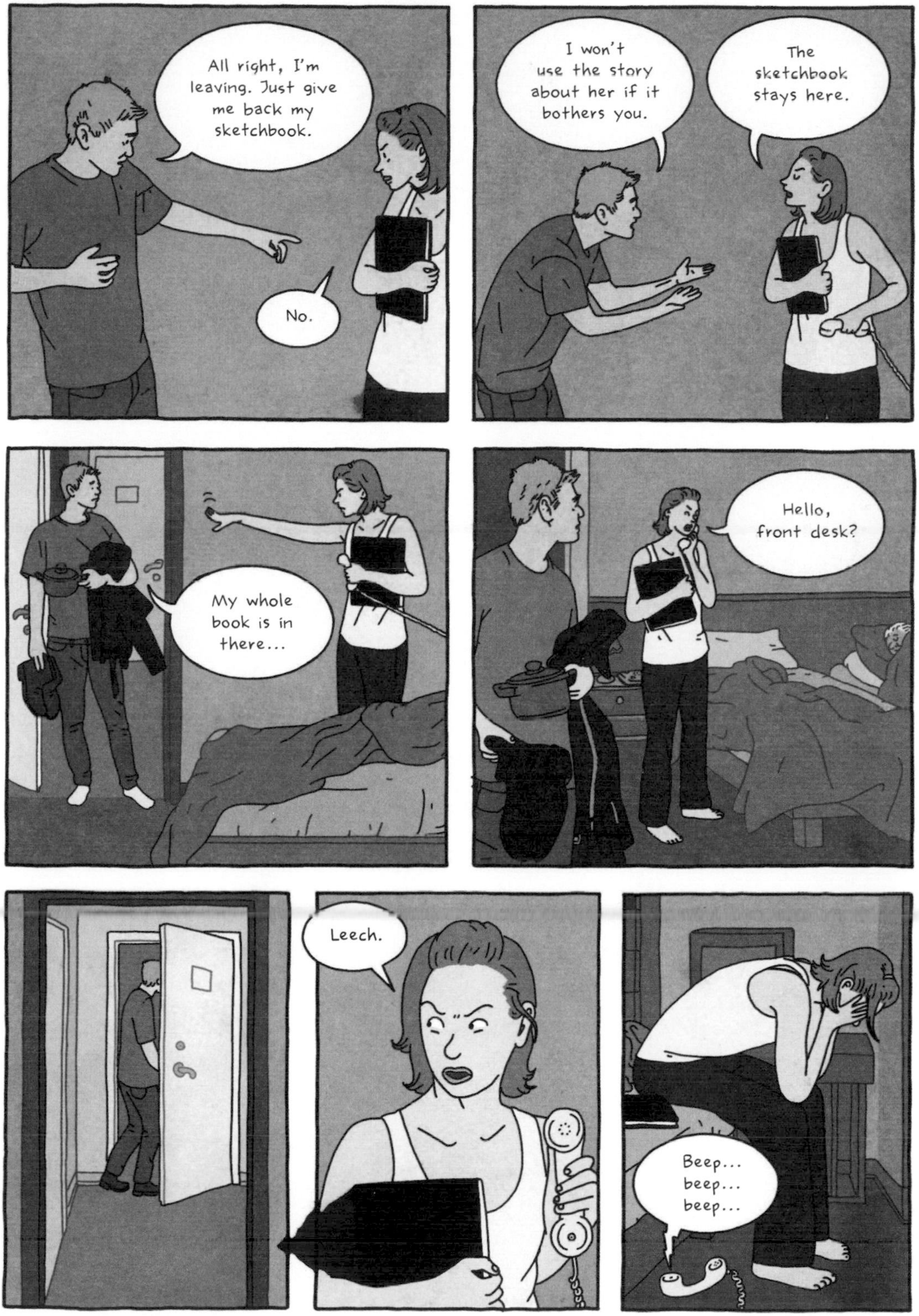
All right, I'm leaving. Just give me back my sketchbook.
No.
I won't use the story about her if it bothers you.
The sketchbook stays here.
My whole book is in there...
Hello, front desk?
Leech.
Beep... beep... beep...

DAY SIX

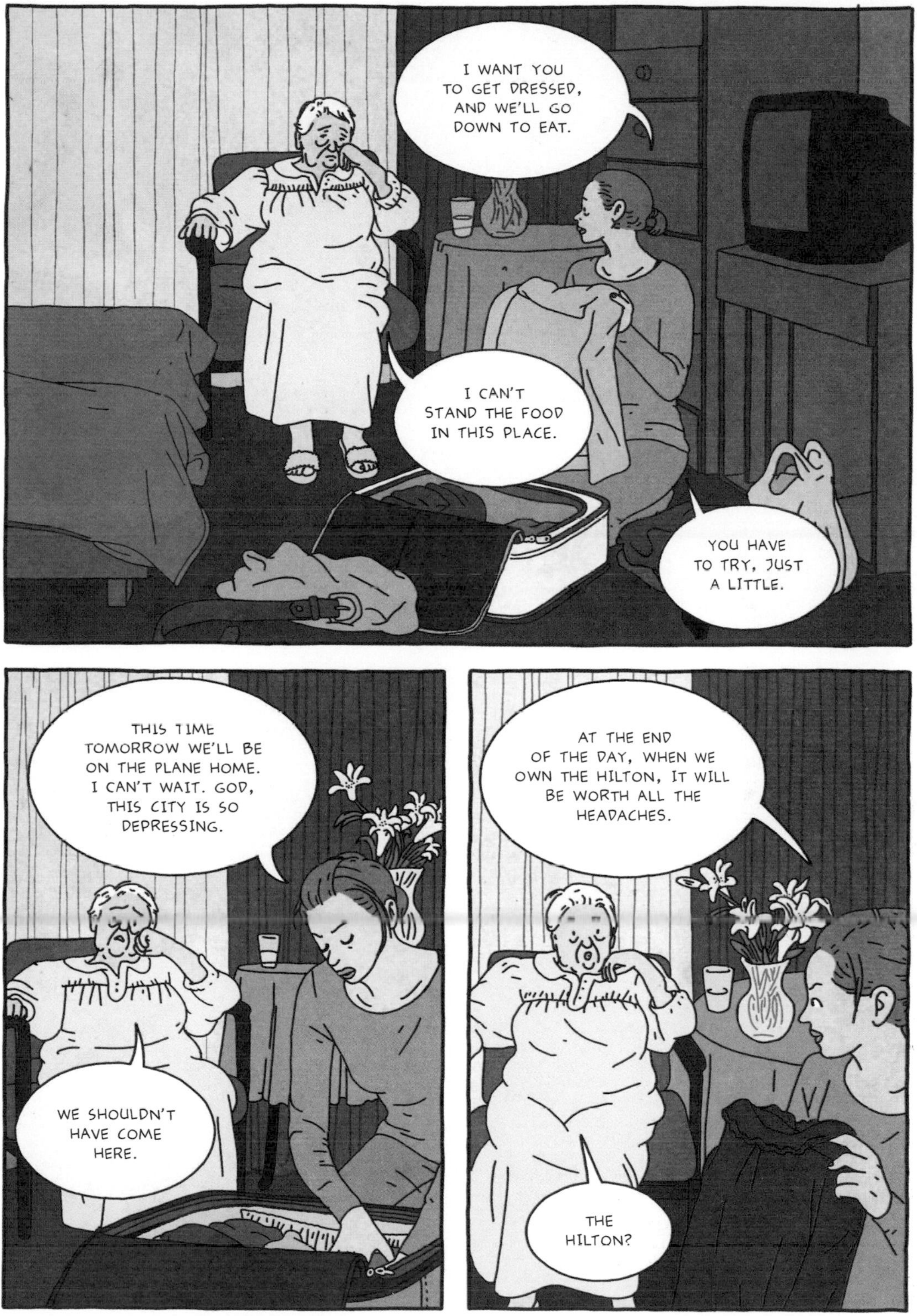
I WANT YOU TO GET DRESSED, AND WE'LL GO DOWN TO EAT.
I CAN'T STAND THE FOOD IN THIS PLACE.
YOU HAVE TO TRY, JUST A LITTLE.
THIS TIME TOMORROW WE'LL BE ON THE PLANE HOME. I CAN'T WAIT. GOD, THIS CITY IS SO DEPRESSING.
WE SHOULDN'T HAVE COME HERE.
AT THE END OF THE DAY, WHEN WE OWN THE HILTON, IT WILL BE WORTH ALL THE HEADACHES.
THE HILTON?

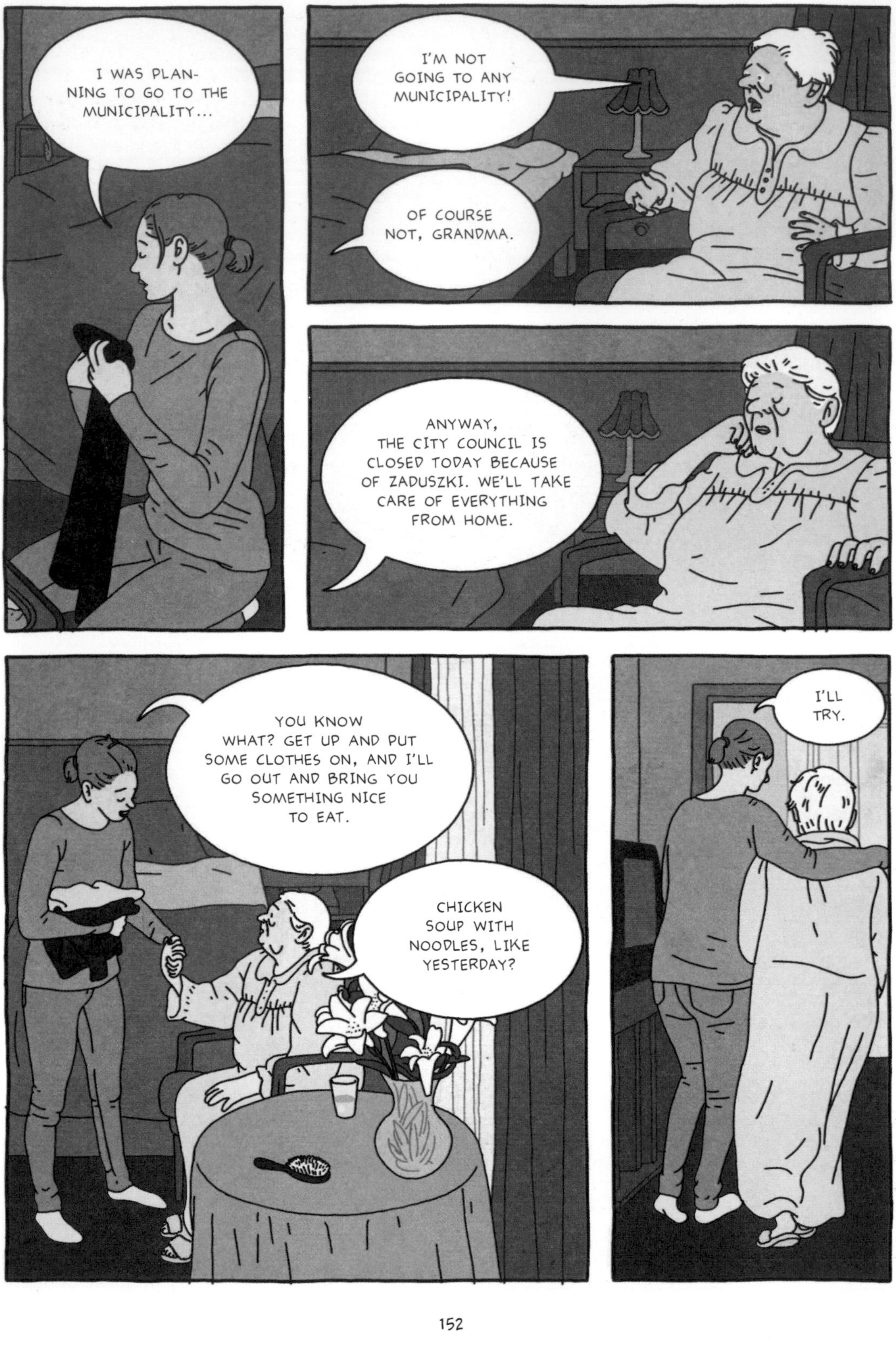
I WAS PLANNING TO GO TO THE MUNICIPALITY...
I'M NOT GOING TO ANY MUNICIPALITY!
OF COURSE NOT, GRANDMA.
ANYWAY, THE CITY COUNCIL IS CLOSED TODAY BECAUSE OF ZADUSZKI. WE'LL TAKE CARE OF EVERYTHING FROM HOME.
YOU KNOW WHAT? GET UP AND PUT SOME CLOTHES ON, AND I'LL GO OUT AND BRING YOU SOMETHING NICE TO EAT.
CHICKEN SOUP WITH NOODLES, LIKE YESTERDAY?
I'LL TRY.

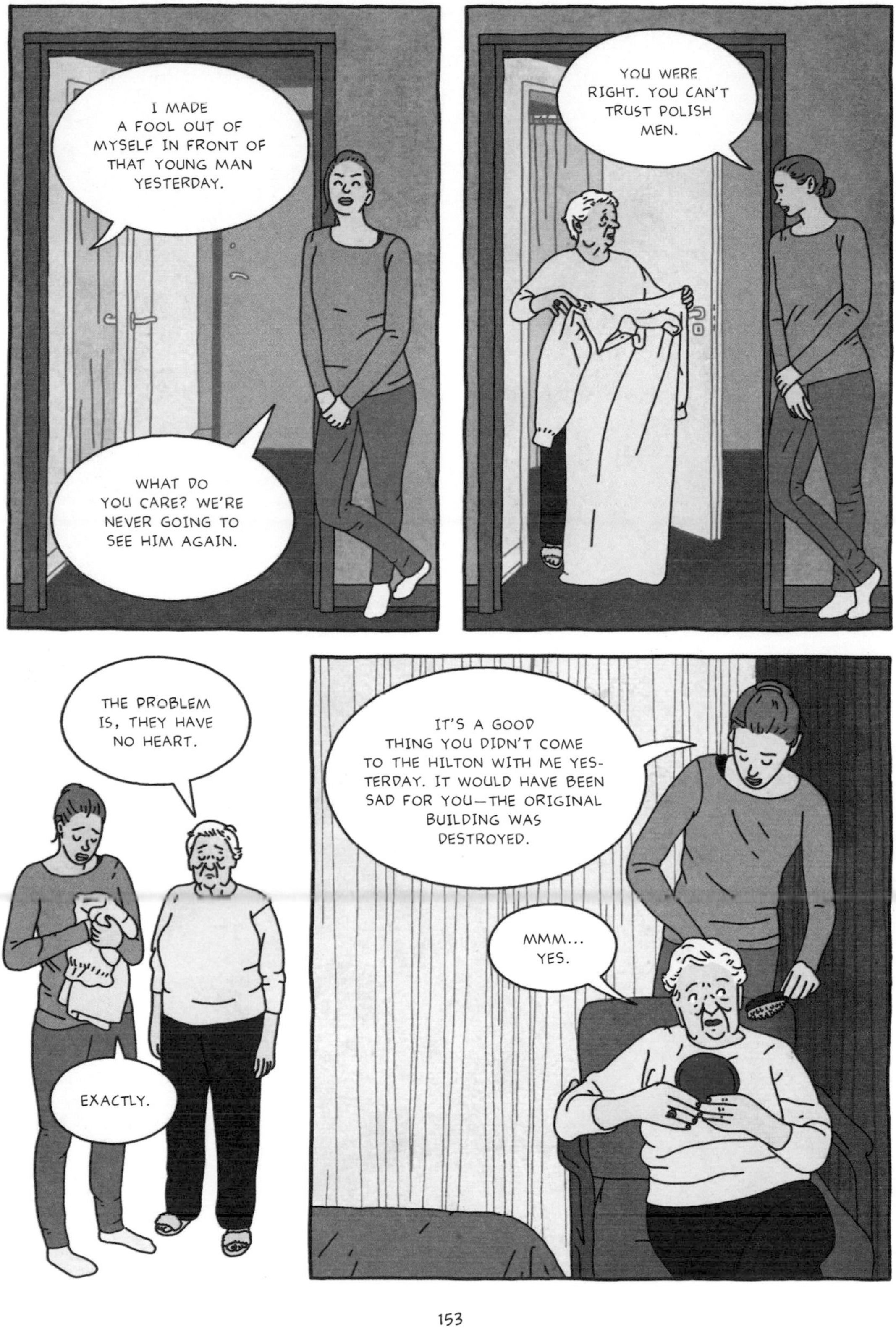
I MADE A FOOL OUT OF MYSELF IN FRONT OF THAT YOUNG MAN YESTERDAY.
WHAT DO YOU CARE? WE'RE NEVER GOING TO SEE HIM AGAIN.
YOU WERE RIGHT. YOU CAN'T TRUST POLISH MEN.
THE PROBLEM IS, THEY HAVE NO HEART.
EXACTLY.
IT'S A GOOD THING YOU DIDN'T COME TO THE HILTON WITH ME YES-TERDAY. IT WOULD HAVE BEEN SAD FOR YOU—THE ORIGINAL BUILDING WAS DESTROYED.
MMM... YES.

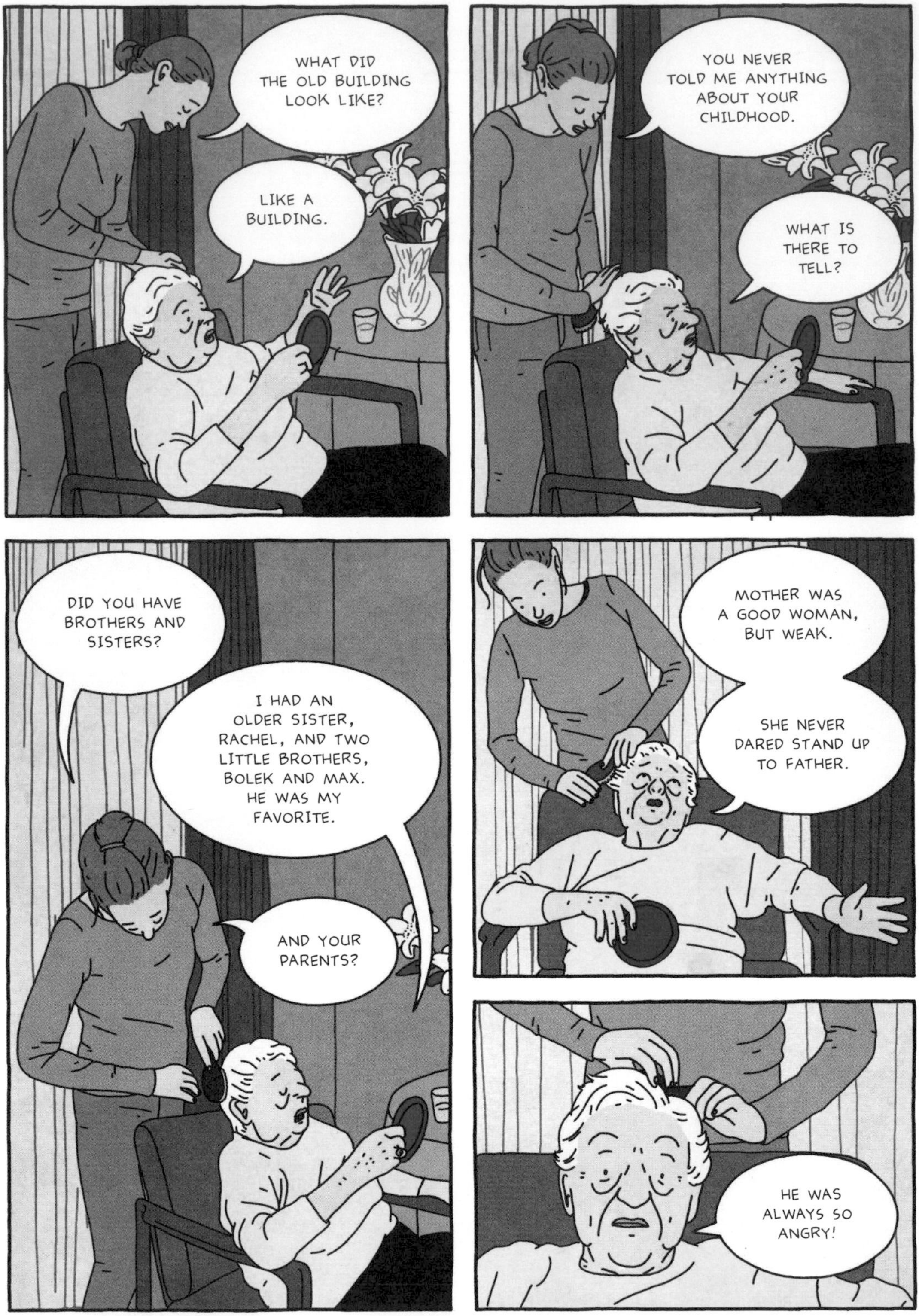
WHAT DID THE OLD BUILDING LOOK LIKE?
LIKE A BUILDING.
YOU NEVER TOLD ME ANYTHING ABOUT YOUR CHILDHOOD.
WHAT IS THERE TO TELL?
DID YOU HAVE BROTHERS AND SISTERS?
I HAD AN OLDER SISTER, RACHEL, AND TWO LITTLE BROTHERS, BOLEK AND MAX. HE WAS MY FAVORITE.
AND YOUR PARENTS?
MOTHER WAS A GOOD WOMAN, BUT WEAK.
SHE NEVER DARED STAND UP TO FATHER.
HE WAS ALWAYS SO ANGRY!

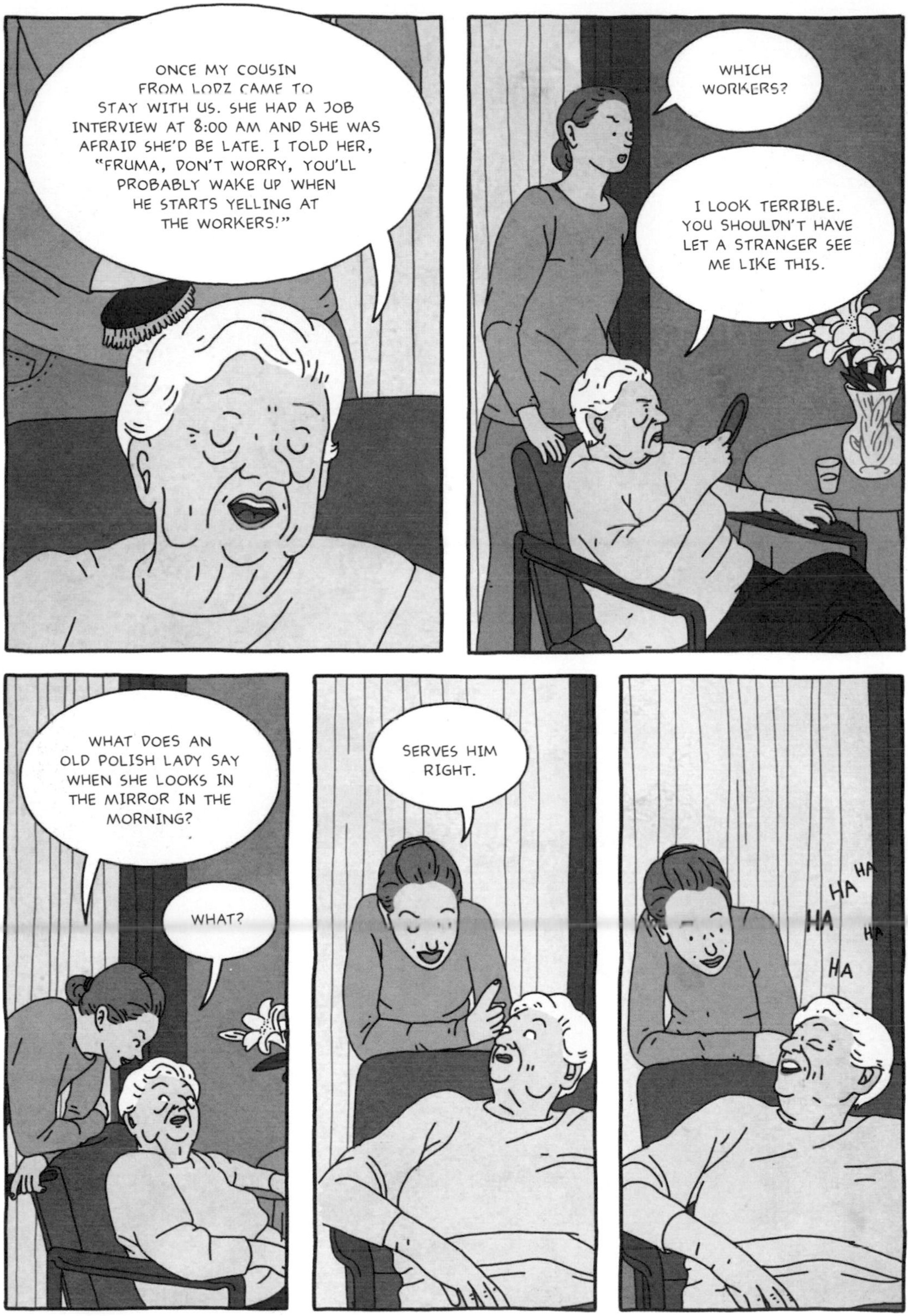
ONCE MY COUSIN FROM LODZ CAME TO STAY WITH US. SHE HAD A JOB INTERVIEW AT 8:00 AM AND SHE WAS AFRAID SHE'D BE LATE. I TOLD HER, "FRUMA, DON'T WORRY, YOU'LL PROBABLY WAKE UP WHEN HE STARTS YELLING AT THE WORKERS!"
WHICH WORKERS?
I LOOK TERRIBLE. YOU SHOULDN'T HAVE LET A STRANGER SEE ME LIKE THIS.
WHAT DOES AN OLD POLISH LADY SAY WHEN SHE LOOKS IN THE MIRROR IN THE MORNING?
WHAT?
SERVES HIM RIGHT.
HA HA HA HA HA

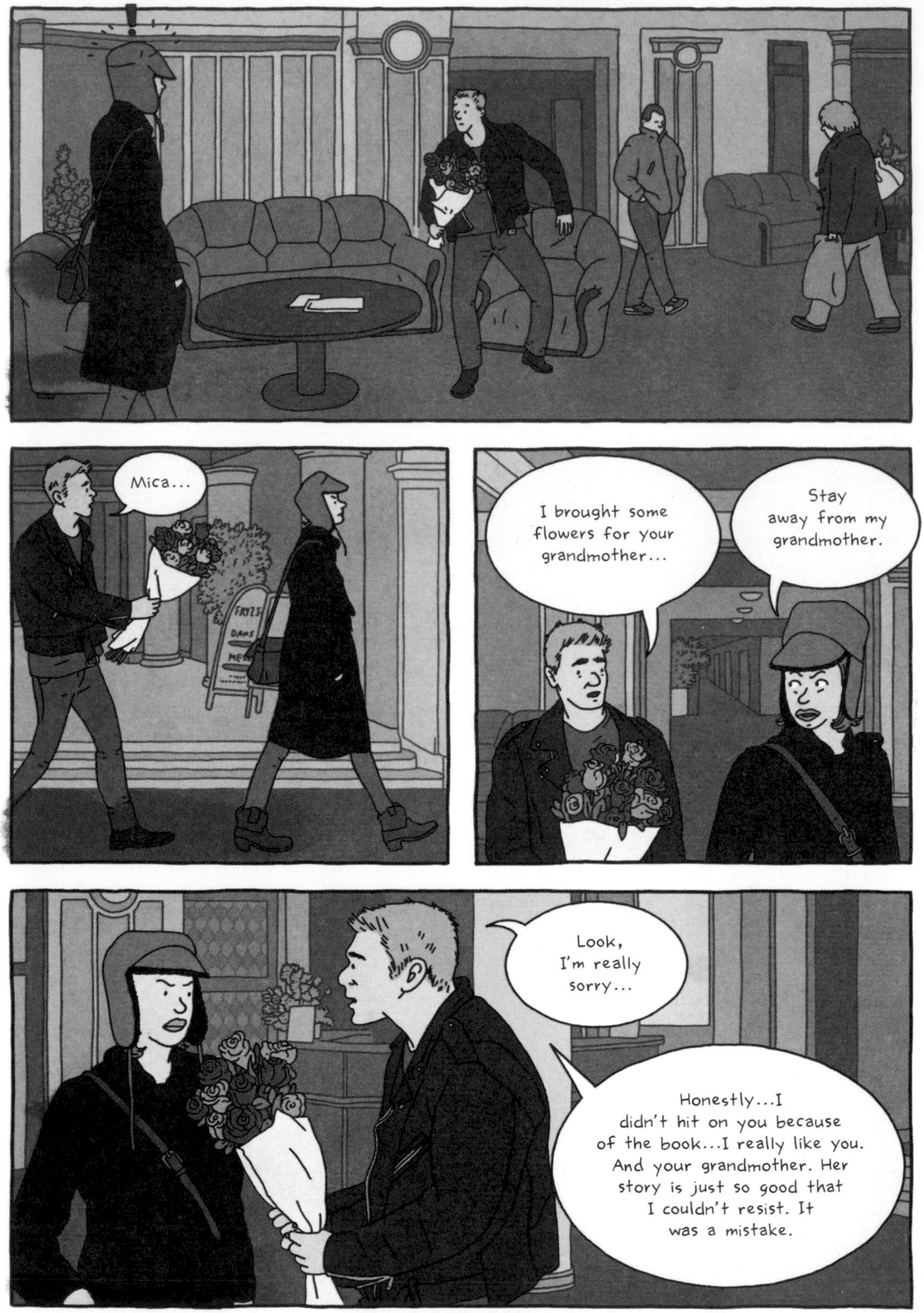
Mica...
I brought some flowers for your grandmother...
Stay away from my grandmother.
Look, I'm really sorry...
Honestly...I didn't hit on you because of the book...I really like you. And your grandmother. Her story is just so good that I couldn't resist. It was a mistake.

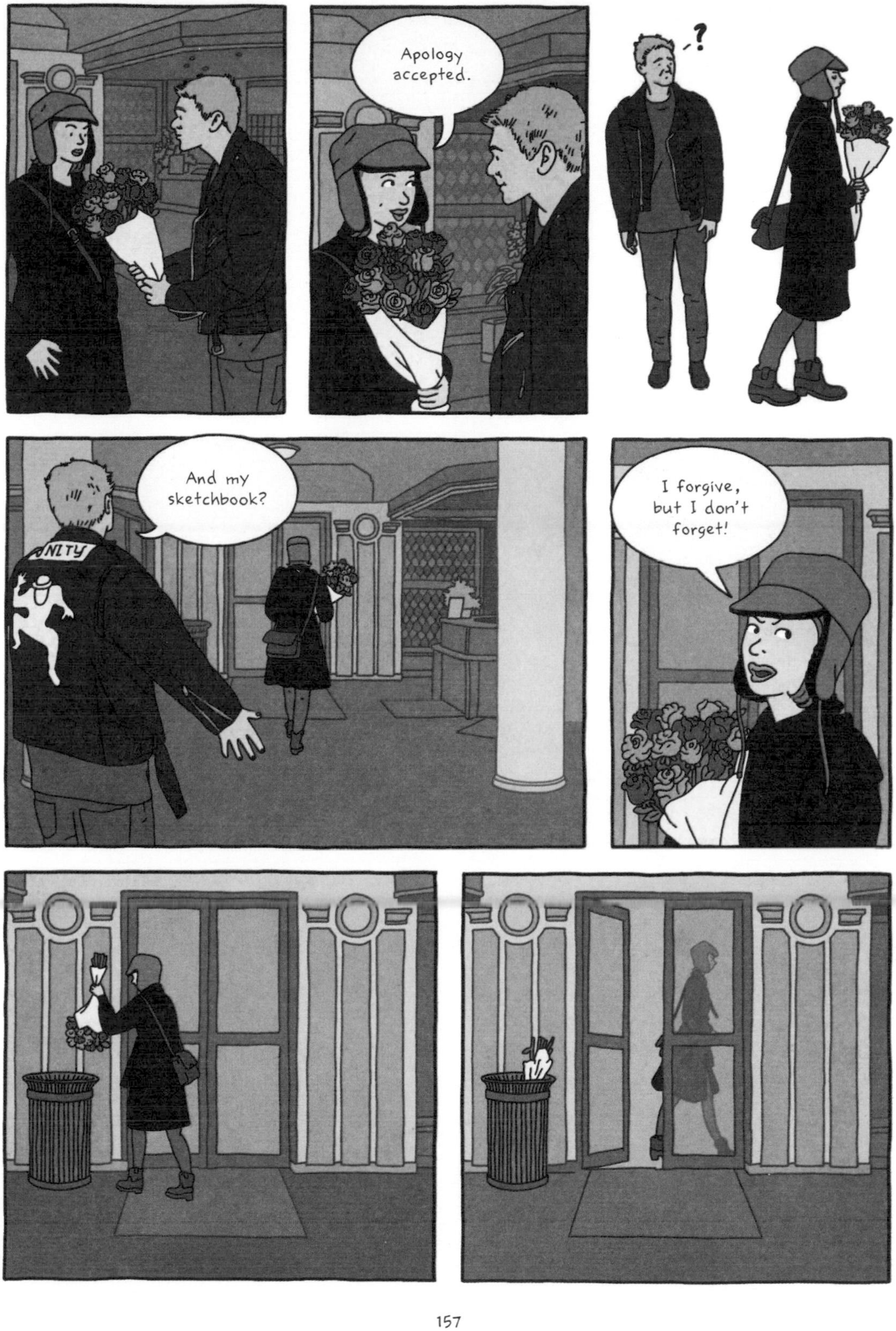

Apology accepted.
?
And my sketchbook?
NITY
I forgive, but I don't forget!

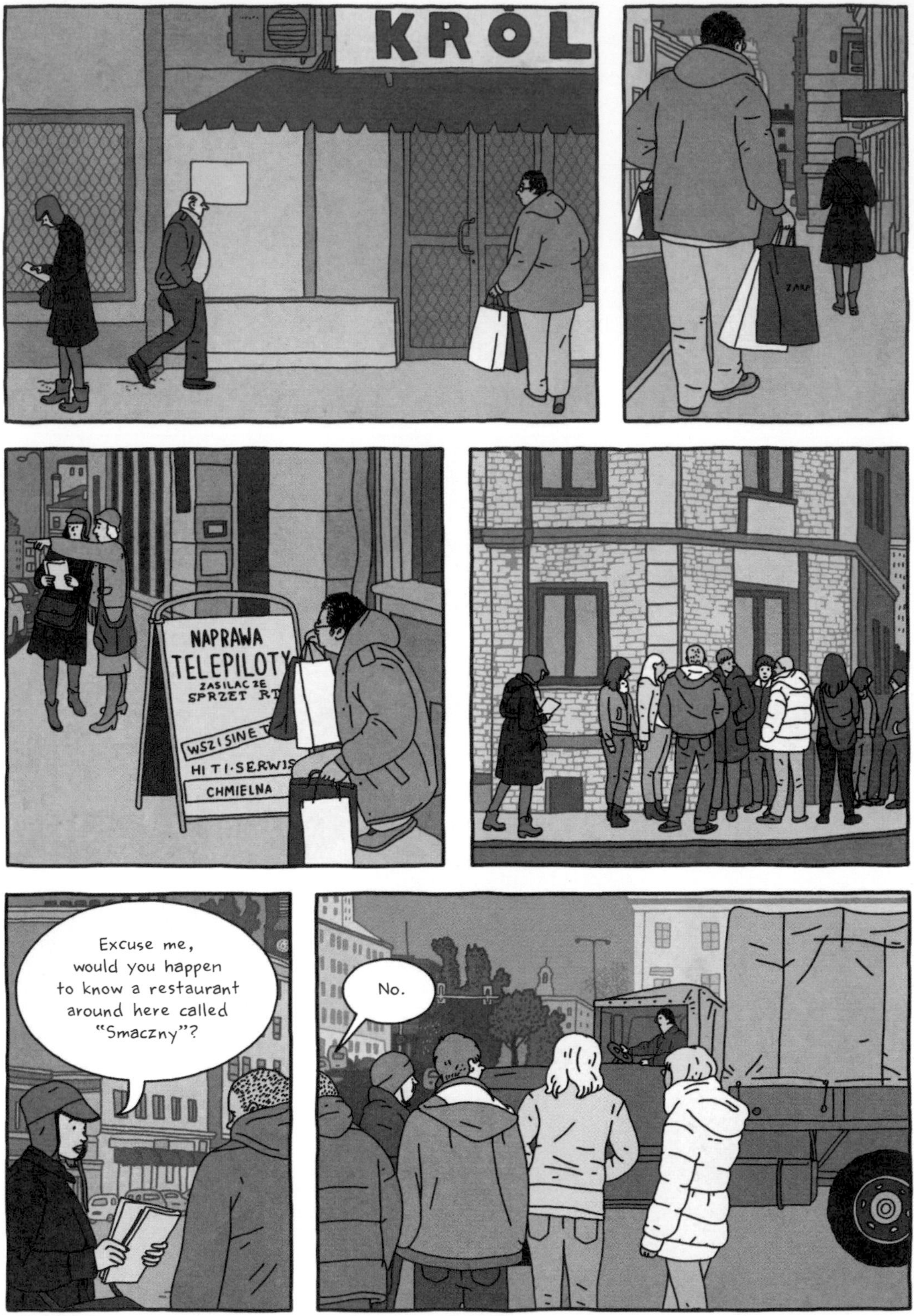
KRÓL
NAPRAWA
TELEPILOTY
ZASILACZE
HI TI·SERWIS
CHMIELNA
Excuse me, would you happen to know a restaurant around here called "Smaczny"?
No.

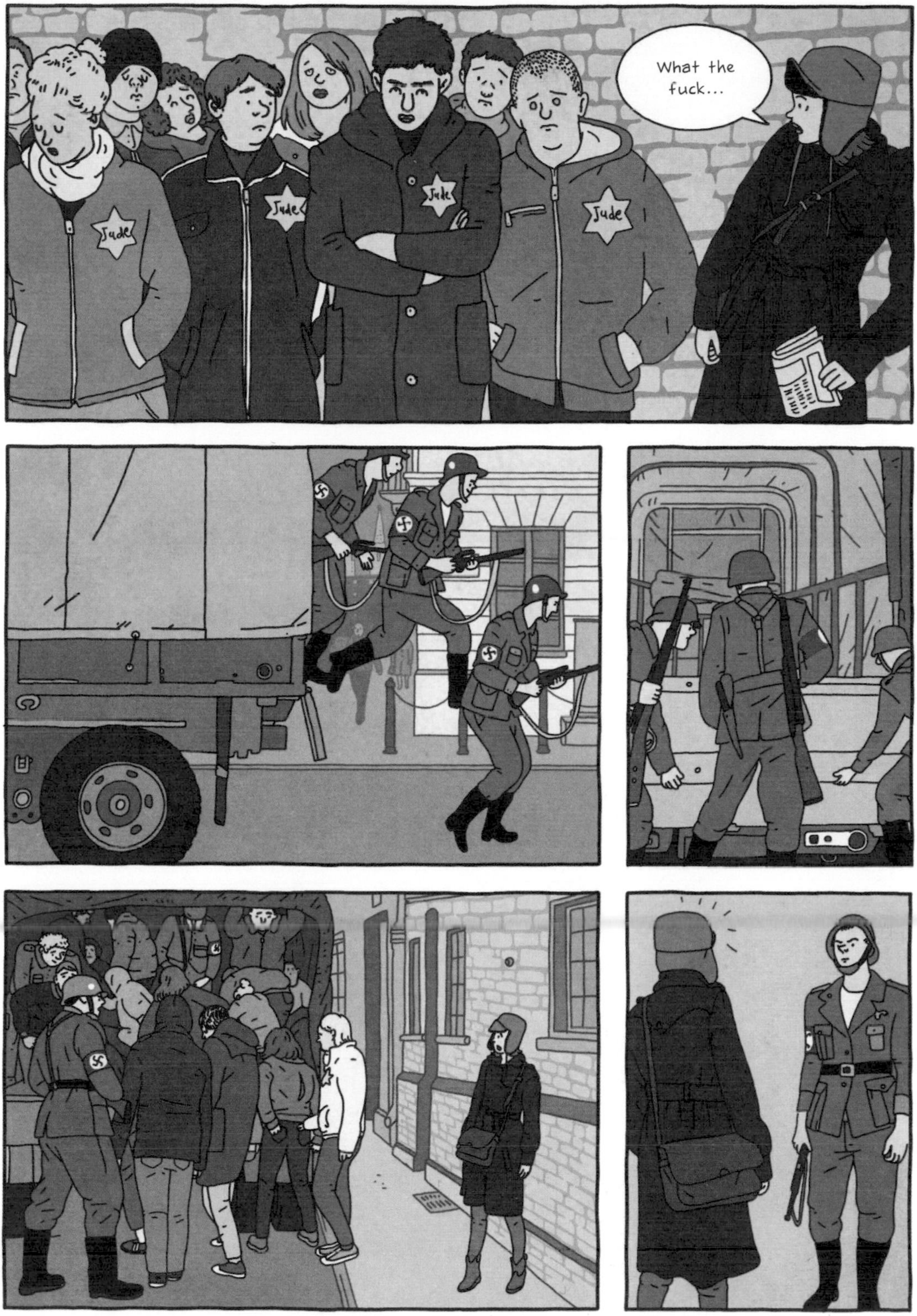
Jude
Jude
Jude
Jude
What the fuck...

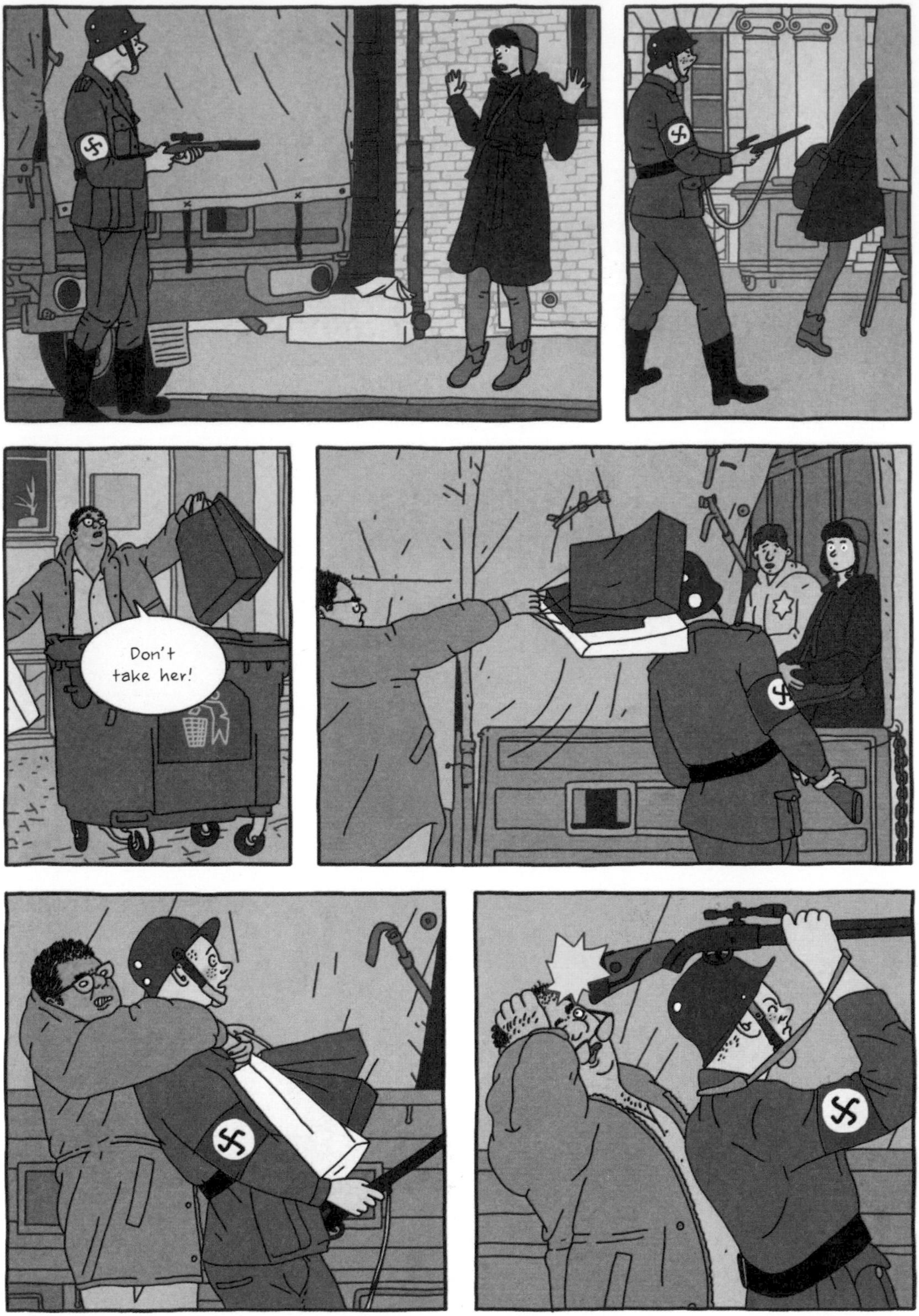
Don't take her!

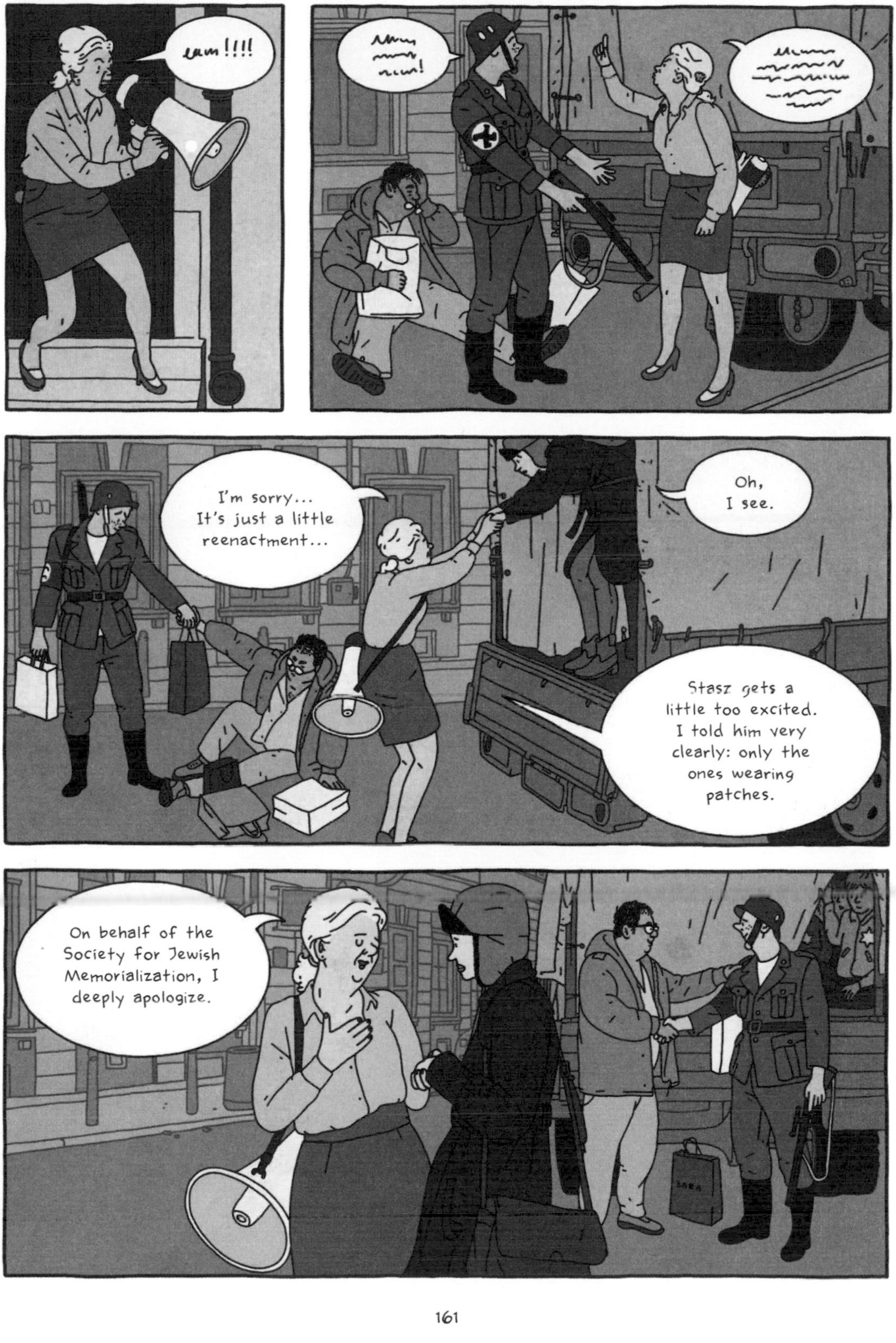
I'm sorry...
It's just a little
reenactment...
Oh,
I see.
Stasz gets a
little too excited.
I told him very
clearly: only the
ones wearing
patches.
On behalf of the
Society for Jewish
Memorialization, I
deeply apologize.

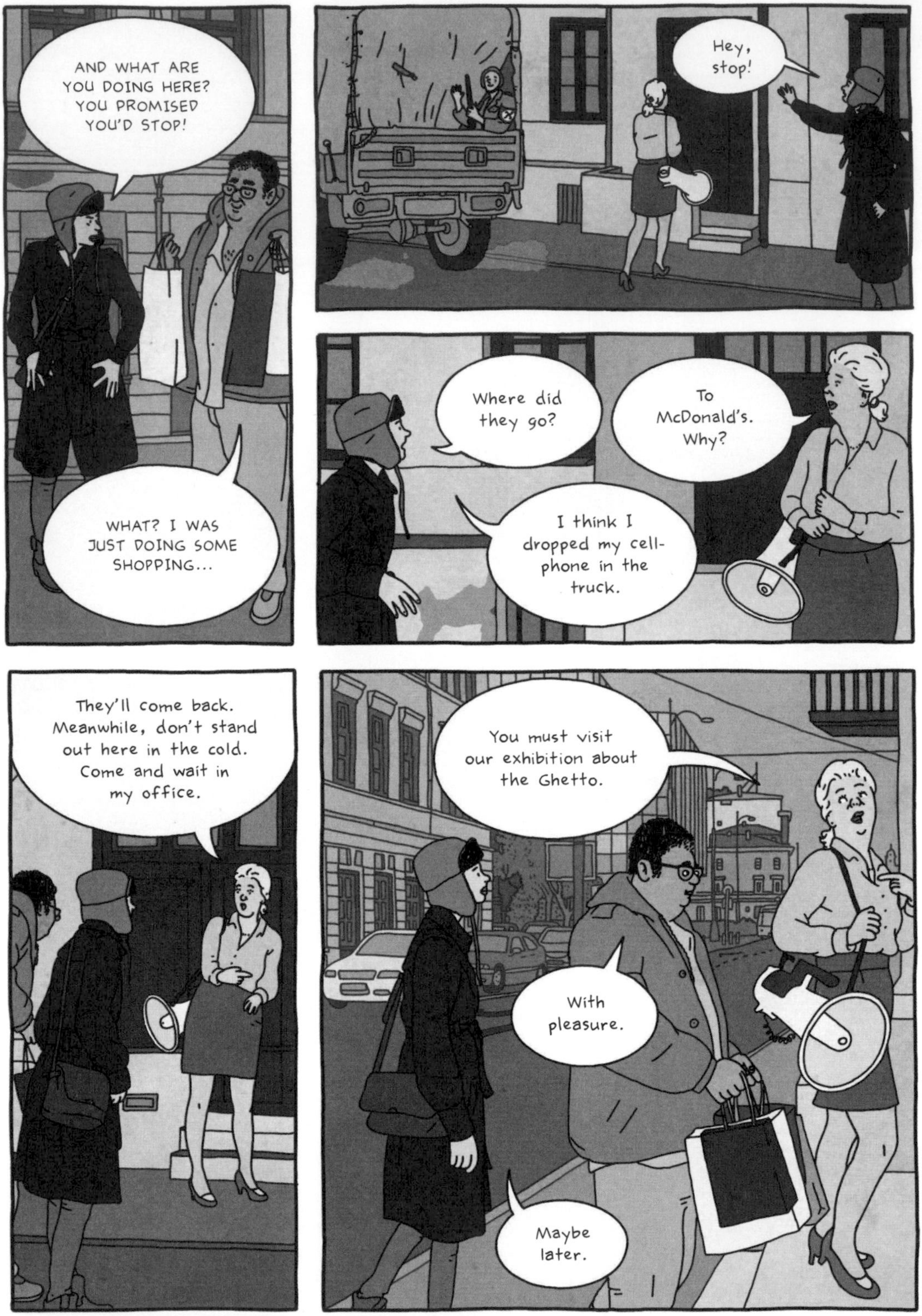

AND WHAT ARE YOU DOING HERE? YOU PROMISED YOU'D STOP!
WHAT? I WAS JUST DOING SOME SHOPPING...
Hey, stop!
Where did they go?
To McDonald's. Why?
I think I dropped my cell-phone in the truck.
They'll come back. Meanwhile, don't stand out here in the cold. Come and wait in my office.
You must visit our exhibition about the Ghetto.
With pleasure.
Maybe later.

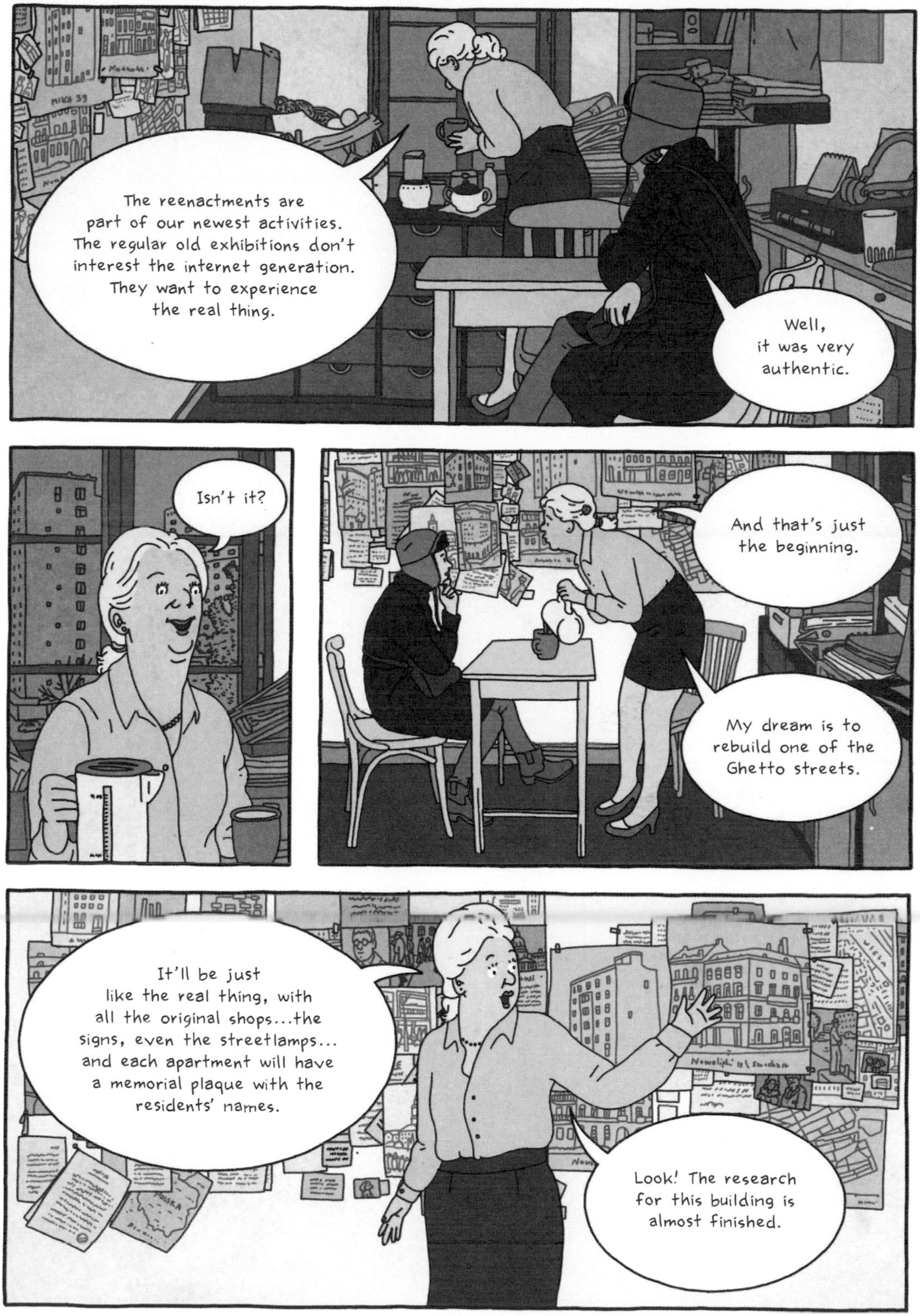
The reenactments are part of our newest activities. The regular old exhibitions don't interest the internet generation. They want to experience the real thing.
Well, it was very authentic.
Isn't it?
And that's just the beginning.
My dream is to rebuild one of the Ghetto streets.
It'll be just like the real thing, with all the original shops...the signs, even the streetlamps... and each apartment will have a memorial plaque with the residents' names.
Look! The research for this building is almost finished.

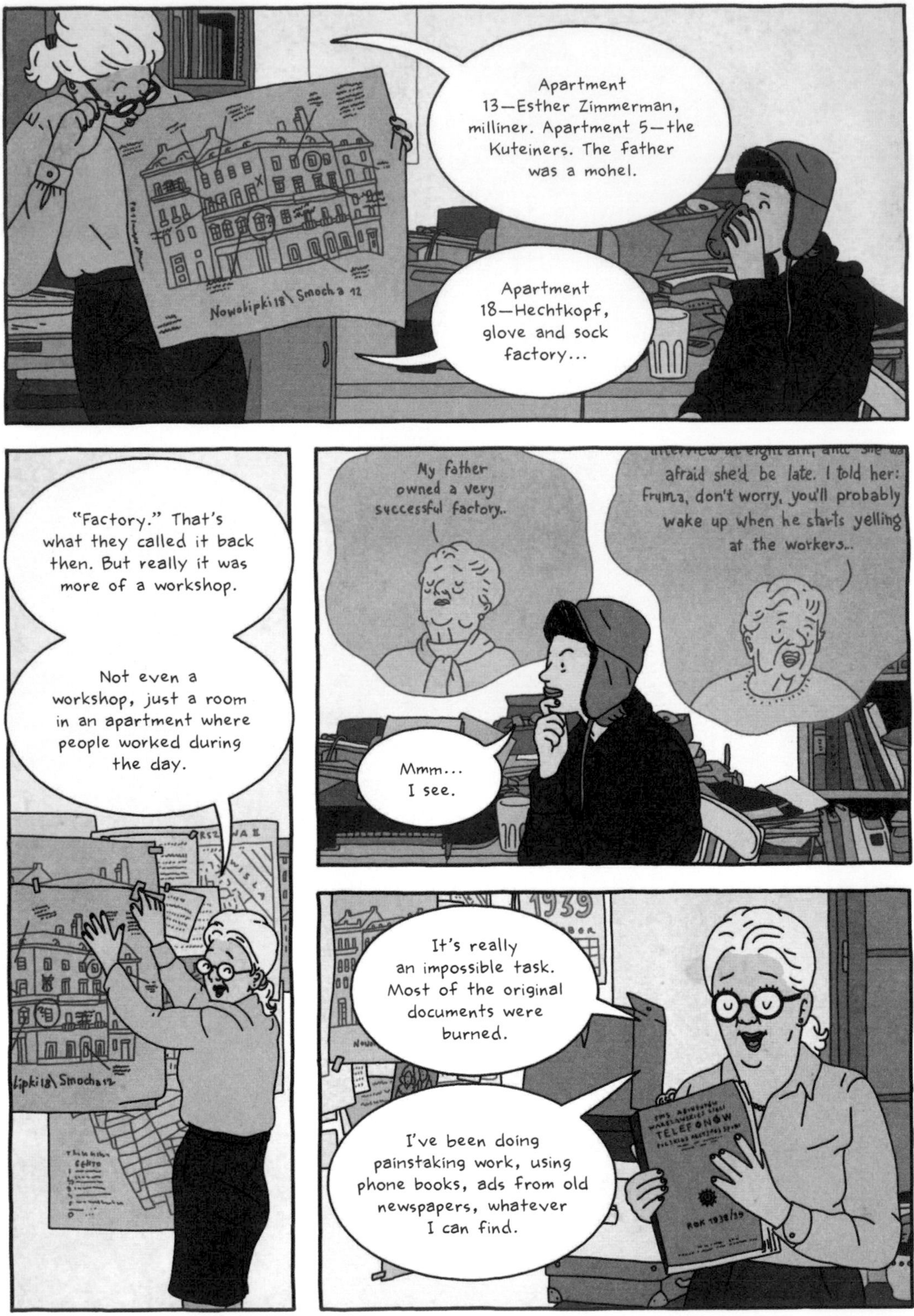
Apartment 13—Esther Zimmerman, milliner. Apartment 5—the Kuteiners. The father was a mohel.
Apartment 18—Hechtkopf, glove and sock factory...
Nowolipki18\ Smocha 12
"Factory." That's what they called it back then. But really it was more of a workshop.
Not even a workshop, just a room in an apartment where people worked during the day.
My father owned a very successful factory..
afraid she'd be late. I told her: Fruma, don't worry, you'll probably wake up when he starts yelling at the workers..
Mmm... I see.
It's really an impossible task. Most of the original documents were burned.
I've been doing painstaking work, using phone books, ads from old newspapers, whatever I can find.
1939
TELEFONÓW
ROK 1938/39

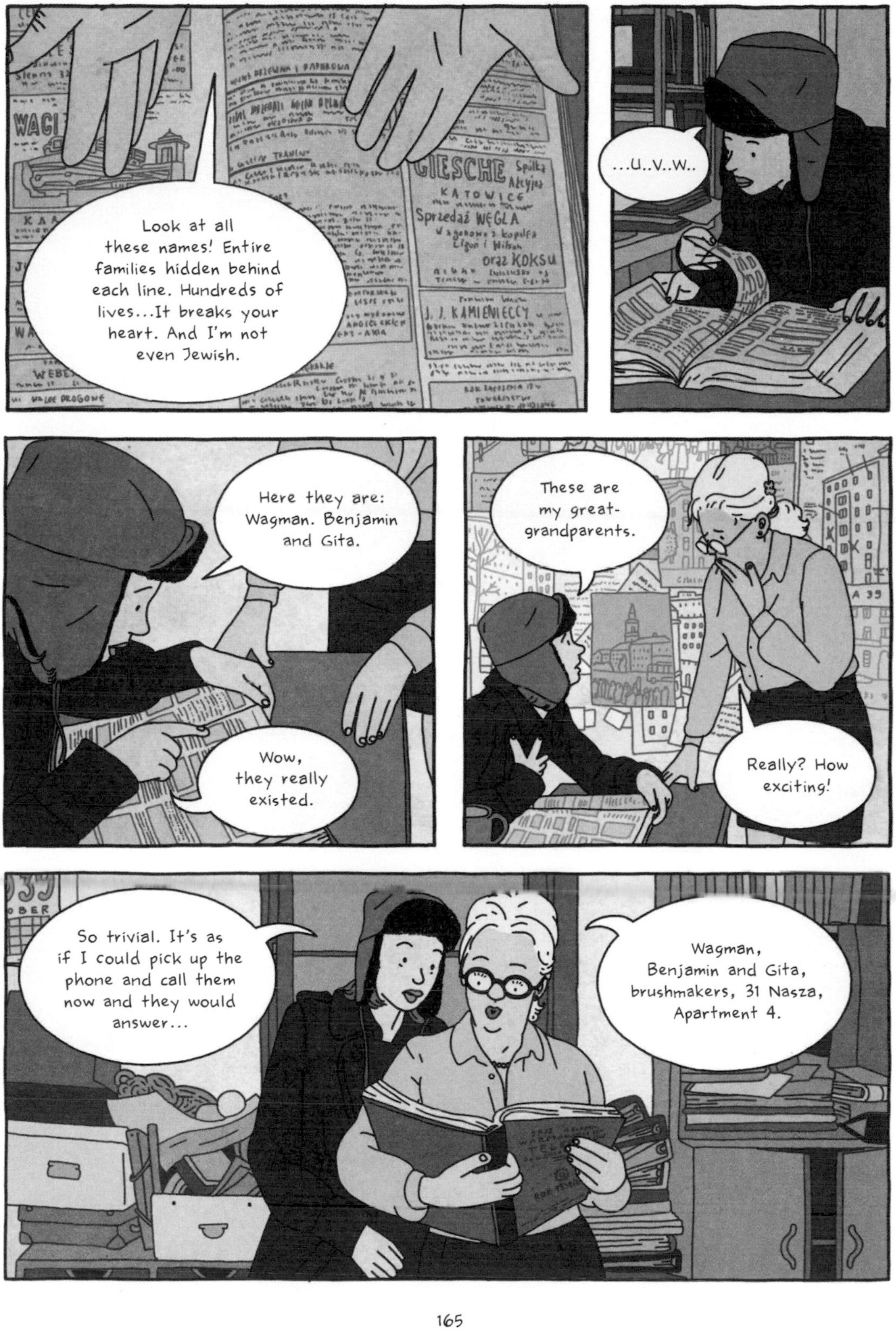
Look at all these names! Entire families hidden behind each line. Hundreds of lives...It breaks your heart. And I'm not even Jewish.
...U..V..W..
Here they are: Wagman. Benjamin and Gita.
Wow, they really existed.
These are my great-grandparents.
Really? How exciting!
So trivial. It's as if I could pick up the phone and call them now and they would answer...
Wagman, Benjamin and Gita, brushmakers, 31 Nasza, Apartment 4.

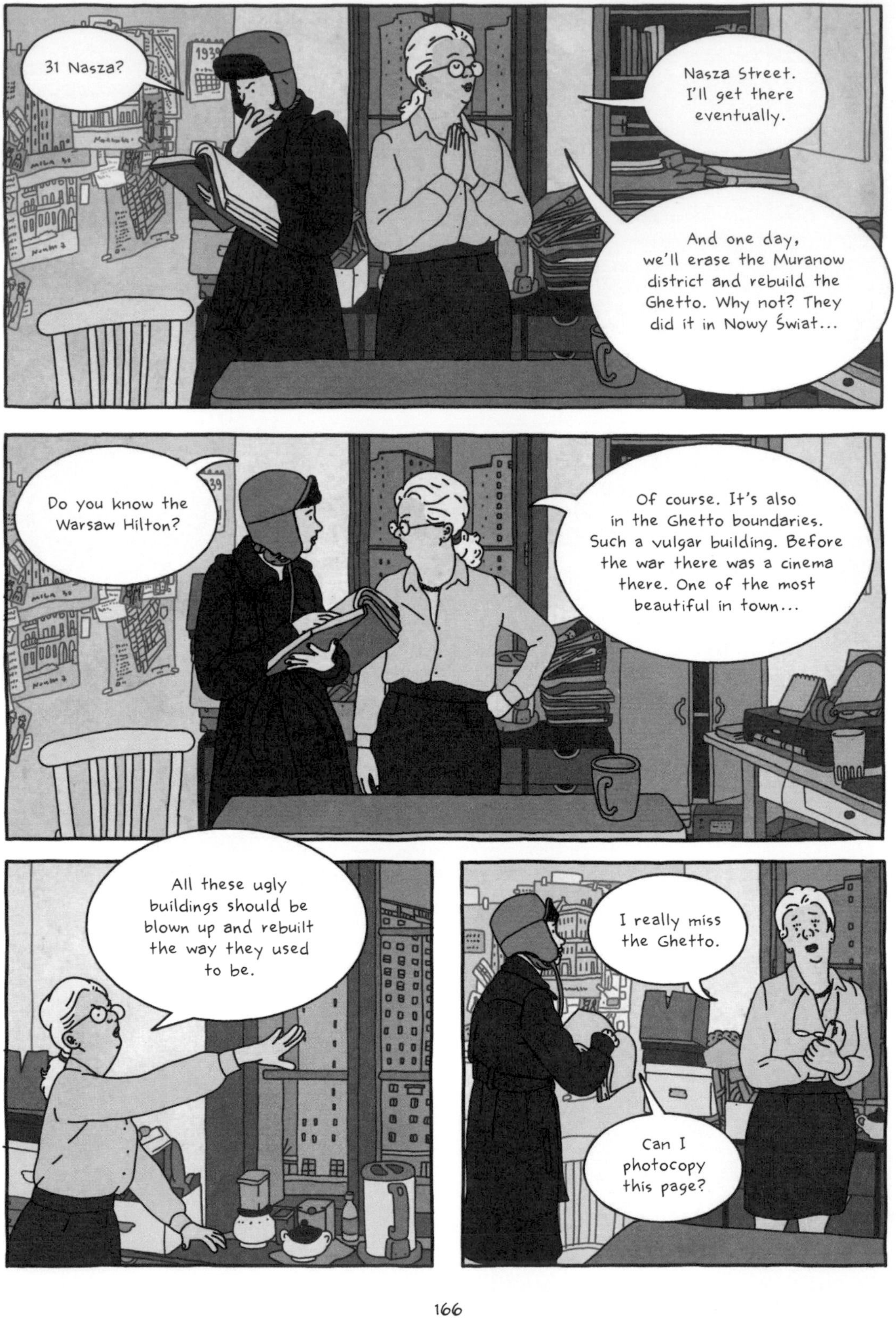
31 Nasza?
Nasza Street. I'll get there eventually.
And one day, we'll erase the Muranow district and rebuild the Ghetto. Why not? They did it in Nowy Świat...
Do you know the Warsaw Hilton?
Of course. It's also in the Ghetto boundaries. Such a vulgar building. Before the war there was a cinema there. One of the most beautiful in town...
All these ugly buildings should be blown up and rebuilt the way they used to be.
I really miss the Ghetto.
Can I photocopy this page?

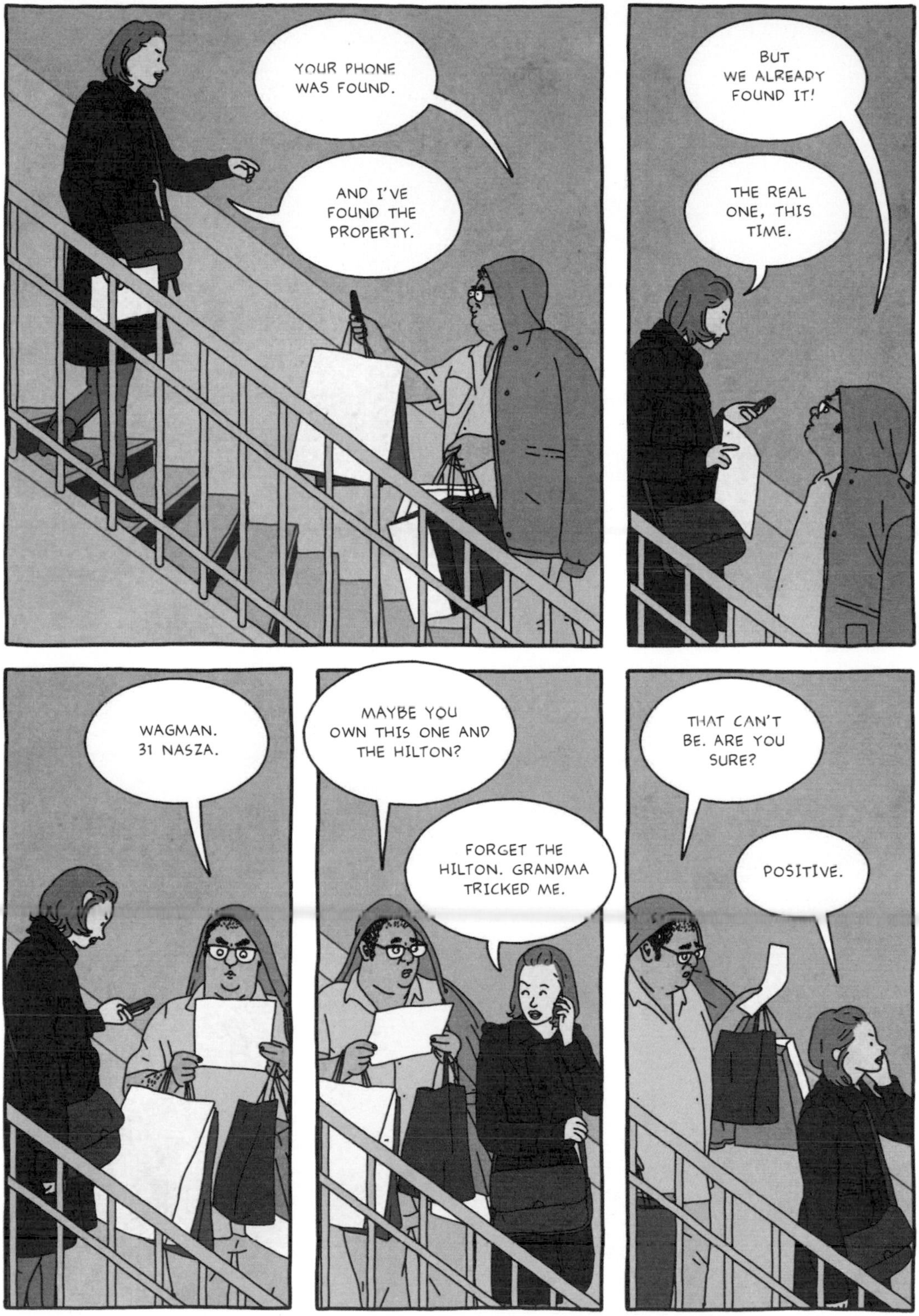
YOUR PHONE WAS FOUND.
AND I'VE FOUND THE PROPERTY.
BUT WE ALREADY FOUND IT!
THE REAL ONE, THIS TIME.
WAGMAN. 31 NASZA.
MAYBE YOU OWN THIS ONE AND THE HILTON?
FORGET THE HILTON. GRANDMA TRICKED ME.
THAT CAN'T BE. ARE YOU SURE?
POSITIVE.

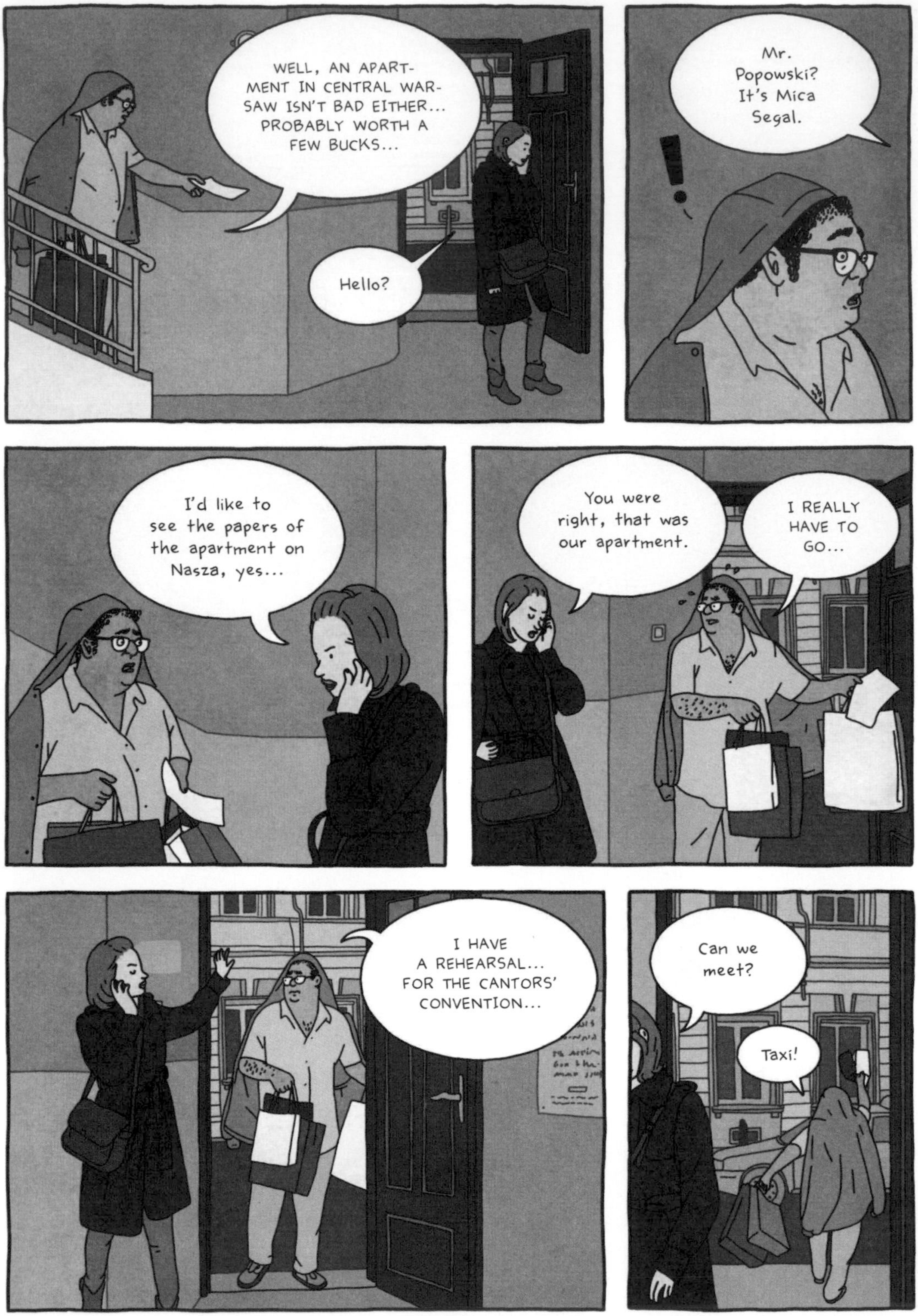
WELL, AN APARTMENT IN CENTRAL WARSAW ISN'T BAD EITHER... PROBABLY WORTH A FEW BUCKS...
Hello?
Mr. Popowski? It's Mica Segal.
!
I'd like to see the papers of the apartment on Nasza, yes...
You were right, that was our apartment.
I REALLY HAVE TO GO...
I HAVE A REHEARSAL... FOR THE CANTORS' CONVENTION...
Can we meet?
Taxi!

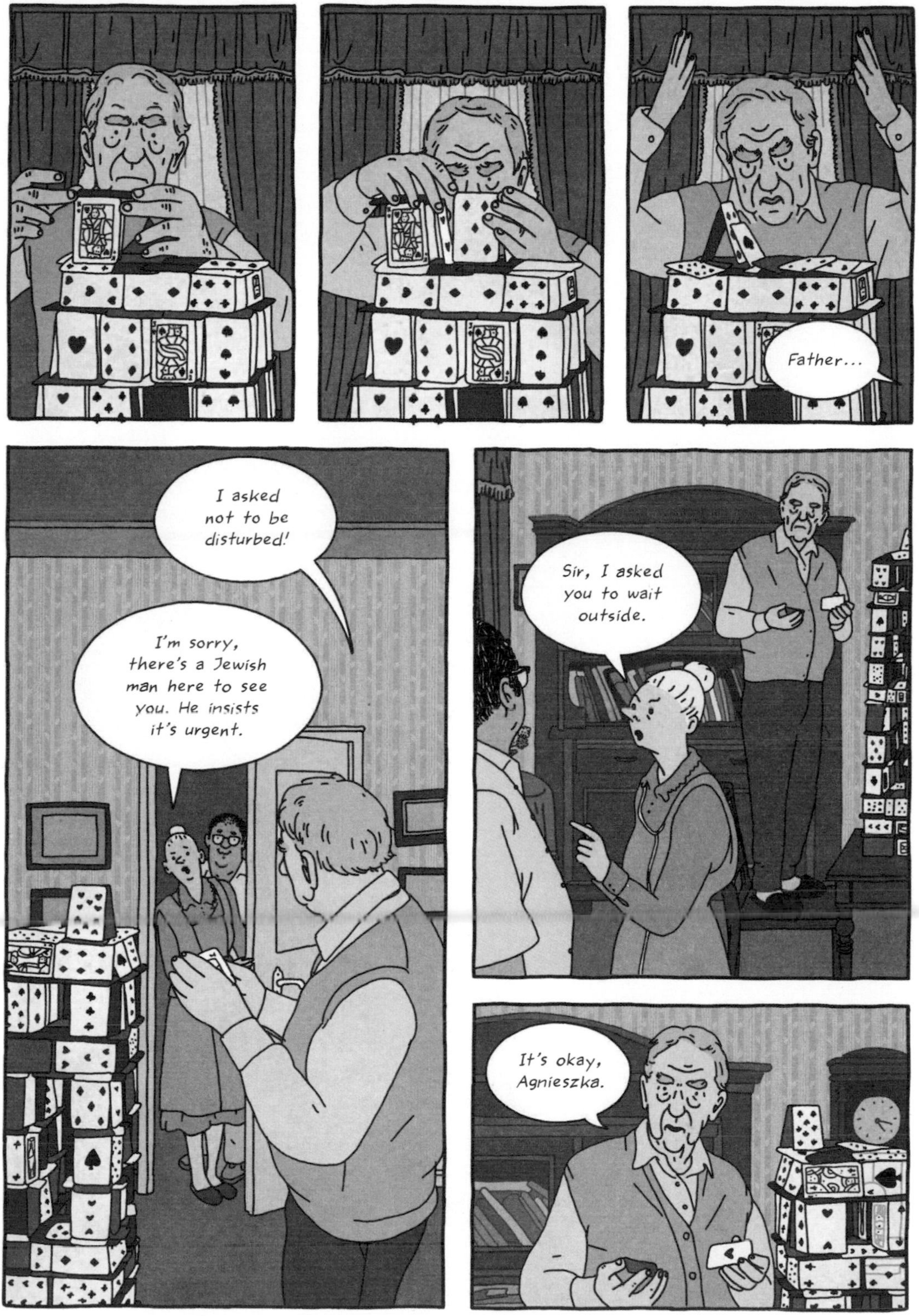
Father...
I asked not to be disturbed!
I'm sorry, there's a Jewish man here to see you. He insists it's urgent.
Sir, I asked you to wait outside.
It's okay, Agnieszka.

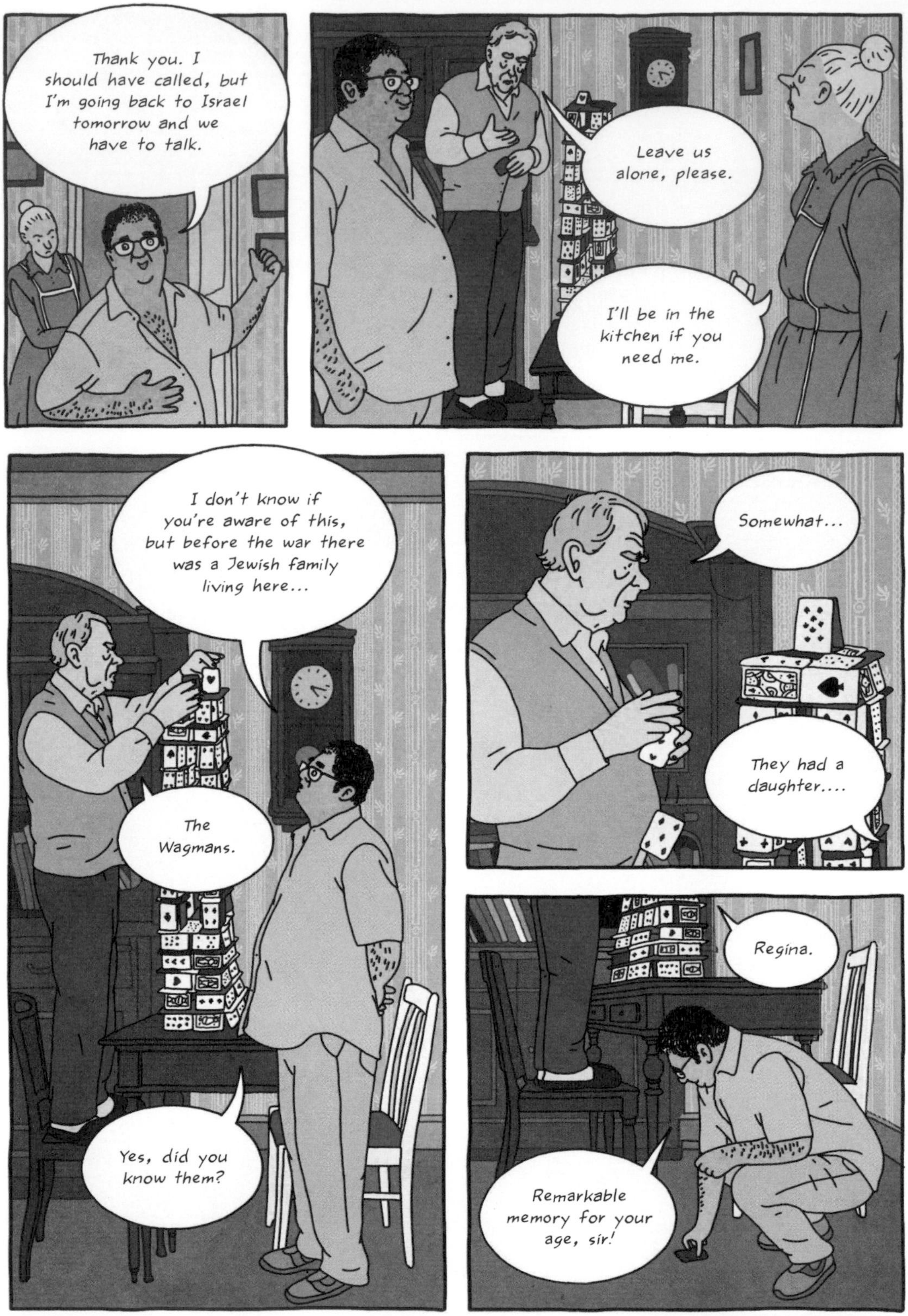
Thank you. I should have called, but I'm going back to Israel tomorrow and we have to talk.
Leave us alone, please.
I'll be in the kitchen if you need me.
I don't know if you're aware of this, but before the war there was a Jewish family living here...
The Wagmans.
Yes, did you know them?
Somewhat...
They had a daughter....
Regina.
Remarkable memory for your age, sir!

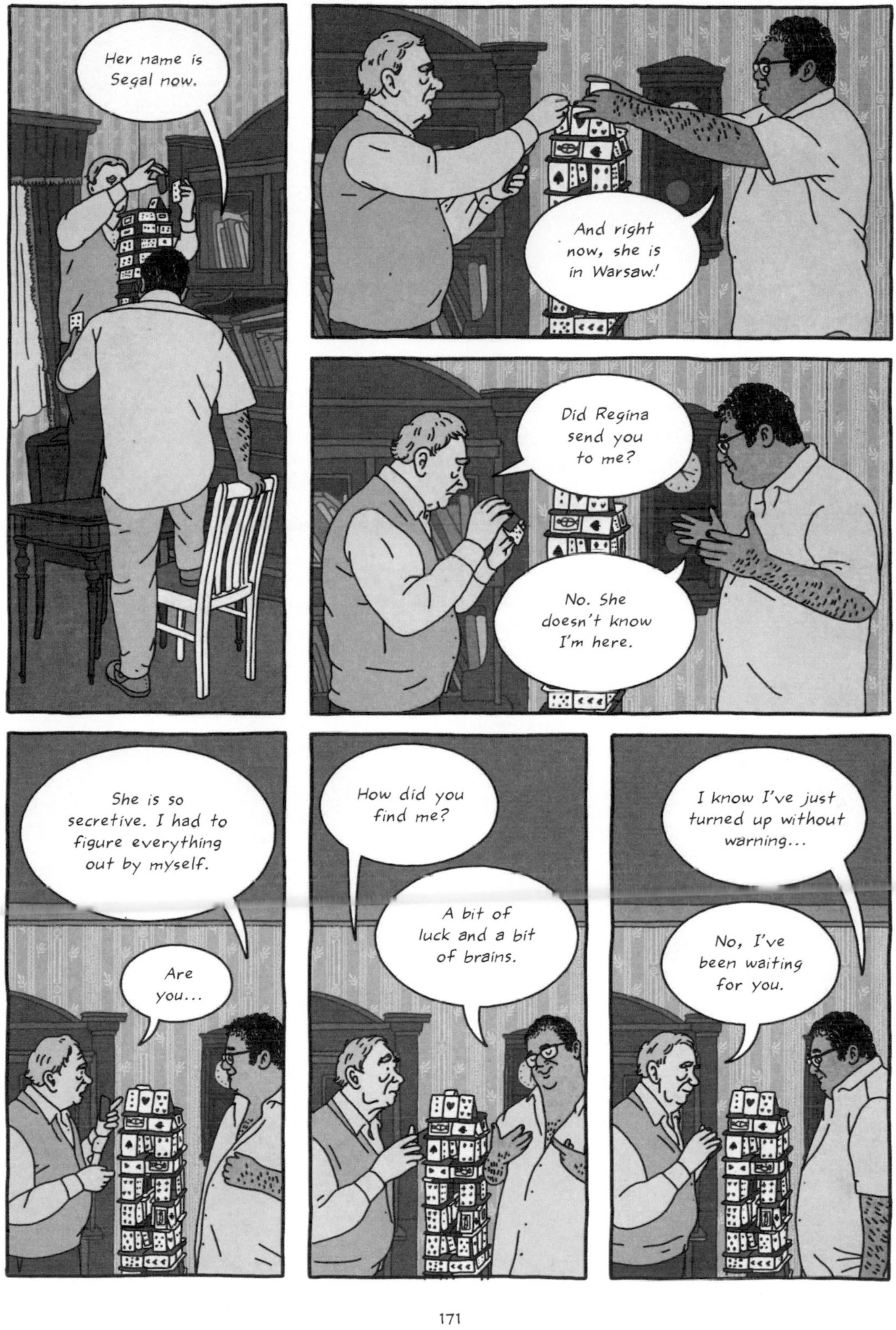
Her name is Segal now.
And right now, she is in Warsaw!
Did Regina send you to me?
No. She doesn't know I'm here.
She is so secretive. I had to figure everything out by myself.
Are you...
How did you find me?
A bit of luck and a bit of brains.
I know I've just turned up without warning...
No, I've been waiting for you.

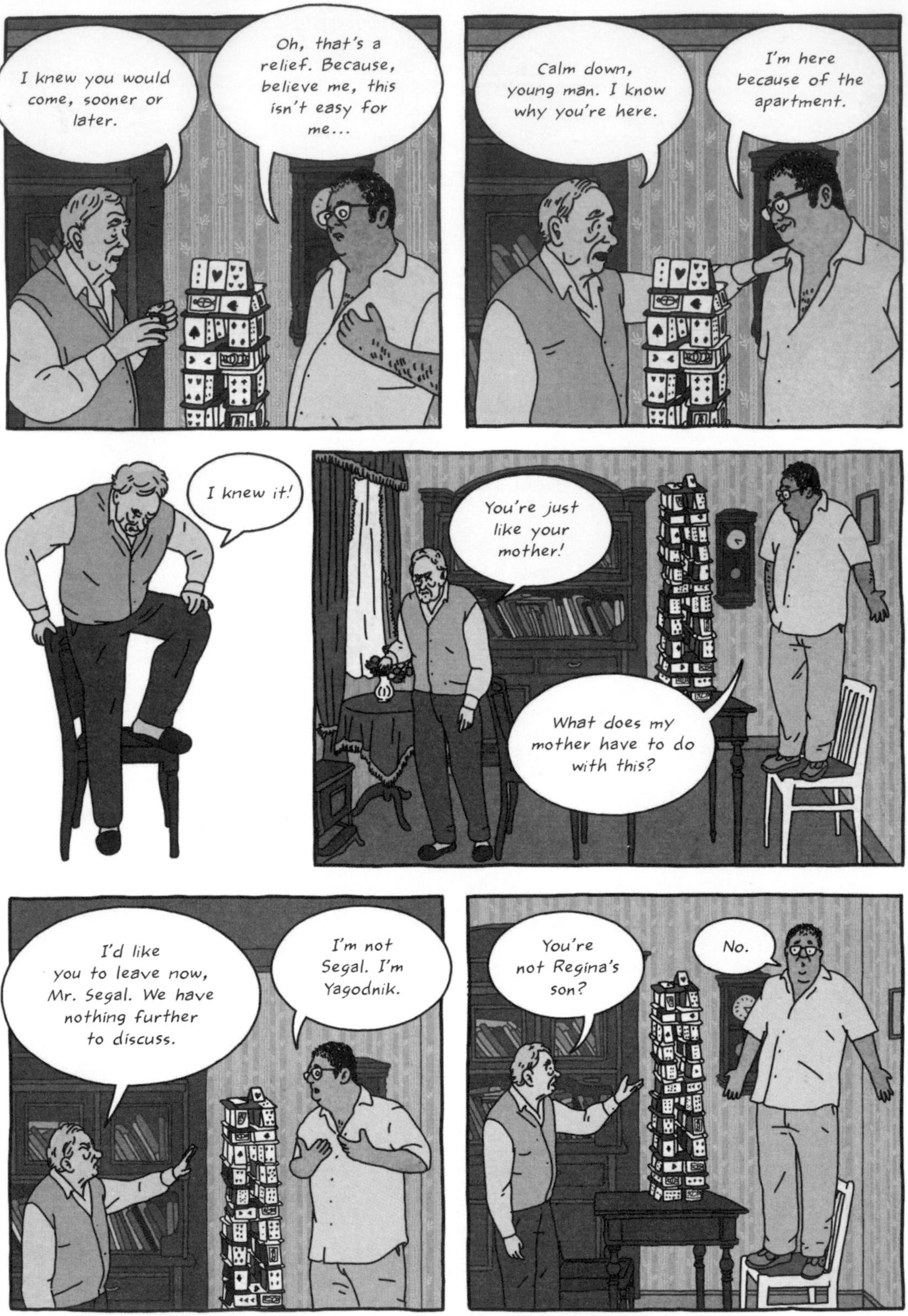
I knew you would come, sooner or later.
Oh, that's a relief. Because, believe me, this isn't easy for me...
Calm down, young man. I know why you're here.
I'm here because of the apartment.
I knew it!
You're just like your mother!
What does my mother have to do with this?
I'd like you to leave now, Mr. Segal. We have nothing further to discuss.
I'm not Segal. I'm Yagodnik.
You're not Regina's son?
No.

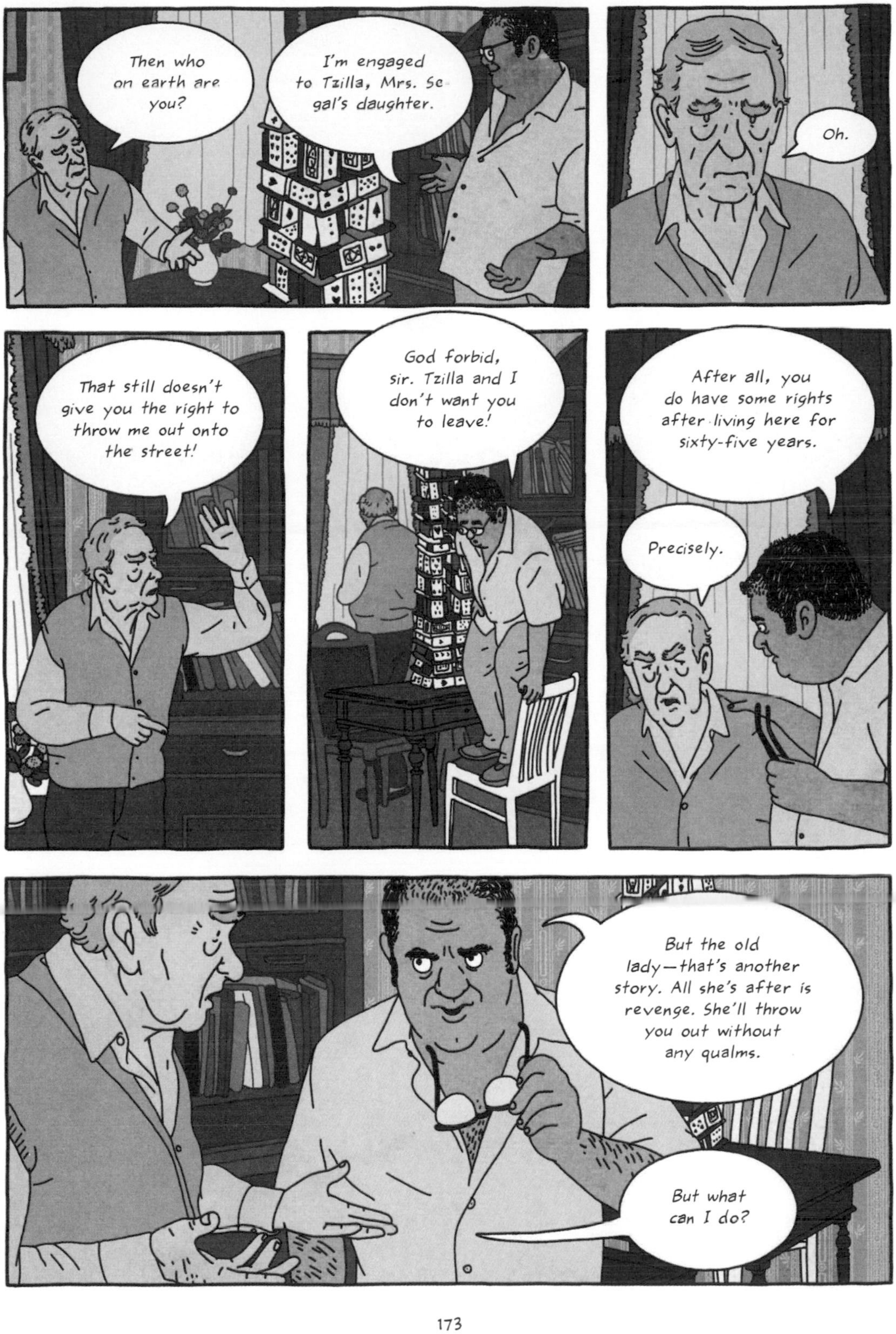
Then who on earth are you?
I'm engaged to Tzilla, Mrs. Se-gal's daughter.
Oh.
That still doesn't give you the right to throw me out onto the street!
God forbid, sir. Tzilla and I don't want you to leave!
After all, you do have some rights after living here for sixty-five years.
Precisely.
But the old lady—that's another story. All she's after is revenge. She'll throw you out without any qualms.
But what can I do?

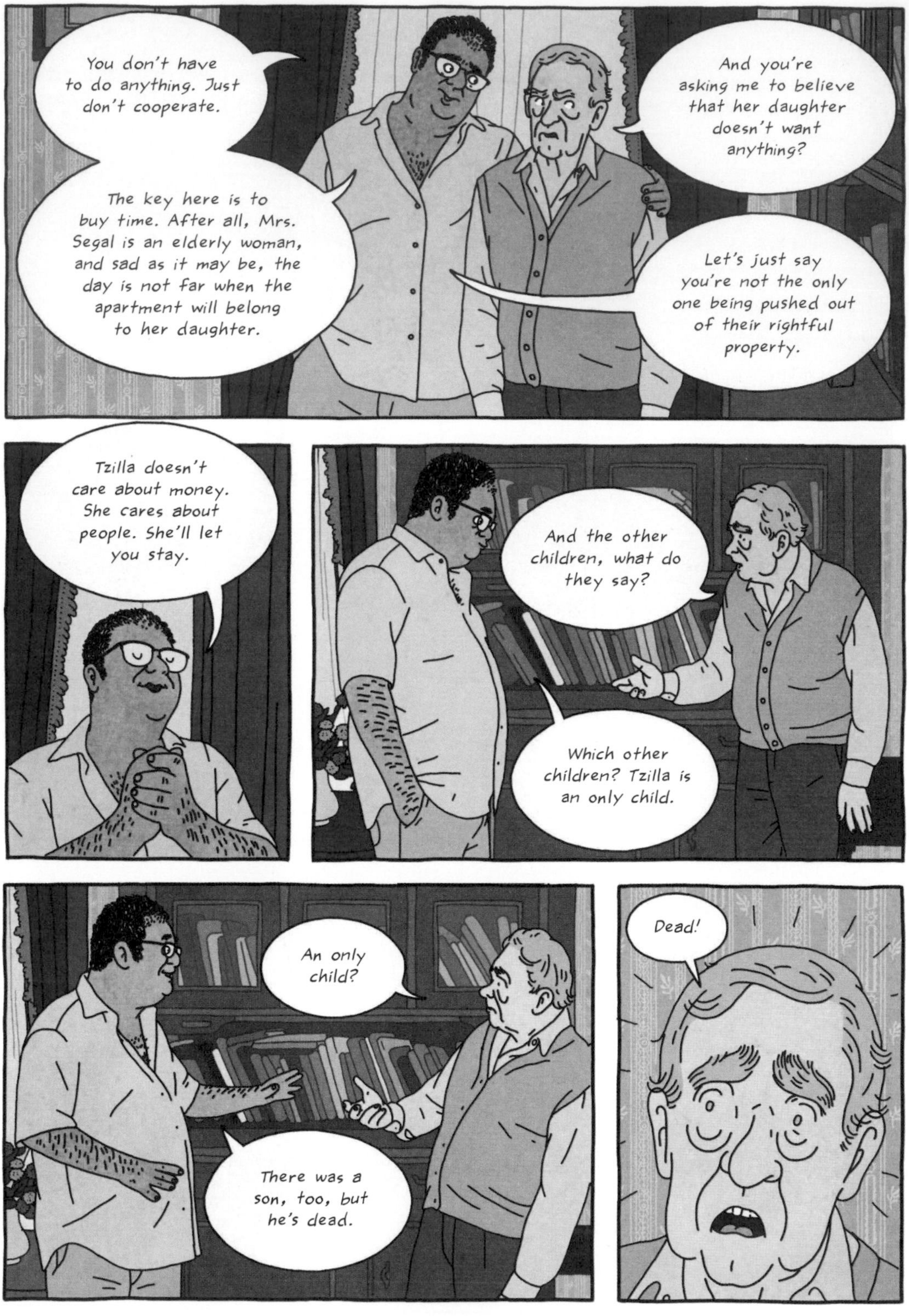
You don't have to do anything. Just don't cooperate.
The key here is to buy time. After all, Mrs. Segal is an elderly woman, and sad as it may be, the day is not far when the apartment will belong to her daughter.
And you're asking me to believe that her daughter doesn't want anything?
Let's just say you're not the only one being pushed out of their rightful property.
Tzilla doesn't care about money. She cares about people. She'll let you stay.
And the other children, what do they say?
Which other children? Tzilla is an only child.
An only child?
There was a son, too, but he's dead.
Dead!

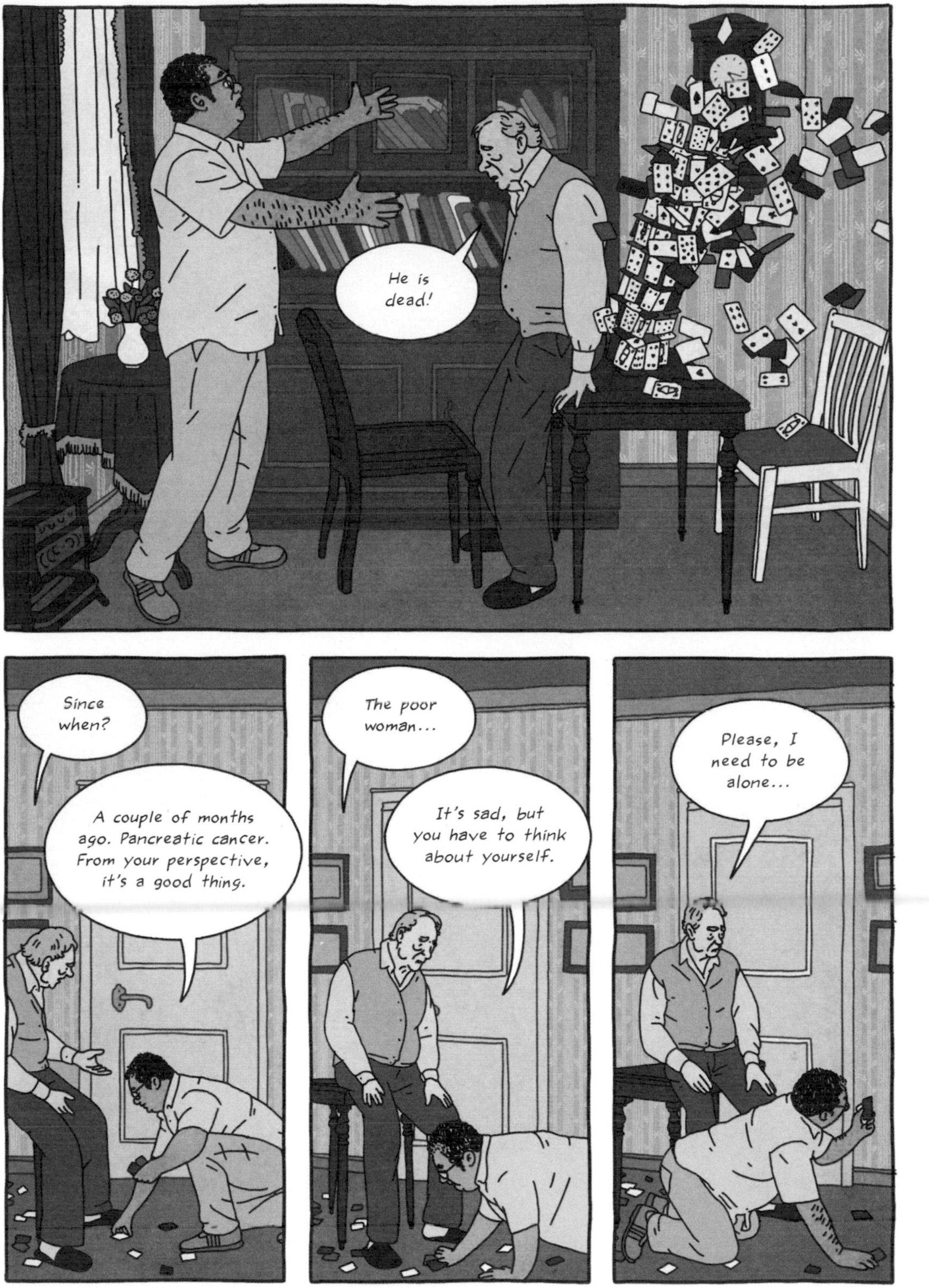

He is dead!
Since when?
A couple of months ago. Pancreatic cancer. From your perspective, it's a good thing.
The poor woman...
It's sad, but you have to think about yourself.
Please, I need to be alone...

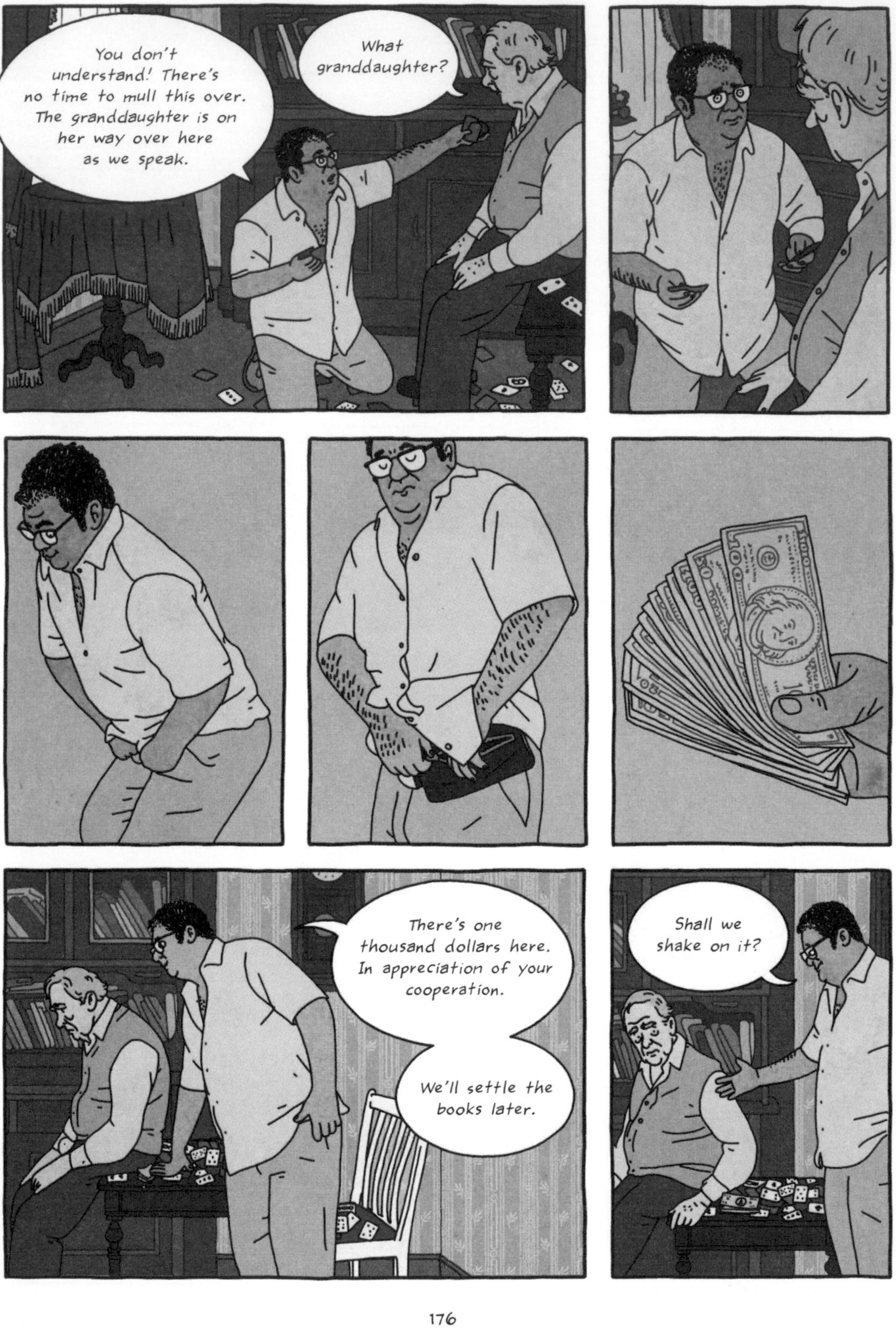
You don't understand! There's no time to mull this over. The granddaughter is on her way over here as we speak.
What granddaughter?
There's one thousand dollars here. In appreciation of your cooperation.
We'll settle the books later.
Shall we shake on it?

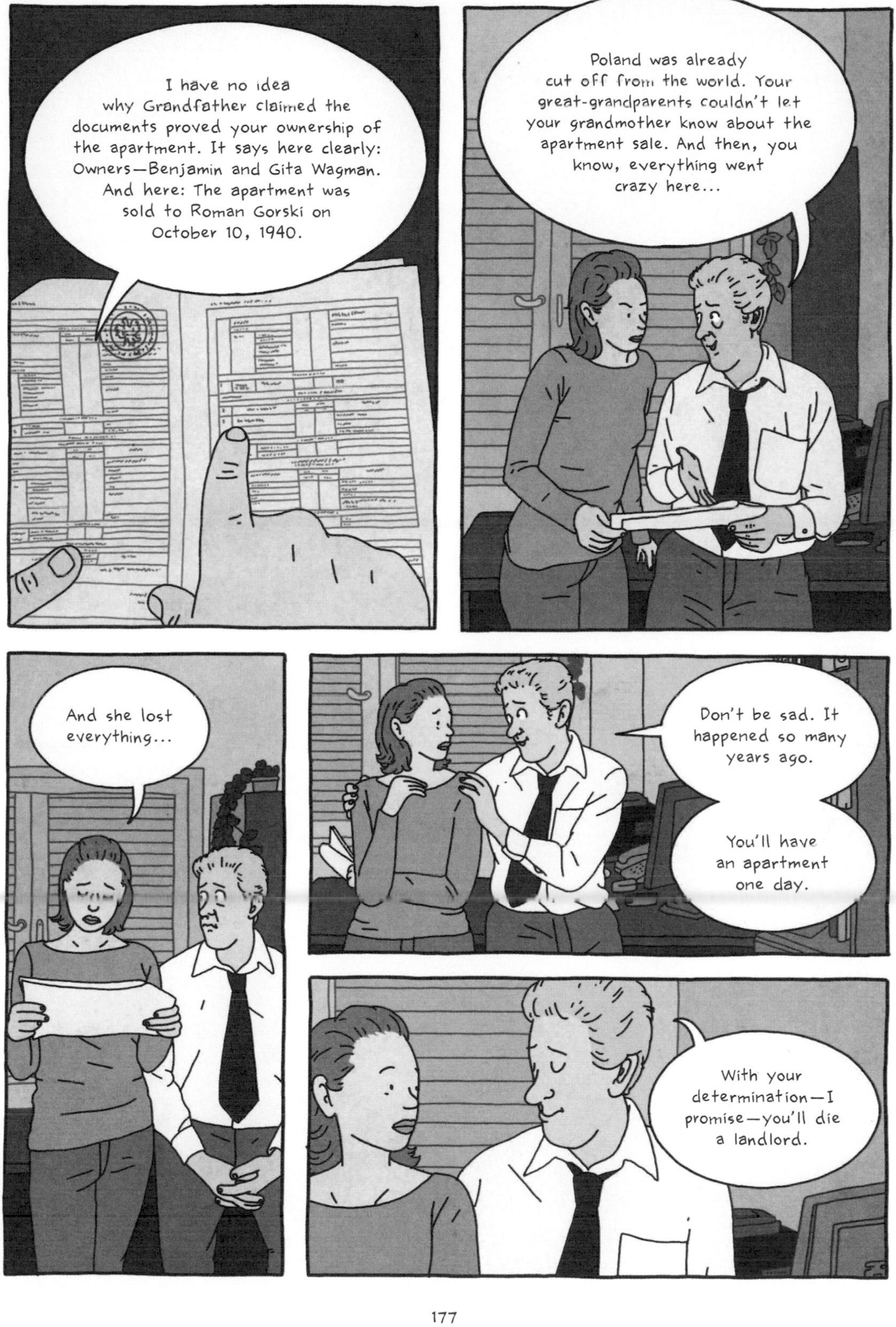
I have no idea why Grandfather claimed the documents proved your ownership of the apartment. It says here clearly: Owners—Benjamin and Gita Wagman. And here: The apartment was sold to Roman Gorski on October 10, 1940.
Poland was already cut off from the world. Your great-grandparents couldn't let your grandmother know about the apartment sale. And then, you know, everything went crazy here...
And she lost everything...
Don't be sad. It happened so many years ago.
You'll have an apartment one day.
With your determination—I promise—you'll die a landlord.

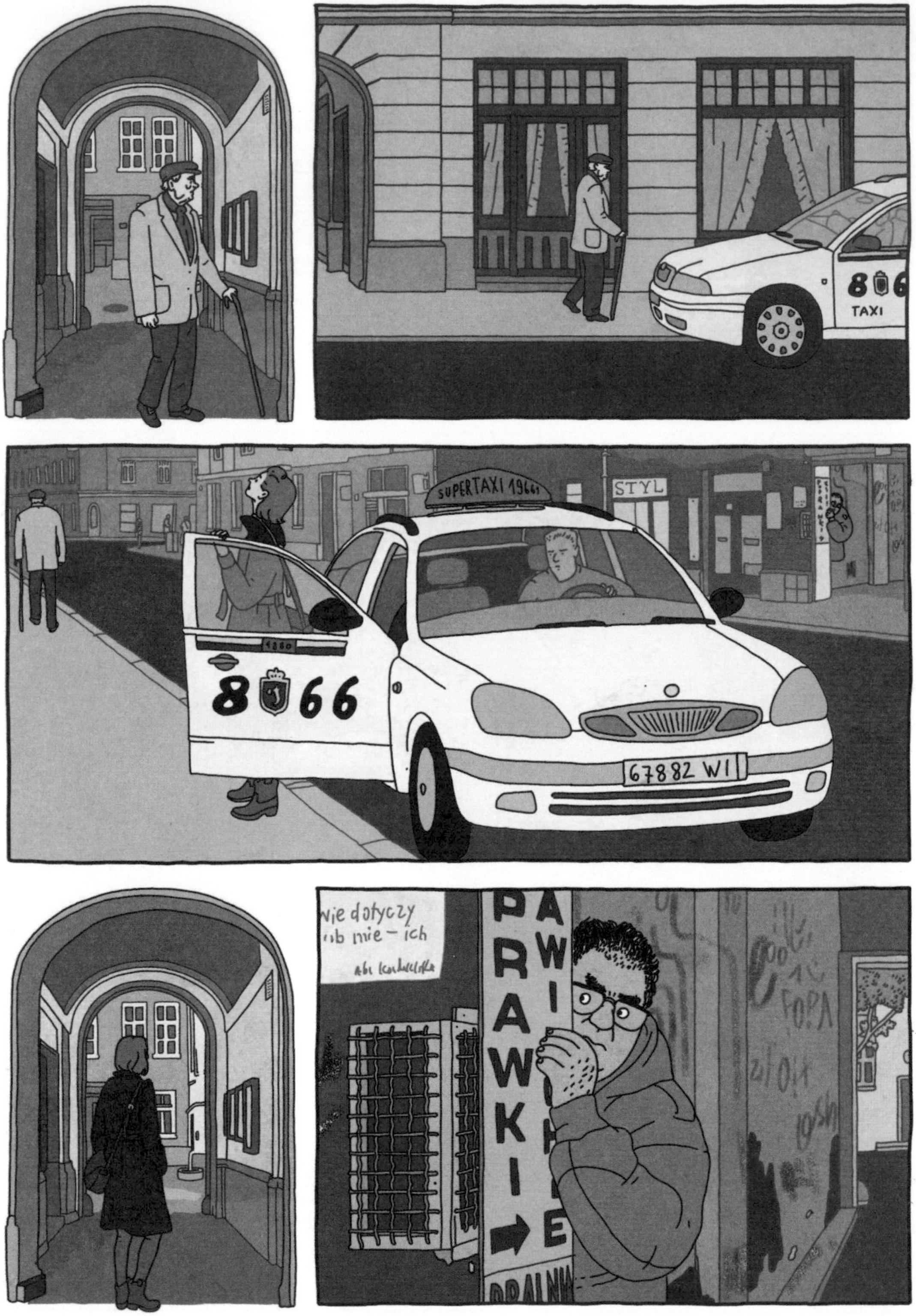

TAXI
SUPERTAXI 19661
STYL
8 66
67882 WI
wie dotyczy
ob nie - ich
PRAWKI

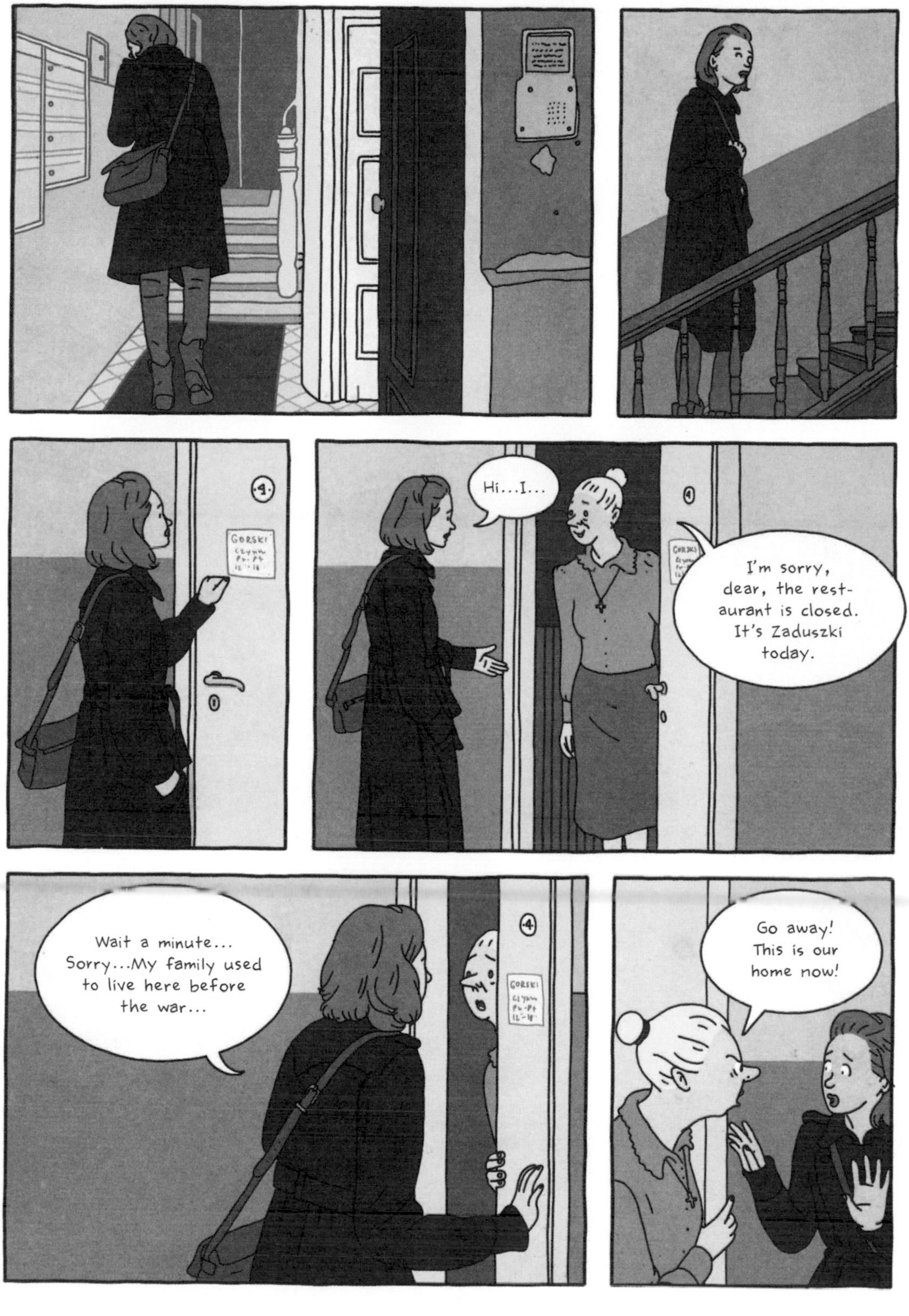
GORSKI
Hi...I...
I'm sorry, dear, the restaurant is closed. It's Zaduszki today.
Wait a minute... Sorry...My family used to live here before the war...
GORSKI
Go away! This is our home now!

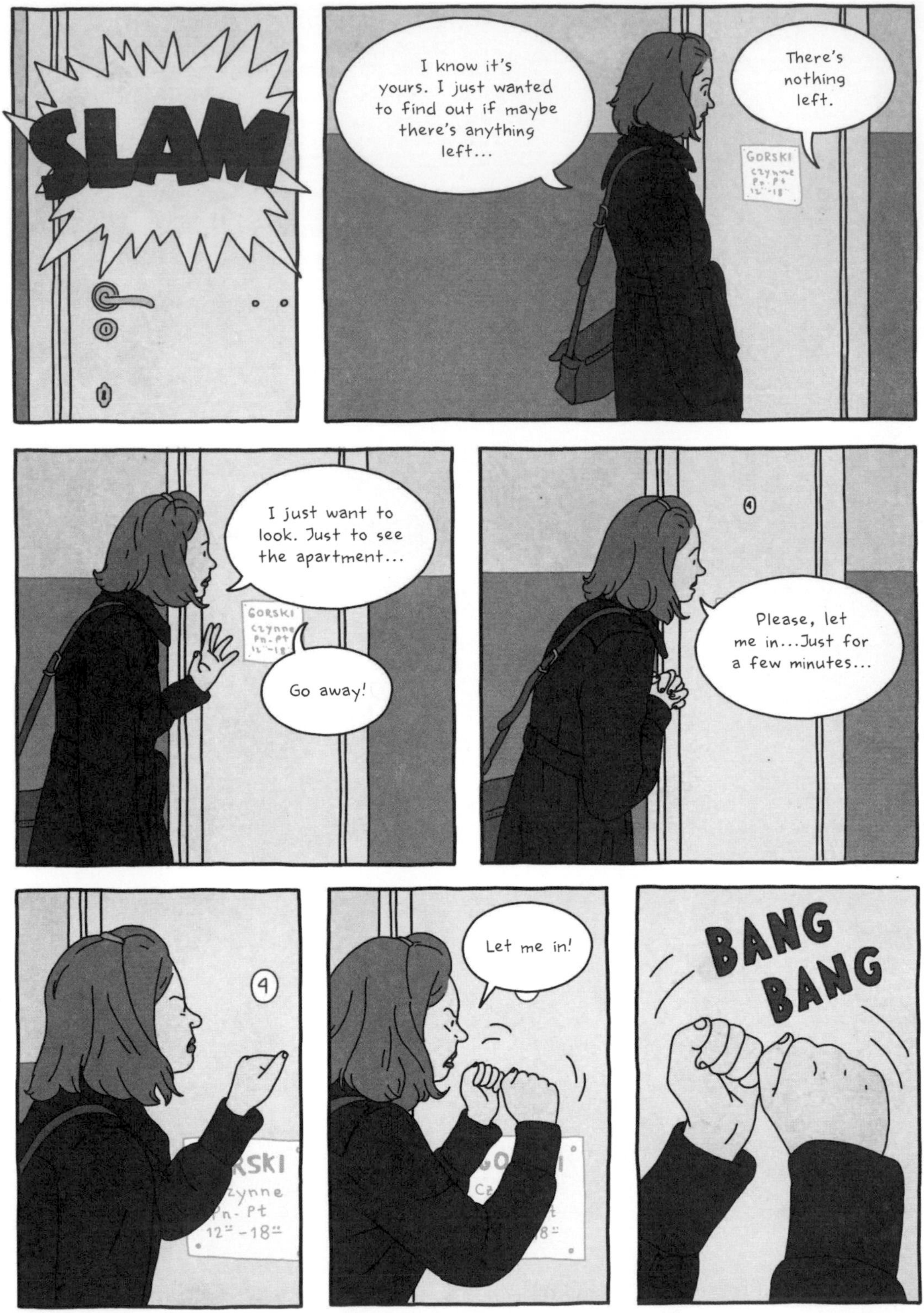
SLAM
I know it's yours. I just wanted to find out if maybe there's anything left...
There's nothing left.
GORSKI
I just want to look. Just to see the apartment...
GORSKI
Go away!
Please, let me in... Just for a few minutes...
Let me in!
BANG
BANG

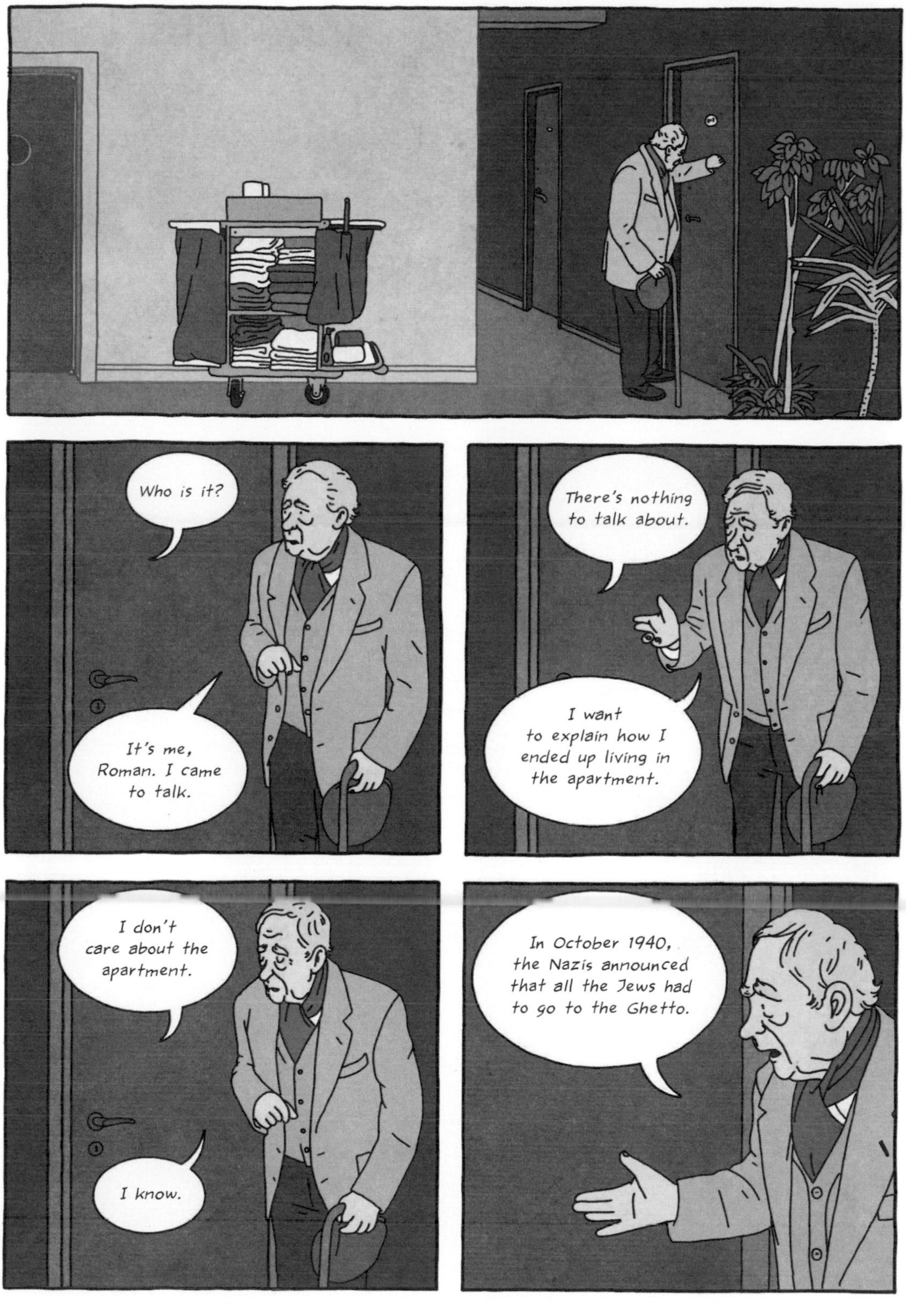
Who is it?
It's me, Roman. I came to talk.
There's nothing to talk about.
I want to explain how I ended up living in the apartment.
I don't care about the apartment.
I know.
In October 1940, the Nazis announced that all the Jews had to go to the Ghetto.

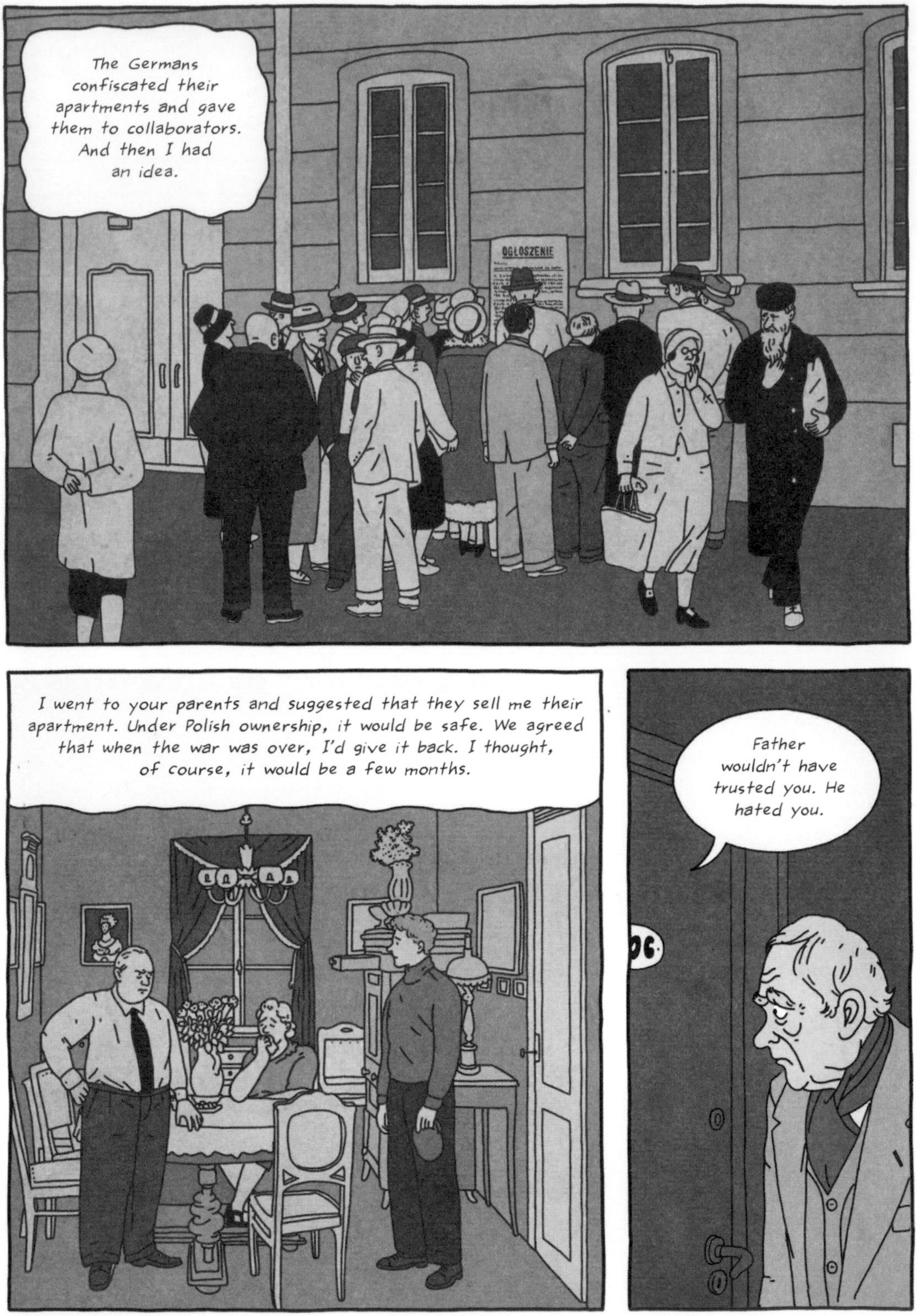
The Germans confiscated their apartments and gave them to collaborators. And then I had an idea.
OGŁOSZENIE
I went to your parents and suggested that they sell me their apartment. Under Polish ownership, it would be safe. We agreed that when the war was over, I'd give it back. I thought, of course, it would be a few months.
Father wouldn't have trusted you. He hated you.

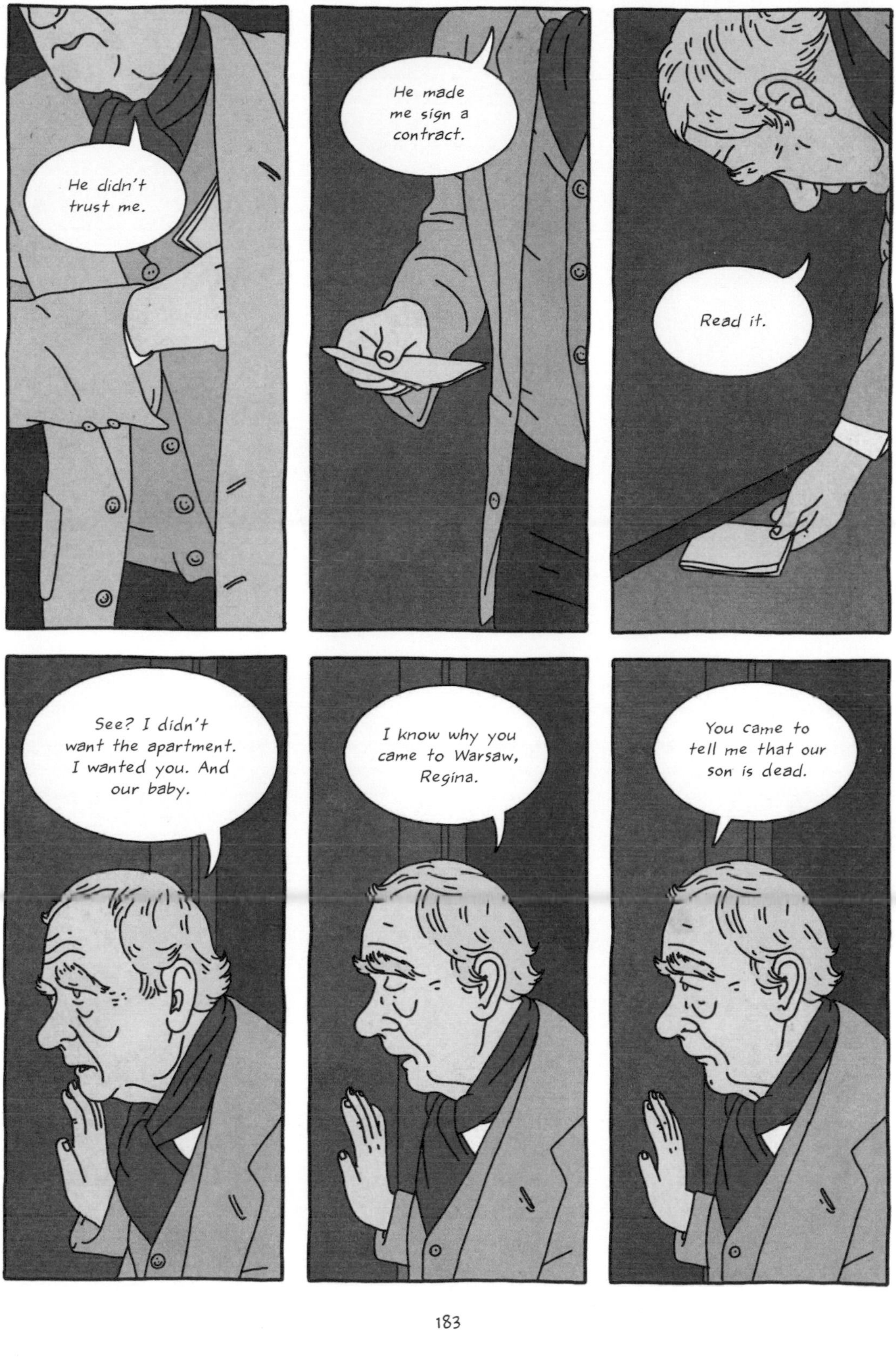
He didn't trust me.
He made me sign a contract.
Read it.
See? I didn't want the apartment. I wanted you. And our baby.
I know why you came to Warsaw, Regina.
You came to tell me that our son is dead.

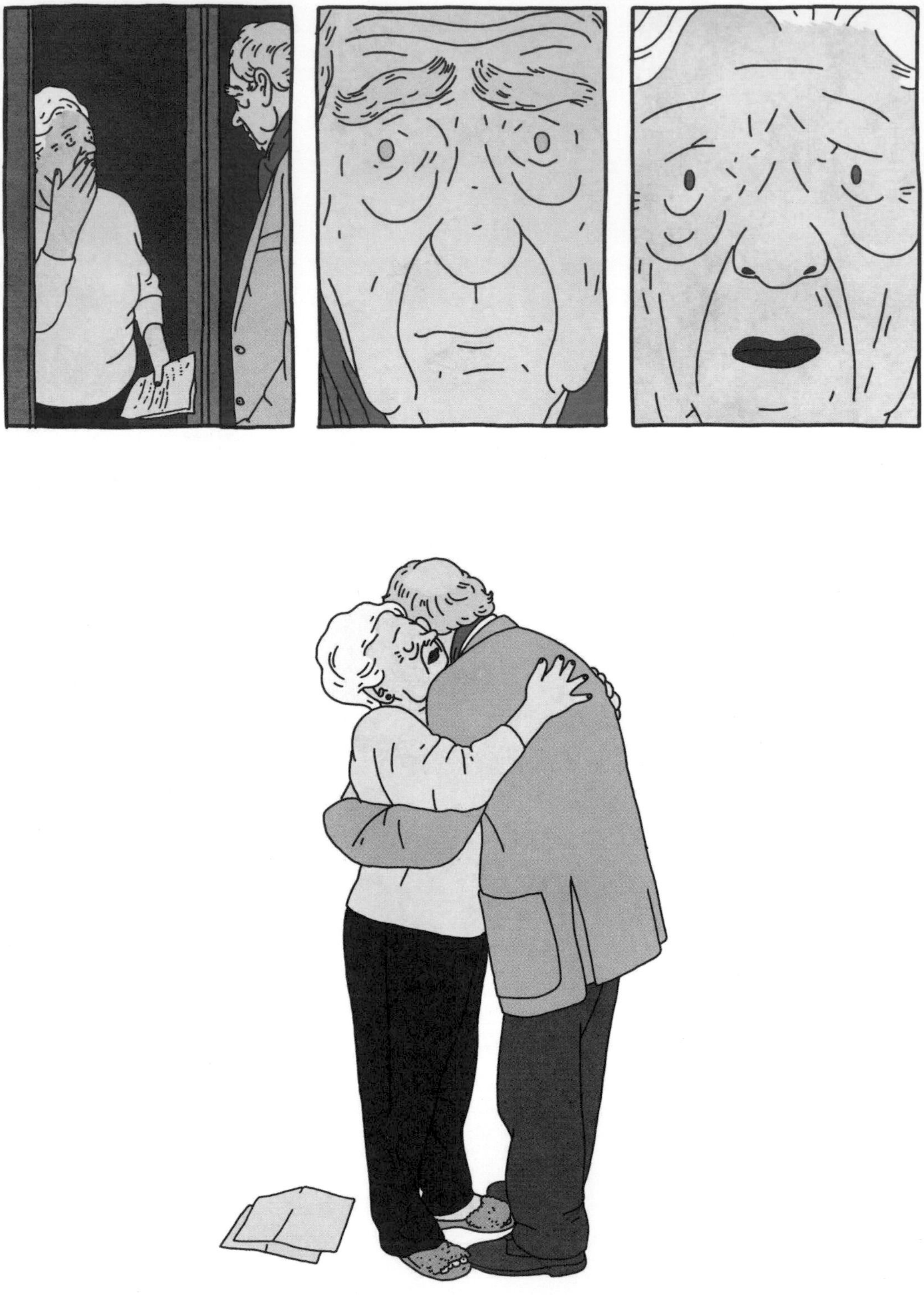

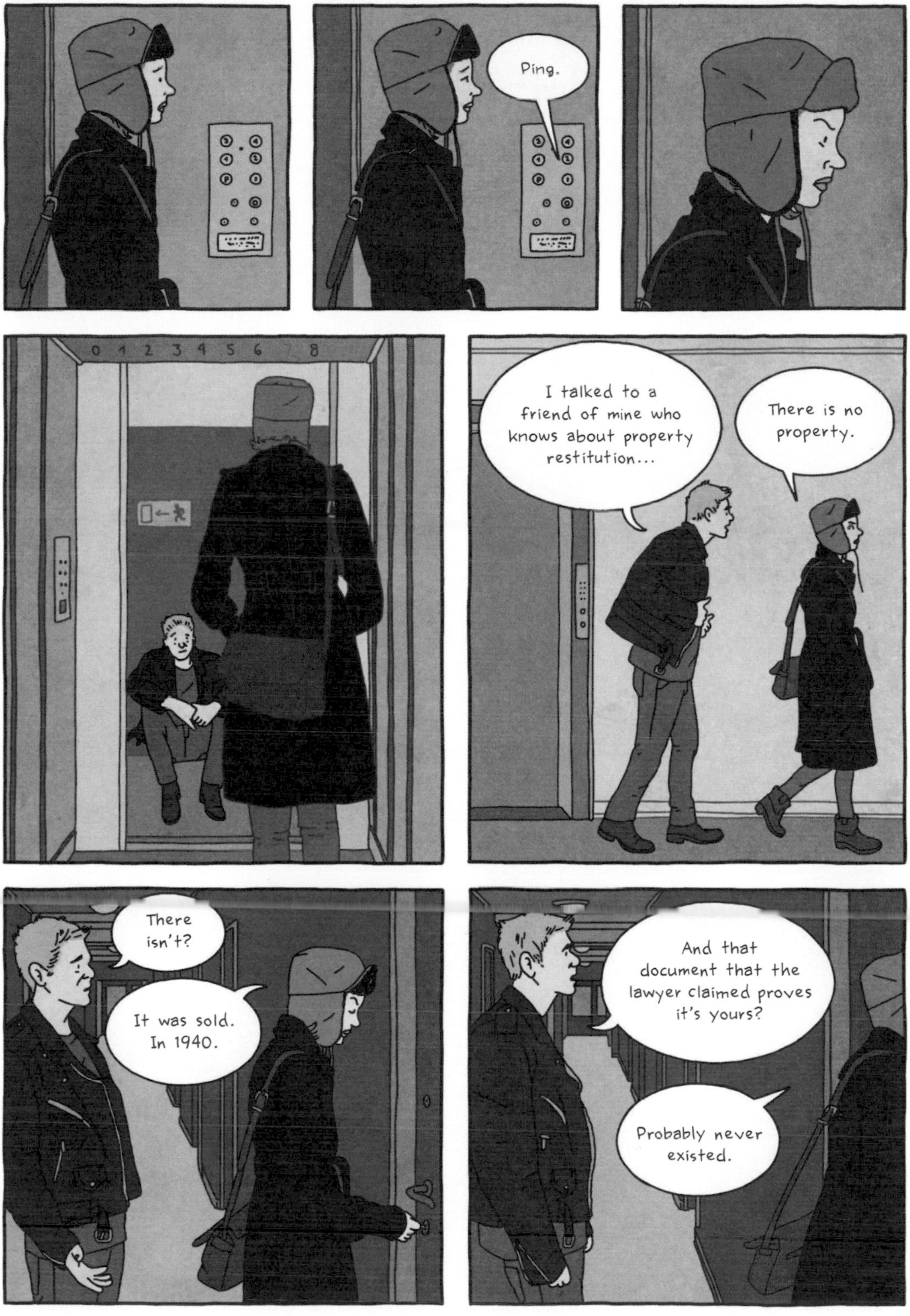
Ping.
0 1 2 3 4 5 6 7 8
I talked to a friend of mine who knows about property restitution...
There is no property.
There isn't?
It was sold. In 1940.
And that document that the lawyer claimed proves it's yours?
Probably never existed.

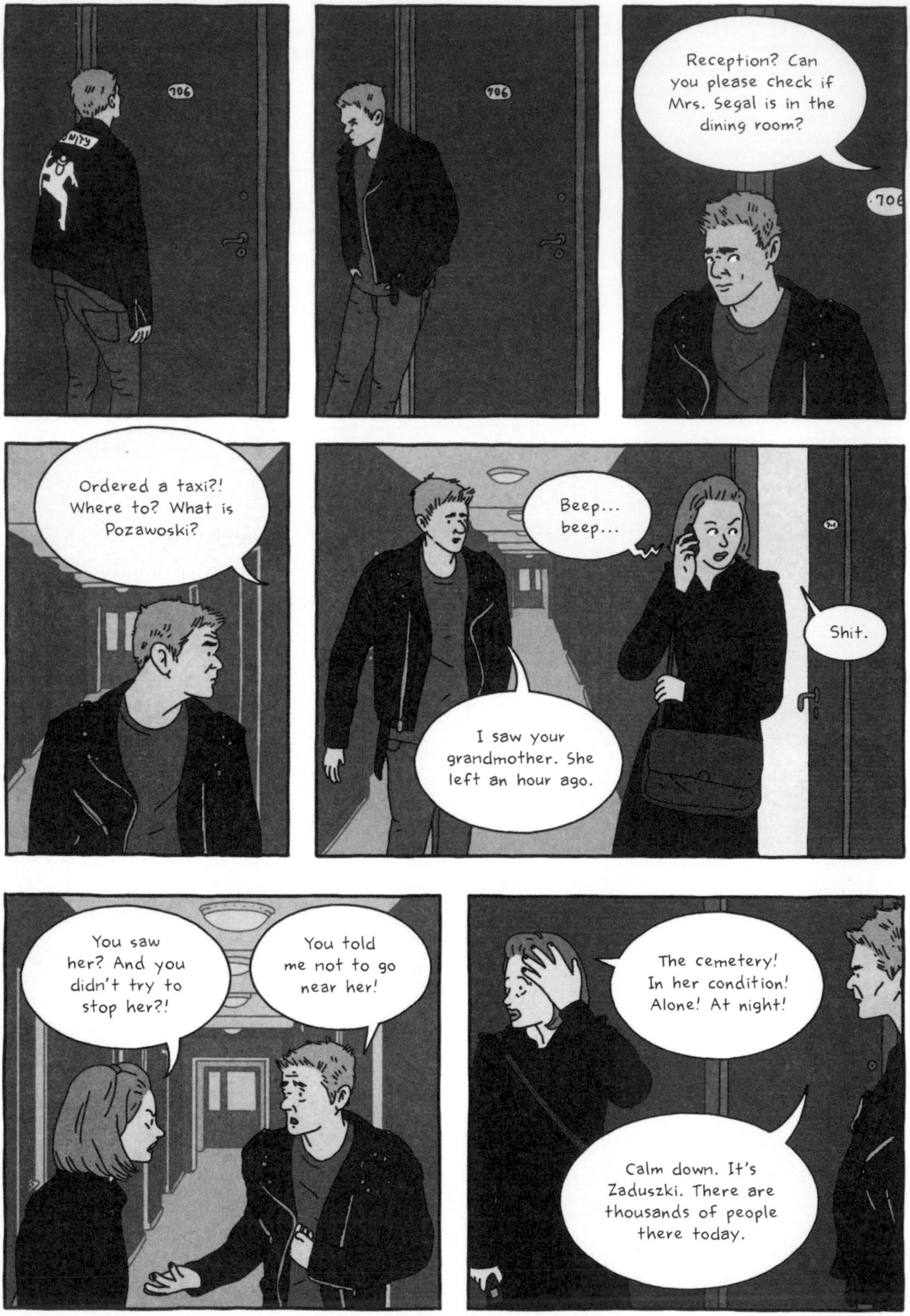
706
706
Reception? Can you please check if Mrs. Segal is in the dining room?
706
Ordered a taxi?! Where to? What is Pozawoski?
Beep... beep...
Shit.
I saw your grandmother. She left an hour ago.
You saw her? And you didn't try to stop her?!
You told me not to go near her!
The cemetery! In her condition! Alone! At night!
Calm down. It's Zaduszki. There are thousands of people there today.

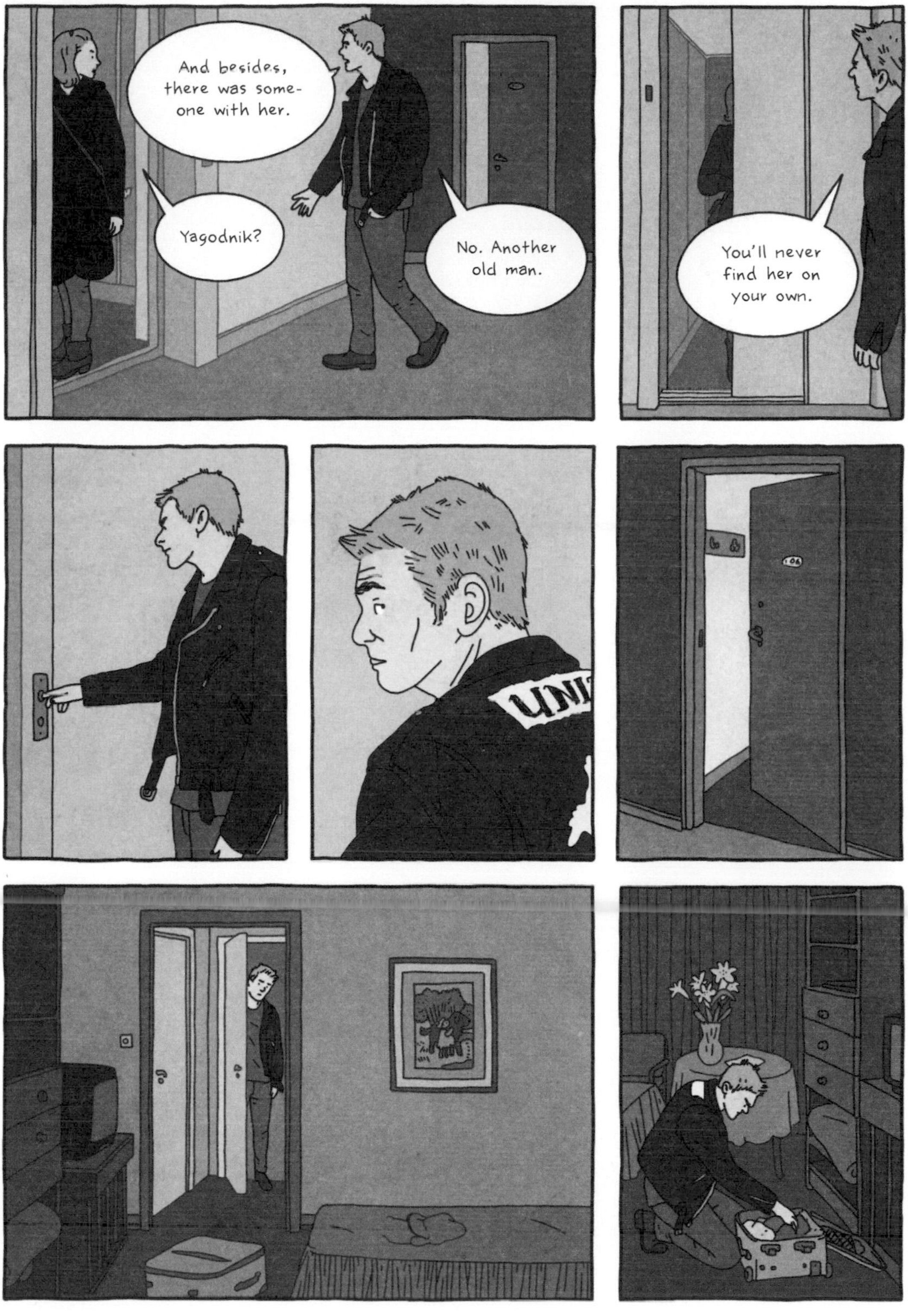
And besides, there was someone with her.
Yagodnik?
No. Another old man.
You'll never find her on your own.
UNI

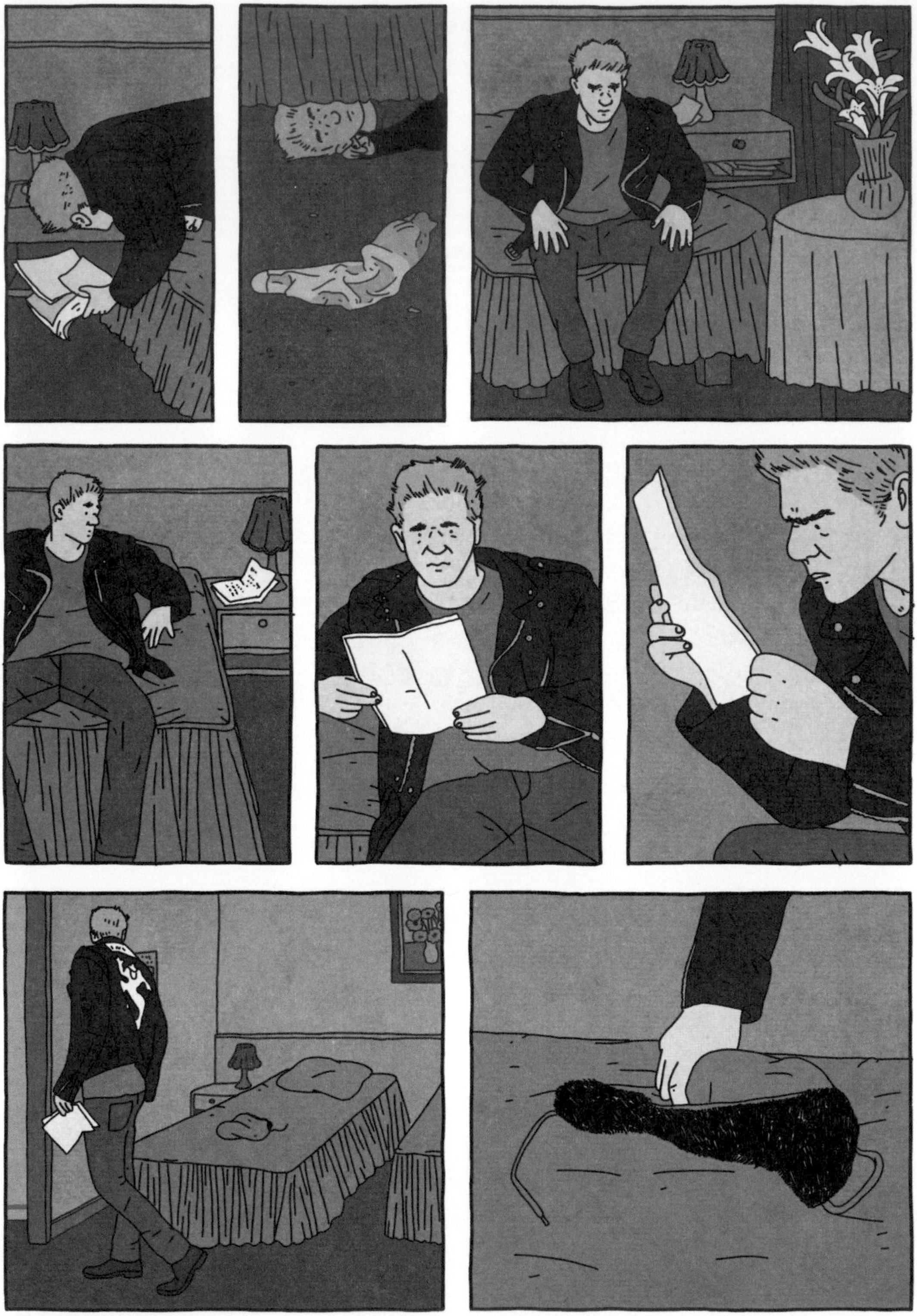

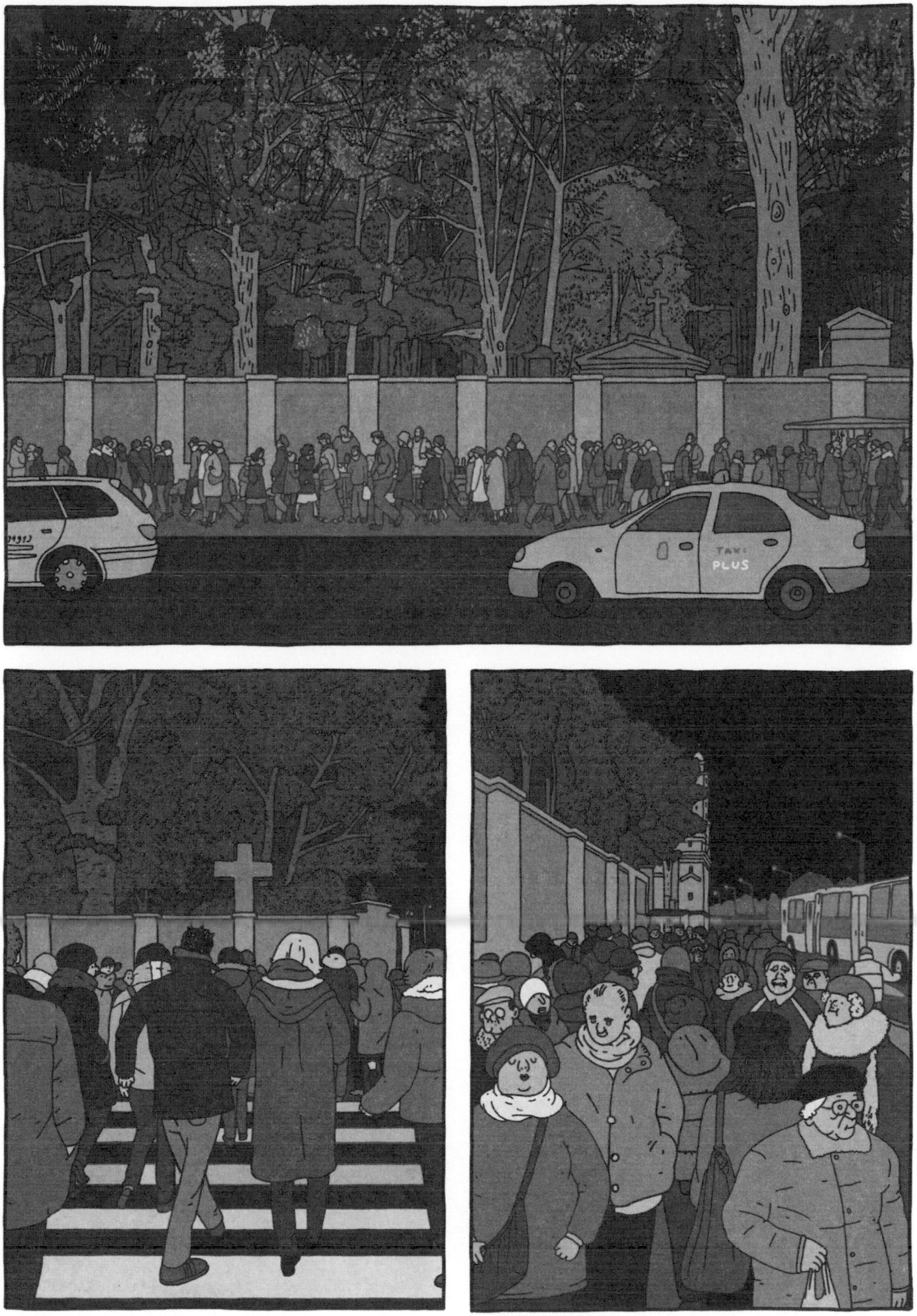
TAXI
PLUS

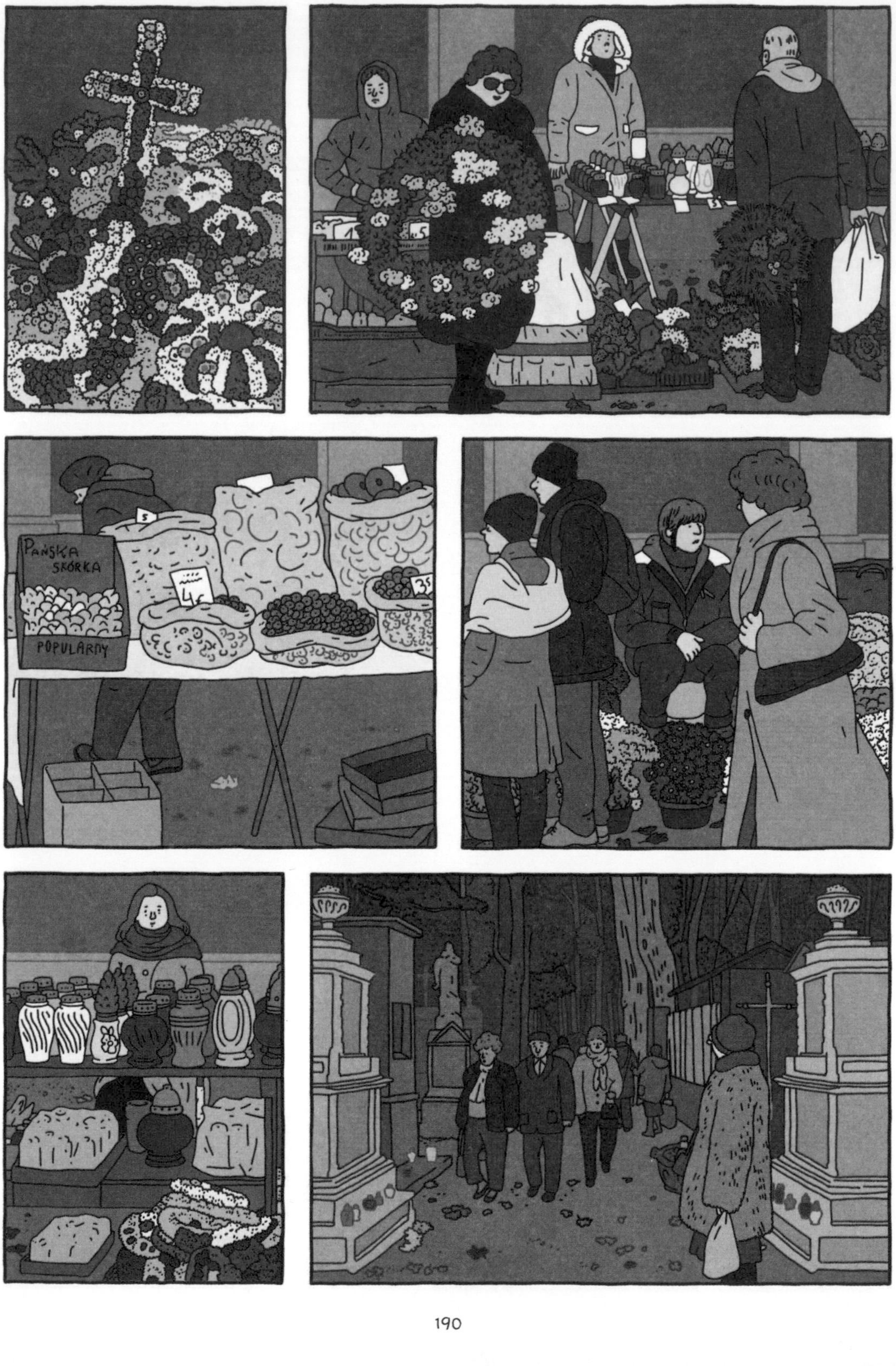
PAŃSKA SKÓRKA
POPULARNY

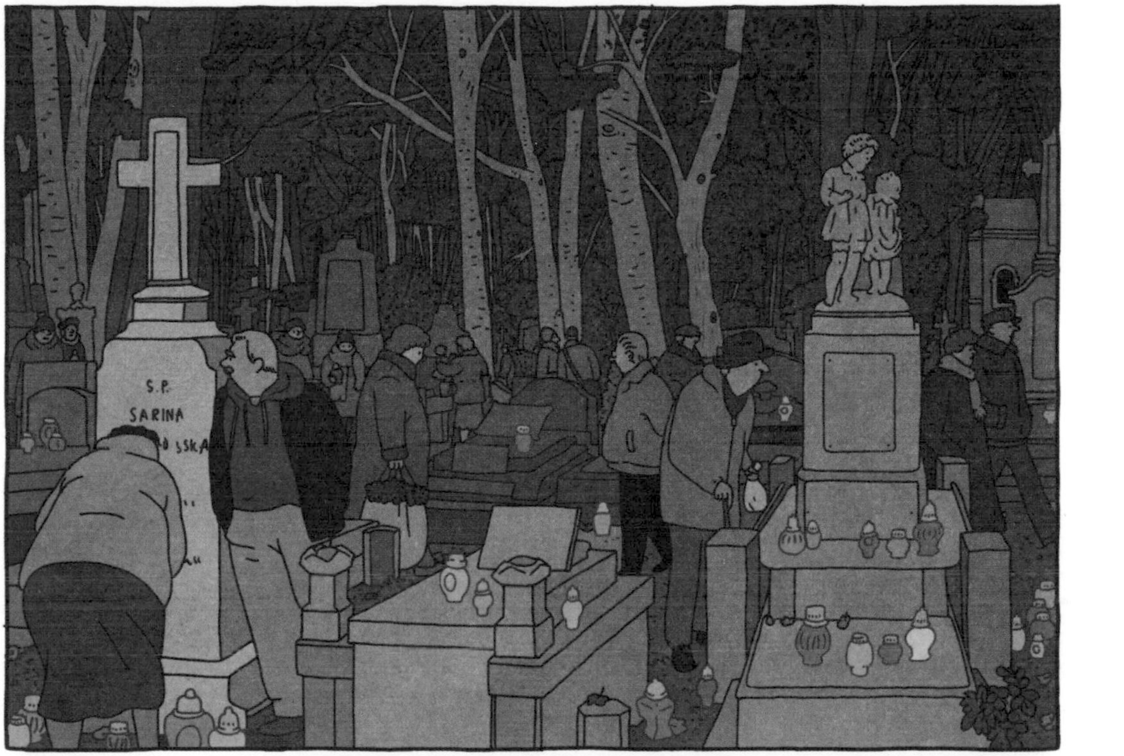
S.P.
SARINA

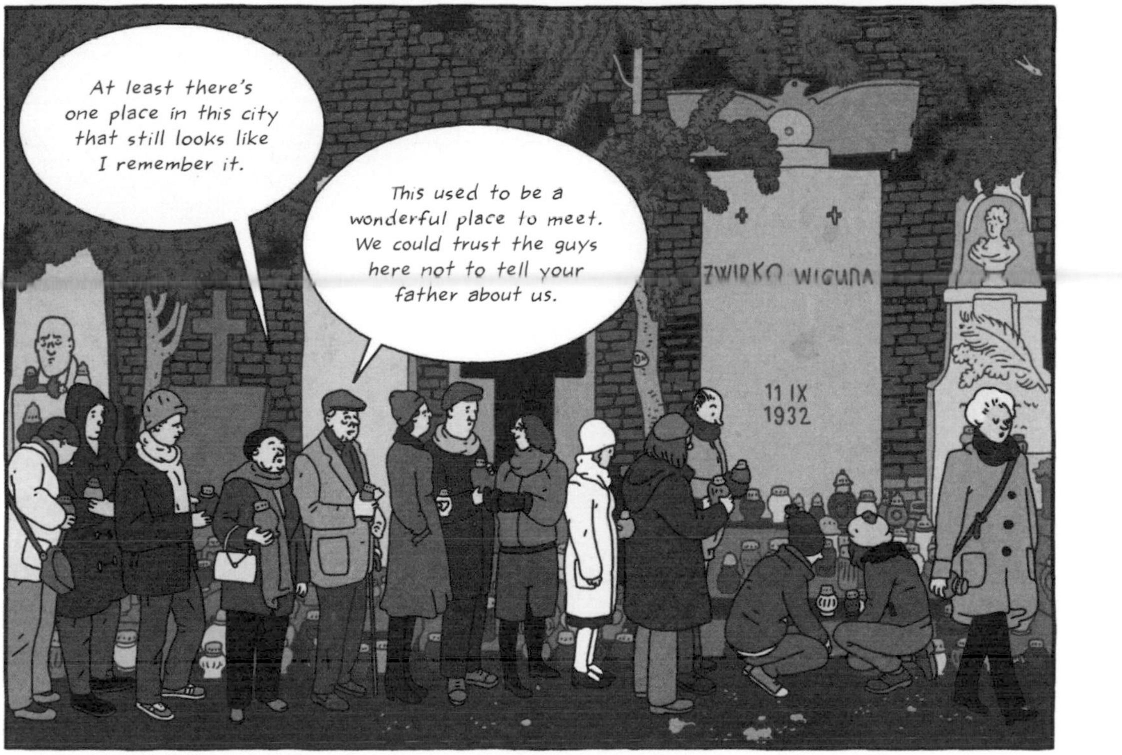
At least there's one place in this city that still looks like I remember it.
This used to be a wonderful place to meet. We could trust the guys here not to tell your father about us.
ZWIRKO WIGURA
11 IX
1932

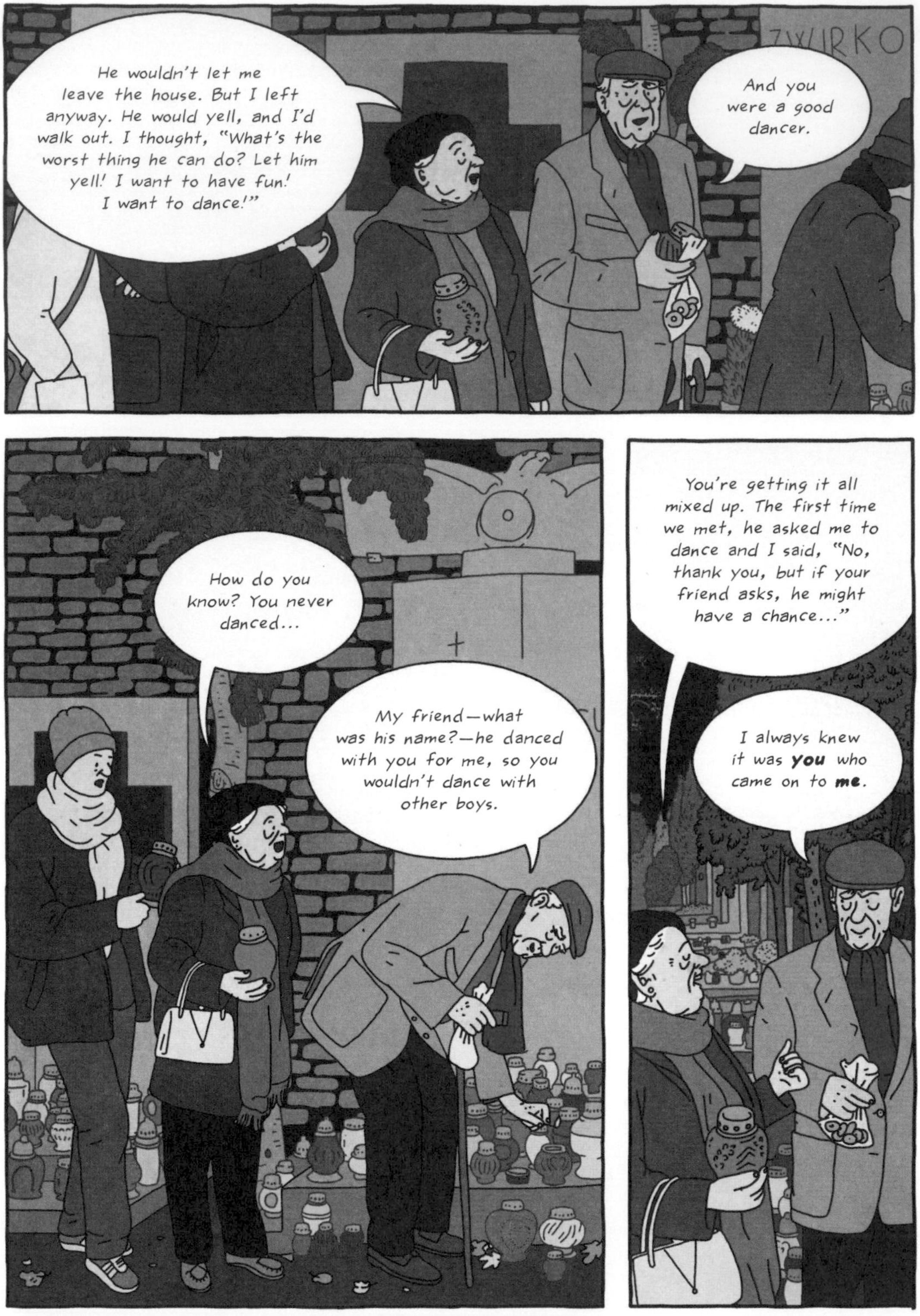
He wouldn't let me leave the house. But I left anyway. He would yell, and I'd walk out. I thought, "What's the worst thing he can do? Let him yell! I want to have fun! I want to dance!"
And you were a good dancer.
ZWIRKO
How do you know? You never danced...
My friend—what was his name?—he danced with you for me, so you wouldn't dance with other boys.
You're getting it all mixed up. The first time we met, he asked me to dance and I said, "No, thank you, but if your friend asks, he might have a chance..."
I always knew it was **you** who came on to **me**.

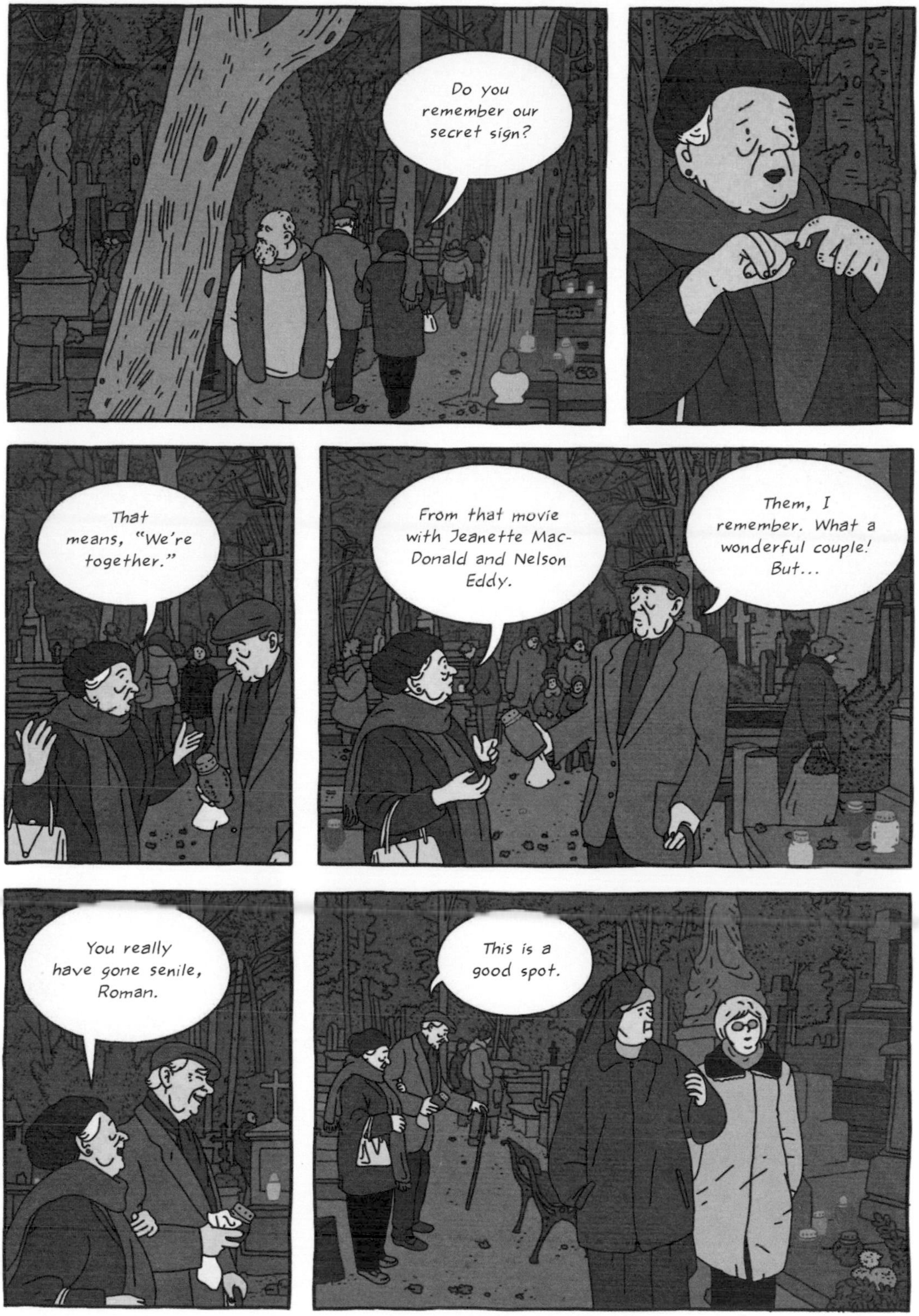
Do you remember our secret sign?
That means, "We're together."
From that movie with Jeanette Mac-Donald and Nelson Eddy.
Them, I remember. What a wonderful couple! But...
You really have gone senile, Roman.
This is a good spot.

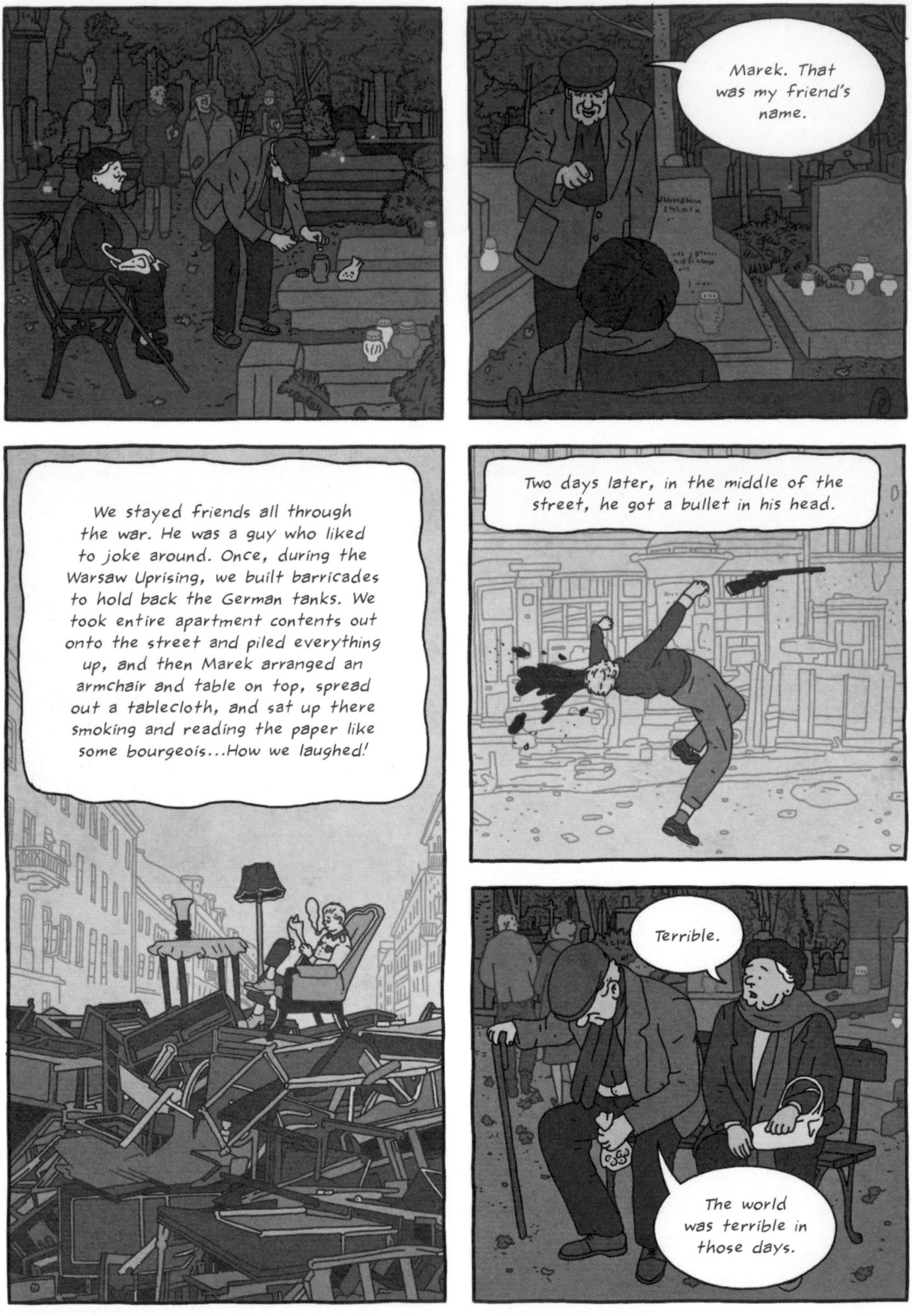
Marek. That was my friend's name.
We stayed friends all through the war. He was a guy who liked to joke around. Once, during the Warsaw Uprising, we built barricades to hold back the German tanks. We took entire apartment contents out onto the street and piled everything up, and then Marek arranged an armchair and table on top, spread out a tablecloth, and sat up there smoking and reading the paper like some bourgeois...How we laughed!
Two days later, in the middle of the street, he got a bullet in his head.
Terrible.
The world was terrible in those days.

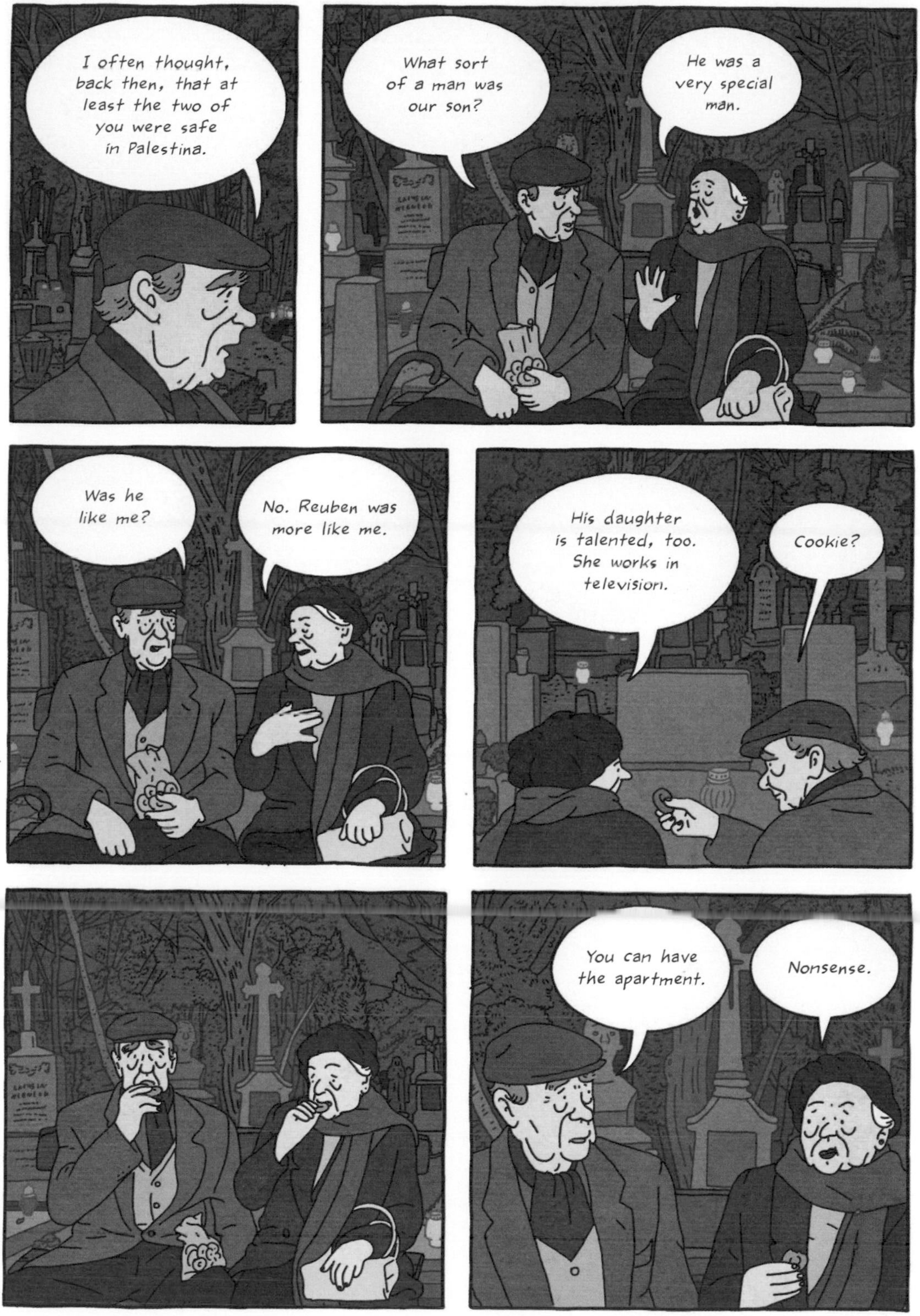
I often thought, back then, that at least the two of you were safe in Palestina.
What sort of a man was our son?
He was a very special man.
Was he like me?
No. Reuben was more like me.
His daughter is talented, too. She works in television.
Cookie?
You can have the apartment.
Nonsense.

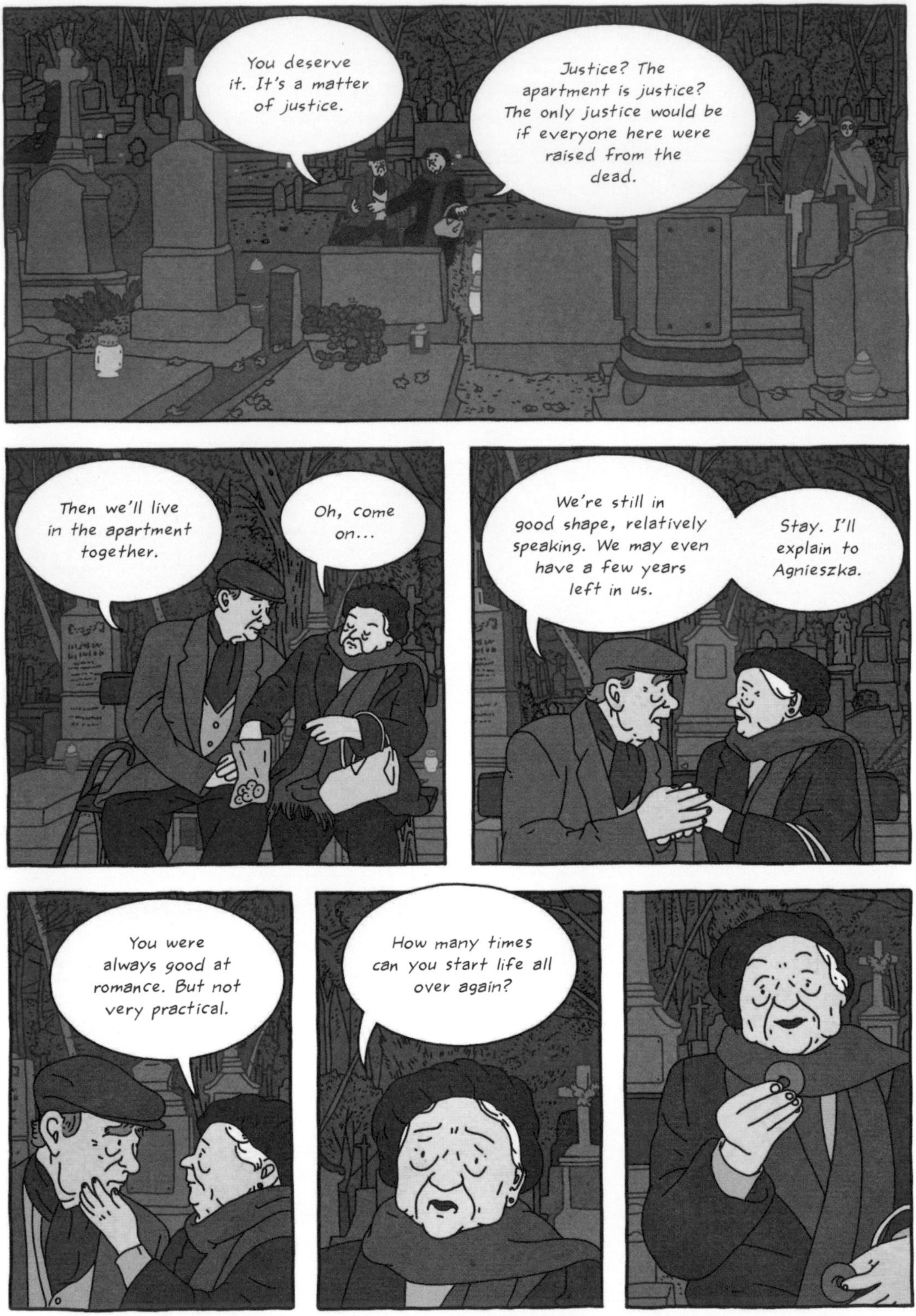
You deserve it. It's a matter of justice.
Justice? The apartment is justice? The only justice would be if everyone here were raised from the dead.
Then we'll live in the apartment together.
Oh, come on...
We're still in good shape, relatively speaking. We may even have a few years left in us.
Stay. I'll explain to Agnieszka.
You were always good at romance. But not very practical.
How many times can you start life all over again?

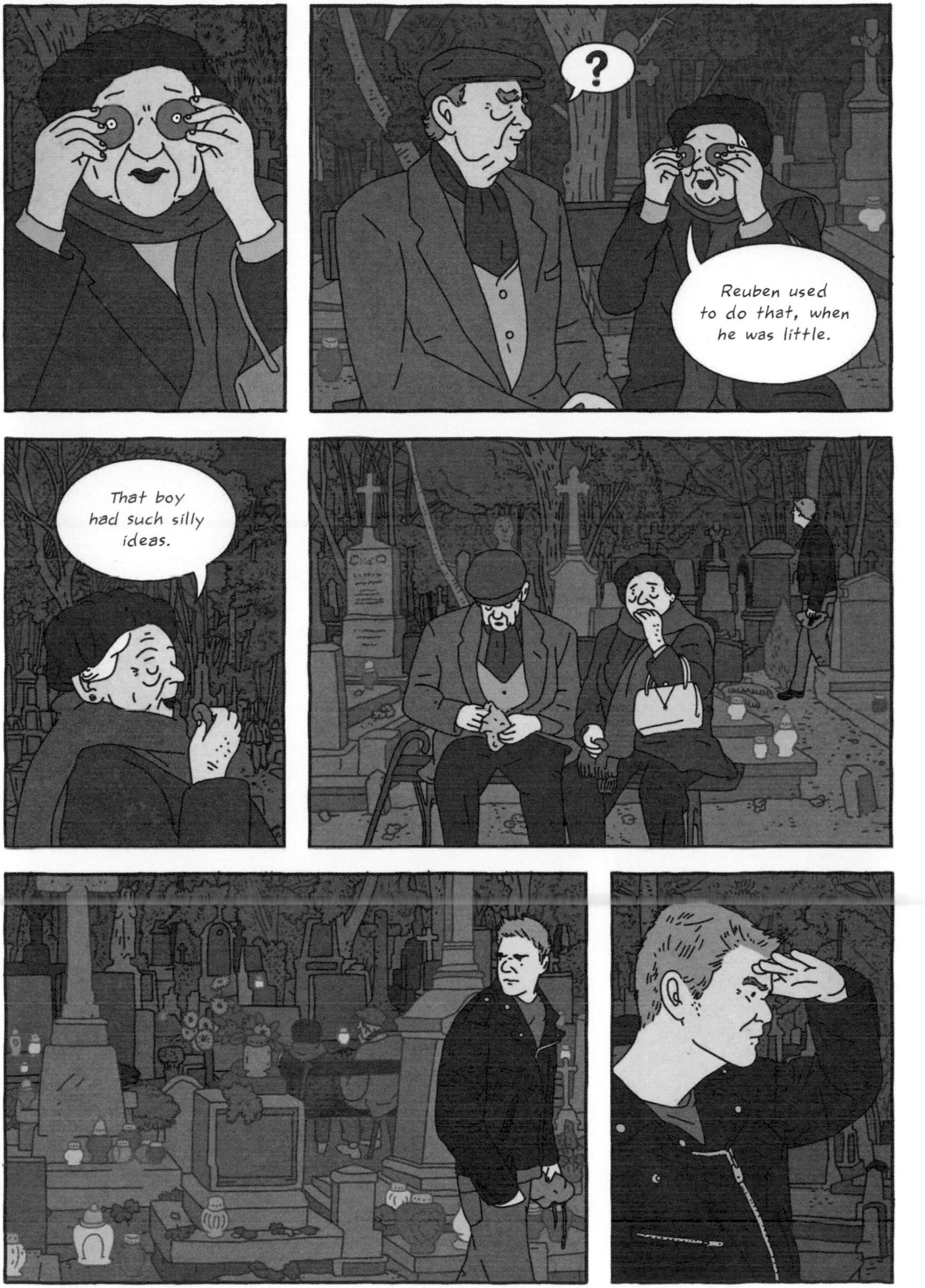
?
Reuben used to do that, when he was little.
That boy had such silly ideas.

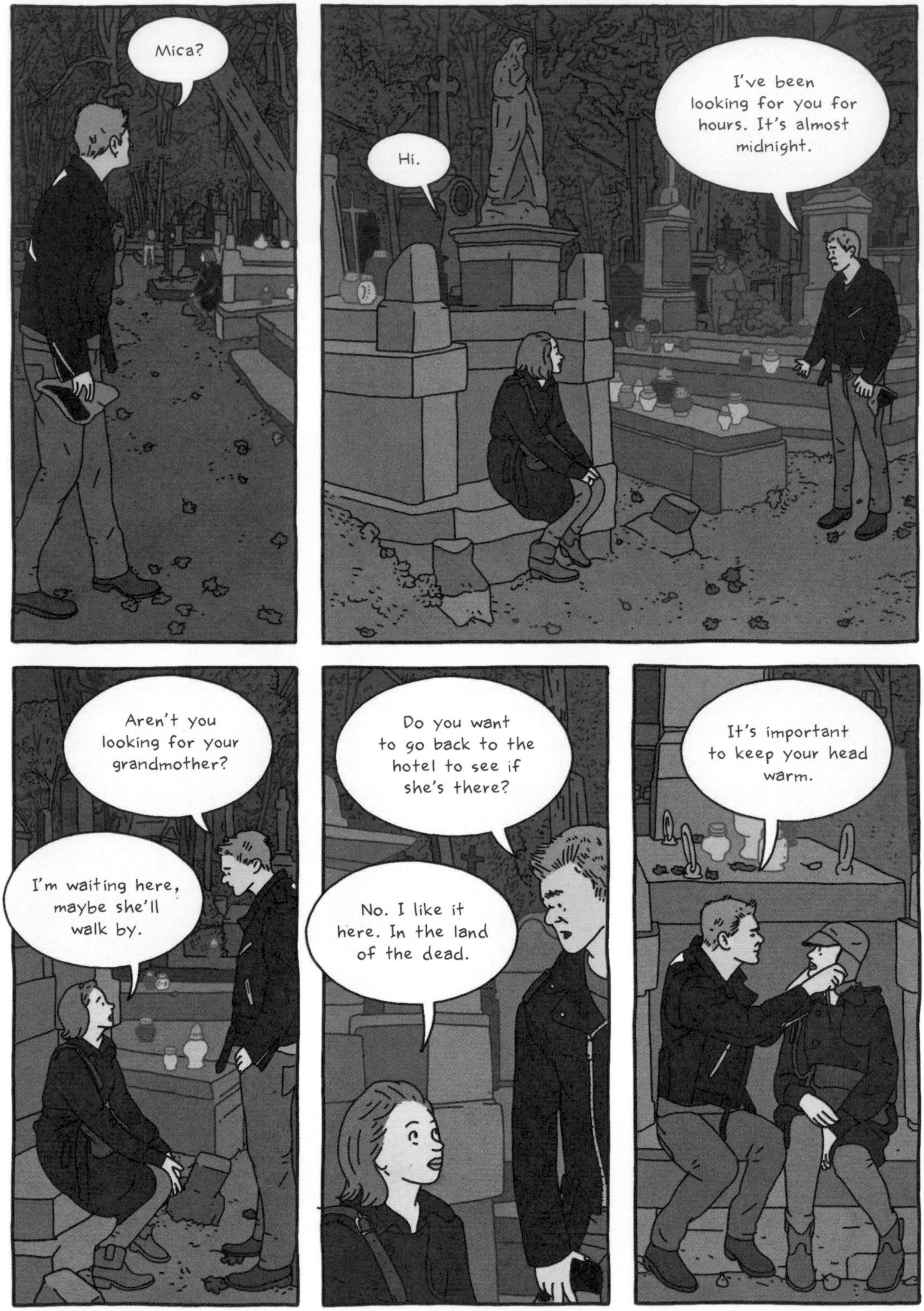
Mica?
Hi.
I've been looking for you for hours. It's almost midnight.
Aren't you looking for your grandmother?
I'm waiting here, maybe she'll walk by.
Do you want to go back to the hotel to see if she's there?
No. I like it here. In the land of the dead.
It's important to keep your head warm.

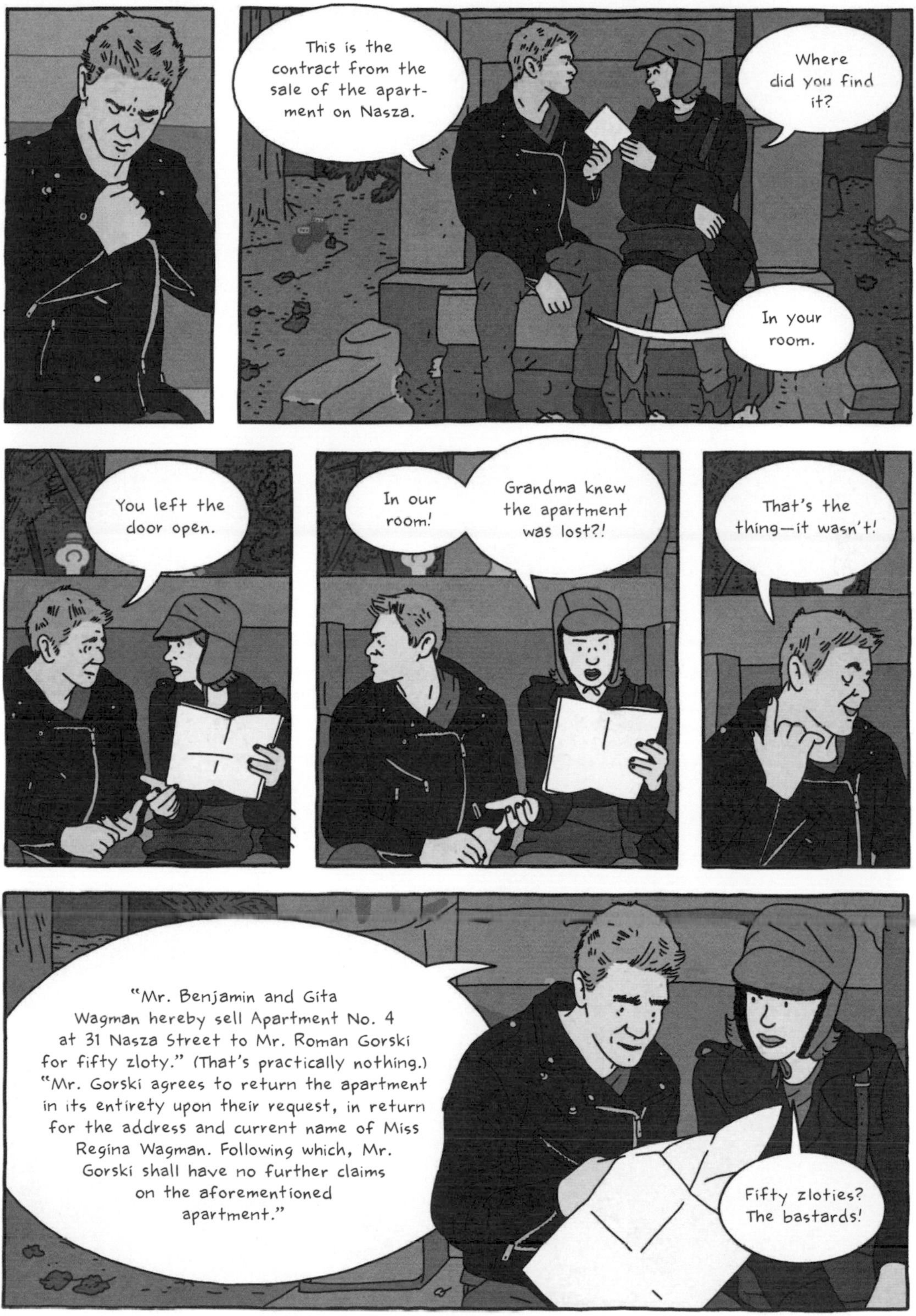
This is the contract from the sale of the apartment on Nasza.
Where did you find it?
In your room.
You left the door open.
In our room!
Grandma knew the apartment was lost?!
That's the thing—it wasn't!
"Mr. Benjamin and Gita Wagman hereby sell Apartment No. 4 at 31 Nasza Street to Mr. Roman Gorski for fifty zloty." (That's practically nothing.) "Mr. Gorski agrees to return the apartment in its entirety upon their request, in return for the address and current name of Miss Regina Wagman. Following which, Mr. Gorski shall have no further claims on the aforementioned apartment."
Fifty zloties? The bastards!

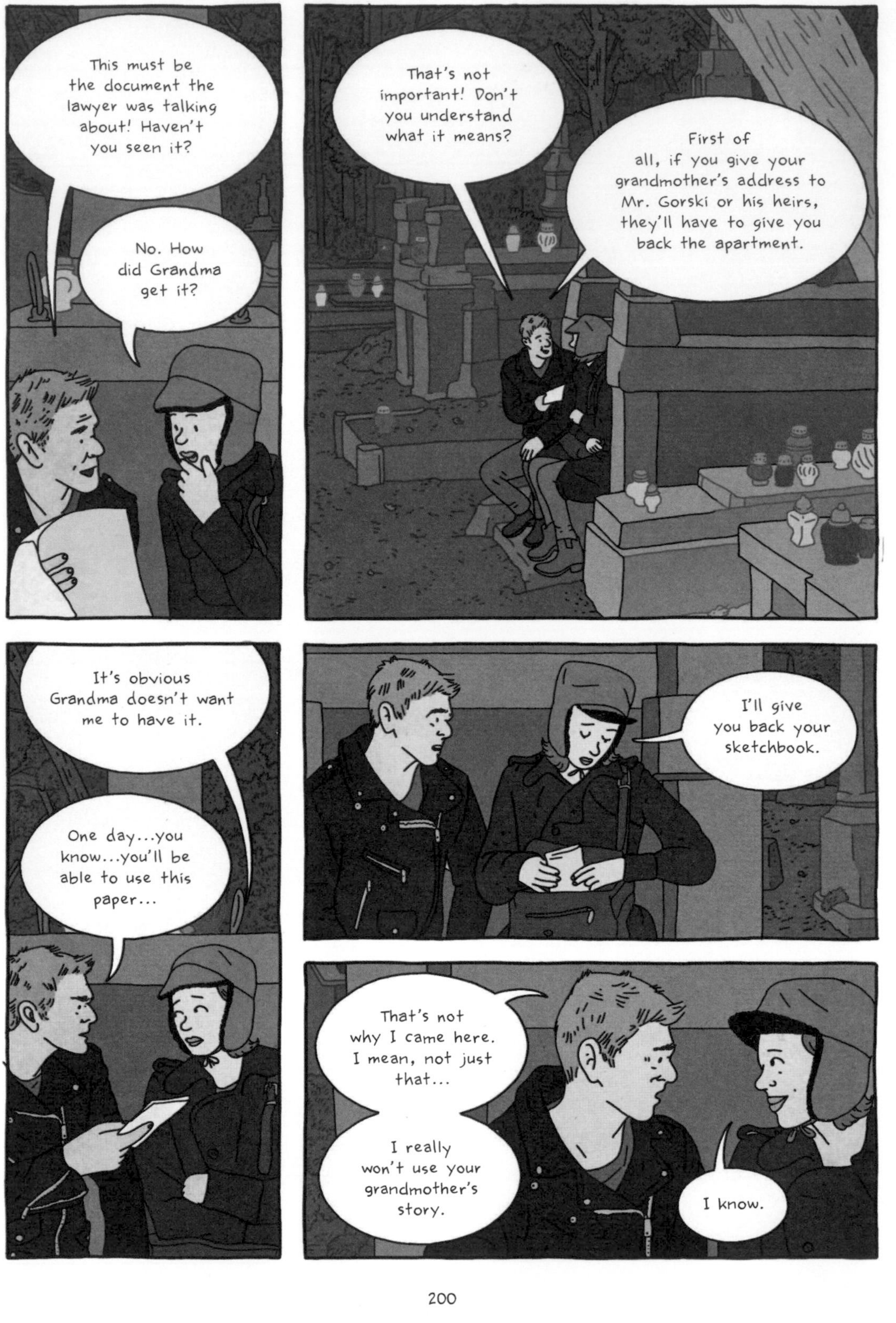
This must be the document the lawyer was talking about! Haven't you seen it?
No. How did Grandma get it?
That's not important! Don't you understand what it means?
First of all, if you give your grandmother's address to Mr. Gorski or his heirs, they'll have to give you back the apartment.
It's obvious Grandma doesn't want me to have it.
One day...you know...you'll be able to use this paper...
I'll give you back your sketchbook.
That's not why I came here. I mean, not just that...
I really won't use your grandmother's story.
I know.

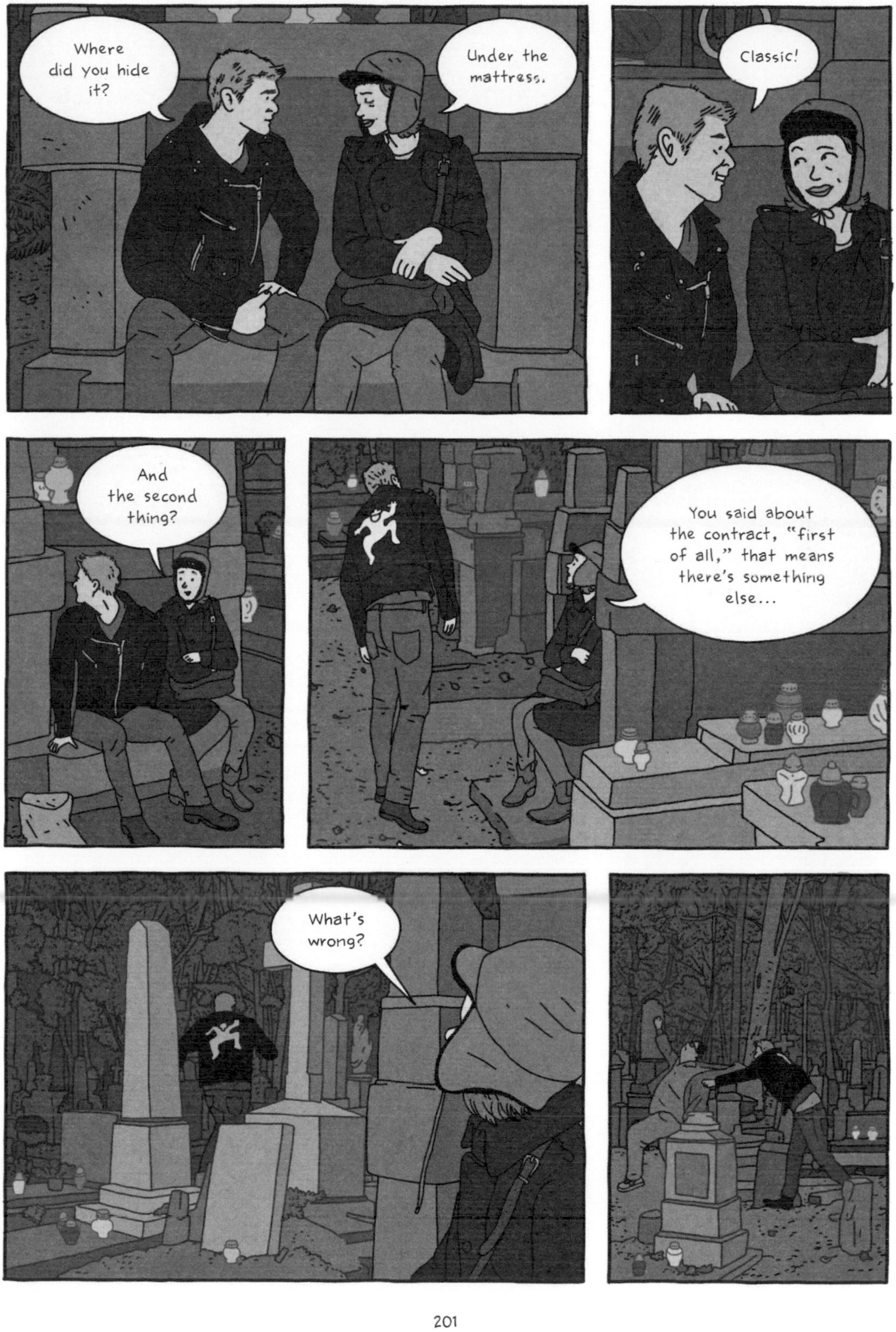
Where did you hide it?
Under the mattress.
Classic!
And the second thing?
You said about the contract, "first of all," that means there's something else...
What's wrong?

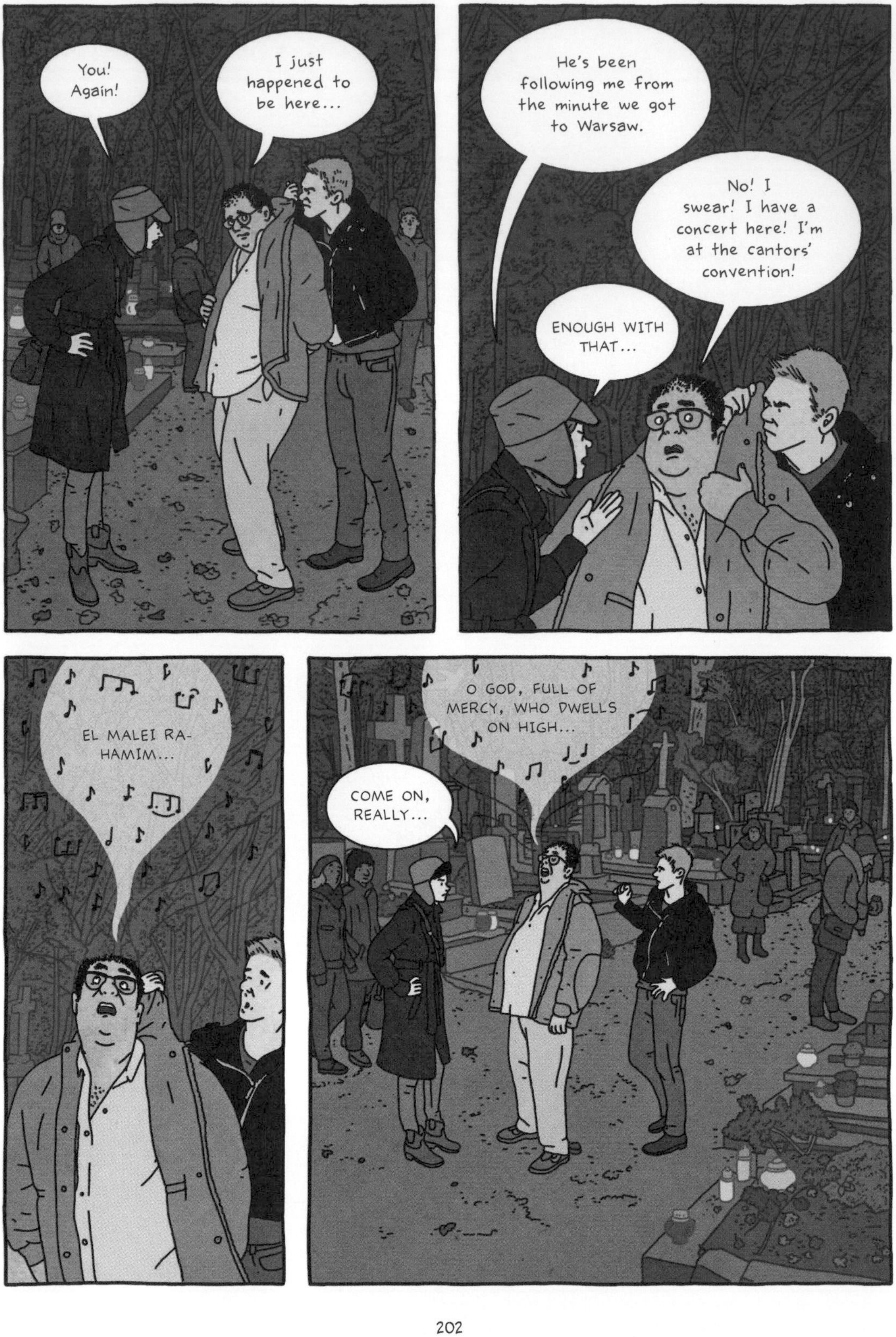
You! Again!
I just happened to be here...
He's been following me from the minute we got to Warsaw.
No! I swear! I have a concert here! I'm at the cantors' convention!
ENOUGH WITH THAT...
EL MALEI RA-HAMIM...
O GOD, FULL OF MERCY, WHO DWELLS ON HIGH...
COME ON, REALLY...

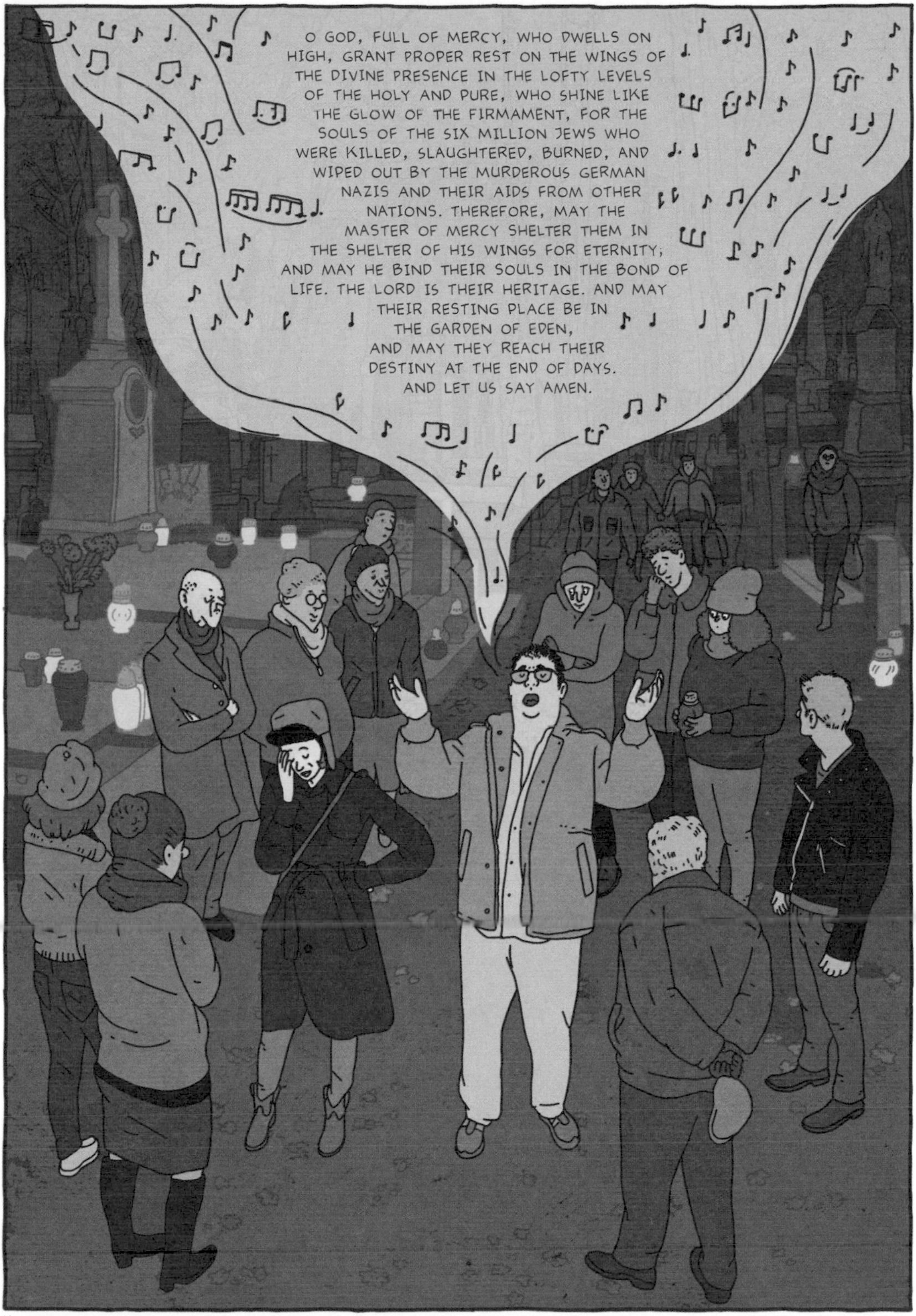
O GOD, FULL OF MERCY, WHO DWELLS ON HIGH, GRANT PROPER REST ON THE WINGS OF THE DIVINE PRESENCE IN THE LOFTY LEVELS OF THE HOLY AND PURE, WHO SHINE LIKE THE GLOW OF THE FIRMAMENT, FOR THE SOULS OF THE SIX MILLION JEWS WHO WERE KILLED, SLAUGHTERED, BURNED, AND WIPED OUT BY THE MURDEROUS GERMAN NAZIS AND THEIR AIDS FROM OTHER NATIONS. THEREFORE, MAY THE MASTER OF MERCY SHELTER THEM IN THE SHELTER OF HIS WINGS FOR ETERNITY; AND MAY HE BIND THEIR SOULS IN THE BOND OF LIFE. THE LORD IS THEIR HERITAGE. AND MAY THEIR RESTING PLACE BE IN THE GARDEN OF EDEN, AND MAY THEY REACH THEIR DESTINY AT THE END OF DAYS. AND LET US SAY AMEN.

*A version of the Jewish funeral prayer, adapted for the remembrance of Holocaust victims, recited throughout Israel at Holocaust Remembrance Day ceremonies.

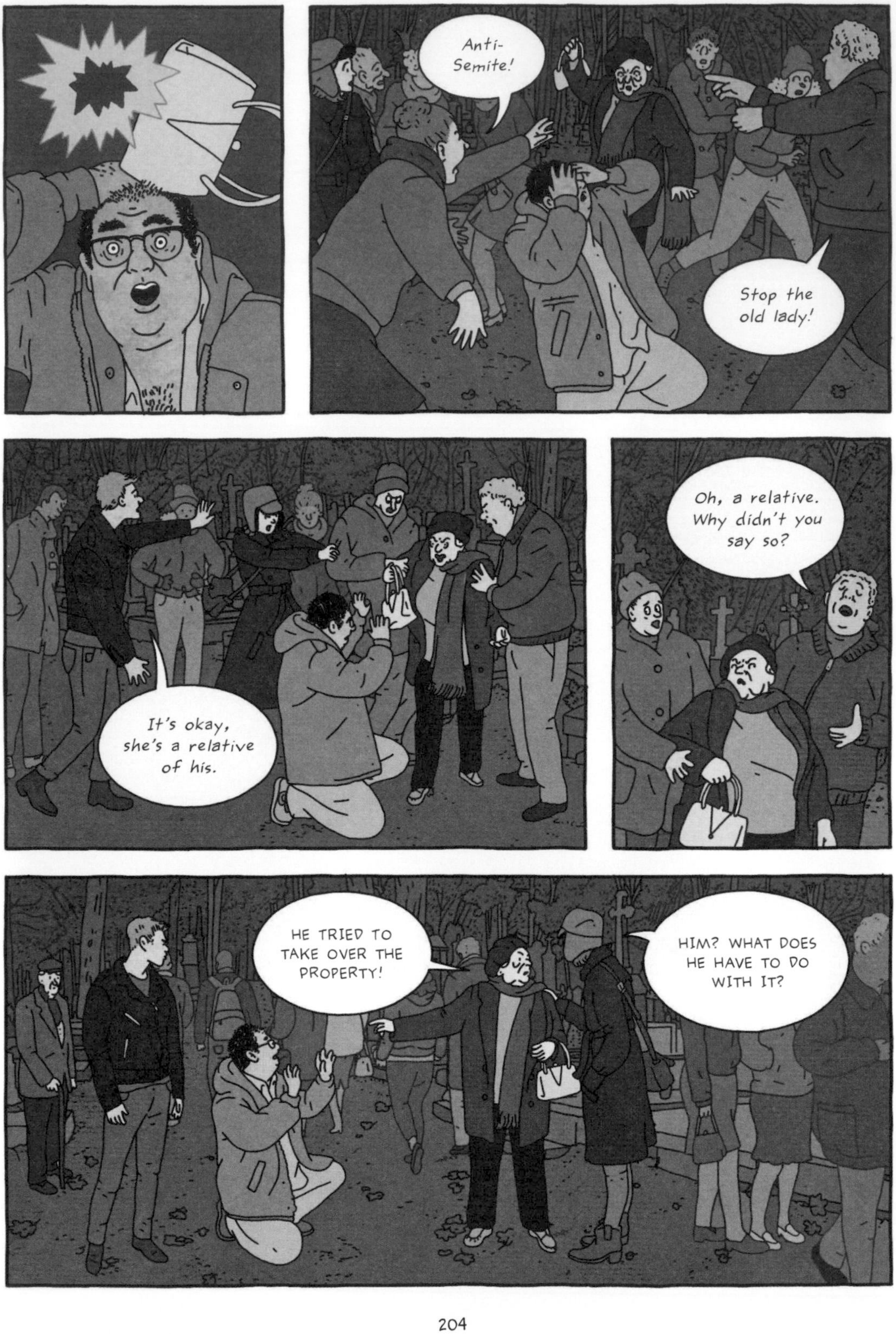
Anti-Semite!
Stop the old lady!
It's okay, she's a relative of his.
Oh, a relative. Why didn't you say so?
HE TRIED TO TAKE OVER THE PROPERTY!
HIM? WHAT DOES HE HAVE TO DO WITH IT?

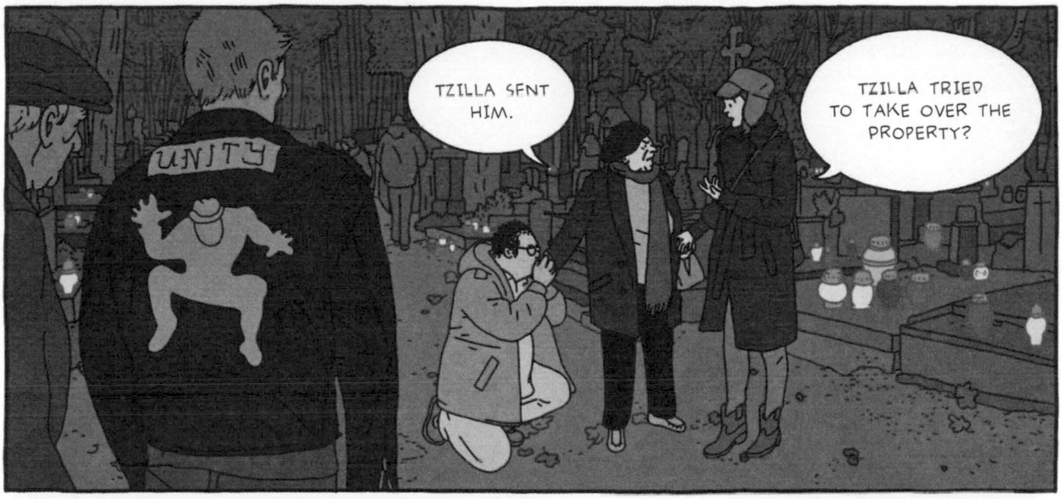
TZILLA SENT HIM.
TZILLA TRIED TO TAKE OVER THE PROPERTY?
UNITY

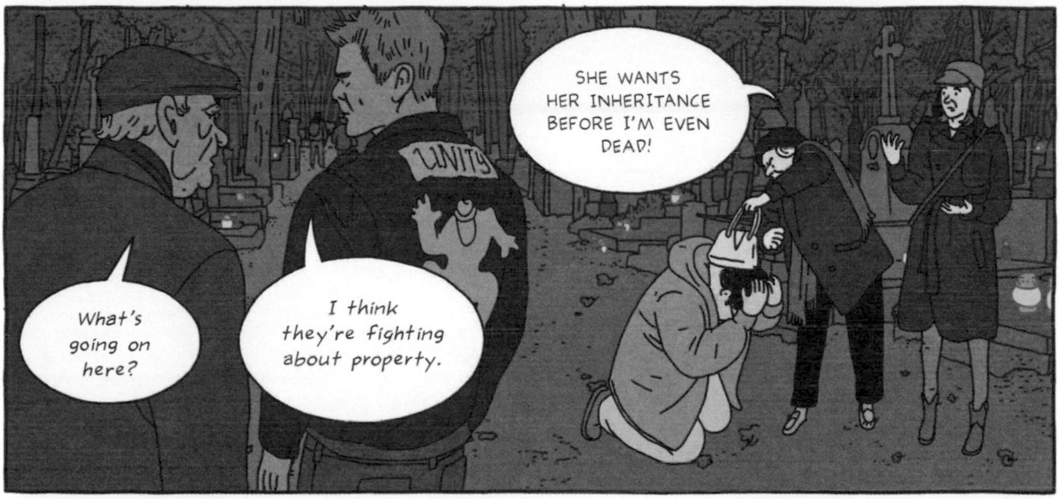
SHE WANTS HER INHERITANCE BEFORE I'M EVEN DEAD!
What's going on here?
I think they're fighting about property.

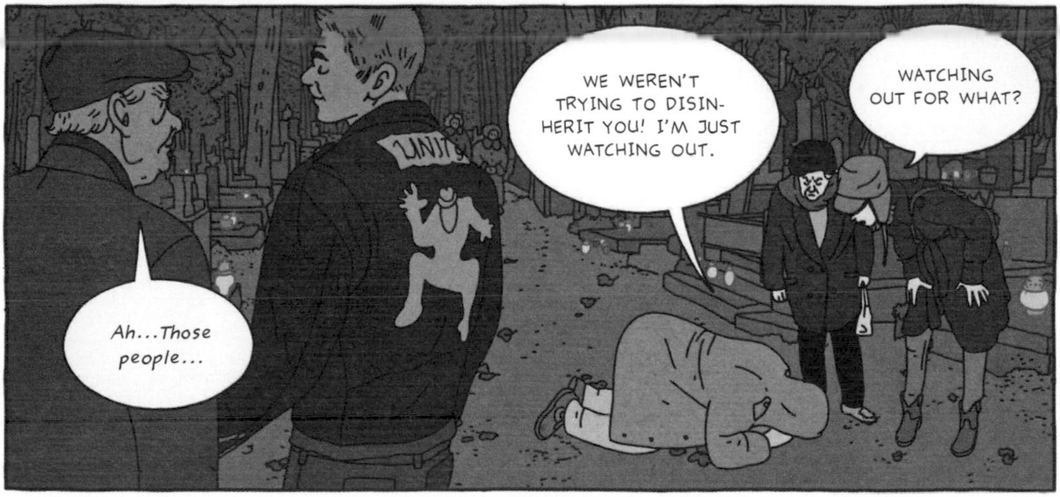
WE WEREN'T TRYING TO DISIN-HERIT YOU! I'M JUST WATCHING OUT.
WATCHING OUT FOR WHAT?
Ah...Those people...

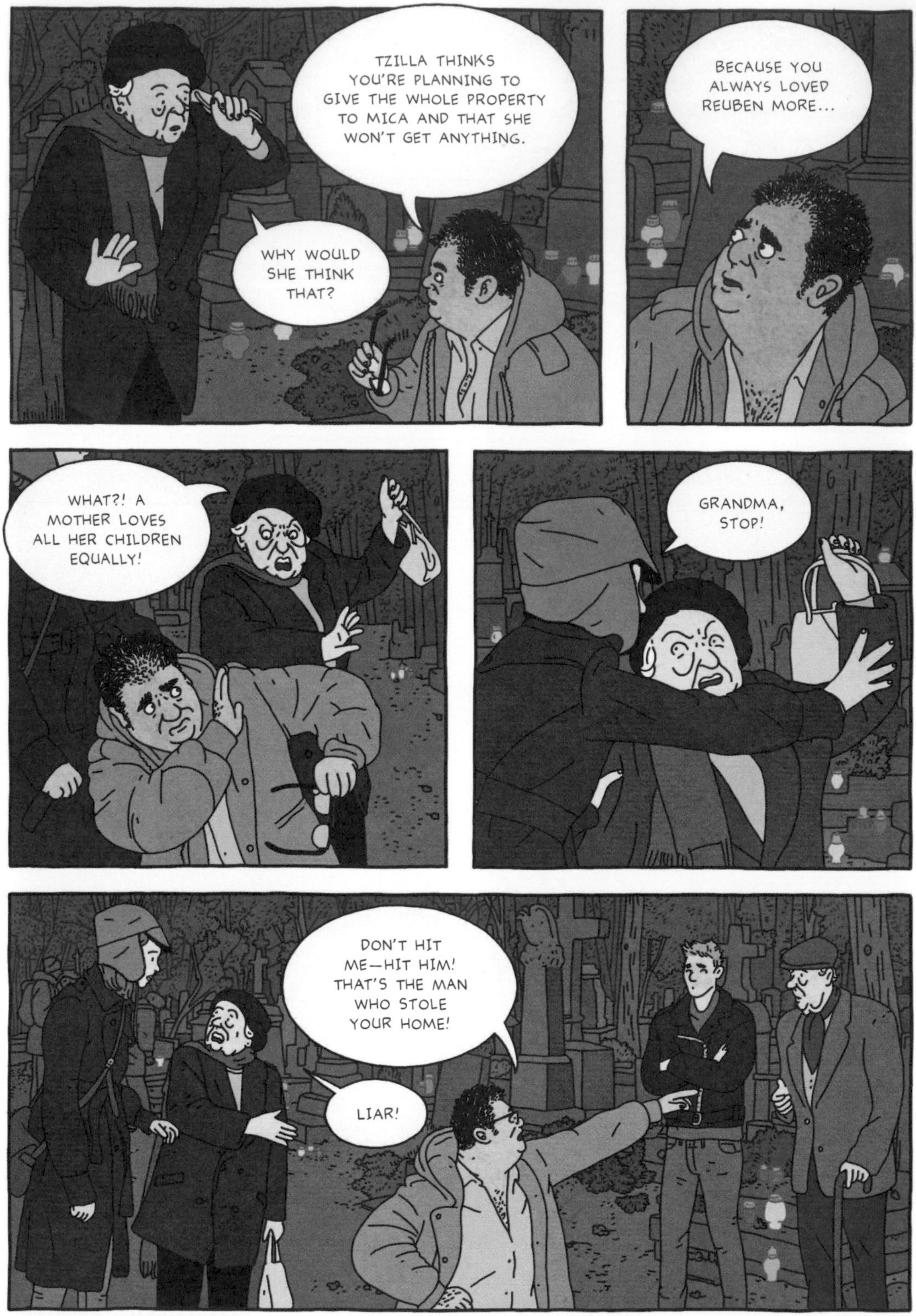
TZILLA THINKS YOU'RE PLANNING TO GIVE THE WHOLE PROPERTY TO MICA AND THAT SHE WON'T GET ANYTHING.
WHY WOULD SHE THINK THAT?
BECAUSE YOU ALWAYS LOVED REUBEN MORE...
WHAT?! A MOTHER LOVES ALL HER CHILDREN EQUALLY!
GRANDMA, STOP!
DON'T HIT ME—HIT HIM! THAT'S THE MAN WHO STOLE YOUR HOME!
LIAR!

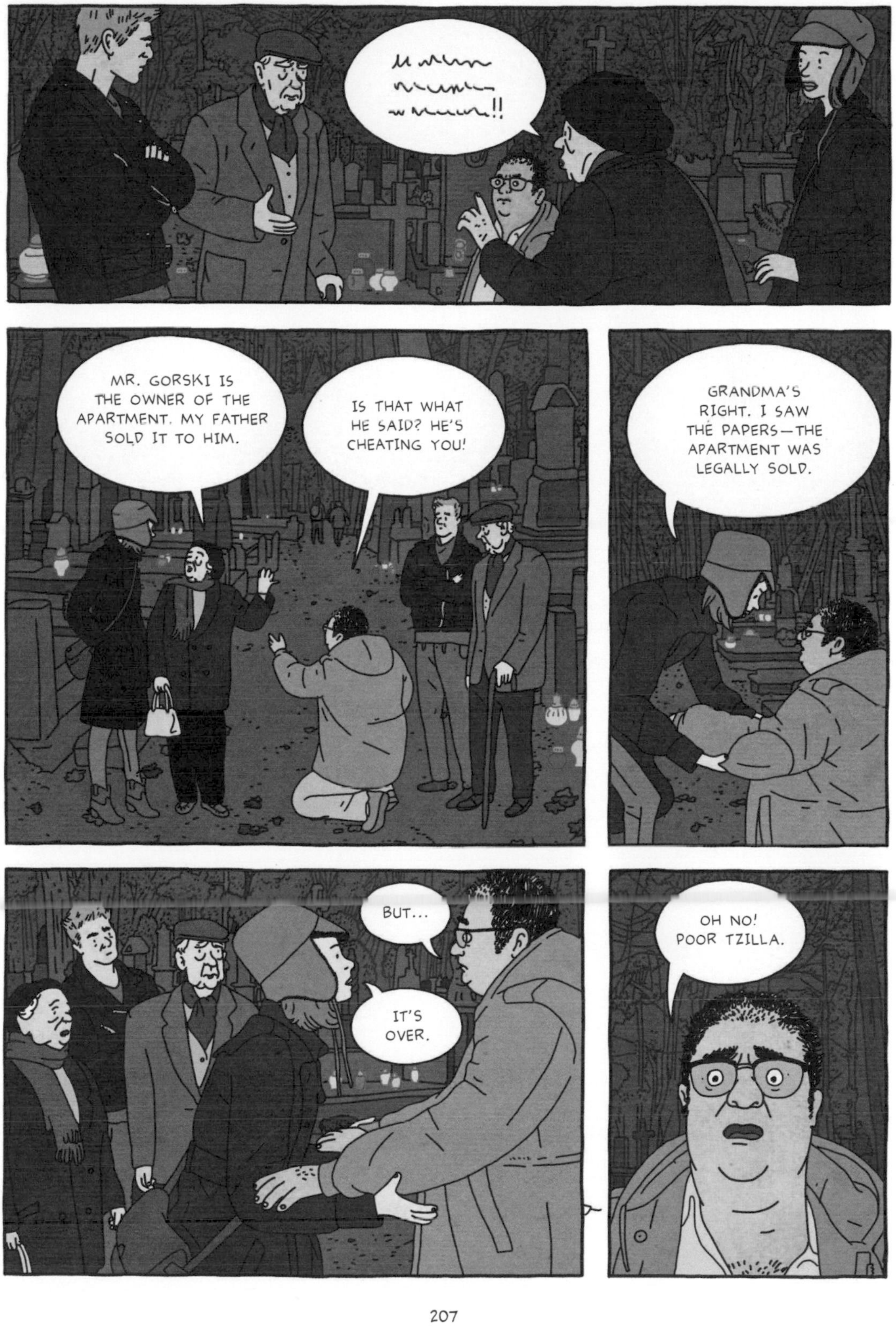
MR. GORSKI IS THE OWNER OF THE APARTMENT. MY FATHER SOLD IT TO HIM.
IS THAT WHAT HE SAID? HE'S CHEATING YOU!
GRANDMA'S RIGHT. I SAW THE PAPERS—THE APARTMENT WAS LEGALLY SOLD.
BUT...
IT'S OVER.
OH NO! POOR TZILLA.

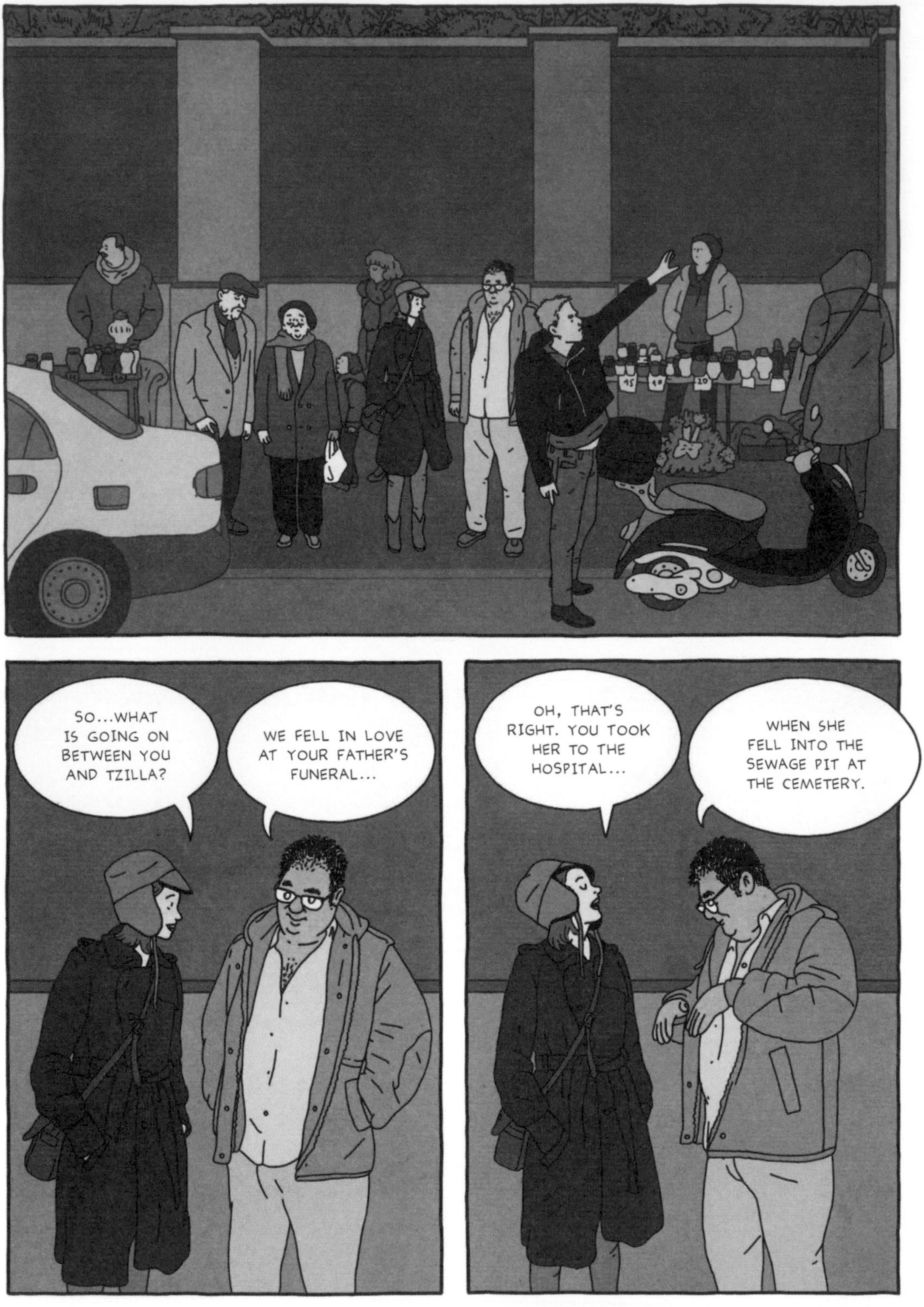
SO...WHAT IS GOING ON BETWEEN YOU AND TZILLA?
WE FELL IN LOVE AT YOUR FATHER'S FUNERAL...
OH, THAT'S RIGHT. YOU TOOK HER TO THE HOSPITAL...
WHEN SHE FELL INTO THE SEWAGE PIT AT THE CEMETERY.

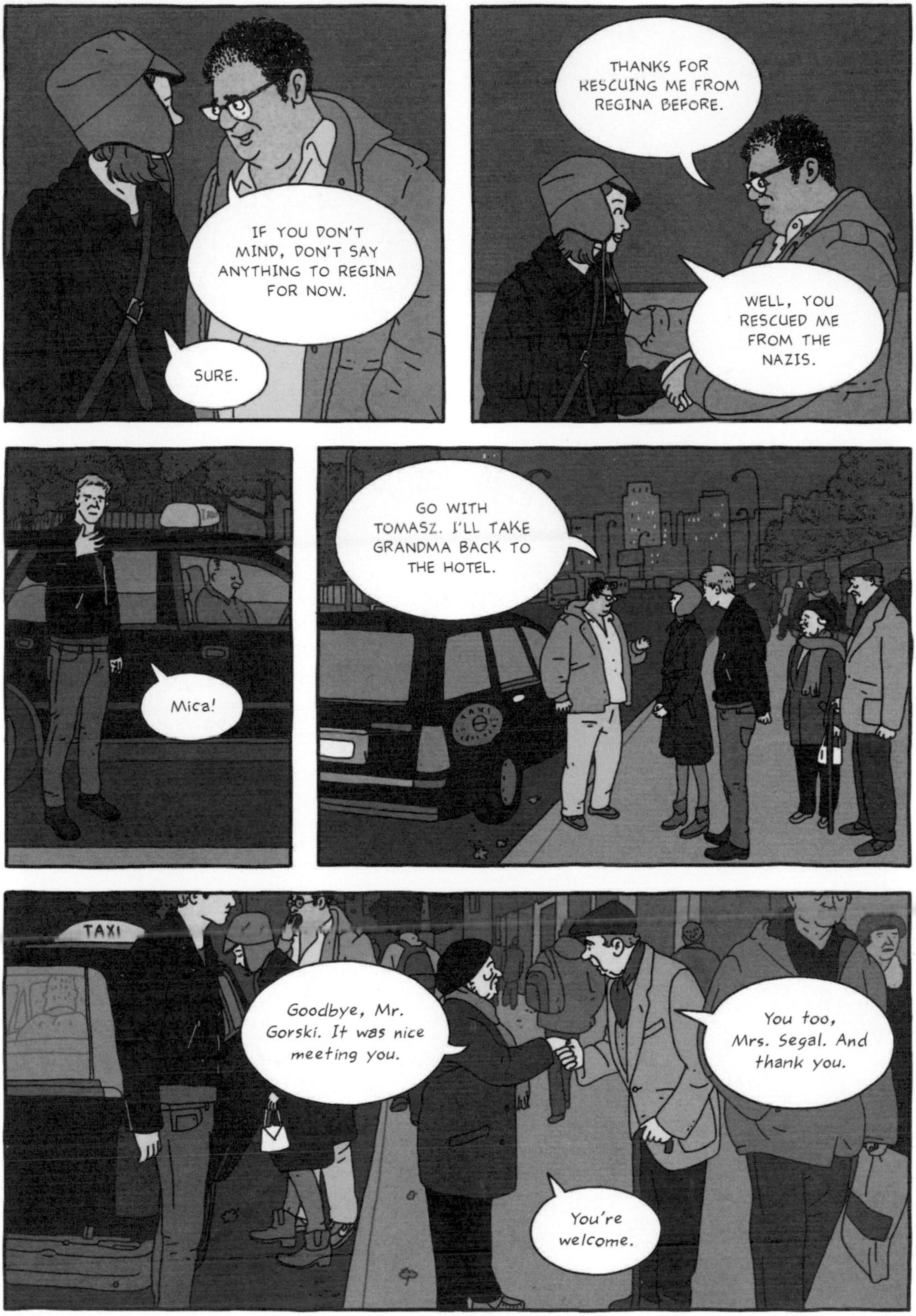
IF YOU DON'T MIND, DON'T SAY ANYTHING TO REGINA FOR NOW.
SURE.
THANKS FOR RESCUING ME FROM REGINA BEFORE.
WELL, YOU RESCUED ME FROM THE NAZIS.
Mica!
GO WITH TOMASZ. I'LL TAKE GRANDMA BACK TO THE HOTEL.
TAXI
Goodbye, Mr. Gorski. It was nice meeting you.
You too, Mrs. Segal. And thank you.
You're welcome.

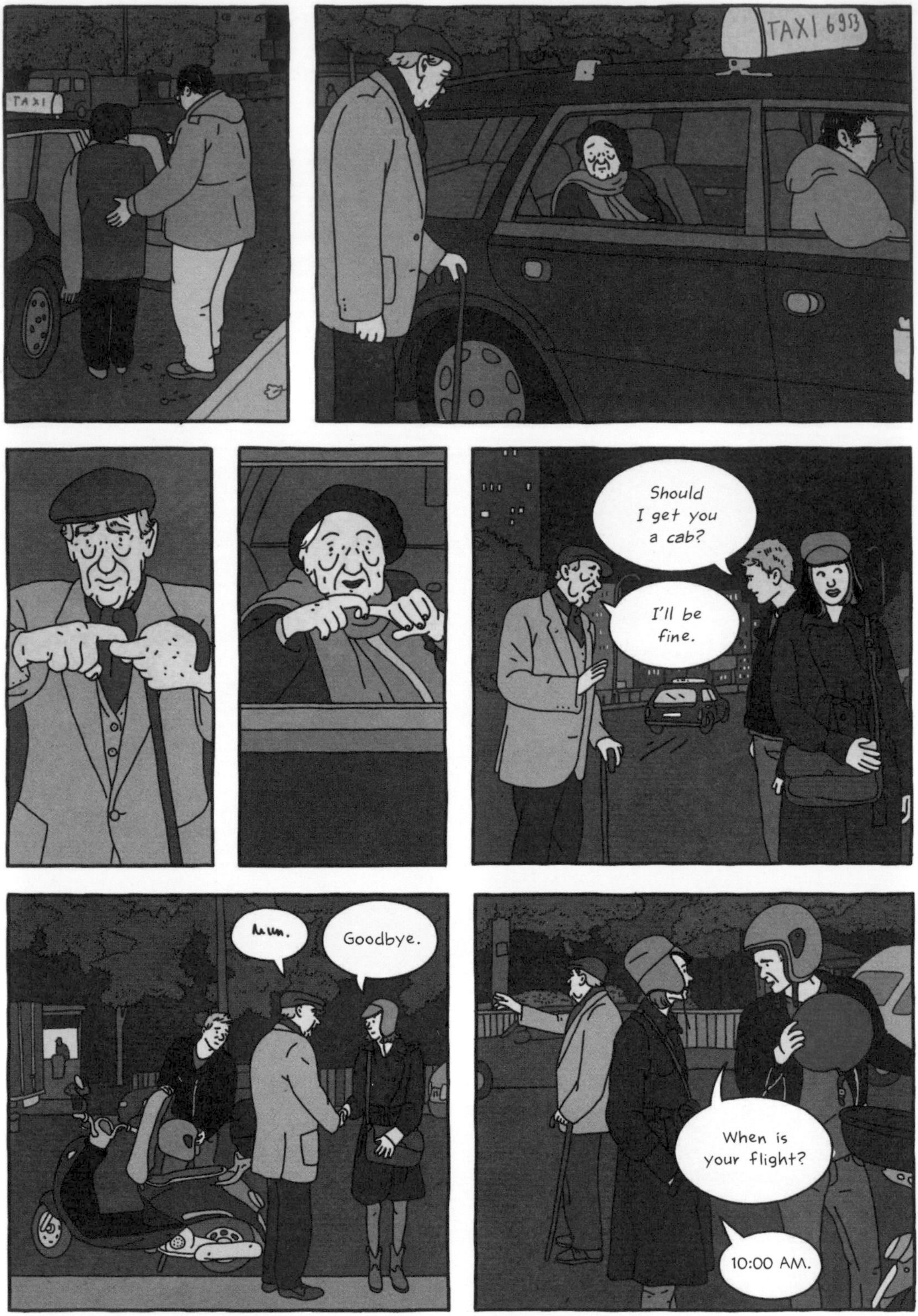
TAXI
TAXI 6953
Should I get you a cab?
I'll be fine.
Goodbye.
When is your flight?
10:00 AM.

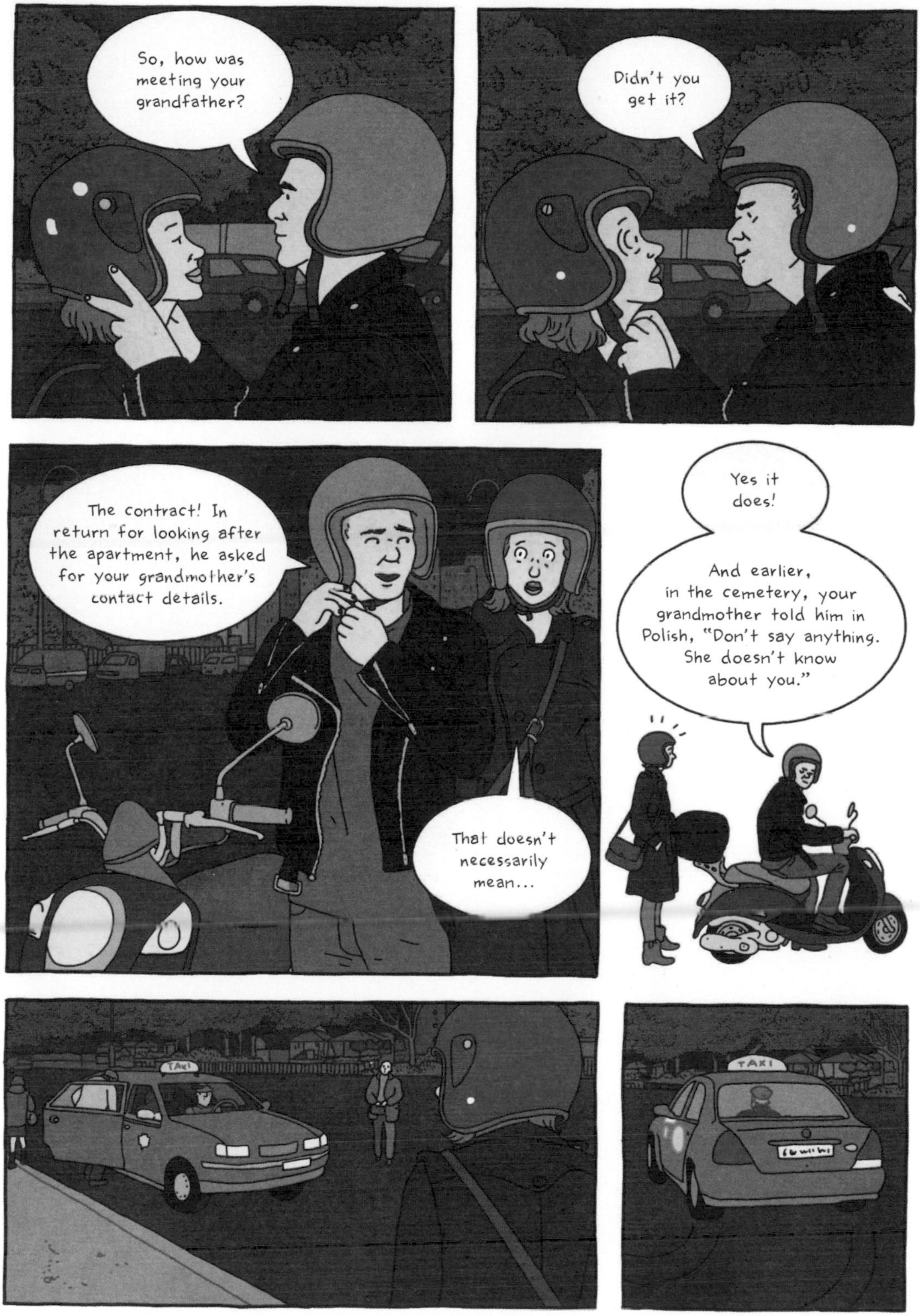
So, how was meeting your grandfather?
Didn't you get it?
The contract! In return for looking after the apartment, he asked for your grandmother's contact details.
That doesn't necessarily mean...
Yes it does!
And earlier, in the cemetery, your grandmother told him in Polish, "Don't say anything. She doesn't know about you."
TAXI
TAXI

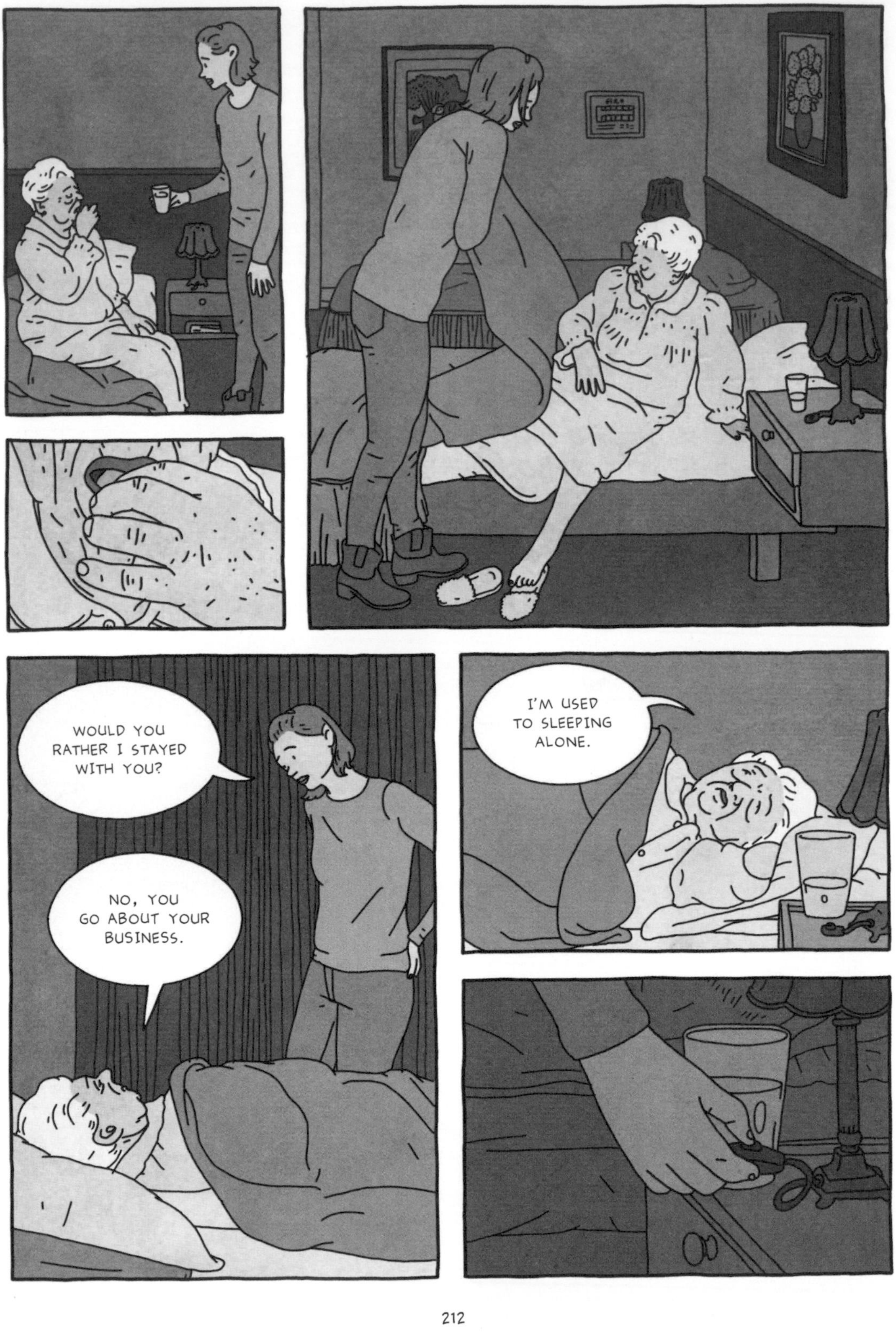
WOULD YOU RATHER I STAYED WITH YOU?
NO, YOU GO ABOUT YOUR BUSINESS.
I'M USED TO SLEEPING ALONE.

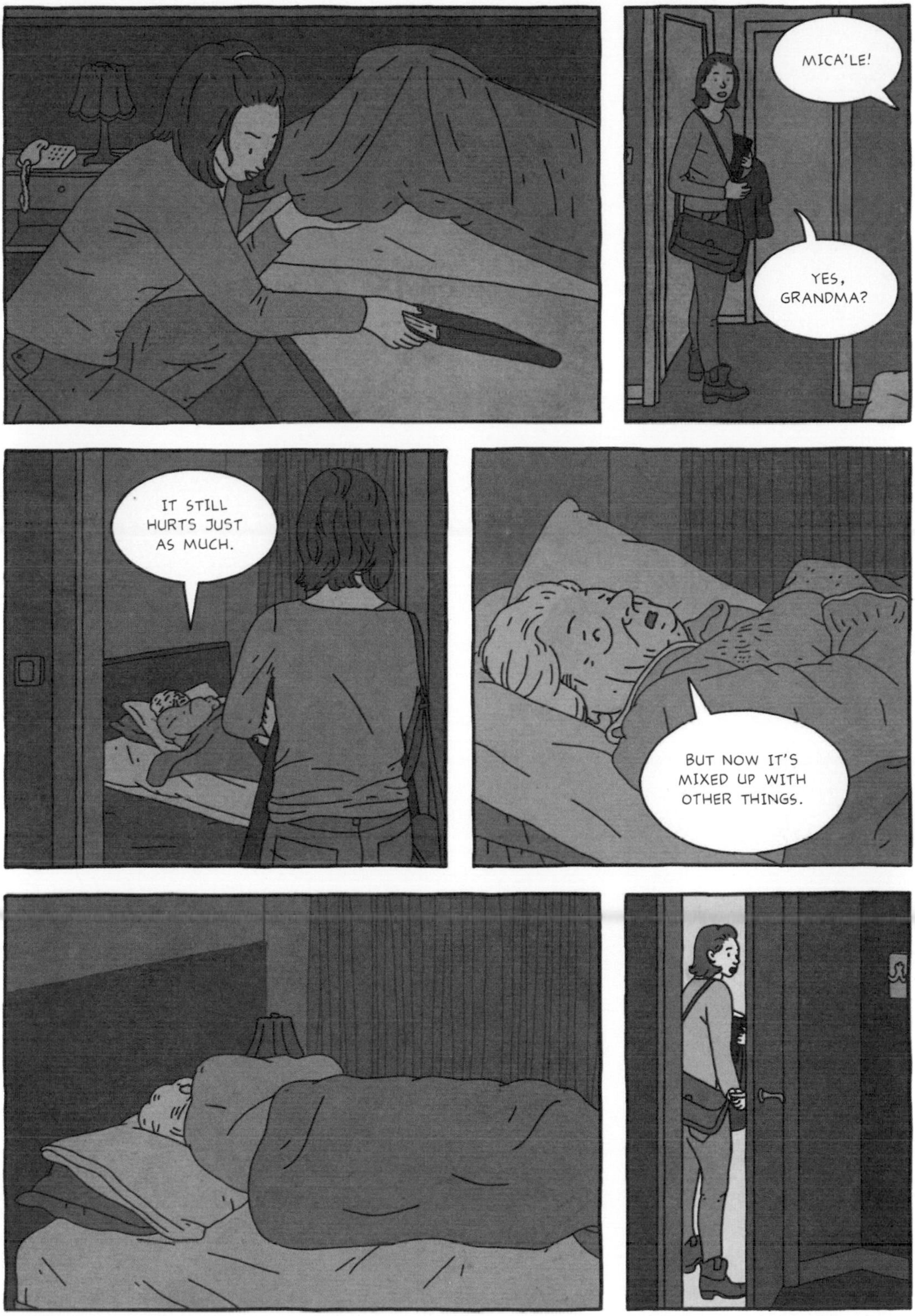
MICA'LE!
YES, GRANDMA?
IT STILL HURTS JUST AS MUCH.
BUT NOW IT'S MIXED UP WITH OTHER THINGS.

DAY SEVEN

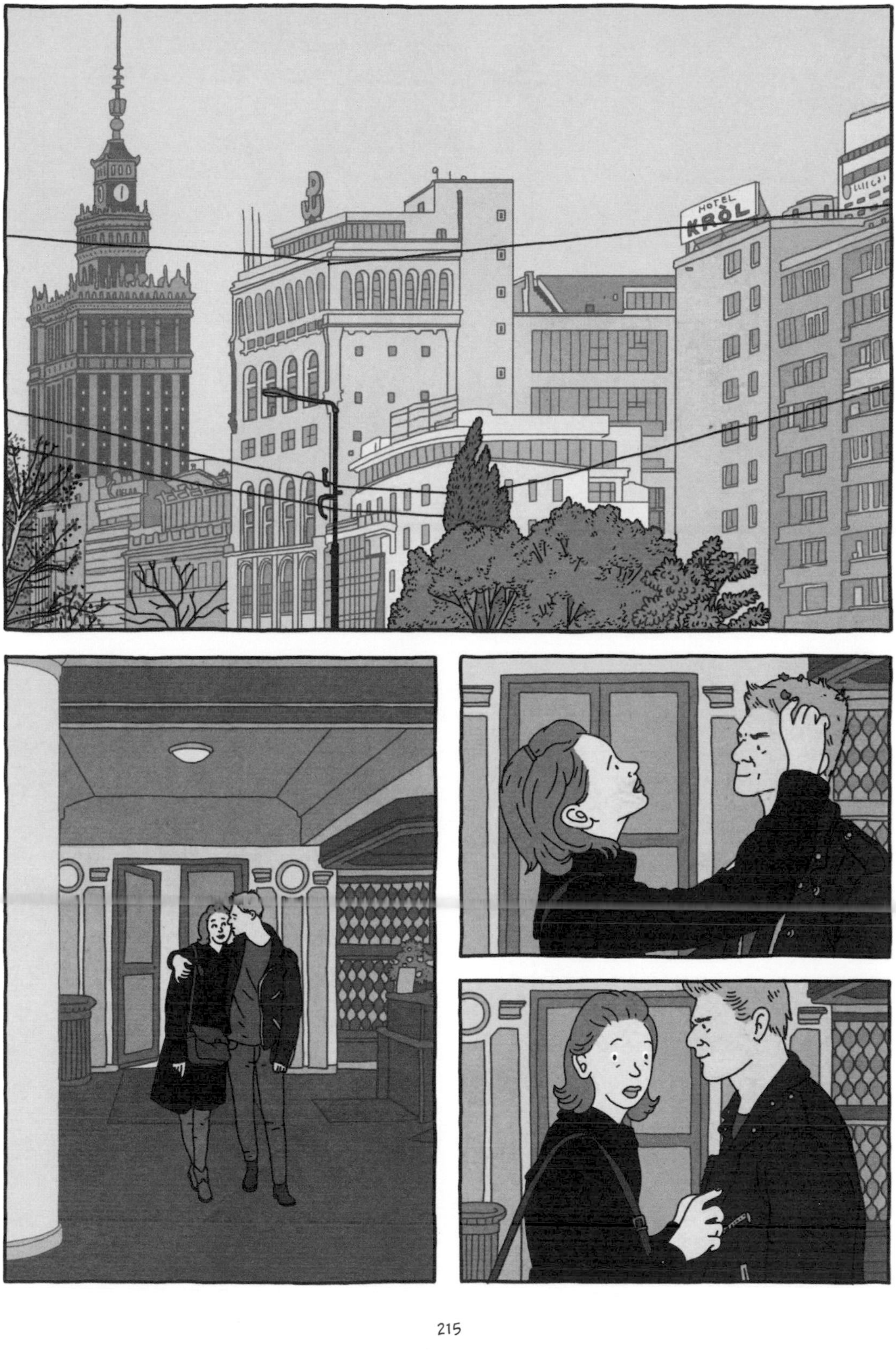
HOTEL
KRÓL

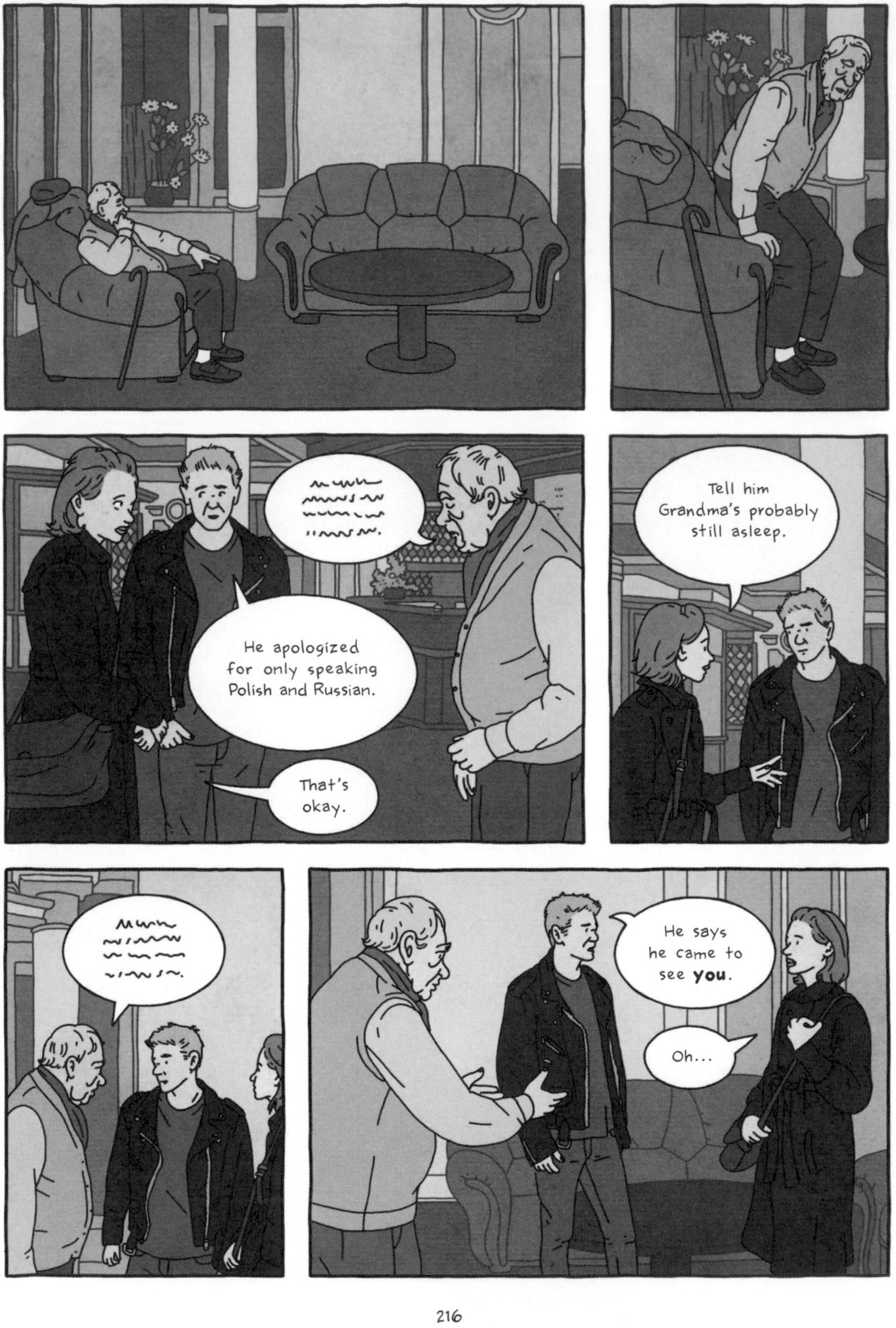
He apologized for only speaking Polish and Russian.
That's okay.
Tell him Grandma's probably still asleep.
He says he came to see **you**.
Oh...

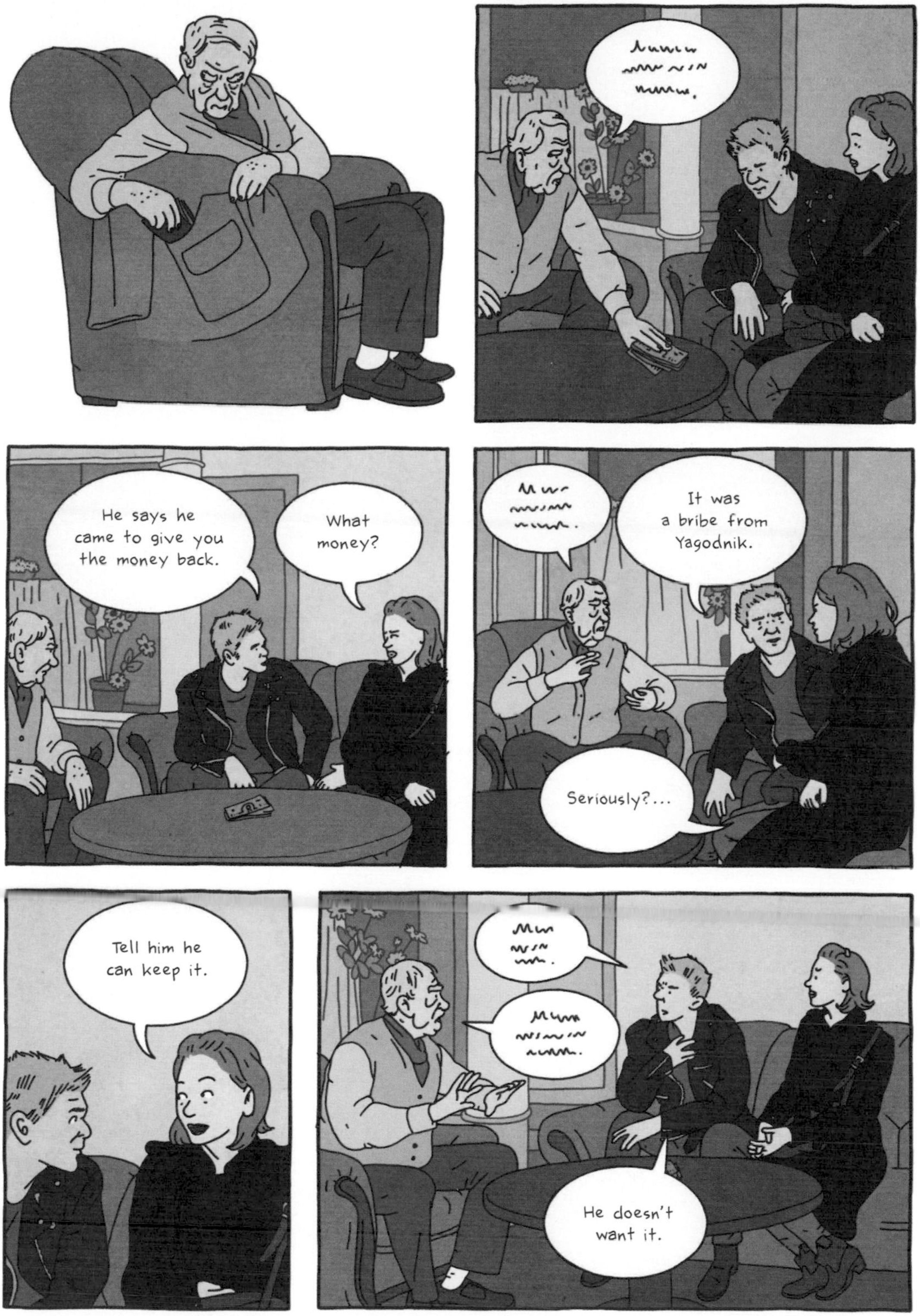
He says he came to give you the money back.
What money?
It was a bribe from Yagodnik.
Seriously?...
Tell him he can keep it.
He doesn't want it.

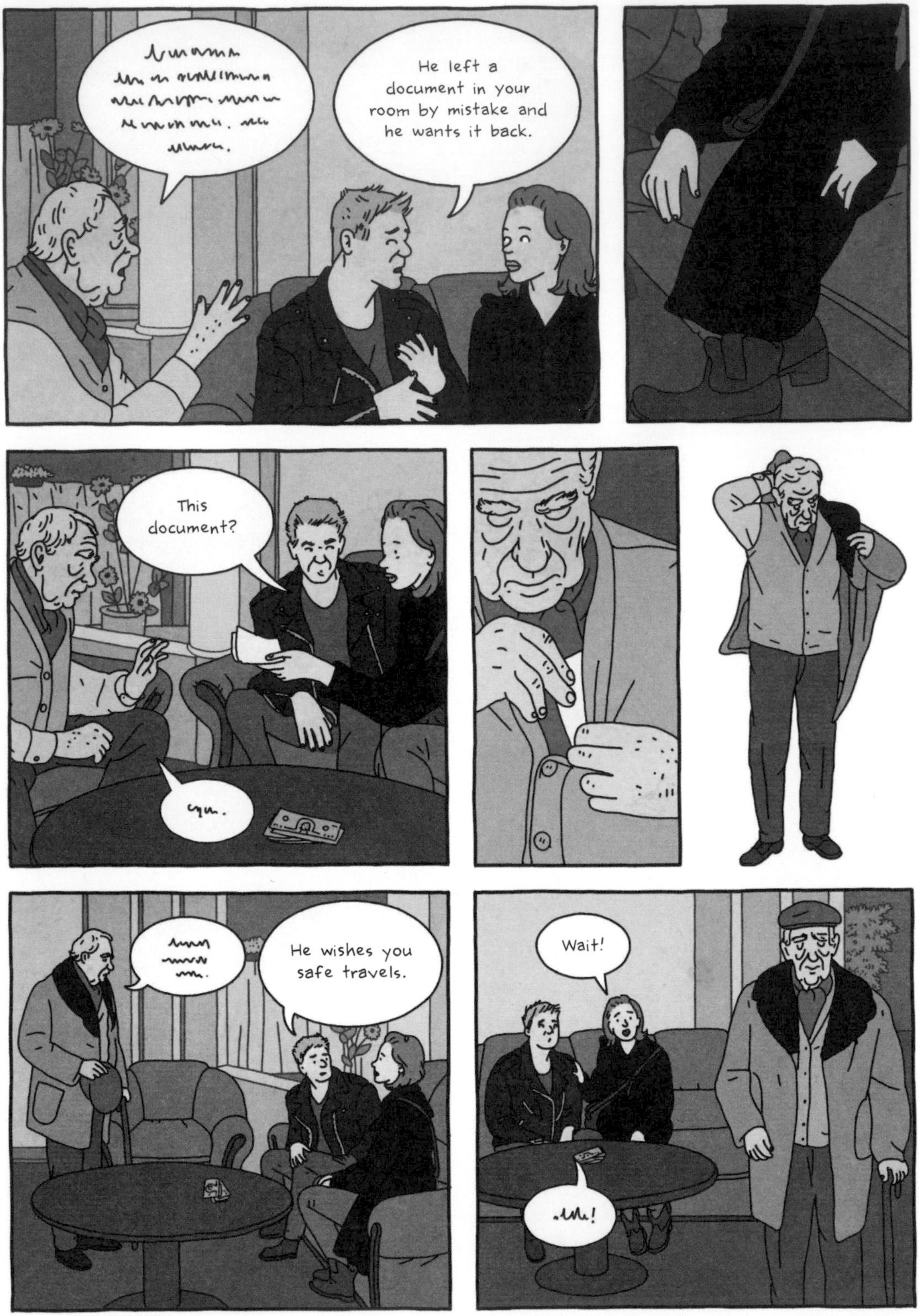
He left a document in your room by mistake and he wants it back.
This document?
He wishes you safe travels.
Wait!

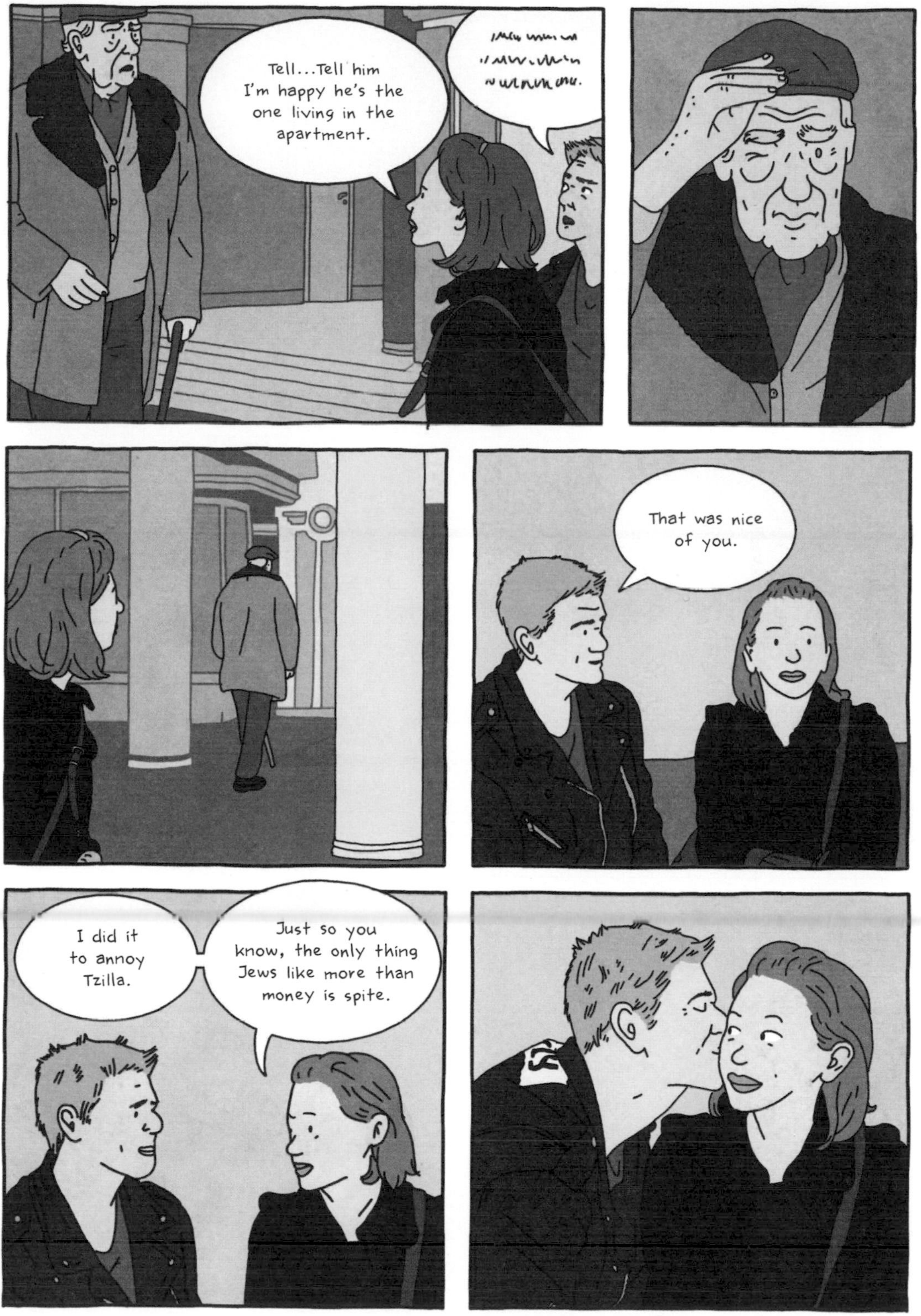
Tell...Tell him I'm happy he's the one living in the apartment.
That was nice of you.
I did it to annoy Tzilla.
Just so you know, the only thing Jews like more than money is spite.

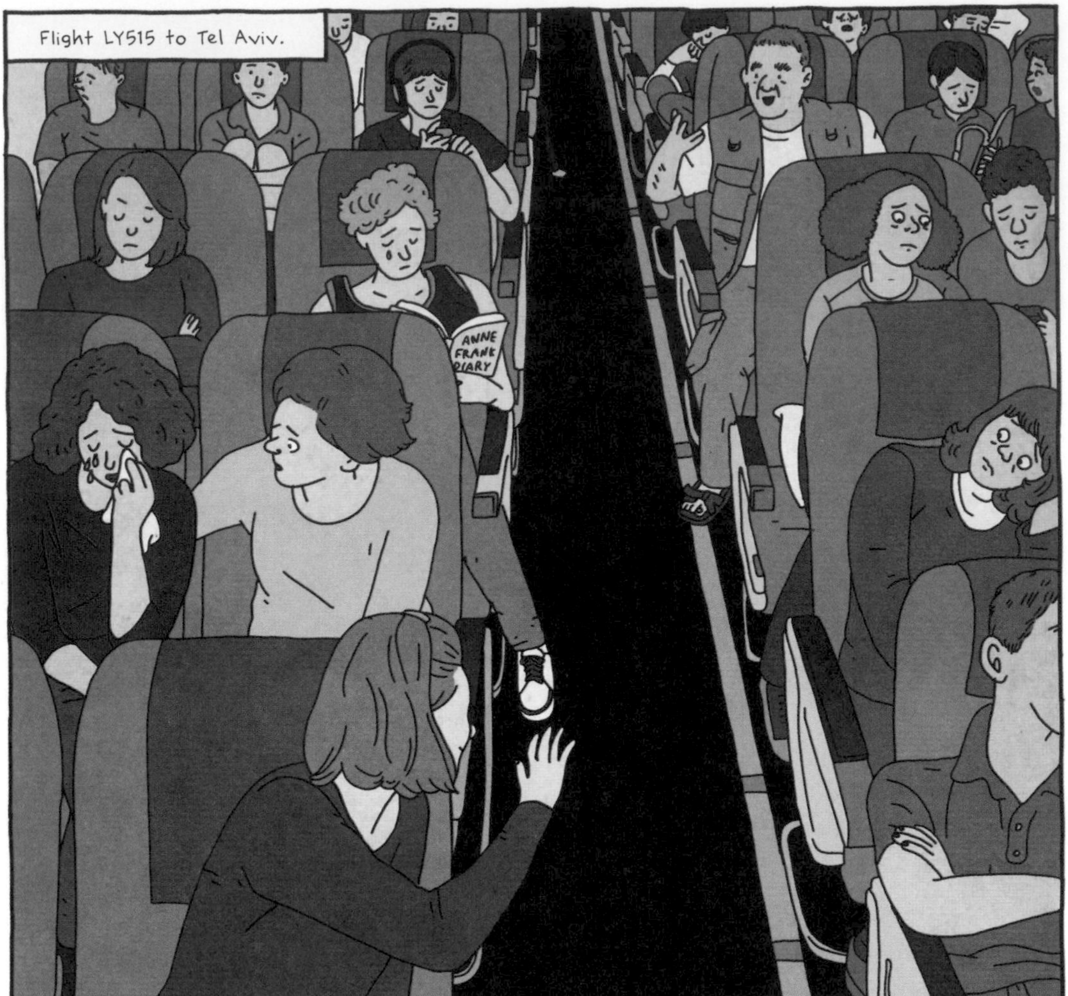
Flight LY515 to Tel Aviv.
ANNE FRANK DIARY

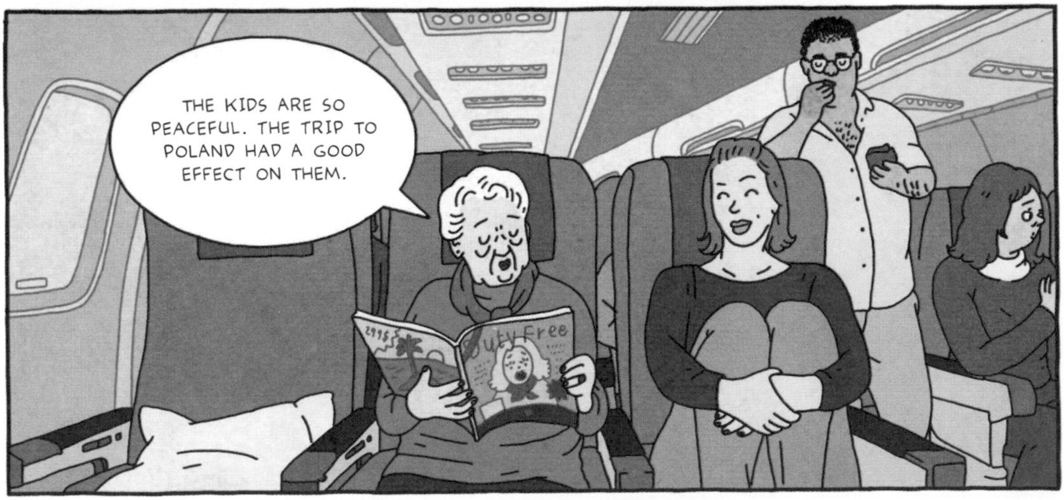
THE KIDS ARE SO PEACEFUL. THE TRIP TO POLAND HAD A GOOD EFFECT ON THEM.
Duty Free

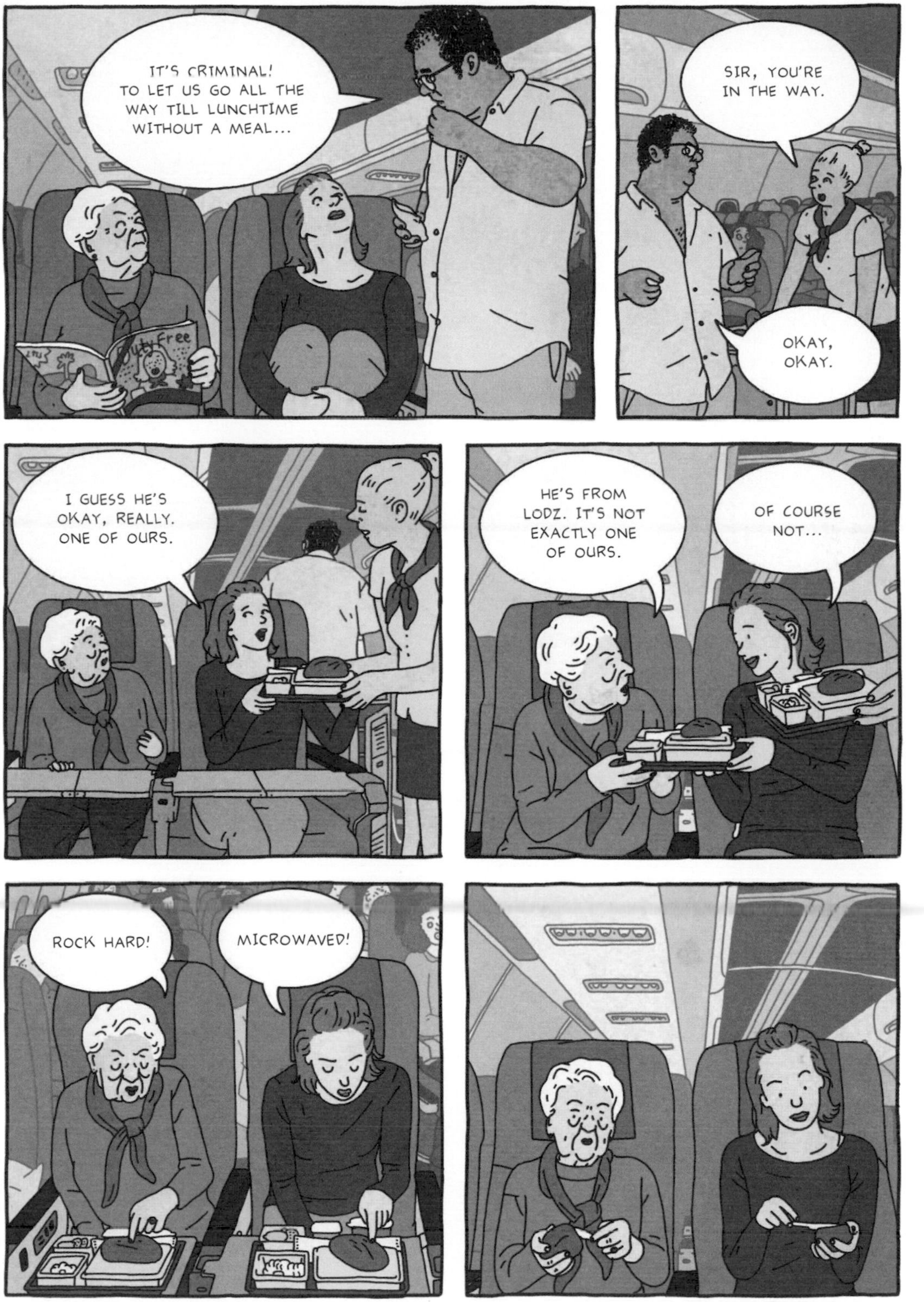
IT'S CRIMINAL! TO LET US GO ALL THE WAY TILL LUNCHTIME WITHOUT A MEAL...
SIR, YOU'RE IN THE WAY.
OKAY, OKAY.
I GUESS HE'S OKAY, REALLY. ONE OF OURS.
HE'S FROM LODZ. IT'S NOT EXACTLY ONE OF OURS.
OF COURSE NOT...
ROCK HARD!
MICROWAVED!

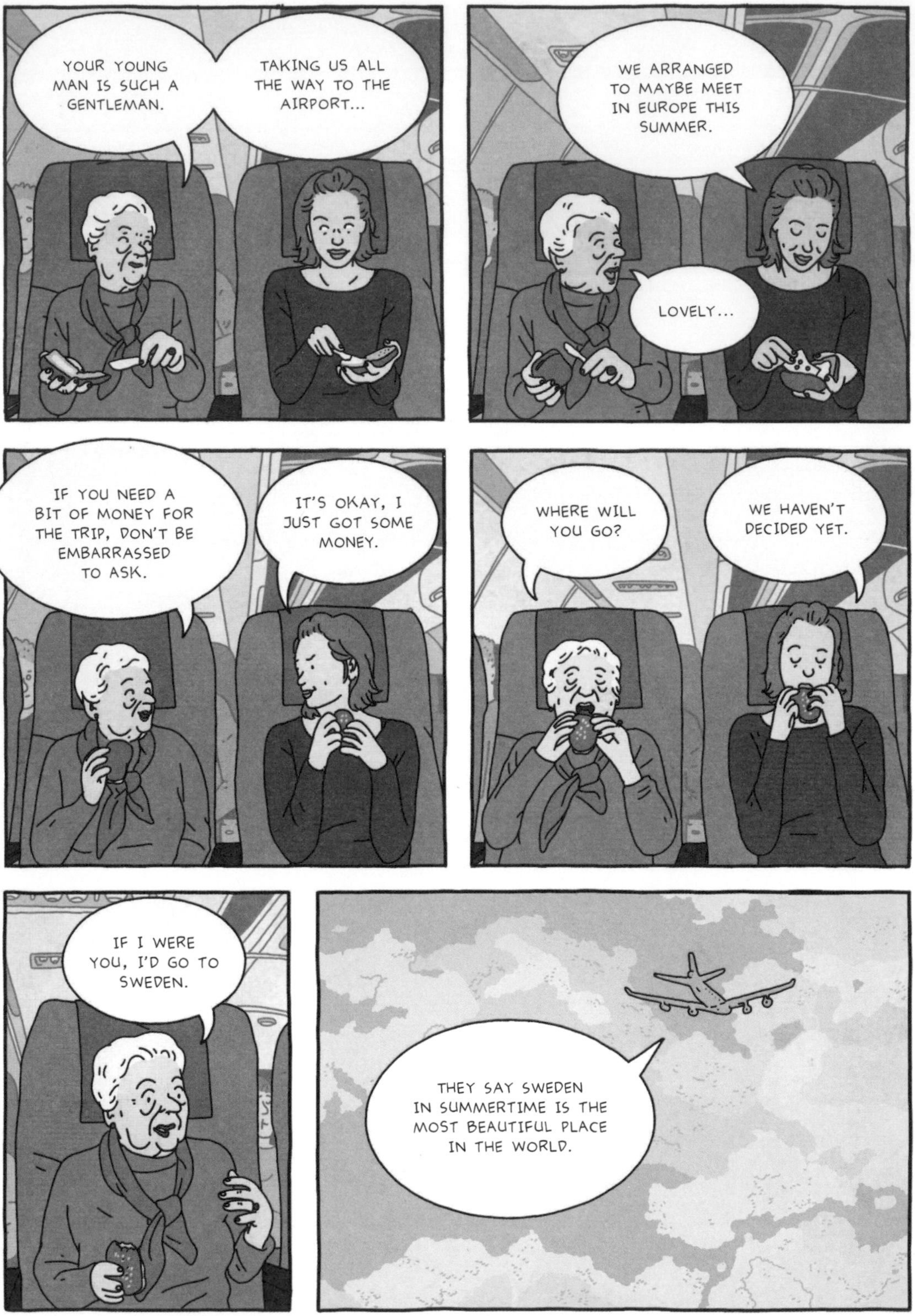
YOUR YOUNG MAN IS SUCH A GENTLEMAN.
TAKING US ALL THE WAY TO THE AIRPORT...
WE ARRANGED TO MAYBE MEET IN EUROPE THIS SUMMER.
LOVELY...
IF YOU NEED A BIT OF MONEY FOR THE TRIP, DON'T BE EMBARRASSED TO ASK.
IT'S OKAY, I JUST GOT SOME MONEY.
WHERE WILL YOU GO?
WE HAVEN'T DECIDED YET.
IF I WERE YOU, I'D GO TO SWEDEN.
THEY SAY SWEDEN IN SUMMERTIME IS THE MOST BEAUTIFUL PLACE IN THE WORLD.

CREDITS

Translator (from Hebrew) JESSICA COHEN
Story editor TIRZA BIRON
Story doulas YIRMI PINKUS & DANA MODAN
Drawings in Tomasz's sketchbook ASAF HANUKA

COMICS ACTORS

Regina Segal DVORA KEDAR
Mica Segal RUTIE BEN-EFRAT
Avram Yagodnik URI HOCHMAN
Tomasz Novak ISHAI GOLAN
Roman Gorski ALEX PELEG
Agnieszka Gorski BATIA KOLTON
Manager of the Society for Jewish Memorialization/Tzilla LILIAN BARRETO
Accountant Popowski ALON NOYMAN
Fotoplastikon operator YIRMI PINKUS
Shopwoman MERAV SALOMON
Yoram OFER BERGMAN
Young Regina MICHAL BERGMAN
Young Roman OFIR TENENBAUM
Nazi soldier IDO MOSES
Production manager and props SIVAN BEN-HORIN
Costumes YAEL SHENBERGER & THE CAMERI THEATRE
Location finder in Warsaw DOMINIKA WĘCŁAWEK
Color assistants HILA NOAM & MICHAL BERGMAN

Special thanks to TERESA SMIECHOWSKA

The characters in this book (the Polish ones, anyway) are fictitious. Any similarity to real persons, living or dead, is coincidental and not intended by the author.

First edition: May 2013. Printed in China. 10 9 8 7 6 5 4 3 2 1

Library and Archives Canada Cataloguing in Publication: Modan, Rutu; The Property / Rutu Modan. ISBN 978-1-77046-115-4. I. Graphic novels. I. Title. PN6790.I73M63 2013   741.5'95694   C2012-907117-X

Published in the USA by Drawn & Quarterly, a client publisher of Farrar, Straus and Giroux: 18 West 18th Street; New York, NY 10011; Orders: 888.330.8477. Published in Canada by Drawn & Quarterly, a client publisher of Raincoast Books: 2440 Viking Way; Richmond, BC V6V 1N2; Orders: 800.663.5714

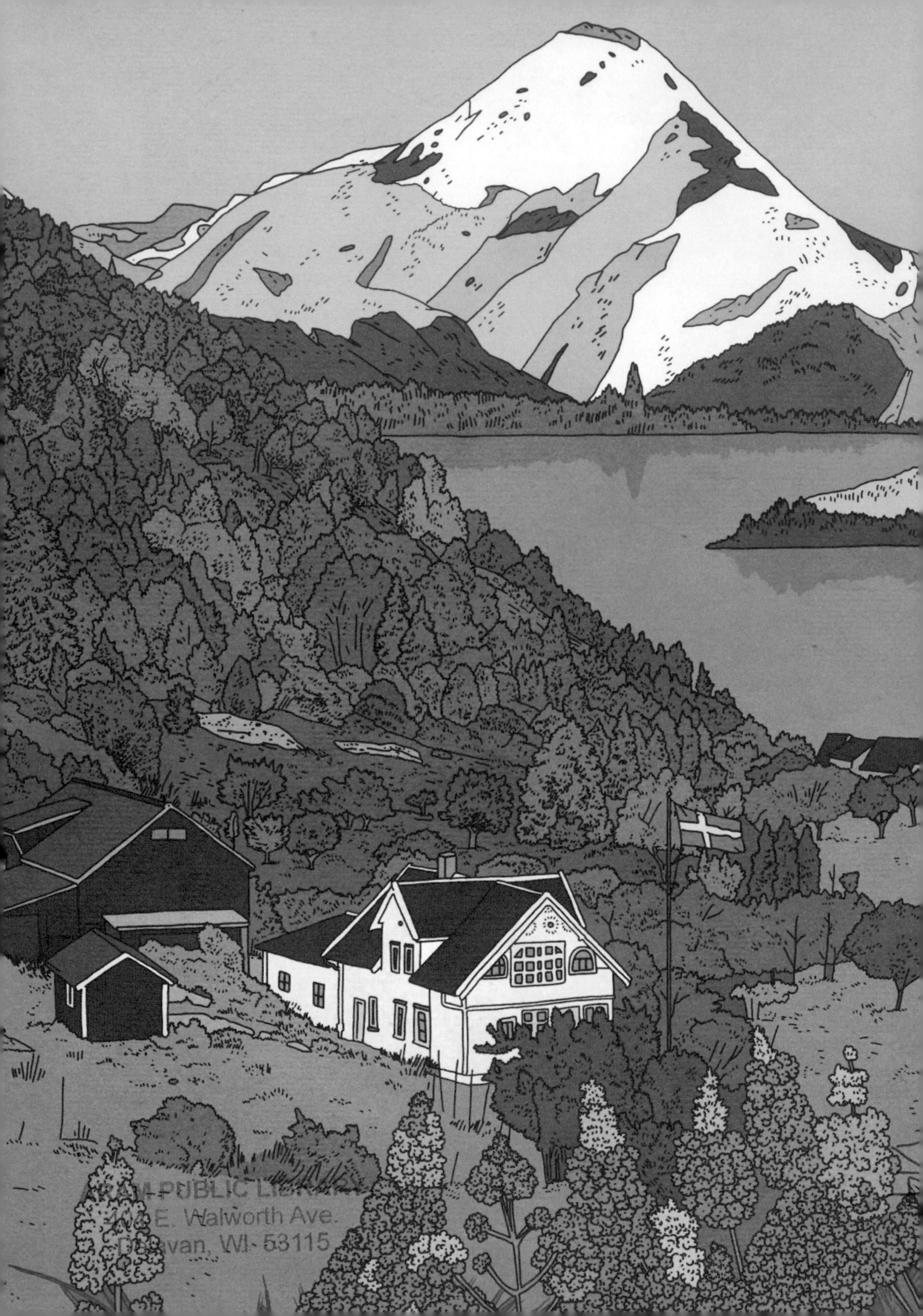